SNOWBELT CITIES

SNOWBELT CITIES

Metropolitan Politics in the Northeast
and Midwest since World War II

EDITED BY

RICHARD M. BERNARD

INDIANA UNIVERSITY PRESS
Bloomington and Indianapolis

The paper used in this publication meets the minimum requirements of American
National Standard for Information Sciences—Permanence of Paper for Printed
Library Materials, ANSI Z39.48-1984.

∞™

Manufactured in the United States of America

Library of Congress Cataloging-in-Publication Data

Snowbelt cities : metropolitan politics in the Northeast and Midwest
since World War II / edited by Richard M. Bernard.

p.   cm.

ISBN 0-253-31177-2 (alk. paper)

1. Cities and towns—Snowbelt States.   I. Bernard, Richard M.,
1948-

HT123.5.A162S66   1990

307.76′4′0973—dc20

89-19931
CIP

1 2 3 4 5 94 93 92 91 90

For
Gus and Estella Bowman

CONTENTS

ACKNOWLEDGMENTS

The contributors to this volume owe much to a number of individuals and institutions for their support and encouragement during the drafting of our manuscripts. In addition to these contributions, noted at the beginning of each chapter, much support has come to me during the time that I have acted as editor, and I wish to acknowledge that support here.

My first debt is to the contributors and to John Gallman and Lauren J. Bryant of the Indiana University Press, who put up with my academic globetrotting from China to the Middle East to New Zealand, faithfully forwarding revised manuscripts to diverse corners of the globe with no complaints as to the costs of postage or the inconvenience of delays. The quality of this volume is a tribute to their perserverence and skills.

The University of Canterbury in Christchurch, New Zealand, where I held a Fulbright Fellowship during 1988, was the site of much of the preliminary editorial work on this book. I am most grateful to officials at Auburn University at Montgomery, Alabama, which was then my home base, for allowing me to set aside my duties and to accept the fellowship. In particular, I appreciate the support that I received from Drs. Guinavera A. Nance, Marion C. Michael and John D. Fair. In New Zealand, I enjoyed the support of Laurence A. Cox, Executive Director of the New Zealand–United States Educational Foundation. At Canterbury in particular, Brian Wearing and the staff of the American Studies Program and Professor W. David McIntyre and the members of the Department of History were most kind and supportive of a visiting American colleague. Geographers Christopher J. Smith, on leave from SUNY–Albany, and J. Ross Barnett, and historians Leonard E. Richardson and Ian C. Campbell criticized earlier versions of the book's introduction, as did historian Mark I. Gelfand of Boston College.

As always, my greatest debt is to my wife, Terry, and our children, Benjamin and Emily, and to our extended families, whose support and encouragement were as important in the completion of this project as in all other phases of life. This book is dedicated to Terry's parents.

Richard M. Bernard

SNOWBELT CITIES

I

INTRODUCTION
SNOWBELT POLITICS

Richard M. Bernard

If the 1970s were the decade in which Americans discovered the Sunbelt, the 1980s mark the era of rediscovery for the urbanized regions of the Northeast and Midwest.[1] Once the focus of media attention, the Sunbelt and its youthful glow began to fade just as northern lights brightened, recharged by promises of high-tech prosperity. Where once the press hailed the sunny climes below the 37th parallel, it now deplores that region's shady trouble spots, folded away where the sunlight of economic development never shines.[2] By contrast, story after story highlights downtown re- newal and neighborhood rejuvenation from Boston to Indianapolis, from Milwaukee to Baltimore. Forty years after the Second World War—barely two decades since the Sunbelt's first gleam—the mature and settled cities of the Snowbelt appear ready to light the nation's way to economic modernization for the twenty-first century.

Unfortunately for that region, however, there is little substance behind the bright claims of Snowbelt advocates. Without question, some cities and states above the Potomac, Ohio, and Missouri rivers have revived their economies and reinvigorated their public images. Who has not heard of Michael Dukakis's "Massachusetts economic miracle"? It is equally true, however, and more characteristic of the region, that other areas have failed to prevent relative decline. Cleveland, Detroit, and the state of Michigan, among others, have not kept pace with the expansive Sunbelt. Those northern communities that have rebuilt and retooled their economies are now beginning to meet the regional challenge, but those that have not face ever grayer winters of discontent.[3]

Since the close of World War II, the combined populations of the Snowbelt states, bounded by Maine, Minnesota, Missouri, and Maryland, have continued to grow but at slower and slower rates. The region's population expanded by only 30.7 percent between 1950 and 1980, including a major drop in its growth rate in the 1970s. In the first eight years of the 1980s, the period of alleged Snowbelt revival, the region grew by only 2.6 percent, restrained largely by lethargy in the

1

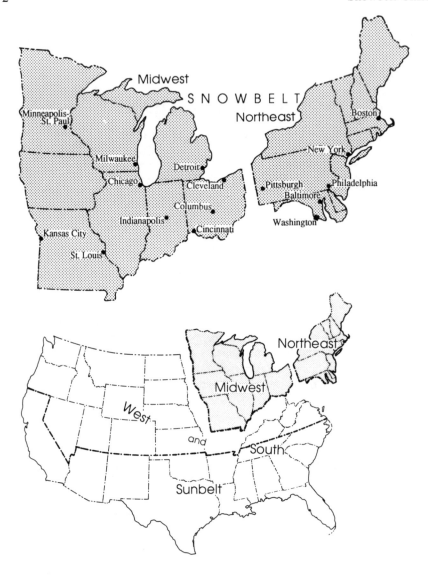

Map 1.1

Regions of the United States

TABLE 1.1
Regional Population Growth Rates
1950–1987[4]

	1950–60	*1960–70*	*1970–80*	*1950–80*	*1980–88*
Total U.S.	18.6	13.4	11.4	59.3	8.5
Snowbelt	15.4	10.6	2.3	30.7	2.6
(Northeast)	(14.1)	(10.8)	(0.8)	(27.5)	(3.6)
(Midwest)	(16.9)	(10.4)	(3.9)	(34.1)	(1.6)
South and West	22.2	16.5	21.3	72.7	13.9
(Sunbelt)	(25.9)	(18.3)	(22.5)	(82.5)	(15.4)
(Other Areas)	(13.9)	(12.0)	(18.1)	(50.7)	(8.4)

Sources: U.S. Censuses of Population, 1950–1980, and *U.S. Department of Commerce News* (CB88–205), December 30, 1988.

For definitions, see note 3.

Midwest. By contrast, the states of the South and West added over 20 percent to their population totals in the 1950s and again in the 1970s, and among these states, those in the Sunbelt grew even faster. In every postwar decade, the growth of these outer regions exceeded that of the Northeast and Midwest by substantial margins. In the turnaround decade of the 1970s, the difference in rates was stunning as the South and West grew over nine times faster than the Snowbelt. Even more remarkable in light of the media's northward focus, the difference in the 1980s is substantial, with the South and West expanding at a rate over five times faster than their rivals.

This gap between public perception and fact is the result of incomplete reporting. Although commentators have accurately noted declines in the rates of southern and western growth, most have failed to compare those declines to the continued low levels of expansion in the North. The recession years of the early 1980s caused a slowdown in all American migration, not just that to the South and West. Although the latter area, especially the oil-dependent states from Louisiana to Wyoming, did suffer slowdowns, the current, more sedate growth of the South and West still far exceeds that of the reviving areas of the Northeast and the dormant ones of the Midwest. In the South and West, eighteen states have exceeded the 7.4 percent national growth rate of the 1980s. In all of the Snowbelt, only New Hampshire has advanced so quickly. Michigan, Ohio, and Iowa are actually losing population.

Growth rates for metropolitan areas also reflect a continuing regional disparity. From 1980 to 1986, the populations of fifty-seven of the country's 281 metropolitan areas grew by over 15 percent. All fifty-seven were in the South and West, fifty-two of them in the Sunbelt, and, of these, forty-seven in California, Florida, and Texas alone. Conversely, fifty-nine of the seventy areas that lost population in these six years were in the Snowbelt, forty-four of them in the economically hard-hit Midwest. Among the major metropolitan areas of the Snowbelt, Detroit, Cleveland,

Pittsburgh, and Milwaukee continue to lose population despite major civic efforts to reverse their melancholy fortunes.[5]

The locus of the problem is not hard to find. It is downtown, or, more broadly, it is within the central cities of the Northeast and Midwest. Between 1980 and 1986, eleven of the sixteen largest metropolitan areas in the Snowbelt region lost population in their central cities (counting as one the losses in Minneapolis and St. Paul in that compound metropolitan area). Only New York, Chicago, Boston, Columbus, and Indianapolis are growing. Beyond the central cities, Cleveland and Pittsburgh even lost population in their suburbs (see appendix, Table A.2).

The clearest factor contributing to the decline of these urban areas is their economic difficulties. Every municipal executive and chamber of commerce director in the northern states knows that moneymaking opportunities are the keys to population growth and regional stability, yet few in the general public realize the startling extent to which these opportunities have evaporated in the Northeast and Midwest. This is largely because some analysts have relied on relatively encouraging regional comparisons of the growth rates of average household incomes. In fact, one report, based solely on this measure, went so far as to announce that the 1970s "power shift" to the South and West had reversed in the 1980s. Proclaiming that the Northeast had risen again, this study suggested that "businesses that want to go where consumer markets are strong may find themselves looking to the east."[6]

Total personal income figures, broken down by region, suggest a much different conclusion, one more in line with current population trends and not nearly so favorable to new entrepreneurs in the cities of the East Coast. Although the Northeast did record the country's largest gains in average household income, 1980–1986 (with the larger gains limited to Vermont, New Jersey, Connecticut, and Massachusetts), the region's proportion of the nation's total personal income declined. In line with a continuous trend since World War II, the Northeast's share of the nation's total income fell from 26 percent in 1980 to only 22 percent six years later. In fact, by this measure, the Midwest was the more stable of the two northern regions, retaining its 24 percent share throughout the 1980s. Outside the Snowbelt, the trends were upward. The South and the West, which at the end of the war had taken in less than 40 percent of the nation's total income, generated wages and salaries in the postwar period at such a rapid rate that they reached parity with the Northeast and Midwest in 1980. Since that time, the total income of these outer regions has further increased so that theirs is now the majority share.[7]

The relative decline of the Snowbelt and rise of the South and West are also apparent in the figures for total income derived from both the industrial sector, traditionally the stronghold of the Northeast and Midwest, and the emerging services sector, often associated with the Sunbelt. By 1982, the Snowbelt accounted for only 57 percent of the nation's total income from manufacturing (down from 77 percent in 1946) and a mere 51 percent of the nation's income from the service industries (down from 60 percent). The hopes of northern commentators notwithstanding, entrepreneurs seeking to increase their total profits from regional consumer markets have moved, and continue to move, south and west, pausing in their efforts only to sidestep general economic downturns.

TABLE 1.2
Regional Shares of National Personal Income,
1946, 1960, 1970, 1980, and 1985
(percentages)

	1946	1960	1970	1980	1985
Total U.S.	100	100	100	100	100
Snowbelt	61	58	56	50	46
(Northeast)	(34)	(31)	(30)	(26)	(22)
(Midwest)	(28)	(27)	(26)	(24)	(24)
South and West	39	42	44	50	54
(Sunbelt)	(26)	(30)	(32)	(37)	(NA)
(Other Areas)	(13)	(12)	(12)	(13)	(NA)

Sources: U.S. Department of Commerce, Bureau of Economic Analysis, *State Personal Income: Estimates for 1929–1982* . . . (Washington: U.S. Government Printing Office, 1984), Table 1; and U.S. Bureau of the Census, Current Population Reports, Series P-60, No. 156, *Money Income of Households, Families, and Persons in the United States: 1985* (Washington: U.S. Government Printing Office, 1987), Table 32.

TABLE 1.3
Regional Shares of National Personal
Income from Manufacturing and
Services,
1946, 1960, 1970, and 1982
(percentages)

	Manufacturing				Services*			
	1946	1960	1970	1982	1946	1960	1970	1982
Total U.S.	100	100	100	100	100	100	100	100
Snowbelt	77	70	65	57	60	58	57	51
(Northeast)	(42)	(35)	(31)	(27)	(36)	(34)	(34)	(30)
(Midwest)	(34)	(34)	(34)	(30)	(24)	(24)	(23)	(21)
South and West	23	30	35	43	40	42	43	49
(Sunbelt)	(17)	(23)	(27)	(33)	(29)	(31)	(32)	(37)
(Other Areas)	(6)	(7)	(8)	(10)	(11)	(11)	(11)	(12)

Source: U.S. Department of Commerce, Bureau of Economic Analysis, *State Personal Income: Estimates for 1929–1982* . . . (Washington: U.S. Government Printing Office, 1984), Tables 7–8.
*The census category "services" excludes substantial sectors of the economy such as banking and finance, government, transportation, and construction.

In the 1970s and 1980s several factors have contributed to these trends, working against the older businesses in the Northeast and Midwest and in favor of the newer ones in the South and West, and especially those in the Sunbelt.[8] Probably the most frequently cited of these factors is an alleged regional imbalance in the distribution of federal funds. A "second civil war" of words on this issue has come forth from the halls of Congress and from various think-tanks that supply lawmakers with their ammunition. Both sides claim their own regions are underfunded, and both sides seemingly have proof.[9]

In recent volleys, Bernard L. Weinstein and Richard W. Wigley, writing for the Sunbelt Institute, argued that in the Fiscal Year 1986 budget there was a "significant redistribution of federal funding" for grants-in-aid to state and local governments and for "total defense procurement" that was highly favorable to the New England and Mid-Atlantic regions. In response, Diane DeVaul and David Sorenson of the Northeast-Midwest Institute, noted that grants-in-aid and defense procurement account for only 37 percent of the total federal budget, omitting, among other items favorable to the South and West, spending for military installations. DeVaul and Sorenson preferred to view the regional distribution of the entire federal budget and with it the regional collection of federal taxes. Balancing total federal funds received against total taxes paid, these researchers concluded that the Northeast-Midwest region "paid $22 billion more in federal taxes than it received from federal spending. The South and West, in contrast, gained $68.8 billion more in federal spending than they paid in taxes."[10]

In this confrontation, DeVaul and Sorenson are right, but for the wrong reasons. The Snowbelt researchers correctly refocused attention away from subsections of the federal budget to an overview of all federal spending, but they were wrong to leave the impression that imbalanced spending is at fault. In fact, considering all the factors that go into the writing of the budget, the regional distribution of spending in relation to the total populations of each area is remarkably even-handed and fair. In Fiscal Year 1986, the Snowbelt, with 45 percent of the population, received 44 percent of the federal largess. The South and West, with 55 percent of the people, brought home 56 percent of the money. Within the Snowbelt, there is some dispartiy in federal spending, with the Northeast faring better than the Midwest, but even here the differences were small. The Northeast obtains about a percentage point worth of funding more than it should and the Midwest about two percentage points less. These surprisingly reasonable distributions represent very little change since 1977, the first year of the administration of President Jimmy Carter, and this too is remarkable given President Ronald Reagan's redirection of priorities toward pro-Sunbelt defense spending and away from pro-Snowbelt social spending.[11]

If the regional distributions of total federal spending are proportional to the population distribution, and not a case of "robbing St. Petersburg to pay St. Paul" or vice versa, what explains the net annual shifting of billions of dollars from the Snowbelt to Washington and of even more billions from Washington to the Sunbelt?[12] The answer is taxes. There are substantial regional differences in the total amounts of taxes paid by the individuals and businesses located in the Snowbelt and by those in the South and West. Taxable personal and corporate incomes are higher in the Northeast and Midwest than in other parts of the country, and, as a result, these regions send more money to Washington than do other areas. Once popular, stiff graduated taxes favored the poor over the rich and therefore extracted less from the poorer South (if not from the West) than from the richer northern states. Reagan-inspired tax cuts, which reduced the taxes of higher-income individuals more than those of lower-income people, reduced the Northeast and Mid-

TABLE 1.4
**Regional Distribution of Federal
Spending, FY 1977 and FY 1986, and Regional
"Balances of Payments"
with Washington, FY 1986**

	% Total Pop. in 1977	% Total Federal Spending FY 1977	% Total Pop. in 1986	% Total Federal Spending FY 1986	% Fed. Taxes Paid 1986	Balance of Payments FY 1986 (millions)*
Snowbelt**	49.1	47.6	45.2	43.9	48.8	− $15,957
(Northeast)	(24.9)	(28.1)	(22.9)	(24.4)	(26.7)	(− 5,768)
(Midwest)	(24.2)	(19.6)	(22.3)	(19.5)	(22.1)	(− 10,189)
South and West	50.9	52.3	54.8	56.1	51.2	+ 62,478
(Sunbelt)	(37.2)	(36.7)	(40.7)	(40.2)	(38.3)	(+ 33,287)
(Other Areas)	(13.7)	(15.6)	(14.1)	(15.9)	(12.9)	(+ 29,091)

Sources: U.S. Bureau of the Census, *1982 Census of Governments*, Vol. VI, *Topical Studies*, No. 4, *Historical Statistics on Governmental Finances and Employment* (Washington: U.S. Government Printing Office, January 1985), Table 29; U.S. Community Services Administration, *Geographic Distribution of Federal Funds in Summary: A Report of the Federal Government's Impact by State, County, and Large City, Fiscal Year 1977.* "Comparison of Federal Funds by States with State Rankings of Selected Demographic Characteristics" and "State Summary Operations." (Washington: Community Services Administration, n.d.); Diane DeVaul and David Sorenson, "A Regional Analysis of the Entire Federal Budget." (Washington: Northeast-Midwest Institute, August 6, 1987), Tables 1–2.

*Totals vary from those of the DeVaul and Sorenson study because of differing regional groupings of the states.

**Excludes the District of Columbia.

west's disadvantage. Taxes, then, and not spending, are to blame for regional imbalances-of-payments with Washington. The real issue, therefore, is not the geographic fairness of spending patterns, but whether pro-Sunbelt graduated taxes or pro-Snowbelt tax reductions are more appropriate.

All this does not, of course, argue that the federal government had no role in creating economic challenges for the Northeast and Midwest. Even the fairest of distributions of federal funds has considerable impact in promoting the fortunes of relatively backward areas. Federal spending, including direct defense spending which clearly favors the South and West, certainly helps those outlying regions. It just does not help them in the disproportionate and unreasonable manner that Snowbelt supporters have charged.[13]

Rather than federal funding imbalances, the greatest of the pro-Sunbelt factors is the often-reported changing nature of the international economy, which in the late 1970s and early 1980s made American industry as a whole less competitive in world markets. Although U.S. industry has continued to expand in the last two decades, its rate of expansion has slowed, and its dominance has disappeared. In the 1970s alone, American manufacturers lost some 23 percent of their share of world export markets. Because the Snowbelt was more industrialized than the other parts of the country, it was hardest hit by Japanese, German, and Third World competition. It is no coincidence that job losses in some of these states, particularly New York, Pennsylvania, Illinois, and Michigan, have been severe. Certainly other regions have also been hurt, but their commitment to lighter industries and to services has insulated them against the severity of the foreign challenge. For example, in the 1970s the rate of growth in capital investment in manufacturing fell in all regions, but the decline was relatively minor in the South and West. Investment growth rates in those states now handily surpass those of the Northeast and Midwest. In fact, there are now more American manufacturing jobs outside the Snowbelt than within it, something unthinkable at the end of the Second World War.[14]

A third factor said to favor Sunbelt economic development and to hurt the cities of the Northeast and Midwest is that great intangible, a "good business climate." Although many are now skeptical of the specific attractiveness of state and local industrial recruitment programs with their tax incentives, creative financing, and amenities giveaways, few dispute the advantages that political climates favorable to business expansion give to the economic development and population growth of the South and West.[15]

Perhaps the most widely quoted measure of state business environments is that compiled by Grant Thornton, an accounting and managerial consulting firm based in Chicago. The Grant Thornton index is a simple ranking of the forty-eight contiguous states on a variety of business related factors, including governmental fiscal policies and regulated employment costs, labor costs, energy and resources costs, and selected quality-of-life issues. Grant Thornton's June 1987 ranking was not as favorable to the Sunbelt as some earlier reports, but it still pointed out substantial advantages to business in the general manufacturing climates of the South and West. In the report's grand summary, where the lower the index number the better for business, the Snowbelt states earn an average ranking of 29.5 (26.5 for the Northeast and 33.6 for the Midwest). Both the South and the West, as a whole, and the Sunbelt, as a subregion, received scores of 21.2. The industrial promotion slogan of one southern state says it all: "Alabama, Open for Business."[16]

If the "Heart of Dixie" is open for business, Alabama and the rest of the South and West are also open for pleasure. A final factor hailed as favorable to those areas is their informal, slow-paced, outdoor lifestyles. The relative newness of these areas, their attractive climates (warmer in the Sunbelt, sunnier in all the West save the northern Pacific coast), and their lower population densities have made daily life easier and more comfortable in the view of many migrants. A number of studies have attempted to measure regional differences in quality of life, but the outcomes of all such research depend directly on which variables the researchers choose. For example, in the 1981 edition of the popular *Rand McNally Places Rated Almanac*, New York led the nation in its support for the arts, but the "Big Apple" lost cultural points for its relative lack of bowling alleys and neighborhood taverns. On these important subpoints, the nation's cultural leaders were Billings, Montana, and Eau Claire, Wisconsin.[17]

Preference surveys, which set aside reality to measure popular perceptions, also have difficulties. Most preference surveys have shown more Americans inclined to praise the South and West over the Northeast and Midwest, a factor of some importance in determining the reasons why people migrate. Yet, because of the imprecision of these surveys and the vagueness of their linkage to actual decisions to migrate, the only accurate way to test the importance of such preferences is to count movers. This method just brings the argument full circle and makes it moot. Certainly, lifestyle preferences work to the disadvantage of the Snowbelt, but the importance of their effects cannot be known.

Throughout the decade of the 1980s, these factors have played extensive roles in the rise of the South and West and the fall of the Northeast and Midwest. The helpful effects of total (if not relative) federal spending, lower federal tax bites, "good business climates," and appealing weather and lifestyles have aided the Sunbelt at the same time that international competition has hurt the North. These factors continue to favor expansion in the South and West and to despoil the best efforts by Snowbelt leaders to return that region to its former prominence.[18] Those predicting a quick thaw in the Snowbelt's economy and an early return to the warmth of prosperity have thus far found only a false spring.

Still, the seasons may change again. Proponents of regeneration in the northern urban core suggest that the Northeast and Midwest enjoy certain long-term advantages that will allow their economies to revive and cause those of the South and West to stagnate. Although stated in many ways, these advantages often boil down to two points, one positive for the Snowbelt and the other negative for its rivals. On the positive side, the Snowbelt provides strong support for education and training, certainly stronger support than found below the Mason-Dixon line. By almost any measure, the Northeast and Midwest spend more on their public schools, producing better-educated work forces than those available in the South. Vis-à-vis the western states, however, the Snowbelt's position is reversed, for it trails the West in measures of public support for schools. Thus, in a very general sense, the Northeast and Midwest's records on education place them midway between the other regions.[19]

On the negative side, Snowbelt advocates have argued that the cities of the South and West face enormous costs associated with the building of highways, utilities, hospitals, and the like to support their growing populations. Conversely, they argue, the slow-growing cities of the Northeast and Midwest built up their facilities decades ago and now have construction costs largely behind them.

Clearly, the building of sturdy infrastructures is an important cost of economic development and growth. Almost as expensive as construction, however, is the maintenance of older facilities in good working order. Streets must be both paved and repaired; utilities must be installed and serviced; hospitals must be built and modernized. Although the construction costs related to the development of urban infrastructures concentrate in the growing regions of the South and West, the burden for maintenance of similar but older facilities falls heavier on the Northeast and Midwest.[20]

Both the construction of facilities and their upkeep are expensive, and if the regional rates of spending on highways, sewage disposal, and hospitals are indicative

of total infrastructure costs, the South and West spend hardly more than the Snowbelt. In 1981–82, the national average for spending on these items was $344 per
capita. Snowbelt states and their local governments spend $341; those in the South
and West spent $347. In fact, since most of the increases in spending have come
in the upper portions of the West, the Sunbelt's per capita figure exactly matched
that of the Snowbelt at $341.[21]

In the future, this balance between construction and maintenance may tip against
the South and West if the population growth in those regions continues to outstrip
that of the Northeast and Midwest, but even then several factors suggest that the
accompanying tax burdens on the newer areas will not prove much greater than
those on the older ones. First, as costs rise in the South and West so too will tax
collections from new businesses and residents. Second, the South and West are
areas that traditionally provide lower levels of services to their residents. They
spend less on welfare, but also less on sidewalks, parks, and bridges. Southern and
western voters may continue to ask less of their governments than northern voters
consider minimal. Third, the South and West's subsequent maintenance costs for
their new facilities should be lower than the Snowbelt's costs for repairs on their
older ones. Finally, since the outlying regions are building up their facilities in an
age of federal support, albeit declining federal support, the taxpayers of the Northeast and the Midwest can expect to share in their rivals' capital costs.[22]

All in all, the elements influencing growth in the South and West strongly suggest
continued expansion in those areas. It is unlikely that the growing costs necessary
for southern education and the build-up of urban infrastructures in the South and
West will be enough to detract from the advantages that these regions offer to new
businesses and new people.[23] And the implication that the Northwest and Midwest
will gain return migrants, fleeing from the newly tax-burdened South and West,
appears overstated at best.

With both their economic and demographic power declining, the states of the
Snowbelt are also losing their political strength in the nation's capital, although the
partisan impact of that shift has yet to be fully felt. From the founding of the Republic through the election of 1968, the voters of the Northeast and Midwest had
the power to elect the president and a majority of the House of Representatives
regardless of the preferences of voters elsewhere. But for some time, migration had
caused the relative strength of these older areas to dwindle, and by the 1960s their
majorities in the 535-vote electoral college and the 435-member House had shrunk
to one vote in each. The 1970 census wiped away that edge and put the Northeast
and Midwest on the political defensive for the first time. In the elections of 1972,
1976, and 1980, the South and West enjoyed a thirteen-vote majority in the electoral
college, and after the 1980 census, that margin jumped to forty-five votes. If projections for 1990 hold, the margin will jump again to seventy-three votes. California
alone will have fifty-three electoral votes; Texas will tie New York for second at
thirty-three.[24]

Today, 54 percent of the nation's electoral tally comes from the South and West.
Beginning with the 1992 election, that figure should stand at 57 percent. Symbolic
of this shift in strength, every elected president since John F. Kennedy has come

TABLE 1.5
**Electoral Votes by
Region, 1960–1988**

	1960	1964 1968	1972 1976 1980	1984 1988	% Electoral Vote in 1984 and 1988
Total U.S.	537	535	535	535	100.0
Snowbelt	276	268	261	245	45.8
Change		− 8	− 7	− 16	
(Northeast)	(145)	(139)	(135)	(126)	(23.6)
Change		− 6	− 4	− 9	
(Midwest)	(131)	(129)	(126)	(119)	(22.2)
Change		− 8	− 3	− 7	
South and West	261	267	274	290	54.2
Change		+ 6	+ 7	+ 16	
(Sunbelt)	(164)	(173)	(181)	(193)	(36.1)
Change		+ 9	+ 8	+ 12	
(Other Areas)	(97)	(94)	(93)	(97)	(18.1)
Change		− 3	− 1	+ 4	

Source: *Guide to U.S. Elections*, 2d ed. (Washington: *Congressional Quarterly*, 1985), p. 1125.

from the Sunbelt, and in 1964, 1968, and 1980, two major candidates came from that region. In 1988, transplanted Yankee George Bush, a former Houston congressman, carried the Sunbelt banner.

In recent elections, the Democratic presidential candidates have had to rely on the declining Snowbelt states as last bastions of support. Since the days of Franklin Roosevelt, white ethnic and black voters in the cities of the Northeast and Midwest have swung the electoral votes of many northern states toward the Democrats. In 1968 when Hubert Humphrey won nine of the nineteen Snowbelt states, in 1976 when Jimmy Carter won ten, and in 1988 when Michael Dukakis took seven, the Democrats were competitive in this area. Beyond the Snowbelt, however, the Democrats have been in trouble.

Except for Carter's near-sweep of the South in 1976, the Democrats have carried only two southern states in all the presidential contests from 1968 through 1988 put together. In 1968, Humphrey captured Texas, and, in 1980, Carter carried his home state of Georgia. In the West, things were worse. In 1968, Humphrey carried the state of Washington. That was the only state from the Great Plains to the Pacific coast to vote Democratic from that year until 1988 when Dukakis took Washington and Oregon. When the polls have closed in the Central Time zone, the lights have gone out for the Democrats.

The fact that the Snowbelt, an area competitive in presidential elections, is declining in population while the pro-Republican South and West are growing bodes further ill for the Democrats. Recent Sunbelt migrations have forced the redistribution of electoral votes in ways that have strengthened the Republicans, in part (it is suggested) by swinging marginal states to the GOP and in part by adding electoral votes to states already in that party's column. Because recent elections have not been close, however, such changes have as yet proven to be of little consequence. For example, in 1968 reapportionment added only eight electoral votes to Richard Nixon's already ample total. Reapportionment gave Gerald Ford five additional votes in 1976, but these were not nearly enough to close the gap between him and Carter. In the Bush landslide of 1988, the Republican gained six reapportioned votes.[25]

In the House of Representatives, the loss of Snowbelt seats and the addition of ones from the South and West might well have enhanced Republican strength had it not been for Democratic control over the redrawing of district lines. With Democrats in charge of most state capitals, their party officials usually dictated the boundaries of new congressional districts, reforming them to their own advantage. As a result, during Nixon's 1972 landslide victory over George McGovern, the Democrats lost only two seats due to reapportionment in redrawn congressional districts. In 1982, with Republican President Reagan quite popular, the Democrats actually gained eleven reapportioned and redistricted seats.[26]

Thus, the migration of people out of the Snowbelt has caused declines in Democratic electoral votes in the presidential races, but so far only small and meaningless declines. The migration has not caused any disruption in Democratic control of the House of Representatives. Still, the demographic trends are against the Democrats, a fact that has caused some commentators to forecast a "Republican lock" on the electoral college, though there is no similar prediction of Republican control over access to the doors to the lower house chamber.

In summation, from the vantage point of the late 1980s, Snowbelt advocates seem to view their region's economic future through rose-colored glasses but its political hopes through a lens of dark blue. The region's spokespersons are too quick to predict a regional economic revival, for the Northeast and Midwest's share of the nation's population and income continues to fall, driven down more by market forces than federal favoritism. Winter continues above the Potomac, Ohio, and Missouri rivers.

Overly optimistic about Snowbelt economic prospects, Snowbelt politicos, especially Democrats and liberals, are solemnly pessimistic about their area's loss of political clout. Though a bit premature, this pessimism becomes ever more warranted as current population trends add to Republican power.

Once a nation where the lights of snow-covered northern factories lit up a vast underdeveloped hinterland to the south and west, the United States of the late twentieth century now enjoys the sunshine of growth and economic development across its outer reaches. Certainly, the recharged lights of Boston, Indianapolis, Milwaukee, and Baltimore are brightening, but whether they and those of their Snowbelt counterparts can outshine the sun remains to be seen.

If the competition among cities and regions for economic development has been intense, so too has the competition among urban political groups and their leaders for the right to run municipal governments and to direct efforts toward economic advancement. This competition has been no less intense in the slower-growing cities of the Northeast and Midwest than in the more rapidly expanding municipalities of the South and West. In all four areas, the major thrust of urban politics has been toward the control and acceleration of economic development activities.

During the twenty-year span from the end of the Second World War to the mid-1960s, the primary competitors for the control of Snowbelt cities were business leaders, working-class ethnics, and progressive reformers. Although each of these three largely white, male groups endorsed the concept of growth as necessary to the bettering of living conditions within cities, the similarities among the three groups stopped there. Each patterned itself after a different organizational model; each modified the growth goal to suit its own needs; and each used different means to achieve its ends.

As befitted their training, outlook, and daily contacts, business leaders developed their efforts on a corporate model, applicable both to their own political campaigns and to the post-election governance of their cities. They viewed mayors and councils as municipal boards of directors, constituted to set overall policy and keep efforts focused on the great goal of economic advancement. As municipal directors, these businessmen thought that they best understood the needs of their cities. In their view, most of these needs could be met through enhanced economic development, and because, as businessmen, they knew best how to make local businesses prosper, they felt little need to consult the city's rank and file about policy decisions. City managers and their staffs of bureaucrats were in place to carry out council policy directives and handle customer complaints. At election time, business people centered their efforts on the elevation or continuation of one of their own as mayor, placing a secondary but important emphasis on the election of friendly council members. Generally, their efforts were sufficient to seat compliant governing bodies, though on occasion business representatives had to show individual council members the advantages to their constituents, and sometimes to themselves, of cooperation with business's agenda. When pressed by hostile council forces, business leaders also turned to the courts for the protection and nurture of their schemes. Although lacking the complete societal control that some of their counterparts enjoyed along the emerging southern rim, Snowbelt businessmen were, nonetheless, major participants in determining the fate of all major cities of the Northeast and Midwest.[27]

The extent to which postwar business leaders controlled power, either independently or through coalitions with other groups, varied across the Snowbelt. Indianapolis, perhaps the most "middle American" of all large cities, was, in the days of Chamber of Commerce Executive Vice President William Henry Book and the "39 Club," archetypal in its pattern of business control over city government. In Detroit, businessmen, led by the nation's leading automakers, were almost as strong. In Pittsburgh and St. Louis, business executives such as Richard Mellon and August Busch worked successfully with ethnic leaders to mold public policy in directions favorable to business interests. In pre-home-rule Washington, businessmen joined with southern congressmen to block the political ambitions of blacks.

The second major urban power group, one sometimes at odds with business leadership, consisted of white working-class ethnics, clinging together as remnants of stereotypical urban political machines of the late nineteenth century. For this group, there was no conscious selection of a role model. Its members simply carried on in much the same manner as their fathers, allowing for certain modernizing adjustments. These included the admission to the machines of new immigrant groups, though usually not black groups, and modifications of traditional rewards systems to take into account the rising educational level of the organization's followers. In the manner of the machines of old, these modern ethnic organizations sought stability and the retention of their power and benefits, goals that were easily compatible with the growth goal of businessmen provided that the ethnics received their share of the spoils. At election time, ethnic politicians worked very hard for their candidates, especially those running for council positions. They contested the mayoral races, and occasionally their candidates won, but generally their strength was in ward-level contests, not citywide. Once in office, ethnic representatives viewed themselves not as corporate directors but as power brokers, there to gain the best bargains possible for their constituents and their organizations. In the ensuing give-and-take, ethnic leaders matched business representatives in attempts to coopt unaligned and opposing council members into arrangements beneficial to those involved. Often this meant quiet deals between business leaders and ethnic representatives to gain support for development in the central city and thus to generate both profits and jobs.[28]

The mid–twentieth century archetypal ethnic political organization was Chicago's Cook County machine. This coalition, originally brought together by Anton Cermak, was known through the 1930s and 1940s as the Kelly-Nash machine. Renamed in the 1950s for its most effective leader, Mayor Richard J. Daley, the machine cooperated with local business interests and maintained enormous power over the distribution of the benefits of Chicago's growth until the mayor's death in 1976. In other cities, ethnically based machines found their authority challenged. In Boston, James Michael Curley and his old Irish pols had to share power with younger, reform-minded Irish pols. In Baltimore, Thomas D'Alesandro, Sr.'s ethnic machine held firm but only by admitting blacks and other outsiders to its membership.

Apart from the dealmakers stood the postwar reformers, many of them only recently separated from their starched service uniforms and equally stiff international ideals. Like the urban progressives at the turn of the century, these high-minded individuals, many of them political novices, chose the businessmen's corporate model as the best for action and governance. Also like their spiritual forebears, these reformers went further than their commercial and industrial contemporaries in calling for propriety over property. In the manner of the progressives, they worked for the creation of efficient governments free from corruption and waste, an effort that became an end in itself, surpassing even economic growth in importance. Certainly the reformers believed in growth, but they placed their emphasis on the nature of government rather than its potential for profit generation. At the polls, they found some limited success, generally doing better when they endorsed a reform-minded candidate from another power group than when they tried in a straightforward manner to elect one of their own. In some cities, the reformers found greater success in the courthouse than at the polling place as dedicated prosecutors sought countless indictments against the greedy and careless.[29] Occasionally, the reformers won at the polls. In Kansas City, for example, the reformers took control when Pendergast officials were removed from office and jailed, and as the "Citizen's Association," they consolidated their control through the leadership of longtime City Manager L. Perry Cookingham. In Philadelphia, the reform-oriented Greater Philadelphia Movement also came to power, but only through the support of the business community. In New York, competing reformers carved up Tammany Hall and struggled to share in its former power, power that was in fact almost totally in the hands of Robert Moses, the great regional planner. In Milwaukee, a reformer won as well, but his situation was unique. As America's only big-city socialist mayor, Frank Zeidler had to share power with both business and ethnic leaders.

During the 1960s, three new factors entered into American municipal politics and catalyzed changes in the participant groups and their relative power. Culminating a process begun in the late nineteenth century, migration of black and Hispanic minorities into northeastern and midwestern cities became so large that their bloc votes became factors in almost every city and deciding factors in some. These increases in minority populations coincided with the civil rights movement and the increased role of the federal government in urban affairs. Together these three reshaped city politics and gave rise to three new challengers for urban political power: blacks; neighborhood activists, and especially "yuppies"; and white suburbanites. As in the case of the earlier groups, men generally held the leadership positions in these groups, but unlike the earlier groups, women shared some power.

Next to the overall decline in the populations of central cities, the most significant demographic change affecting the political life of late twentieth-century Snowbelt cities was the marked rise in central-city black populations. For some cities, the most significant change early in the next century will be the growth in the number of Hispanics. From the eve of the Second World War to 1980, Baltimore's population went from 19 percent black to 54 percent black. In Detroit, the black increase was from 9 percent to 63 percent; in Washington, from 18 percent to 70 percent. Based on 1980 census counts, blacks now constitute over one-third of the populations of these major Snowbelt cities plus those of St. Louis, Cleveland, Chicago, Philadelphia, and Cincinnati. In the region's sixteen largest metropolitan areas, blacks form at least 20 percent of the central-city populations in all but the twin city metropolis of Minneapolis (8 percent) and St. Paul (5 percent). In a few areas, most notably Washington (17 percent) and New York (10 percent), a significant proportion of the suburban population is also black. Hispanics account for 20 percent of New York City's population and 14 percent of Chicago's. Almost 5 percent of New York's suburban population is Hispanic (see Table A.4).[30]

Although the civil rights movement with its southern focus on *de jure* segregation had little direct effect on the lives of northern blacks, it did provide a good deal of inspiration to them and to other minority groups desiring to increase their own political power. Seeing the courageous efforts of southern blacks to gain political and social rights caused black people in the North to reconsider their own political, social, and economic conditions and the potential for bringing about changes in them. Only in the movement for voting rights, however, did minorities in north-eastern and midwestern cities find civil rights tactics that were directly applicable to their own needs. Impressed by massive southern drives to register blacks, and to a less extent Hispanics, northern black leaders initiated similar efforts.

Additional inspiration and guidance to neighborhood groups (black, Hispanic, and Anglo) and to predominantly white suburbs came from the federal government. President Lyndon Johnson's Great Society channeled millions of dollars into the urban political arena where neighborhood and suburban groups fought ever harder for their shares, blessed with at least a small degree of federal protection. In this regard, most notable among LBJ's projects were the Community Action Program and the Model Cities Program. The former required "maximum feasible partici-pation" by the recipients of its benefits as a guarantee that the poor would have some role in decisions affecting their neighborhoods. The Model Cities Program gave similar standing to suburban communities in the area-wide distribution of certain funds. General revenue sharing and community development block grants absorbed and replaced many of these programs during the Nixon and Ford years. These new initiatives also provided substantial funding to support municipal ac-tivities, although much of the money shifted beyond the reach of neighborhood groups. The Nixon/Ford programs, together with subsequent Reagan budget cuts, steadily reduced neighborhood, if not suburban, input on spending priorities, but not before many young leaders had learned the ways of bureaucratic politics.

Among those anxious for a chance to govern their cities were a number of very able black newcomers. The greatest change in twentieth-century urban politics in the Snowbelt as well as the Sunbelt has been the coming to power of blacks, an arrival signaled by the 1967 mayoral victories of Carl Stokes in Cleveland and Richard Hatcher in Gary, Indiana. For some time, black voters had provided im-portant support to white machines in selected cities, most notably in William H. Thompson's prewar mayoral campaigns in Chicago. Now, black leaders stepped forward to head local tickets and to form organizations of their own.

In organizing their followers, blacks looked to the old immigrant machines for a model in struggles to get power and benefits previously withheld from them. To the extent that they were underdogs, wrongly denied a place in the American political system, their struggles took on the aura of moral crusades for racial justice. They were that, but they were also the most recent in a line of self-interested efforts to gain the spoils of municipal office. On election day, black precinct workers labored as hard as their white ethnic predecessors to get out large bloc votes. Over time, they became successful. Black candidates, and to a lesser extent pro-black white candidates, have sometimes carried 90 percent and more of the vote in black neigh-borhoods and in the process have won their cities' highest offices.

Stokes's win in Cleveland was the first mayoral victory by a black in a major American city, but it did not mark any sort of permanent turnover of the city to black control. Lacking a significant base of support, Stokes became the first black mayor of a major city to give power over to a white successor. At the other extreme, black population majorities appear to have taken permanent control of Detroit and Washington, D.C., beginning with the elections of Coleman Young (1973) and Walter Washington (1974). In a racially divided city still polarized by its 1967 riot, Young, a union activist with a checkered past, had to overcome both automakers and white autoworkers. In the nation's capital, Mayor Washington, the appointed chief executive, immediately won election in his own right once district residents gained the opportunity to vote. The all-black 1987 Baltimore mayor's race in which young attorney Kurt Schmoke defeated Acting Mayor Clarence "Du" Burns, an old-line politician, may also have signaled a shift of that black-majority city to permanent black leadership. Somewhat more tenuous were the 1983 victories of black candidates in Chicago and Philadelphia where, like Cleveland, blacks are not in the majority. In the Windy City, Congressman Harold Washington won startling victories over the split forces of the riotous Daley machine and a Republican candidate with racist support. Less remarkable was City Manager Wilson Goode's relatively low-key win in Philadelphia, though his 1987 reelection over tough white ethnic spokesman and former mayor Frank Rizzo came in a boisterous, no-holds-barred contest. Black control in Chicago ended in 1989 when acting Mayor Eugene Sawyer, put in place by the votes of white aldermen, and Alderman Timothy Evans fought over Washington's black constituency, allowing Richard M. Daley to win the election. Whether Goode's political career can survive the continuing fallout of an ill-placed police bomb remains to be seen.

Once elected, black officeholders learned quickly the art of compromise and dealmaking, for, lacking majorities in all but a handful of cities, they had to form alliances to win key votes. At first, blacks leaders such as Harold Washington often sided with white reformers such as Chicago's "Lakefront Liberals" who were commited to human equality and anxious to add racial justice to their other liberal causes. More recently, however, some black leaders, such as Goode and Schmoke, have tied their fortunes to those of business in drives for local economic redevelopment. Sawyer, a longtime Daley machine functionary, and other black politicians have worked closely with ethnic council members as concerned as themselves over the distribution of government's benefits.

As long as black leaders associated their demands with calls for racial and, to a lesser extent, economic justice, they found friends in the press ready to ennoble their efforts and vilify those of the opposition. Support also followed black attempts to promote economic development. But the more that some blacks acted like ward politicians and spoilsmen, the less favorable was their media treatment. If reporters judged black leaders guilty of corruption, admiration ended and hostility ensued. Local courthouses then became forums for the airing of both white charges of black malfeasance in office and black countercharges of racism through selective prosecution.[31]

In addition to minority groups, the 1970s and 1980s brought forth other, less likely, political contenders among neighborhood activists. Sometimes these were longtime community residents, but often as not, they included young professionals and managers ("yuppies," in the language of the mid-1980s), who moved into old central-city areas to restore properties and "gentrify" neighborhoods. With the zeal of converts, some of these newcomers became stronger advocates of neighborhood causes than were their more settled neighbors. Patterning themselves after the National Association for the Advancement of Colored People, these new-age reformers idealistically sought racial justice and, in their own self-interest, the preservation of their new neighborhoods and their property values. At city hall they worked when possible with blacks and other minorities to slow downtown growth machines and to rechannel funds to residential areas. At the courthouse, they resorted to legal obstruction of selected economic development projects thought to jeopardize urban communities. Although these groups were rarely able to attain citywide power, they did prove capable of forcing decision makers to spare and revive certain areas otherwise doomed to the wrecking ball and concrete mixer.

In Cincinnati, neighborhood political organizations began to vie for power with the established Republican and Democratic parties long before the term "yuppie" entered the American vocabulary. As early as the mid-1950s, when city officials began to shift the focus of city planning from downtown to neighborhoods, liberal local organizations rose and supported, first in coalition with Democrats and then, when abandoned, on their own, anti-development candidates and causes. Some urban sub-areas, such as Cincinnati's Over-the-Rhine and West End neighborhoods, have successfully stalled redevelopment efforts. Boston's South End, Washington's Georgetown District, Chicago's Near Northside, Milwaukee's Sherman Park, and Baltimore's Fell's Point—upper-, middle-, and lower-class neighborhoods with white, black, and mixed residents—are among the many that have similarly slowed or stopped the wheels of unwanted progress.

As these struggles wax and wane in the central cities, others are developing along the urban peripheries where suburban white populations and their governments are becoming more active in metropolitan area politics. Responding to such encouragements as those offered under Johnson's Model Cities Program, the leaders of outlying areas have joined efforts to promote growth while seeking a centrifugal redistribution of its benefits. If the business elite of the cities hoped to form central-city governments into model coporations, suburban leaders, more often than not business people themselves, are trying to make their communities into models of small commercial operations. Like small business people, they are largely concerned with stability, in this case as a means of protecting their cities' quality of life. To the extent that they seek any changes, suburban leaders look longingly at the idealistic goal of greater local control and independence from their central cities. They also want the self-serving goal of increased power and benefits. Unlike the other groups, however, suburban leaders do not focus attention on elections, for only rarely do their constituents vote in area-wide contests. Rather they direct their energies into courthouse struggles for suburban rights, state capital skirmishes over central-city expansion and other territorial infringements, and federal hearing room rows over the allocation of funds. And, as the nation shifts attention from the "urban crisis" of the central cities and the need-based categorical responses of the 1960s to more general municipal concerns and formula-based revenue sharing and block grants, these smaller, more affluent communities are doing ever better in their challenges to central-city hegemony. Although in this volume few of the authors address this metropolitan phase of urban politics, the rising power of the outer areas may soon shift the entire focus of urban political conflict to the bureaucratic struggles pitting governments against governments.

In this book, contributors consider the histories of the politics of twelve of the sixteen largest metropolitan areas of the Northeast and Midwest. In three of these, business interests were clearly in control.[32] Robert G. Barrows tells the story of Indianapolis, where businessmen have faced little opposition to their leadership or their commercially oriented plans for urban redevelopment and expansion. Zane L. Miller and Bruce Tucker analyze the equally successful efforts of conservative council members in Cincinnati to bridge party differences in order to stifle reformers and neighborhood advocates. Michael P. Weber considers the generally, but not completely, successful attempts of Pittsburgh's business interests to gain the co-operation of mayors whose bases of support were in the old ethnic neighborhoods.

In two of the cities, old-style political machines have lingered well into the 1980s. In the Northeast, Mark I. Gelfand examines Boston, where the ascendancy of "southie" ward politician Raymond Flynn has extended a long tradition of Irish control. In the Midwest, Richard M. Bernard looks at Milwaukee, where the down-fall of Zeidler, the last socialist mayor, led to his replacement by Democrat Henry Maier, who during his twenty-eight years in office created a modern bureaucracy-based machine rooted in German and Polish neighborhoods but supported by the pro-redevelopment forces of business.

In four of the cities, as noted earlier, ethnic and business politicians have given way to blacks. Joseph Arnold discusses the peaceful transfer of power from modern machine mayor Donald Schaefer to black leaders when Schaefer won the Maryland governorship. Arnold R. Hirsch traces the rise and fall of Chicago's Cook County machine, which saw control of that city slip out of the hands of Mayor Daley's white successors and into those of Harold Washington. Carolyn Teich Adams dem-onstrates a similarly complex shift in Philadelphia from businessmen to reformers to white ethnics, and then back to reformers, before the election of black Mayor Goode. And Steven J. Diner presents a much more straightforward tale of the victory of blacks in Washington over businessmen and southern congressmen.

Finally, in the remaining three cities, uneasy alliances of business people, white ethnics, reformers, and minorities have kept local politics in turmoil. Thomas F. Campbell chronicles the remarkable pluralism of Cleveland's politics, where black Mayor Stokes lost power to resurgent white ethnic populists who in turn surrendered to the city's business elite. Daniel J. Walkowitz discusses the rough-and-tumble world of New York politics during and after the age of Robert Moses, concluding with the rise to power of the irascible Edward Koch; and John Clayton Thomas analyzes affairs in Kansas City, where businessmen and reformers vied for control.

Together, these essays present an intricate pattern of urban political competition among the leaders of business, white ethnics, reform movements, blacks, neigh-borhoods, and to a lesser extent suburbs. Aside from the neighborhood protection-ists, these groups generally agreed on the growth-oriented policies long advocated by business, something that they have in common with their counterparts in the cities of the South and West. The relative power of the non-business groups and their effectiveness in challenging business on the means for achieving that growth and over the distribution of its benefits, however, sets these cities apart from those of the Sunbelt and forms the bases of the Snowbelt's postwar metropolitan politics.

NOTES

1. Carl Abbott, *Urban America in the Modern Age, 1920 to the Present* (Arlington Heights, IL: Harlan Davidson, 1987); Kenneth Fox, *Metropolitan America: Urban Life and Urban Policy in the United States, 1940–1980* (Jackson: University Press of Mississippi, 1986); Jon C. Teaford, *The Twentieth Century American City: Problem, Promise, and Reality* (Baltimore: Johns Hopkins University Press, 1986). On the rise of the Sunbelt, see Carl Abbott, *The New Urban America: Growth and Politics in Sunbelt Cities* (Chapel Hill: University of North Carolina Press, 1981); Richard M. Bernard and Bradley R. Rice, eds., *Sunbelt Cities: Politics and Growth since World War II* (Austin: University of Texas Press, 1983); Blaine A. Brownell and David R. Goldfield, eds., *The City in Southern History: The Growth of Urban Civilization in the South* (Port Washington, NY: Kennikat Press, 1977); David R. Goldfield, *Cotton Fields and Skyscrapers: Southern City and Region, 1607–1980* (Baton Rouge: Louisiana State University Press, 1982); Bradford Luckingham, *The Urban Southwest: A Profile History of Albuquerque, El Paso, Phoenix, Tucson* (El Paso: Texas Western Press, 1982); Gerald Nash, *The American West in the Twentieth Century* (Englewood Cliffs, NJ: Prentice Hall, 1973); Kirkpatrick Sale, *Power Shift: The Rise of the Southern Rim and Its Challenge to the Eastern Establishment* (New York: Random House, 1975); and Alfred J. Watkins and David C. Perry, eds., *The Rise of the Sunbelt Cities* (Beverly Hills, CA: Sage Publications, 1977).

2. John Helyar, "Sun Belt's Economy Booms in Many Cities, But Rural Regions Lag," *New York Times,* January 15, 1988; *Shadows in the Sunbelt: Developing the Rural South in an Era of Economic Change: A Report of the MDC Panel on Rural Economic Development, May 1986* (Chapel Hill, NC: MDC, Inc., 1986); Michael Kinsley, "The Frost Belt's Revenge," *Washington Post National Weekly Edition,* April 14, 1986; "The Dark Side of the Sun Belt," *Newsweek,* July 19, 1982, pp. 46–50; "Worries on the Rise in the Sun Belt, Too," *U.S. News and World Report,* June 15, 1981, p. 31. See also Steven C. Ballard and Thomas E. James, eds., *The Future of the Sunbelt: Managing Growth and Change* (New York: Praeger, 1983).

3. On the uneven responses to the Sunbelt challenge, see Gary Gappert, ed., *The Future of Winter Cities: Urban Affairs Annual Reviews,* Vol. 31 (Newbury Park, CA: Sage Publications, 1987; Barry Checkoway and Carl V. Patton, eds., *The Metropolitan Midwest: Policy Problems and Prospects for Change* (Urbana: University of Illinois Press, 1985); Larry Sawers and William K. Tabb, eds., *Sunbelt/Snowbelt: Urban Development and Regional Restructuring* (New York: Oxford University Press, 1984); and Edward W. Hanten, Mark J. Kasoff, and F. Stevens Radburn, eds., *New Directions for the Mature Metropolis: Policies and Strategies for Change* (Cambridge, MA: Schenkman, 1980).

4. This study employs rather standard regional definitions: The "Northeast" includes Pennsylvania, Maryland, the District of Columbia, and the states to their north and east. The "Midwest" includes the states from Ohio through Minnesota, Iowa, and Missouri. Together, these two regions comprise the "Snowbelt." The other states constitute the "South and West," which includes the "Sunbelt," as defined in Bradley R. Rice, "Searching for the Sunbelt," *American Demographics* 3 (March 1981): 22–23, to include those states below the 37th parallel along the northern borders of North Carolina, Tennessee, Arkansas, Okla-

homa, New Mexico, and Arizona. In a variation from that study, however, this one puts all of California in the Sunbelt. The "Other Areas" include the remaining southern and western states, i.e., border states, the upper Plains, the Rockies, and the Pacific Northwest.

5. *U.S. Department of Commerce News* (CB87–116), July 24, 1987. One of the reasons northeastern and midwestern cities continue to fall in population rankings is their inability to match southern and western cities in the annexation of land. Largely hemmed in by suburbs, few Snowbelt cities have had this option, and only Milwaukee, Kansas City, Columbus, and Indianapolis have added as much as 5 percent to their land areas since 1960. Seymour Sacks, George Palumbo, and Robert Ross, "The Cold City: The Winter of Discontent?" in Gappert, ed., *Future of Winter Cities,* pp. 13–34.

6. McKinley L. Blackburn and David E. Bloom, "Regional Roulette," *American Demographics* 10 (January 1988): 32–37. The quotation is from p. 32.

7. The reason for the regional differences between the per household income growth rates and growth rates of total personal incomes is largely explained by two factors. First, as Blackburn and Bloom admit, there are more two-income households in the Northeast, and their proportion of the total number of households is rising faster in that region than elsewhere. This certainly increases the per household earnings of the region, but it does not necessarily add to the region's total income. Second, migration is transplanting more low-income households from the Northeast to the South and West than vice versa, causing a rise in per household earnings in the Northeast and a rise in the total earnings of the other areas.

8. In the early 1970s, the period of Sunbelt takeoff, only about 2 percent of employment losses in the North were due to plant relocations. Peter M. Allaman and David L. Birch, "Components of Employment Change for States by Industry Groups, 1970–1972," (Cambridge, MA: Joint Center for Urban Studies of M.I.T. and Harvard University, September 1975). Moreover, well over 90 percent of the northern firms that moved did so within their own region. James P. Miller, "Manufacturing Relocations in the United States: 1969–1975," in Richard B. McKenzie, ed., *Public or Private Choices?* (San Francisco: Cato Institute, 1981). See also John C. Raines, Lenora E. Berson, and David McI. Gracie, eds., *Community and Capital in Conflict: Plant Closings and Job Loss* (Philadelphia: Temple University Press, 1982); Sally K. Ward, "Economic Ownership in U.S. Communities: Corporate Change, 1961–75," *Social Science Quarterly* 62 (March 1981): 139–150; and Barry Bluestone and B. Harrison, *Capital and Communities: The Causes and Consequences of Private Disinvestment* (Washington: The Progressive Alliance, 1980).

9. Robert Jay Dilger, *The Sunbelt/Snowbelt Controversy: The War over Federal Funds* (New York: New York University Press, 1982), summarized the origins of the modern regional struggle over federal funds. See also "The Second War between the States," *Business Week,* May 17, 1976, pp. 82ff.

10. Weinstein and Wigley, "Regional Biases in Federal Funding," Center for Enterprising, Southern Methodist University, Dallas, Texas, July 1987 (photocopy), 44 pp.; John Rees, Bernard L. Weinstein, and Harold T. Gross, "Regional Patterns of Military Procurement and Their Implications," *ibid.,* September 1988 (photocopy), 69 pp.; DeVaul and Sorenson, "A Regional Analysis of the Entire Federal Budget," Northeast-Midwest Institute, Washington, D.C., August 6, 1987 (photocopy), 14 pp. The quotation is from their unpaginated introduction. See also John W. House, ed., *United States Public Policy: A Geographical View* (Oxford, U.K.: Clarendon Press, 1983).

11. Robert K. Whelan, "The Impacts of Reagan Administration Budget Cutbacks on States and Cities in the Sunbelt," unpublished paper presented at the conference on "The Sunbelt: A Region and Regionalism in the Making?" Miami, Florida, November 5, 1985.

12. Stephen Sandelius and Charles R. Foster, "Economic Shift to Sunbelt Reflected in Foreign Policy," *International Perspectives* [Canada] (May/June 1981), p. 12.

13. In Fiscal Year 1986, the Snowbelt with 45.6 percent of the population received only 36.1 percent of the nation's defense funds. The Northeast gained in almost exact proportion to its population, and the Midwest with 22.3 percent of the population obtained only 13.3 percent of the Pentagon's money. In contrast, the South and West with 54.8 percent of the

people captured 63.9 percent of the defense dollars. In the Sunbelt, the figures were 40.7 percent and 47.0 percent. DeVaul and Sorenson, Table 4. In 1983, only 264 of the nation's 647 military bases were in the Snowbelt. U.S. Department of Defense as quoted in *USA Today,* December 20, 1983. In Fiscal Year 1984, only 18 percent of the Snowbelt's metropolitan areas had net gains from Pentagon spending over tax monies sent to support the military, but 45 percent of those in the Sunbelt did. James R. Anderson, *Bankrupting American Cities: The Tax Burden and Expenditures of the Pentagon by Metropolitan Area,* 1984 ed. (Lansing, Michigan: Employment Research Associates, n.d.). See also Roger Lotchin, "The Origins of the Sunbelt-Frostbelt Struggle: Defense Spending and City Building," unpublished paper presented at the Sunbelt conference (see note 11); and Ann R. Markusen, "Defense Spending: A Successful Industrial Policy?" *International Journal of Urban and Regional Research* 10 (March 1986): 105–122.

14. John Agnew, *The United States in the World Economy: A Regional Geography* (Cambridge: Cambridge University Press, 1987); B. Bluestone and B. Harrison, *The Deindustrialization of America: Plant Closings, Community Abandonment, and the Dismantling of Basic Industry* (New York: Basic Books, 1982); L. E. Browne *et al.,* "Regional Investment Patterns," *New England Economic Review* (July/August 1980): 5–23. See also Ann R. Markusen, Peter Hall, and Amy K. Glasmeier, *High Tech America: The When, How, Where and Why of the Sunrise Industries* (London: Allen and Unwin, 1986); Allen J. Scott and Michael Storper, eds., *Production, Work, Territory: The Geographical Anatomy of Industrial Capitalism* (London: Allen and Unwin, 1986); Manuel Castells, ed., *High Technology, Space, and Society,* Vol. 27, *Urban Affairs Annual Reviews* (Beverly Hills, CA: Sage Publications, 1985); and Peter Hall and Ann Markusen, *Silicon Landscapes* (London: Allen and Unwin, 1985). At this writing, there are indications that American industry is reviving, thanks largely to the drop in value of the American dollar. The regional effect of this revival is unclear. See *Time,* March 14, 1988, pp. 48–50.

15. Bernard L. Weinstein *et al., Regional Growth and Decline in the United States* (New York: Praeger, 1985). Although no one disagrees on the linkage of economic development and growth, many nationwide are now questioning the desirability of the effects of unchecked development on their communities. This is especially true in southern California where a pro-growth record is now a political liability. Robert Reinhold, "Area's Growth Imperils Mayor in Los Angeles," *New York Times,* September 9, 1987. Even some southerners are having second thoughts. James C. Cobb, *Industrialization and Southern Society, 1877–1984* (Lexington: University Press of Kentucky, 1985), and *The Selling of the South: The Southern Crusade for Industrial Development, 1936–1980* (Baton Rouge: Louisiana State University Press, 1982); and Alfred J. Watkins, "Good Business Climates," *Dissent* 27 (1980): 476–84.

16. *The Eighth Annual Study of General Manufacturing Climates of the Forty-Eight Contiguous States of America* (Chicago: Grant Thornton, 1987). On the factor of state tax rates, see also Donald Phares, "State and Local Tax Burdens across the Fifty States," *Growth and Change* 16 (April 1985): 34–42; Steven Gold, "How and Why State Tax Rates Differ," *State Legislatures* 11 (March 1985): 6–7; and Roy Bahl, *Financing State and Local Government in the 1980s* (New York: Oxford University Press, 1984). For a dissenting view on the importance of low state tax rates, see Thomas R. Dye, "Taxing, Spending, and Economic Growth in the American States," *Journal of Politics* 42 (1980): 1085–1107. Much of the South and West's great advantage on the Grant Thornton index lies in the strongly probusiness states of the northern Great Plains; North Dakota, Nebraska, and South Dakota, respectively, earn the highest rankings. The Snowbelt, in fact, is much aided by the inclusion of Missouri (ranking: 6), a state at the border of the Midwest and the Plains. Without it, the Snowbelt's collective average rank would have jumped to 32.6. Conversely, oil-burdened Louisiana (45) pulled down the South and West's average, which without Louisiana would have been 19.4. For a critical review of the Grant Thornton and similar indices, see Charles L. Skoro, "Rankings of State Business Climates: An Evaluation of Their Usefulness in Forecasting," *Economic Development Quarterly* 2 (May 1988): 138–52.

17. Richard Boyer and David Savageau, *Rand McNally Places Rated Almanac: Your Guide to Finding the Best Places to Live in America* (Chicago: Rand McNally, 1981 and 1985). In both its 1981 and 1985 editions, the almanac listed about half its top fifty cities in the Snowbelt and about half in the South and West. Similarly, it split its choices for "super-solid and solid areas" about evenly. But the compliers of this popular study shattered their consistency, and some suggested their credibility, by replacing Atlanta as the nation's most livable city with Pittsburgh. To most Americans, the thought of Pittsburgh as America's best was, at the very least, a little surprising.

18. Bernard L. Weinstein and John Rees, "Sunbelt/Frostbelt Confrontation?" *Society* 17 (May/June 1980): 17–21.

19. Grant Thornton (1987), pp. 63–67, and *The Chronicle of Higher Education,* November 4, 1987, pp. A27–A31. For a dissenting view on the importance of state spending on education, see Dye, "Taxing, Spending, and Economic Growth."

20. As Dye puts it, "Newer states are uncluttered with obsolescent capital infrastructures and the habits and characteristics of past eras." Dye, "Taxing, Spending, and Economic Growth."

21. U.S. Bureau of the Census, *1982 Census of Governments,* Vol. VI, *Topical Studies,* No. 4, *Historical Statistics on Governmental Finances and Employment* (Washington: U.S. Government Printing Office, January 1985), Tables 24 and 29. Other factors also go into the costs of infrastructures, but the Census Bureau did not list these expenses separately.

22. This sort of federal assistance was woven through the recommendations of *The President's National Urban Policy Report, 1980,* prepared by President Carter's Department of Housing and Urban Development though ignored by the Reagan administration. See also John Kasarda, "The Implications of Contemporary Redistribution Trends for National Urban Policy," *Social Science Quarterly* 61 (December 1980): 373–400.

23. Richard B. McKenzie, "Myths of Sunbelt and Frostbelt," *Policy Review* 20 (Spring 1982): 103–14; Christopher Ross, "Regional Patterns of Organizational Dominance: 1955–1975," *Sociological Quarterly* 23 (Spring 1982): 207–19; Ward, "Economic Ownership."

24. The projected figures are from a press release of Election Data Services, Inc., Washington. See *New York Times,* February 5, 1988.

25. Based on figures from the *Congressional Quarterly's Guide to U.S. Elections,* pp. 1120–1121, 1125, the states won by Nixon in 1968 had added fifteen electoral votes as a result of the 1960 census count and had lost only seven, leaving Nixon with a net gain of eight electoral votes. Humphrey's states had gained only four electoral votes while losing ten, lowering his total by six votes. The states that voted for George Wallace, running on the American Party ticket, had lost four votes. Similarly, the states supporting Ford in 1976 had gained seven votes from the 1970 census and had lost but two, netting the incumbent five extra votes. Those states for Carter had gained only four votes and lost nine, leaving Carter with a net loss of five votes. In 1988, those states for Bush had gained a net of six votes after the 1980 census, while those for Dukakis had lost an equal number. Fred M. Shelley and J. Clark Archer, "Post-War Presidential Elections in the Sunbelt"; Kenneth C. Martis, "Critical Elections and Realignment in Sunbelt Voting: Congressional Elections, 1960–1984"; and Richard Morrill, "Redistribution, Reapportionment and Regionalism," unpublished papers presented to the Sunbelt conference (see note 11 above); *Time,* November 21, 1988, p. 33.

26. These figures, based on the *Congressional Quarterly's Guide to U.S. Elections,* pp. 1118–1119, result from comparisons of net losses by each party in the states that lost congressmen after each reapportionment with net gains in those states that gained. The published figures for California are incorrect and require crosschecking with the state's lists of congressional winners. As reapportionment caused the fortunes of the Democrats to fade, so too did it affect those of liberals, but, as the 1988 election made clear, the causes of the liberals' decline are multiple. As in the case of the Democrats, the portion of their decline attributable to reapportionment is likely rather small. On the foreign policy issue, Sandelius and Foster,

"Economic Shift," suggest that more Sunbelt representation may create a more isolationist Congress, but, for similar reasons, their argument seems overdrawn.

27. Harvey Molotch, "The City as a Growth Machine: Toward a Political Economy of Place," *American Journal of Sociology* 82 (September 1976): 309–32, argues that pro-growth people were more drawn to city officeholding than others and that they created a pro-growth ethos that became "the political and economic essence of virtually any given locality's growth" (pp. 309–10). The seminal work on this subject is Paul E. Peterson, *City Limits* (Chicago: University of Chicago Press, 1981), which argues that virtually all U.S. cities have a political consensus that favors attempts to make their cities competitive and that assumes that all residents will benefit. Both Peterson's supporters and critics agree that such a consensus exists, but they disagree on the degree to which all share in the benefits of growth: R. Scott Fosler and Renee A. Berger, eds., *Public-Private Partnership in American Cities* (Lexington, MA: D. C. Heath, 1982); Susan S. Feinstein, *Restructuring the City: The Political Economy of Urban Revolt* (New York: Longman, 1983); Katharine L. Bradbury, Anthony Downs, and Kenneth A. Small, *Urban Decline and the Future of American Cities* (Washington: The Brookings Institute, 1982); Roger Friedland, *Power and Crisis in the City: Corporations, Unions, and Urban Policy* (New York: Schocken Books, 1983). On urban politics in the Sunbelt, see Richard M. Bernard, "Metropolitan Politics in the American Sunbelt," in Raymond A. Mohl, ed., *Searching for the Sunbelt* (Knoxville: University of Tennessee Press, forthcoming).

28. On the waning days of political machines, see John H. Mollenkoft, *The Contested City* (Princeton: Princeton University Press, 1983); Harvey Boulay and Alan DiGaetano, "Why Did Political Machines Disappear?" *Journal of Urban History* 12 (November 1985): 25–49; Kenneth R. Mladenka, "The Urban Bureaucracy and the Chicago Political Machine: Who Gets What and the Limits of Political Control," *American Political Science Review* 74 (December 1980): 991–98; and Glenn Abney and Thomas P. Lauth, "A Comparitive Analysis of Distributional and Enforcement Decisions in Cities," *Journal of Politics* 44 (February 1982): 193–200.

29. The seminal work on these reformers, indeed on postwar municipal politics, is Edward C. Banfield and James Q. Wilson's *City Politics* (Cambridge, MA: Harvard University Press, 1963), which argues that the nature of city politics was an uneven acculturation of groups to the recurrent reform ethos.

30. See also Annemette Sorensen and Karl E. Taeuber, "Indexes of Racial Residential Segregation for 109 Cities in the United States, 1940 to 1970," *Sociological Focus* 8 (April 1975): 125–42; and Douglas S. Massey and Nancy A. Denton, "Trends in the Residential Segregation of Blacks, Hispanics, and Asians: 1970–1980," *American Sociological Review* 52 (December 1987): 802–25.

31. Rufus Browning, Dale Rogers Marshall, and David Tabb, *Protest Is Not Enough* (Berkeley: University of California Press, 1984); Rufus Browning and Dale Rogers Marshall, eds., "Black and Hispanic Power in City Politics: A Forum," Special Issue of *PS* 19 (Summer 1986); William E. Nelson, Jr., and Philip J. Meranto, *Electing Black Mayors: Political Action in the Black Community* (Columbus: Ohio State University, 1977); Michael B. Preston, "Limitations on Black Urban Power: The Case of Black Mayors," in Louis H. Masotti and Robert Lineberry, eds., *The New Urban Politics* (Cambridge, MA: Harvard University Press, 1976); Charles H. Levine, *Racial Conflict and the American Mayor* (Lexington, MA: D. C. Heath, 1974); Leonard Cole, "Electing Blacks to Municipal Office: Structural and Social Determinants," *Urban Affairs Quarterly* 10 (September 1974): 17–39.

32. As originally designed, this volume was to cover all sixteen of the largest metropolitan areas in the Northeast and Midwest, but well into the writing process some contributors discovered that they were unable to meet their commitments and withdrew from the project.

II

BALTIMORE

SOUTHERN CULTURE AND
A NORTHERN ECONOMY

Joseph L. Arnold

It is important to remember that Baltimore lies just below the Mason-Dixon line. It is a Snowbelt city with a southern past. During the Civil War a large number of its men fought for the Confederacy, and as late as 1948 the city still erected statues of Robert E. Lee and Stonewall Jackson in its public squares.[1] Until the 1950s Baltimore's public schools and many other facilities were racially segregated, even if its black voters were never disfranchised and segregation was not as universal as it was farther south. By the 1980s Baltimore had shed most of its southern orientation, but the tradition of Dixie can be seen in much of its post–World War II history.[2]

Baltimore has one of the best natural harbors on the Chesapeake Bay. The core city of the eighteenth and nineteenth centuries is located on the Middle Branch of the Patapsco River, five miles above its confluence with the bay. From here the famous Baltimore clippers sailed, but this old "Inner Harbor" is no longer used for shipping. Today it has become the central focus of the city's Harborplace renewal area.

Today a city of 80 square miles, Baltimore is surrounded on three sides by the 600 square miles of Baltimore County. As late as 1945, contractors had only begun to expand the city's housing, industries, and port facilities into the lower end of the county. Today almost half of the entire county is suburbanized, and development has spilled over into the more distant counties of Harford, Carroll, and Howard. The northern section of Anne Arundel County, which abuts part of the city's southern boundary, is an 80-square-mile area containing the Baltimore-Washington International Airport, office and industrial parks, and very large residential developments. The Baltimore metropolitan region now covers slightly over 400 square miles, and its southern suburbs are rapidly merging with the outer suburbs of the much larger and wealthier Washington D.C. metropolitan region.

Locked, it now seems permanently, into its present municipal boundaries, Baltimore City encompasses about 20 percent of the land, 28 percent of the population, and 23 percent of the assessed wealth in the metro area. There are no significant local or municipal governments within the five surrounding counties, so in theory, at least, city-county cooperation should be quite easy. In fact, that has not proven to be the case. A regional planning council was created in 1963, but it has only advisory authority. In 1968, a proposed new constitution for the state provided for the creation of metropolitan governments, but fearful suburbanites voted it down.[3] There are some metro-wide programs in such areas as water supply, highways, and mass transit, but in more sensitive areas such as schools, local taxes, or public housing there is no cooperation and no serious discussion. This is understandable, since the greatest asset the suburban counties possess is their separateness from the city's poverty, crime, and high taxes.

In spite of Baltimore's dwindling size and wealth, it continues to serve five major functions in the metro region that raise it above the level of just another specialized sub-area. First, it is the center of Maryland's cultural life, the state's principal communications and financial headquarters, and its primary entertainment and tourist attraction. Second, the city has the largest concentrations of low-income housing (public and private) and low-skilled jobs in the state. The city has attracted, or imprisoned some might say, 44 percent of Maryland's low income households. Third, Baltimore holds 45 percent of the state's black population and is the center of Maryland's black cultural, economic, and social life (even though a number of middle-class black families have joined the flight to the suburbs and 14 percent of the region's black population live outside the city). Fourth, the north end of the city, anchored by Johns Hopkins University, two elite private colleges, and a number of expensive prep schools, contains one of Maryland's wealthiest and most prestigious residential areas. There, many of the city's leaders live in $300,000 homes and send over 90 percent of their children to private schools. Fifth, the city serves as a magnet for attracting increasing numbers of white, affluent, childless "back-to-the-city" people who are gentrifying many of the inner city's historic and architecturally interesting neighborhoods. These functions are not easily compatible, and the efforts to sustain a city composed of such different elements form a major theme in the history of Baltimore during the past four decades.

The changes that have come about in Baltimore reflect factors common to the nation's other older industrial cities: the suburbanization of middle-class populations followed by outmovement of retail and wholesale trade; the influx of poor, mostly black, rural immigrants; and the general decline of central-city employment. Local industry is in shambles. Baltimore's population declined by 180,000 between 1960 and 1985, and total city employment declined by over 50,000 jobs—the majority of which were high-paying, blue-collar manufacturing jobs. During the same period the surrounding counties increased their employment by over 100,000 jobs, and their populations rose by over 600,000. Total employment in the city is expected to rise somewhat in the early 1990s, but over 80 percent of the increase will come from relatively low-paying service and retail trade jobs. By 1990 manufacturing will comprise only 10 percent of the city's employment base.[4]

The city's history as a major manufacturing center lasted only about 80 years. Before the twentieth century, Baltimore's prosperity depended primarily on commercial activities. The nineteenth century was its glory era of tall ships and pioneer railroading. Manufacturing was clearly secondary. By the 1880s, however, Baltimore's leaders concluded that the city could not continue to rely so heavily on commerce and launched an effort to attract manufacturing plants. The city's industrial base grew moderately in the 1880s and 1890s and then more rapidly after 1900. Clothing factories, chemical plants, foundries, steel mills, and auto assembly plants spread out behind the wharves.

By the 1930s Baltimore had come to resemble quite closely the industrial cities of the North, but the transition occurred at a slow, leisurely pace that failed to disturb the southern attitudes of its businessmen or working classes. Baltimore's business leaders tended to be gracious and sophisticated southern gentlemen who were regarded as cautious plodders in both business and civic affairs. When the city's businessmen talked about the "fast track," they were probably discussing the horse races at Pimlico, where the annual Preakness race was one of Baltimore's great social events. The city's working classes, while not entirely docile, were clearly less militant than their counterparts in other northern cities.[5] One of Baltimore's attractions for nationwide corporations was its weak labor movement and low wage scales. Major firms such as General Motors, Western Electric, Bethlehem Steel, Lever Brothers, and Armco Steel located plants in and around Baltimore.

In contrast to its economy, Baltimore's social, cultural, and political life appeared to change very little between 1880 and 1945. The city retained much of its nineteenth-century structure and flavor. John Gunther, after touring the city in 1947, wrote that it had more the atmosphere of the eighteenth century.[6] H. L. Mencken, Baltimore's most famous resident, delighted in the sluggish backwardness of its residents and the pre-industrial charm of its streets, alleys, and row houses. He made a career out of excoriating the city's "boosters" who in Babbitt-like fashion sought to bring the city "up to date."[7] In 1945 Baltimore probably still had a larger proportion of its nineteenth-century physical plant than any other major city, and its population still bore a close resemblance to the one that had resided there in 1860. The majority were native-born whites who traced their roots to rural Maryland or other southern states. Baltimore had the smallest percentage of eastern and southern European immigrants of any city in the Northeast, but a larger share than any city of the South. It had more black residents than any city of the Northeast, but whites kept them firmly in place through a southern system of legal and social segregation.

The majority of Baltimore's black residents lived in stark poverty, squeezed into three terribly overcrowded, blighted ghettos surrounding the central business district. Blacks were barred from attending the University of Maryland (U.S. Supreme Court Justice Thurgood Marshall was forced to go out of state to get his law degree). They could not eat at the city's famous restaurants, try on clothes at any department store, join the Chamber of Commerce, swim at the municipal pools and beaches, or play tennis on the municipal tennis courts.[8] Since the end of the Civil War, most of Baltimore's black voters had been Republicans, but because they earned no rewards for their loyalty, they began after 1935 to move into the Democratic party. There they were also largely ignored.

That Baltimore of 1945 now looks very remote. During the following forty years the city underwent a more profound change than in any other time in its long history. First, the numerical dominance of its black residents and the rise to power of black leaders has transformed the social and political life of the city. Black residents became a majority of the population in the mid-1970s and a majority of the electorate in the early 1980s. In 1987 the city elected its first black mayor. Second, the economic structure, physical plant, and much of the neighborhood environment of the city has changed profoundly and, for the most part, very positively. Some view redevelopment of the city's downtown, centered on the now famous Inner Harbor area, as the most successful redevelopment project in urban America and a most powerful symbol of the "Baltimore Renaissance." Other areas of the city have also experienced profound alteration. The majority of Baltimore's 266 neighborhoods now have a very different socioeconomic profile than they exhibited in 1945 or even in 1965. The changes present a complex patchwork of improvement, deterioration, and rebirth. On balance, the majority of the city's neighborhoods have shared at least modestly in the city's renaissance, but opinions differ sharply on this aspect of the city's progress. Certainly the large number of dilapidated and abandoned homes in many city neighborhoods stand as visible evidence of devastating job losses in the 1970s and 1980s.

There is a close connection between city politics and the Baltimore Renaissance. The political history of the city since 1945 is really two sagas, one revolving around race relations and the other centered on business-government connections, particularly as they relate to urban redevelopment. Close cooperation between city hall and corporate board room has been essential to the success of most urban reconstruction, and Baltimore's business-government relationship has been very close since 1945. The cardinal fact of the city's postwar history is that Baltimore underwent a profound change in city politics with a smoothness that never forced the municipality to divert attention from its slow, steady pursuit of the redevelopment goals set out by its business and government leaders in the late 1940s and early 1950s. A fundamental cautiousness or cultural conservatism on the part of Baltimore's black and white residents, as well as their leaders, helps to explain both the nature and pace of the city's long and somewhat tardy revolutions in politics and redevelopment.

Baltimore's transition from a segregationist polity to a city government led by a black mayor is not unique, but it is remarkable primarily for the general absence of polarization. With the possible exception of the 1968–1971 era, with its urban riots and national level upheavals, racial tensions in Baltimore never reached the level seen in many other cities.

How was racial change achieved without major turmoil? Mayoral leadership was a major factor. For most of the postwar years influential mayors, who combined political power with the legal authority of a "strong mayor" municipal structure, recognized either the inevitability or the justice of giving the city's black voters roles in the party and the municipal government. Each proceeded to advance the black cause, though generally with great caution or, as some black leaders charged, with great foot dragging. If the pace of change became too slow, Baltimore's large and well-organized chapter of the National Association for the Advancement of Colored People, led by the remarkable Lillie May Jackson, brought well-timed pressure on the city's white politicians, reminding them how often Baltimore's black voters had tipped the balance in city primary elections and statewide general elections.[9] Nevertheless, change was very gradual. It was so gradual that it never provoked a significant white backlash, yet it was steady enough to keep major black political leaders loyal to the city's dominant Democratic machine. Whites never rallied behind any of the local right-wing radicals who preached "massive resistance" to integration, nor did black residents respond very enthusiastically to black separatists and advocates of violence.

An old Democratic machine dating to the late nineteenth century totally dominated Baltimore politics until the 1960s. Even then a number of the machine's old ward bosses continued to wield local power. For a decade the party wandered without strong leadership or city-wide organization until a new and different coalition of Democrats was constructed by William Donald Schaefer. From 1930 to 1947 the major figure in the Democratic machine was William Curran, a quintessential Irish boss who led an organization dominated by Anglo-American, German, and Irish blocs. Curran was not very popular, however, among the city's Italian, Jewish, or Polish voters whom he made to feel like outsiders, and he had little or no connection to blacks. In 1947 "Tommy" D'Alesandro, the Democratic leader of Baltimore's "Little Italy," combined with local Jewish politicians to take control of city government from the Curran faction. D'Alesandro won the mayor's race—the first Italian and the first Catholic to hold that office.[10]

To arm himself against Curran's inevitable counterattack, D'Alesandro reached out to new groups of Democratic voters. He encouraged the growing numbers of black voters to identify with his faction of the Democratic machine by firmly supporting a program of gradual municipal desegregation. (Baltimore was the first large southern city to begin desegregating its schools after the 1954 *Brown* decision.) He also dispensed a small number of the city's jobs to loyal black party workers. Both policies dismayed a number of his own white city councilmen but brought black politicians into the Democratic machine. Clarence "Du" Burns, who became the first black president of the city council in 1982, received his first municipal job from D'Alesandro in 1951. Overall, D'Alesandro's strategy was successful and his coalition held firm for twelve years.[11]

None of these changes within the city Democratic party helped Baltimore's Republicans who continued to sink into political impotence. The GOP, saddled since the Reconstruction era with the support of the city's black voters, had never been able to attract many white voters. The party had shown some strength in the 1920s but had failed to recover from losses it had sustained during the Great Depression. The last Republican ever elected to the city council left office in 1942, and the only Republican to win the mayor's office since the 1920s was Maryland Governor Theodore McKeldin, a beloved maverick who presented himself to city voters in 1943 and again in 1963 as an "independent" member of the GOP.

Serving as mayor from 1963 to 1967, McKeldin had no organizational support, for there were no Republican councilmen and almost no Republican party in the city. What McKeldin did have was a remarkable personality which made him very popular with both white and black voters. McKeldin was deeply committed to racial equality. As mayor, he pushed racial integration much farther along. In this effort, he enjoyed the discreet help of integrationists within the Democratic machine who deceived white segregationists into thinking that racial changes were the doing of the Republican mayor. Following McKeldin, D'Alesandro's son and namesake served during the riot-torn years of 1967 to 1971. The younger D'Alesandro worked very closely and effectively with the city's black leaders to keep racial strife from deeply dividing the whole city, but the experience soured him on politics, and he declined to run for reelection.

The junior D'Alesandro gave the reins of office over to the influential city council president, William Donald Schaefer, who was elected mayor in 1971. He became the greatest and most powerful mayor in the city's history, staying in the mayor's office until trading it for the governorship in 1987. No one has ever wielded greater authority over the city's Democratic Party or ruled the municipal government so much like a benevolent monarch.

Schaefer began his career in the 1950s as a protégé of the old-time local bosses in the white neighborhoods of West and Northwest Baltimore. As a young councilman, he worked hard and adroitly. Late in the decade, he faced a major personal and political decision when his West Baltimore neighborhood underwent a racial transition and became 90 percent black. Rather than following his white constituents into Baltimore County, as other politicians had often done, Schaefer stayed with his mother in their little row house. By remaining behind, Councilman Schaefer developed a close association with black leaders in the rapidly growing West Baltimore black community, and he became the city's only white politician with a significant black following. With a coalition of black and white neighborhood leaders, politicians, and some influential businessmen, Schaefer rose to become city council president in 1967, and thereafter he probably held more real power than D'Alesandro.

In the primary race for mayor in 1971, Schaefer defeated George Russell, the city's first black state's attorney, by capturing 90 percent of the white vote and 15 percent of the black vote. As Schaefer's power grew and the numbers of black voters and councilmen increased, his black supporters reaped larger rewards and greater responsibilities in the city government. A number of white politicians resented this, but the mayor's defenders knew that, with the exception of the school system, the majority of key posts remained in familiar white hands. White politicians and voters also feared that unseating Schaefer might split the party and bring in a black mayor—a possibility that in the late 1960s and early 1970s was regarded by most Baltimore whites as the final "defeat." During this same period some black leaders complained that racial progress in the city government was too slow, particularly in the upper levels of municipal service and in the awarding of city contracts. These individuals urged black voters to unite behind a challenger from their own race, but the black community remained patient, waiting for the mayor to retire or move on to higher office. Their chance finally came in 1987 when Schaefer was elected governor.[12]

With Schaefer gone and blacks now an estimated 56 percent of the electorate, whites searched longingly for a white mayoral candidate acceptable to black voters. Only one white political leader was thought capable of drawing a large vote from both groups. This was Robert C. Embry, who had been one of Schaefer's closest advisors, the chief architect of the Baltimore Renaissance, and a young man who had always moved easily in the interracial world that was developing in the city. When Embry chose not to run, most observers believed he had decided that it would be too divisive for him to campaign against the several well-qualified black candidates seeking the office.

The race narrowed to two black Democratic leaders, Clarence "Du" Burns and Kurt Schmoke. The aspirants represented two quite different generations and backgrounds. "Du" Burns had worked his way up through the machine over a period of almost forty years, becoming acting mayor upon Schaefer's resignation. He was Schaefer's choice to succeed him. Like the elder "Tommy" D'Alesandro, Burns was largely self-educated and outgoing. He was a very skillful politician with a common touch that made him both a friend and popular symbol for thousands of black Baltimoreans who shared the same humble background and limited formal training. Kurt Schmoke was a thirty-seven-year-old attorney, a high school and college sports star, a graduate of Yale University and Harvard Law School, and a Rhodes Scholar. He had entered politics more than half way up the ladder as the Baltimore City state's attorney.[13]

Although Schmoke defeated Burns in the 1987 primary by a very narrow margin (50.6% to 47.4%), commentators interpreted the results as a sign of the emergence of Baltimore's new middle-class black voters. The media also noted the stronger appeal of the Ivy League attorney to the city's white middle classes. In the general election Schmoke easily defeated his white Republican opponent, Samuel Culotta, by securing over 90 percent of the black vote and 65 percent of the white vote.[14] Thus, the climax of Baltimore's transition to black leadership occurred without polarization or even any noticeable tension.

Schmoke's election also made it clear that the long-standing business-government coalition would remain in place. Throughout his campaign, Schmoke allied himself with business-government policies, saying that Schaefer's ability to "bring business into government" was a significant contribution and that "the next generation of leaders will have to build on that, expand on that."[15]

The forty-year program of physical redevelopment in Baltimore parallels the city's political reconstruction and shares several of the same qualities: a slow pace, cautiousness bordering on timidity, but ultimate triumph.

In 1945 few of Baltimore's leaders saw any reason to undertake a dramatic program of physical reconstruction. The Second World War brought tremendous economic growth to the city, and many of the war production plants continued to expand as shipping in the port continued to climb. In 1947 Baltimore exported a higher tonnage of goods than New York, becoming the nation's leading exporter. After almost a century of watching their population and economy slip farther behind the other large cities of the nation, Baltimoreans now believed that they were beginning to turn their city's prospects around.

In the midst of all this self-congratulation and optimism, a few city leaders suggested that all was not as well as it seemed. The postwar boom rested on some shaky foundations. Hooper Miles, one of the city's leading bankers and president of the Chamber of Commerce, told the chamber that Baltimore's economic performance since the war was cause for rejoicing but that this prosperity had come to depend more heavily than ever on forces far beyond the control of the city, region, or nation. National and international factors, he said, "form the actual keystone of our economic outlook and security." Even more troubling was that while Baltimore had entered "the big league of really great cities of the country, and indeed the world," it was "suffering from the inertia and self-indulgence that comes from a willingness to rest upon the accomplishments of our historic past." Unless the city's leaders recognized that big-city status had also brought big-city problems requiring vigorous countermeasures, "we will have failed to meet our real obligation to our community."[16]

The list of problems identified by Miles and the city's business leaders were a familiar list in postwar urban America: (1) the decline of the downtown retail and office center; (2) obsolescence of the port facilities; (3) lack of a modern urban highway system; (4) deterioration of the city's housing as middle-income neighborhoods were abandoned to lower-income (mostly black) residents; and (5) the increasing cost of municipal government which pushed the local tax rate up and threatened the city's financial stability. Businessmen did not consider the loss of industry a significant problem at the time, since net total industrial employment in the city was still growing. Only in the 1970s and 1980s did this issue move to the front as a series of factory closings shook the foundations of the city's industrial economy.

The original list of urban problems dealt primarily with physical and economic problems. Largely ignored were the city's serious social and human problems: racial discrimination, low wages, lack of social services, and poor quality instruction in the public schools. Here again, only in the 1970s and 1980s did these issues begin to attract the serious attention of Baltimore's business leaders.

Of the five problems that city leaders did identify in the late 1940s, four have clearly been solved. The port has undergone complete reconstruction, the downtown has turned into a spectacular economic success, an urban super highway system is now in place, and the tax base and tax rate have stabilized. The housing and neighborhood problem remains. Conditions in many sections of the city have improved, while in many others they remain grim or are getting worse.

Reconstruction of the port was a high priority in the postwar years because so much of Baltimore's industry and commerce depended on it. Progress languished, however, until 1956, in part because the city could not afford the huge cost involved but did not want either the state or private contractors to take over this historic municipal function. The other major problem was the railroads' lack of enthusiasm because plans called for much greater truck access to the piers. The opposition of both the city government and the railroads finally gave way due to the formation of an elite businessmen's organization called the Greater Baltimore Committee (GBC). Established in 1955 to breathe life into the timid downtown revival efforts, the GBC gradually became the chief force behind the entire Baltimore Renaissance. The GBC went to the state legislature with the sweeping proposal that the state of Maryland take over the entire port, rebuild it for trucks as well as railroads, and administer it as a state agency. The GBC won the legislative battle, and the city lost control of its port. In one respect, the loss was inevitable, since over the next thirty years much of the new port construction would come outside the municipal boundaries in the Patapsco River's Outer Harbor area. This extramunicipal development left the old Inner Harbor abandoned and unused until the city eventually realized its fabulous potential for urban renewal.[17]

Highway building was the most vexing and politically explosive issue the city faced during the whole forty-year period. One local commentator said, ''It has been Baltimore's Vietnam.'' The city began with a very ambitious and destructive program that envisioned running major new highways through almost every section of the city, but neighborhood groups in areas slated for highway demolition carried on a thirty-year defense of their turf from the bulldozers. As a result highway advocates ended up in the 1980s with less than half of what they originally wanted, but this has proven to be adequate. This contest of wills had both good and bad consequences for the city. On the positive side, limitations on the final highway program saved a number of stable neighborhoods that are now prospering. The political opposition also forced highway administrators to abandon their 1950s and 1960s plans to run an east-west superhighway through the center of the Inner Harbor where it would intersect with the major north-south route near an eighteenth-century waterfront neighborhood called Fells Point. The construction of such a monstrosity would have virtually precluded development of the Inner Harbor renewal project, and the proposed central clover leaf would have destroyed what is now some of the most valuable waterfront property on the East Coast. Instead of following such a destructive path, the final highway plan placed I-95 in a gigantic tunnel running under Ft. McHenry and the Inner Harbor. This underground section is the most expensive single segment of the nation's 40,000 mile interstate highway system, but it is a triumph of rational and sensitive highway planning. Through it, downtown drivers gained easy access to the expressways without intruding too heavily on the surrounding residential, historic, or renewal districts.[18] The unfortunate aspect of Baltimore's highway battles and the city's failure to take more prompt action was that the interstate beltway, located entirely outside the city, opened many years before the city highways. The timing caused many businesses that might have stayed within the municipality to move to office and industrial parks along the Baltimore County beltway.[19]

The central fiscal problem for Baltimore has been the decline of its tax base in the 1960s and 1970s. Nevertheless, the city has a very long history of financial stability and has always kept a high municipal credit rating. One reason is the city's great success in winning state and federal funding. During the 1960s and 1970s Baltimore received far more than its fair per capita share of federal funds, but this input has declined sharply in the 1980s, forcing the state to take up more of the burden, particularly for school funding. In political or administrative terms, the fact that over 40 percent of the municipal budget now comes from the state and federal governments means that the city has lost almost half of its financial independence. The modest growth in its tax base in the 1980s due to downtown renewal and neighborhood gentrification has been helpful, but dependence on the state government will continue to be essential for municipal budget balancing.

The city has also been extremely tight-fisted with its money. It has never granted large salary increases, and the city payroll is modest compared to other larger cities. Its capital budget comes under double scrutiny from city and state governments. City employees have never found a political base strong enough to challenge the mayor, whose authority over budgetary matters is far greater than the more easily influenced city council. Yet even with these many advantages, Baltimore has not been able to remain competitive in its rate of local taxation. The city tax rate has risen from $2.84 per $100 of assessed valuation in 1948 to slightly over $6.00 in the late 1980s—more than twice the Baltimore County rate. This remains one of the chief reasons for the exodus of the city's middle- and lower-middle-income families.[20]

Baltimore's national reputation rests on its downtown renewal program and its close association with developer James Rouse, one of the founding members of the Greater Baltimore Committee. That reputation put the city (and Rouse) on the cover of *Time* magazine in 1981 and brought close to a billion dollars worth of investment capital into an area of the city that in 1960 was largely abandoned and smelled bad.[21]

Downtown renewal goes back to the founding of the GBC in 1955 and its decision to build Charles Center, a 33-acre development just north of the Inner Harbor. This facility was to have offices, plazas, restaurants, and a hotel. The idea drew heavily on the Pittsburgh Golden Triangle project, but it was smaller in scope. The elder D'Alesandro's administration quickly produced the enabling legislation, and voters approved a bond issue to pay the costs. Demolition, however, did not begin until 1961, and the project was not completed until the early 1970s. The area held a large federal office building, commercial offices, a Hilton Hotel, the Morris Mechanic Theater, and a variety of shops and retail stores. Even this modest project was at first difficult to sell to Baltimore's conservative investors. Its promoters later told stories of businessmen who advised them back in 1960 that the project would be a colossal failure but who came back years later to see if they could rent space in it.[22]

Charles Center demonstrated that downtown renewal might work in Baltimore, and it encouraged gradual new building in adjacent areas. By the early 1960s some of the city's leaders suggested that even the old Inner Harbor waterfront might be feasible for renewal, but such talk was still regarded as idle speculation. A few of the city's planners had envisioned the area as a waterfront promenade, and Mayor McKeldin, in his inaugural address of 1963, painted a glowing picture of what the area could become. Serious work was not begun, however, until the early 1970s when the Maryland Science Center (1976) and the Maryland Port Administration's World Trade Center (1977) built striking buildings on the waterfront. At the suggestion of Robert Embry, James Rouse was invited in 1977 to build two pavilions, now called Harborplace, at the center of the Inner Harbor in a style reminiscent of the Quincy Market project that he had done in Boston. With the opening of Harborplace and the National Aquarium in 1980–81, Baltimore's Inner Harbor was finally reborn. As investors grasped the profit potential of the area, a land rush began. Developers began refurbishing every old waterside warehouse they could find and building spectacular new structures. Behind the waterfront, block after block of old rowhouses were rapidly gentrified. The most recent major proposal, one for waterfront housing with adjacent marinas on the site of an abandoned shipyard, calls for an investment of $600 million.[23]

To some degree Baltimore was just plain lucky with the Inner Harbor area. The harbor itself is one of the most splendid natural settings for redevelopment anywhere in the United States, and the very tardiness of its development turned out to be a great advantage. The city's failure to do anything in the Inner Harbor area (it sat vacant for almost twenty years awaiting the construction of the ill-fated highway project) kept it out of the hands of low-investment, piecemeal developers until 1980 when Rouse's Harborplace pavilions opened. Thus, the investment community did not "discover" Baltimore until the beginning of the greatest real estate and land development decade of the century, a coincidence of timing that has allowed the city to reap maximum economic benefits.

In contrast to the ultimate success of Baltimore's downtown and Inner Harbor renewal, progress in the rest of the city has been much more uneven. There is no question that the city became poorer in the 1970s, and some of its neighborhoods have declined significantly. At least one scholar has suggested that Schaefer created an "island of renewal in a sea of decay."[24] Critics charge that his administration spent too much public money downtown and not enough to help declining neighborhoods, to save more of the city's industrial plants, and to develop better employment for those who could not qualify for downtown office jobs. Exactly how much money the city spent on downtown renewal is unknown. It is likely that the city spent more than necessary to get private investors back downtown, but that is a judgment of hindsight. No one could have predicted in the "riot" year of 1968, when Charles Center was still an island of renewal in a downtown sea of commercial decay, that fifteen years later the Inner Harbor would attract more visitors than Disneyland and that tourism would be a $786 million industry in Baltimore, generating over 16,000 new jobs.[25] Until the mid-1970s the GBC and Mayor Schaefer had to work hard to sell potential investors on the economic viability of the area. Not until the latter part of that decade did the rush of buyers begin to make the city's heavy subsidies look unnecessary.

If the Schaefer administration failed to subsidize neighborhood development in a similar manner it did make important nonfinancial contributions to the advancement of those areas. Of real value was the mayor's constant efforts to give residents a sense of pride in their neighborhoods and in their city. A major study of Baltimore's neighborhoods concludes that in the municipal liturgy, "neighborhood is next to motherhood."[26] Throughout his term in office (and for many previous years), Schaefer spent night after night speaking, and listening, at small neighborhood meetings throughout the city. He took complaints about trash, street lights, stray dogs, and crime back to the appropriate city department for action. But he always exhorted local audiences to do things for themselves and to take pride in their street and their neighborhood.

Embry headed the drive to put on a Baltimore City Fair in 1970 at a time when many people, remembering 1968, had put the city out of their minds. The central feature of the fair was to be group of twenty "neighborhood booths," built and staffed by the neighborhood people themselves, offering food, drinks, and information about their locality. Right up to the day it opened on September 25, 1970, its organizers wondered "Is anyone really going to come?" The question was not idle, since the previous May the old Baltimore Flower Mart, an outdoor festival put on by a Baltimore woman's club, had to be closed after unruly inner-city teenagers disrupted it. By the standards of 1970 the first City Fair was a great success, bringing over 300,000 people down to the new Charles Center Plaza. By 1974 the event had grown so large that it moved to the still vacant Inner Harbor. Now there were dozens of neighborhood booths with sophisticated displays and the names of real estate agents who could show good houses at prices far below those seen in the suburbs.[27]

Neighborhood improvement, of course, long predated the Schaefer administration, and the mayor never claimed to have launched the city's neighborhood renaissance. In spite of the vast changes in its racial composition, Baltimore has a very large number of black and white residents committed to stable neighborhood life. It also had a small, but active group of "gentrifiers" long before that term came into use. Tyson Street and Bolton Hill, two locally famous neighborhoods, were gentrified in the late 1940s and early 1950s. By the 1960s young people were buying city houses in working-class districts such as Federal Hill, Fells Point, and Union Square. Other younger families bought large older homes in areas most realtors had expected to slide gradually into decay. Even more important to the city's housing market and neighborhood stability was the steady growth of black home ownership and the development of stable black neighborhoods. Between 1950 and 1970 dozens of neighborhoods changed from white to black and for the first time encompassed some very attractive areas into which middle- and upper-income black families moved. By 1980 racially integrated or predominantly black neighborhoods comprised the majority of all residential acreage in the city, and neighborhood stability was noticeably greater than it had been in 1970. A careful analysis of Baltimore's neighborhoods during the 1970s found "the emergence of middle-class, stable, black or integrated neighborhoods as the most predominant type of neighborhood in the city."[28]

At the close of 1986 the Morris Goldseker Foundation issued a report, *Baltimore 2000: A Choice of Futures,* by Peter Szanton, a distinguished urban policy analyst. The report caused a sensation in official circles and concern among the general public because it concluded that the entire Baltimore Renaissance up to 1986, while very promising and helpful, was not going to solve the city's deeper problems of job losses, unemployment, and middle-class flight or elevate the low level of education and skills possessed by nearly half its residents. Quoting one of the many

Baltimoreans he interviewed, Szanton said, "This city needs a second act."[29] As a second phase, the report suggested the development of a new consensus of opinion on the city's chief goals now that the port facilities, downtown, and highway goals had been clearly achieved. According to Szanton, these goals should be: (1) a dramatic improvement of the city's schools, a system that almost all objective observers told him was simply a failure; (2) a more favorable and attractive climate for the city's most talented college graduates, especially black graduates, who have tended not to return to the city or metropolitan area; (3) a first-class system of public higher education that will attract and hold the most talented youths and serve the city's business, professional, and industrial needs; and (4) closer links to the neighboring Washington, D.C., metropolitan area that is so much larger and wealthier. Echoing Hooper Miles in 1947, Szanton cautioned that there was no "sure test of Baltimore's comparative advantage in the national marketplace. . . . Major investments . . . might turn out to yield little." However, he predicted that to stand still and hope that past successes would carry the city through its present difficulties would wipe out much or all the progress made over the previous decades.[30] Considering the long struggle of the city to hold its own in the years from 1945 to 1986 when the goals were more clear-cut and federal money flowed rather more freely, the agenda for Baltimore's "act two" is very ambitious. Yet, a much broader spectrum of talented people lead the city today than led it in 1945, and they have the invaluable experience of the Baltimore Renaissance upon which to draw for a new assault on the problems of tomorrow.

NOTES

1. *The Sun,* May 2, 1948.
2. Sherry H. Olsen, *Baltimore: The Building of an American City* (Baltimore: Johns Hopkins University Press, 1980), pp. 302–86; Sherry Olson, *Baltimore* (Cambridge, MA: Ballinger Publishing Company, 1976), pp. 17–29; George H. Callcott, *Maryland and America, 1940 to 1980* (Baltimore: Johns Hopkins University Press, 1985).
3. John P. Wheeler, Jr., and Melissa Kinsey, *Magnificent Failure: The Maryland Constitutional Convention of 1967–1968* (New York: The National Management League, 1970).
4. Eric Garland, "The End of Baltimore as a Blue Collar Town," *Baltimore Magazine* 73 (December 1980): 52–58.
5. Jo Ann E. Argersinger, *Toward A New Deal in Baltimore: People and Government in the Great Depression* (Chapel Hill: University of North Carolina Press, 1988), pp. 1–7, 141–77.
6. John Gunther, *Inside U.S.A.* (New York: Harper & Brothers, 1947), p. 639.
7. For Mencken's views on "boosters," see *The Sun,* February 15, 1926. His classic work on the old Baltimore is *Happy Days, 1880–1892* (New York: Alfred A. Knopf, 1940).
8. The Sidney Hollander Foundation and the Baltimore Urban League, *Toward Equality: Baltimore's Progress Report* (Baltimore: The Sidney Hollander Foundation, 1960).
9. Callcott, *Maryland and America,* pp. 145–71.
10. Joseph L. Arnold, "The Last of the Good Old Days: Politics in Baltimore, 1920–

1950," *Maryland Historical Magazine* 71 (1976): 443–48; Callcott, *Maryland and America*, pp. 3–10.

11. There is no biography of D'Alesandro. See the lengthy obituary in *The Sun*, August 24, 1987, and the brief biography in Melvin G. Holli and Peter d'A. Jones, ed., *Biographical Dictionary of American Mayors, 1820–1980* (Westport, CT: Greenwood Press, 1981), pp. 91–92.

12. Robert Douglas, "Will The New Racial Politics Divide and Conquer Baltimore?" *Baltimore Magazine* 73 (October 1980): 60–68; James B. Young, "The Loneliest Man in City Hall: City Council President William Donald Schaefer," ibid., 61 (November 1968): 35–44; Robert Douglas and Mike Powell, "Mayor Schaefer's Shadow Government," ibid., 73 (April 1980): 69–75; and Kevin O'Keefe, *Baltimore Politics, 1971–1986: The Schaefer Years and the Struggle for Succession*, The Georgetown Monographs in American Studies, No. 3 (Washington, D.C.: Georgetown University Press, 1986).

13. Priscilla Cummings, "The Man Who Would Be Mayor," *Baltimore Magazine* 77 (November 1984): 77–79; Mark Cohen "King for a Day: Clarence 'Du' Burns," ibid., 79 (November 1986): 68–75, 144–48; *The Sun*, January 18, September 6, 13, 1987.

14. *The Sun*, September 17, November 4, 1987.

15. *The Sun*, January 18, 1987.

16. Hooper Miles, "President's Annual Report," *Baltimore* 41 (February 1948): 10–11.

17. Norman G. Rukert, *The Port: Pride of Baltimore* (Baltimore: Bodine and Associates, Inc., 1982), pp. 77–78, 105–16; Joseph L. Arnold, *Maryland: Old Line to New Prosperity* (Northridge, CA: Windsor Publications, 1985), pp. 168–72; "Greater Baltimore Committee Formed," *Baltimore* 48 (January 1955): 11; *The Sun*, March 2, 1956.

18. The "Vietnam" comparison was made by local political columnist Neal Friedman in his "City Hall" column in *Baltimore Magazine* 65 (March 1972): 65. The background of the highway plans is in "Master Traffic Plan to Be Based on Radial Arteries, Ring Streets, Downtown Loop," *Baltimore* 42 (July 1949): 12–14; Clark S. Hobbs, "The New East-West Expressway: Tumult and Shouting," ibid., 55 (February 1962): 43–44; and "The East-West Expressway: Which Route?" ibid., 57 (November 1963): 15–17. The reaction of Baltimore neighborhoods to the expressways is briefly examined in Matthew A. Crenson, *Neighborhood Politics* (Cambridge: Harvard University Press, 1983), pp. 243–49.

19. *The Sun*, July 2, 1962; "The Great New Beltway Is a Reality," *Baltimore* 55 (July 1962): 7–10; "Boom Around the Beltway," *Baltimore Magazine* 59 (November 1965): 27–28; Neal A. Brooks and Eric Rockel, *A History of Baltimore County* (Towson, MD: Friends of the Towson Library, 1979), pp. 385–87; Maryland Department of Economic Development, *Community Economic Inventory: Baltimore County, Maryland* (Annapolis: Department of Economic Development, 1963–1987).

20. "The Case of the Soaring Budget," *Baltimore* 57 (November 1963): 48–49; James F. Waesche, "Baltimore's Tax Base: A Crisis of Erosion," *Baltimore Magazine* 67 (March 1971): 25–28; Alan L. Anders, "What New York Can Learn from Baltimore," ibid., 71 (August 1975): 18–21, 41–49; "Baltimore With $52 Million Surplus," *U.S. News and World Report*, October 20, 1975, p. 22; *The Sun*, April 13, 1988.

21. Michael Demarest, "He Digs Downtown: James Rouse and the Urban Redevelopment of Baltimore," *Time*, August 24, 1981, pp. 42–48. One official in the city's promotion and tourism bureau told the author that this cover article probably did more to promote the city as a tourist and investment attraction than all the advertisements and articles that had appeared in newspapers and magazines during the previous ten years.

22. Lenora H. Nast, Laurence N. Krause, and R. C. Monk, eds., *Baltimore: A Living Renaissance* (Baltimore: Historic Baltimore Society, Inc., 1982), pp. 36–49, 56–63, 229–45, 255–58; Henry A. Barnes, "Downtown: Prosperity or Doom?" *Baltimore* 49 (June 1956): 16–21; William G. Ewald, "The Challenge of Downtown Survival," ibid., 54 (October 1961), 36–38; "Charles Center," *Baltimore Magazine* 61 (September 1968): 19–23.

23. "The Inner Harbor: A New Downtown in Thirty Years at a Cost of $260,000,000," *Baltimore Magazine* 57 (October 1964): 12–13; "Rebirth of Baltimore: Phase Two," ibid.,

59 (October 1966): 33–38; Jacques Kelly, "The Master Builders," ibid., 78 (June 1985): 90–103; Eric Garland, "Downtown's High Stakes Showdown," ibid., 77 (June 1984): 64–70.

24. Marc V. Levine, "Downtown Redevelopment as an Urban Growth Strategy: A Critical Appraisal of the Baltimore Renaissance," and Bernard L. Berkowitz, "Rejoinder," *Journal of Urban Affairs* 9 (February 1983): 103–23, 125–32. A summary of Levine's views appeared in *The Sun,* August 10, 1986, under the title, "The Case for Two Baltimores."

25. Tim Wheeler, "The Tourists Are Coming," *Baltimore Magazine* 78 (May 1985): 66–75.

26. Crenson, *Neighborhood Politics,* p. 292.

27. Rawley M. Grav, "City Fair," in Nast et al., eds., *Baltimore,* pp. 12–16.

28. Allen C. Goodman and Ralph B. Taylor, *The Baltimore Neighborhood Fact Book* (Baltimore: Center for Metropolitan Planning and Research, Johns Hopkins University, 1983), p. 58; Eric Garland, "A New Baltimore Emerges: The Changing Face of Our Neighborhoods," *Baltimore Magazine* 77 (April 1984): 58–69.

29. Peter Szanton, *Baltimore 2000: A Choice of Futures* (Baltimore: The Morris Goldseker Foundation, 1986), p. 22.

30. Ibid., pp. 20–22, 46.

III

BOSTON

BACK TO THE POLITICS
OF THE FUTURE

Mark I. Gelfand

On the surface, Boston politics displayed remarkable continuity in the four decades after the Second World War. Four of five mayors served at least two terms, and the fifth had been mayor three times before. Their names—Curley, Hynes, Collins, White, and Flynn—showed that the Irish majority that had dominated Boston's politics since the turn of the century was still in control. Yet beneath this superficial stability, a great change had occurred. If for roughly the first half of the postwar era Bostonians continued to struggle against a static and parochial past, by the 1960s they started to come to grips with the challenges of a dynamic and pluralistic future.

The Old Boston

Boston in 1945 was a city imprisoned by its past, due, in part, to the very length and character of its history. By American standards Boston was old—in 1930 it celebrated the three-hundredth anniversary of the Puritans' arrival. The price the city paid for having so rich a legacy was an antiquated physical structure and advanced cases of ancestor worship and provincialism. For example, Boston without its historic Common was unthinkable, but that sacred turf split the modern commercial section into bitterly competing parts. Similarly, although the streets downtown were probably not, as legend has it, laid out by colonial cows, these narrow and twisty lanes were a nightmare for motorists. And the Puritans' intolerance for dissenters lived on in the Watch and Ward Society and an official censor. Nonconformists no longer feared hanging, but the phrase "Banned in Boston" still bespoke parochial minds.

If the colonial heritage was felt in Boston, the part of the past that held the city in tightest bondage was of more recent vintage; indeed, it stretched back almost exactly a hundred years. With the arrival of Catholic Irish in large waves, beginning in the 1840s, the once homogeneous, Anglo-Saxon, Protestant, Yankee community became a bitterly divided city. Italians, Jews, and others came later, but they were little more than bystanders in the raging Yankee-Irish conflict. Almost no aspect of life in Boston escaped this clash. In few other cities were partisan, ethno-cultural, and class lines so starkly drawn and in few other cities did a predominant socio-economic group (Yankee Republicans) and an emerging political majority (Irish Democrats) display so little restraint in venting their mutual contempt. Each side inflicted damage on the other, but in this mean-spirited clash there was no real winner and only one sure loser: Boston.

The Yankees, with their Brahmin-like families in the lead, inflicted damage in a variety of ways. For one, they withdrew their residences beyond the city limits into suburban enclaves. Although Boston was able to annex several bordering communities in the 1860s and 1870s, the more affluent suburbs rebuffed the Hub's allure of improved municipal services and kept apart. Boston remained a geographically small city of 44 square miles, hemmed in by independent and unsympathetic neighbors whose growing numbers and wealth sharply contrasted with that of the central city; Boston's share of its metropolitan area population ranked among the lowest of America's major cities (see Tables A.2 and A.3).

By leaving the city, the Yankees yielded the local political field to the Irish, but they were still able to use the power of state government to influence municipal affairs. The State House on Beacon Hill looked down on the city, both literally and figuratively. The Yankee-dominated Massachusetts legislature went beyond its customary restraint in local matters and in the early 1900s created a gubernatorially appointed Finance Commission to oversee all aspects of Boston's administration.

The Yankees also restricted the Boston Irish economically. The twentieth-century descendants of the Boston capitalists who made fortunes in the China trade and in textiles lacked the entrepreneurial nerve of their ancestors and sat on their money instead of funding new endeavors. Business in New England consequently suffered, and Boston began to experience a hardening of its economic arteries. More directly, the Yankees who controlled the vast pools of money held by Boston banks and insurance companies signified their displeasure with Boston politics and tax rates by simply not building or investing in the city. Long before the Great Depression, lower-class Bostonians knew the hardships of a stagnant economy.

By behaving in this fashion, the Yankees hastened the realization of their fears of an Irish takeover of Boston, a nightmare come to life in James Michael Curley, who was elected mayor for the first time in 1914. Ruthless in his drive for power and vindication, Curley mined the pent-up frustrations and anger of the Irish for his own political benefit. "His basic source of power," John Gunther wrote in 1947, "was his identification with all the resentments closely cherished by the Irish underpossessed." Curley regularly referred to his Yankee opponents as descendants of those who "got rich selling opium to the Chinese, rum to the Indians, or trading in slaves." By such rhetoric, he promised to be the "Mayor of the Poor," and he delivered in the form of jobs, playgounds, beaches, bath houses, and a first-rate city hospital. Curley dominated the political alignment of Boston for nearly four decades.[1]

Several factors flowing from the efforts of Progressive Era, good-government types contributed to Curley's power. Charter reform in 1909 created a strong mayor system; the council became little more than a footnote in the running of the city. Besides focusing authority in the executive, Progressives also mandated nonpartisan elections; with party organizations cut out of the process, the race for mayor was invariably a personality contest. The absence of strong unions and the abstinence of the Roman Catholic Church meant that the mayor had virtually no competition for the political loyalty of the less privileged. Similarly, the press was not a political force. Until the late 1950s, Boston had several newspapers, but each tended to serve a narrow constituency. None had the opportunity and the inclination to make itself an active force in municipal politics. Only the business community was a constant thorn in the side of this "last of the buccaneers," but it also provided Curley with a perfect foil.[2]

During Curley's heyday the Boston electorate divided into three roughly equal parts. The first, fiercely loyal to Curley, included those lower-income people who crowded into the inner-city neighborhoods of Irish South Boston and Charlestown and the Italian North End and East Boston. A second segment was just as intensely anti-Curley: the Yankees holding firm on Beacon Hill, in the Back Bay, and in other scattered enclaves and the "lace-curtain Irish" moving up the economic ladder. Sitting between these two was an ill-defined group of Bostonians who held no strong feelings one way or the other about Curley and who shifted easily from side to side depending on the specific circumstances of each election.

This volatile middle group made Curley's career something less than an unbroken triumph. Unlike the "bosses" of this era, with whom he was commonly but mistakenly identified, Curley had no machine worthy of the term behind him. Instead of formal organization, Curley relied on good drama, adept strategy and tactics, and personal endurance. Losing his bid for reelection in 1917, Curley prevailed in 1921 and 1929. (He could not run in 1925 because of a new state law, clearly aimed at Curley, prohibiting Boston mayors from serving consecutive terms.) In 1934 he won the governorship, becoming the first of the Boston Irish to occupy the office, but when his two-year term ended, his career went into a nose dive. Contesting four elections (U.S. Senate, gubernatorial, and mayoral twice) between 1936 and 1941, Curley lost them all, and, at age sixty-seven, his political career seemed over.

Just a few days into 1945, Bostonians found themselves without a mayor. Much to the chagrin of the Republicans, who had supported an Irish politician, Maurice Tobin, in the 1937 and 1941 races against Curley and had repealed the state law prohibiting consecutive terms so that Tobin could run again in 1941, Tobin had won the governorship on the Democratic line the previous November. Not only had the Yankees lost the State House, but they also faced the unpleasant prospect that Curley might return to City Hall.

Forecasters of Curley's political demise in 1941 had misjudged the man and his followers. Curley had gained a seat in Congress in 1942 from a district comprising his inner-neighborhood strongholds in Boston and their adjacent working-class suburbs. He was reelected easily in 1944, even though he was under federal indictment for mail fraud. When Tobin won statewide in the same balloting, Curley immediately announced his candidacy for mayor in a special election to fill the vacancy.

The special election was never held. Certain that Curley would have no difficulty topping the field in a short springtime campaign, his enemies opted for delay. A special election had been necessary because state law had granted an acting mayor only a limited array of powers. Rather than let Curley profit from this, Republicans on Beacon Hill and anti-Curley Democrats in the city agreed to new state legislation that conferred all the mayor's powers on the acting mayor until after the regularly scheduled balloting in November and cancelled the special election.

This ploy could put off, but could not prevent, Curley's return. The end of the Second World War led to anxiety among the lower and middle classes that peace would lead to wholesale unemployment reminiscent of the 1930s. Curley's political fortunes had always flourished in times of economic uncertainty, and 1945 was no different. Further, the war years had witnessed an ugly outburst of anti-Semitism in Irish neighborhoods. The number of people involved, mostly teenagers and young adults, was small, but delays by government and church officials in confronting the problem revealed a city under great stress. Although Curley never associated himself with anti-Semitism (his prejudice was confined to Yankees), the tensions in the Irish community worked to his advantage.[3]

Curley also profited from divisions among his political opponents. In the top-vote-getter-take-all arrangement of Boston's elections, Curley fared better when the field was crowded. The 1945 ballot listed six candidates. Only two posed a serious challenge, but their presence caused all the split Curley needed. In the greatest triumph of his career, Curley carried nineteen of twenty-two wards and took nearly as many votes as his two strongest foes combined in winning a near majority. To the joy of his patronage-seeking backers, and the dread of his tax-fearing enemies, he again promised to bring "monumental and constructive" government to Boston.[4]

It was not to be. Within weeks of his election, Curley was in Washington on trial for mail fraud. Of the many legal problems that marked Curley's political career, this one least merited prosecution. Curley's involvement was marginal at most; he became the target not for what he did but for who he was. Although the judge allowed Curley to attend his own inauguration in January 1946, a jury soon returned a guilty verdict. The new mayor of Boston faced a possible forty-seven years in prison and $19,000 in fines. Curley managed to avoid jail for nearly eighteen months, but in June 1947 the judge rejected his final emotional appeal ("You are imposing a death sentence upon me") and committed the 72-year-old Curley to one year in a federal penitentiary.

Curley's impending incarceration created a leadership crisis in Boston. For more than a year Massachusetts's political leaders had known that the mayor was likely to go to prison, but they seemed paralyzed and unable to act. The problem lay with the City Charter which provided for neither automatic removal of a mayor convicted of a felony nor a means for operating the government when a mayor became incapacitated. Because Curley refused to resign, Boston faced government either by a prison inmate or an acting mayor with virtually no power.

The Republicans on Beacon Hill produced a political solution. Many saw an opportunity to get rid of Curley by declaring the mayor's office vacant and having a gubernatorially appointed commission run the city until November 1947 when a special election would be held. But Republican Governor Robert Bradford was not prepared to kick Curley when he was down for fear that this would create a popular backlash in the mayor's favor. Furthermore, Bradford had beaten Tobin for the governorship in 1946 with Curley's help and an appreciative Curley might be useful in 1948. The result was legislation allowing Curley to keep both title and salary but conferring the full powers of mayor on the city clerk. Upon release from jail, Curley would regain his authority.

This so-called "Curley Law," passed in only ninety minutes the night Curley went to prison, had two important results. First, it confirmed to most observers the hypocrisy and self-serving motives of the Yankees, who were shown to be no different than the Irish in subordinating city interests to personal ambition. Bradford's performance, the Boston-based *Christian Science Monitor* claimed, "will remain to astonish future generations as the low ebb of Boston's civic conscience." Second, the "Curley Law" brought to the fore City Clerk John B. Hynes, who would open a new chapter in Boston's political story.[5]

His personal qualities and the climate of the times combined to give Hynes an historic role. Brought up in a lower-class Irish neighborhood, Hynes sought job security as a clerk in the city's Health Department in 1920. Over the next twenty-five years he worked his way to the top of the municipal bureaucracy through competency and a knack for making the right political contacts. Although virtually unknown to the general public, Hynes won wide respect within the government. When the city needed an interim administrator in 1947, Hynes was the obvious choice. In his five months as acting mayor, Hynes adopted prudent fiscal policies and prevented giveaways of lucrative franchises. He returned to the city clerk's position when President Truman commuted Curley's sentence in November, but before stepping down Hynes had made a strong impression on the city's voters which was to pay off two years later.

In 1949 Boston's electorate passed its own judgment on Curley during a period of charter reform. For years, leaders among both the Yankee and "lace-curtain Irish" factions had pushed for a city manager form of government. Neither gained much headway until 1947 when several members of the twenty-two man, ward-based city council were linked to payoffs in the granting of licenses. In a remarkably candid admission, one councilman said: "I'll take a buck, and who in hell doesn't know it. . . . I'd like to see the guy who doesn't take a buck." Although the scandal produced no jail terms, it pressured Beacon Hill to redesign Boston's government. Nonetheless, the state lawmakers and municipal politicians remained firmly opposed to a city manager plan for Boston.

Thanks to the machinations of Curley, the reform proposals submitted to the voters in 1949 offered only slight alterations in the way the city was run. The council was reduced to nine members, all elected at-large. But as the council would remain weak in comparison to the mayor, this modification would be little more than window dressing. More significant were the changes made in the manner of electing the mayor. Elections continued to be nonpartisan, but instead of the top-vote-getter-take-all arrangement, there would be a runoff between the two leading candidates. Although intended to deny Curley the advantage of a divided opposition, this new scheme actually made no difference to Curley's fortunes. For the city's long-term political course, however, the change would be of great importance.[6]

Charter reform won easily in 1949, largely because it was almost totally over-shadowed by the mayoralty contest. Once out of prison, an unrepentant Curley tried but failed to govern as he had in the past, but his body and spirit were no longer up to the task. During his final two years, municipal administration was adrift, and the business community sat on its hands as the city's economic condition worsened. Audacious as ever, Curley at seventy-four sought reelection.

Four candidates challenged the obviously vulnerable incumbent, but the contest soon settled down into a Curley-Hynes battle. Although in 1947 Curley had dismissed the acting mayor's performance with the quip, "I have accomplished more in five hours than has been done in the past five months," Hynes had demonstrated he could handle the job. The city clerk could not match Curley's oratory, but he more than made up for this deficiency with a well-financed and well-organized drive. Republicans worked hard for Hynes, after getting his promise not to seek statewide office in the future. With GOP politicians cooperating with anti-Curley Democrats, Hynes received generous contributions from businessmen and the endorsement of both the Republican *Boston Herald* and the Democratic *Boston Post*.

Hynes pledged to give Boston "a clean, honest and efficient administration." Beyond that, he made no promises. Spartan as it was, the one-issue campaign succeeded in highlighting differences with Curley; it was enough, for example, to lead the *Christian Science Monitor* to drop its long-standing editorial policy of noninvolvement in municipal politics and urge Hynes's election as the way to end "one-man misrule in Boston."

The mayor's response to Hynes was vintage Curley. He stressed his past record in providing jobs and services, and lashed out at Hynes as the "puppet" of Republican "pirates" and the "State Street [the city's financial center] wrecking crew." Such themes were successful in the past, and in 1949 only the candidacy of a Curley-like opponent who siphoned off some of the old campaigner's inner neighborhood strength could beat him. Although Curley received more ballots (126,000) than he had in any of his seven previous races for the mayoralty, he fell short of Hynes's 138,000.[7]

The decade-long tenure (the longest consecutive service for any Boston mayor up to that time) of John B. Hynes brought Curley's career to an end—Hynes buried Curley, if not his legacy, in an avalanche of votes in a 1951 rematch. Administratively, Hynes spoke like a Progressive Era reformer, but he accomplished little. Municipal government under Curley had become a bloated bureaucracy, primarily concerned with supplying public jobs in a depressed labor market. When Hynes left office in 1960, Boston's municipal spending on a per capita basis remained the highest in the nation. Nor could Hynes break the city's highly irregular and arbitrary assessment of commercial property. Under Curley the city commonly assessed land and buildings downtown (mostly owned by Yankees) at higher than market value.

By inflating the total of assessed valuations, Curley was able to keep taxes on homeowners to a minimum. Over-assessment also provided opportunities for Curley and his friends to trade tax abatements for favors. Although Hynes had condemned the system in 1949, tax assessments remained a dirty business because Hynes found the alternatives unpalatable. If assessors listed commercial properties at true market value, the city's overall tax rate would have to go higher, and Hynes was not prepared to risk political suicide in order to do what was "right." The mayor would accept the longer-term approach of adopting a more rational method of assessing all property, but only if the city gained a new source of revenue to relieve the pressure on homeowners. Hynes suggested a payroll or sales tax, but he could not muster the necessary support from other Boston politicians.[8]

Hynes proved equally ill suited to the task of urban redevelopment. Unlike many other big-city mayors of the period, Hynes moved slowly to take advantage of federal urban renewal funds available through the 1949 and 1954 Housing Acts, and he failed to mobilize the business community behind a revitalization program. The mayor's inability to reform tax assessments or stem the rise in tax rates poisoned the redevelopment well, making Boston a mere spectator of the postwar building boom.[9]

The 1955 mayoral election demonstrated how the past still dominated Boston politics. The major challenge to Hynes's bid for a third term came from Johnny Powers, a South Boston native, who was leader of the Democratic minority in the Massachusetts Senate and a powerful figure in the party. Often sounding like Curley, Powers portrayed the election as a conflict between "two philosophies of government—one dedicated to State Street and the banking interests to which the present Mayor has been consistently subservient, and the other a philosophy of government dedicated to the people of Boston." He promised to end "the rule of this city by people who neither live nor pay taxes in Boston." The challenger raised an emotional issue by claiming that Hynes's budget cutting had led to a deterioration of services at Boston City Hospital and to the deaths of fourteen premature babies.

Hynes, after initially focusing on his achievements in shedding Boston's reputation for "venal government" and raising the city's bond rating, lashed out at his opponent as the election neared. Characterizing Powers as a would-be political boss "who wants to sit in the Mayor's chair as a Czar or Caesar," Hynes also intimated that Powers had ties to the underworld. The *Boston Herald*, however, placed the contest in its historical setting. A Powers victory, it claimed, would mean a "reversion to Curleyism: the same old political manipulation of the Mayor's office for selfish ends that brought the city to its low estate before Mr. Hynes took over. It is no accident," declared the Republican *Herald*, "that Curley turned his support to Powers."[10]

In the end, Hynes won 124,500 to 111,400 in a virtual replay of the 1949 contest. Not only was the number of votes separating Hynes from Powers about the same as in the win over Curley six years before, but Powers also captured ten of the eleven wards Curley had won. The old battle lines still held.

To a large extent, it was Hynes's failures, rather than accomplishments that led to a break-up of these patterns. The next four years were not easy ones for Hynes.

His inability to reform tax assessments came back to haunt his new term when, faced with an accumulated budget deficit of $45 million, he had to ask the city council and state legislature for loan authority to bridge the gap. He received it only after making concessions both to rival politicians and bankers. The business community became increasingly frustrated by the mayor's lack of success in curbing municipal spending—the cost of running Boston's government rose 50 percent during his tenure. By necessity the property levy also climbed: in 1959 the tax rate, which had stood at less than $60 per $1,000 of assessed valuation when Hynes took office in 1950, soared above the highly symbolic $100 level, dampening an already poor economic climate.

Even though the announcement of the $101.20 tax rate jolted business in early 1959, the increase was not expected to affect the election that fall. Most political observers assumed that Hynes would not run again and that Powers, now president of the state senate, would win easily. With Powers all but sworn in months before the election, politicians and others hastened to jump aboard his bandwagon. Many Republicans backed him with an eye toward the 1960 statewide contests. Powers and the incumbent Democratic governor were bitter enemies, and with Powers in City Hall their intraparty strife was bound to intensify. Almost all the Democratic officeholders in the city and state came out for Powers. One of his most celebrated backers was the Commonwealth's junior U.S. senator and White House aspirant, John F. Kennedy, who praised the state senate president's "vigorous leadership." Powers's proven capacity to command also appealed to the *Boston Herald,* which four years before had likened him to Curley. It is likely that the *Herald*'s conversion, which was shared by many leading businessmen, was nothing more than expedient acceptance of the inevitable and reflected only a wish to keep lines of communication open to the certain winner.[11]

But an election would have to be held to make it official, and Boston never had a shortage of politicians willing to buck the odds. Four candidates entered against Powers, and two quickly emerged as having the best chance of making it into a runoff. One was Gabriel F. Piemonte, who as a city councilor had earned a reputation for hard work and mastery of municipal administration. Piemonte, however, suffered from one critical, ultimately fatal, political liability: he was Italian in an Irish city.

The other contender was Irish, but he too had a handicap; John F. Collins was confined to a wheelchair because of polio. Raised in a lower middle-class neighborhood, Collins gained a law degree and won election to the state legislature. Although he demonstrated a streak of independence by opposing organized labor and the Democratic governor, he won his party's nomination for attorney general in 1954, a race he lost. The following year he ran for the Boston City Council and won, despite being stricken with polio during the campaign. In 1957 he accepted a gubernatorial appointment to a sinecure. Exuding the "carefree, sunny charm of a curly-haired parochial choir boy grown older," the forty-year old Collins seemed in 1959 to be through with tough political combat.

But the fires of ambition burned deep within Collins, and he saw a weakness in Powers's candidacy. Powers had become the candidate of the "Establishment," and Collins sensed that this could be the senate president's undoing. Running under the banner of "Stop Power Politics," Collins portrayed himself as champion of the average citizen against a closed circle of professional politicians and interest groups. (Although Collins received far fewer endorsements than Powers, he did have some heavyweights on his side, including Mayor Hynes, the Democratic governor, and some prominent Republicans. They provided his campaign with workers and money, but not so much as to tarnish Collins's image as an outsider.)

The preliminary election in September confirmed one fact of Boston political life and raised doubts about another. As expected, the city was not ready for an Italian mayor; Piemonte fell two percentage points (22 to 20 percent, about 2,500 votes) short of Collins in the contest for second place. Powers drew 34 percent, but that was far short of the 55–60 percent his managers had looked for.

The tax issue overshadowed all others in the two-man race, and, in one of the great ironies of Boston politics, Powers, sounding like a Yankee reformer, proposed to cut city spending "by eliminating waste and abuse in city government." Collins was equally vehement in pledges to economize, but he claimed that the only way property tax relief could be accomplished was by a sales tax, a step Powers opposed as being harmful to lower-income families. Hynes had been hinting for years that a sales tax (favored by the financial community) was the city's only salvation, but he never mustered the necessary courage to come out forthrightly for it. By making it central to his campaign, Collins gave an early indication that he was cut from a different mold than the sitting mayor.

As the election drew near, the campaign degenerated into a nasty exchange of character attacks. The candidates traded charges of using their public positions to enrich themselves, and Collins resurrected the question of Powers' reputed ties to organized crime. These allegations gained great attention on the Friday before the Tuesday election, when U.S. Treasury agents made a gambling raid on an East Boston tavern that displayed a huge "Powers for Mayor" sign. The next day's newspapers carried Collins's front-page advertisements with a picture of the tavern and the sign; the accompanying caption read, "This is what I mean by Power Politics."

The voters of Boston chose John Collins by a margin of 114,000 to 90,000, a result that left most observers stunned. Powers took only the two wards in his home base of South Boston and two wards in lower to lower-middle-class Roxbury. Collins piled up big majorities in the middle-class areas around the city's rim. Seeking to explain the upset, analysts pointed to Collins's success in portraying himself as the "people's candidate" and the fortuitous timing of the gambling raid. What no one could know at the time was that Boston was entering a whole new era and that the 1959 election marked the end of the Curley epoch. His legend (he died in 1958) might continue to haunt the city, but Boston would henceforth confront its future instead of fighting its past.[12]

The New Boston

The city along the Charles was moribund as Collins assumed the mayoralty. The 1960 census revealed that Boston's population since 1950 had dropped more than

100,000, a loss of 13 percent, to fewer than 700,000. Most who had left were middle-class. Employment and retail sales in the central business district showed sharp declines over the decade, and, with new commercial construction virtually suspended, the city's tax base in 1960 was 25 percent less than on the eve of the Great Depression. All this, plus the obvious physical deterioration of once fashionable residential areas such as Beacon Hill and the Back Bay, led Moodys Investors Service in late 1959 to lower Boston's bond rating from "A" to "Baa," making it the only city in the country with more than half a million people with so poor a status.[13]

Just as John Kennedy in 1960 had to prove that being young and a Catholic need not bar one from the presidency, so John Collins had to exorcise the belief that all Boston Irish politicians were "crooked or stupid, or both." He succeeded. No major scandal besmirched his two terms in City Hall, and certainly, no one ever publicly called him stupid. Indeed, commentators applied such terms as "shrewd, able, decisive, and tough" to his early decision to make urban renewal the centerpiece of his administration. Making it work would require, however, the full cooperation of business leaders, something Collins encouraged by paring the municipal budget and holding the line on taxes.

State Street proved responsive, for the downgrading of the city's bonds had shaken the financial community. Rather than confront the great uncertainties of insolvency, and hopeful that the new man at City Hall would provide vigorous leadership, fifteen of Boston's most influential businessmen formed a Co-ordinating Committee (soon known as "The Vault," because its initial meetings were held in the boardroom of the Boston Safe Deposit and Trust Company), which began holding biweekly sessions with the mayor.

This unprecedented partnership between City Hall and State Street paid its first dividends in the appointment of Edward J. Logue as director of the urban renewal program. By going out of the city to hire the nationally known Logue, Collins broke with the long-standing Boston practice of filling municipal posts with local people whose primary qualification was loyalty to the mayor. If the appointment demonstrated that Collins was serious about urban renewal, the Co-ordinating Committee proved its commitment by agreeing to pay half of Logue's $30,000 salary.[14]

Working in tandem, Collins, Logue, and the businessmen launched "the most ambitious civic rejuvenation program in the country." With the mayor cutting taxes in four consecutive years and Logue lining up federal urban renewal funds ($200 million in eight years—making Boston the most favored recipient on a per capita basis among the nation's big cities), the business community responded by plowing its own money into planning and building for the downtown district. Together, they worked out a tax plan that put a long-delayed Back Bay redevelopment project back on track and ironed out the differences that had put off action on a huge sixty-acre Government Center that included a new City Hall.

Although downtown renewal captured much attention, the redevelopment administrator was also committed to revival of the city's old and blighted residential neighborhoods. His plans covered a quarter of Boston's total land surface and half its population, but this part of Logue's program did not fare as well as the downtown plans. Boston had long been a city of tightly knit, almost insular neighborhoods,

suspicious of outsiders who sought change. Logue's Irish background and temperament provided him a hearing in these areas, but despite his announced policy of
"planning with people," he met great resistance. In lower-class Charlestown, for
example, where Logue and his staff held more than 130 small meetings with residents over two years, and where the plans he drew up (emphasizing rehabilitation,
not clearance) enjoyed the support of the Catholic Church (the chairman of the
Boston Redevelopment Authority was a priest), public hearings on the proposal
turned into near riots.[15]

Despite these setbacks, Collins's emphasis on urban renewal initially proved
rewarding. His slogan in his 1963 reelection race was "Keep Boston on the Go,"
and Collins had no trouble raising funds to keep that message before the electorate.
The mayor also claimed credit for four successive property tax cuts, although his
critics pointed out that these were at least partially offset by a brand new sewerage
service charge. Easily outdistancing the field in the primary contest, Collins had
no problem in the final head-to-head encounter with Piemonte, taking nearly 60
percent of the vote.

In his second term, however, Collins' political fortunes declined precipitously.
Downtown renewal progressed apace, but there was growing disenchantment in the
neighborhoods with an austerity program that provided the financial foundations
for the new skyscrapers. Tax concessions to the redevelopers could be recouped
only by general property tax increases in three out of four years and slashes in
municipal services. In a city whose residents were accustomed to good police
protection, garbage collection, street lighting, and playgrounds, the cutbacks became a political liability. Running for the Democratic nomination for the United
States Senate in 1966, the mayor lost 21 of the city's 22 wards and the primary.
As in other cities, the urban renewal program in Boston was fraught with political
peril, and because of it Collins was vulnerable.[16]

If Boston had been a latecomer to urban renewal in the 1950s, it was among the
first of the northern cities to feel the civil rights movement of the 1960s. While
police brutality and housing and job discrimination were the focus of protests elsewhere, blacks in Boston complained mostly about segregated schools. For more
than a decade, the prospect, and then the reality, of forced busing threatened to
tear the city apart. Yet, in the end, the politics of Boston emerged remarkably
unchanged.

The black experience in Boston was unlike that in most other northern cities. As
the cradle of the abolitionist movement, Boston had drawn a sizable share of the
black population that left the South in the nineteenth century, but of the huge
migrations of the first half of the twentieth century, the city received relatively
little. With its stagnant economy, Boston held scant attraction for upward-striving
blacks. The result was a black community that was both significantly smaller (5
percent of the total population in 1950, 9.1 percent in 1960; see Table A.4) than
elsewhere and seemingly more established and accepted. A report issued in 1960
by the Harvard-M.I.T. Joint Center for Urban Studies observed: "The fact that the
so-called 'Negro area' [Roxbury] is only one-quarter colored offers a strong contrast
with the ghettos and black belts of other major cities." The report continued:

> But to truly appreciate the difference between the gray of Boston and the black of Chicago's South Side, one merely has to walk the streets of Roxbury. There he will find white and Negro children playing arm-in-arm and colored women gossiping over backyard fences with their white neighbors.

Other commentators painted a less rosy picture, noting the absence of blacks from sales jobs in downtown retail stores (despite a strong state antidiscrimination law), the deterioration of black housing, the near disfranchisement of blacks as a consequence of nonpartisan and at-large elections, and the almost total invisibility of blacks in the pages of Boston's newspapers.[17]

When the ferment of the civil rights movement reached Boston, it was natural that the schools would be the target for action. Once the city's pride, the public school system of the 1960s provided little for either whites or blacks. About a third of its constituency was going to private schools; parents of these children cared little about what happened to the public system. The School Department had become isolated and hidebound.

Primary responsibility for the sad state of the schools fell to the popularly elected, five-member School Committee. Just as the School Department had become a haven for Irish bureaucrats looking for security, the School Committee became a magnet for Irish politicians seeking to advance their careers. Although membership paid no salary, it offered opportunities for dispensing patronage and making contacts. Charting a progressive educational policy was all but impossible in an environment where elected officials and bureaucrats shared a common interest in maintaining the status quo.

Under the provisions of a 1855 state law, Boston and other communities in Massachusetts were prohibited from maintaining a dual school system, but a century later, Boston's schools were segregated in fact, if not in name. This reflected not only discriminatory housing practices but, more importantly, deliberate actions by the School Committee. Black schools were often physically obsolete and staffed by inexperienced or uncaring teachers, a situation graphically depicted in the nationally acclaimed book *Death at an Early Age* (1967). In June 1963 the Boston chapter of the National Association for the Advancement of Colored People and other black groups complained to the School Committee and organized a one-day boycott of the city's schools. The racial issue had been joined, and it produced the first leader of the northern white backlash movement, Boston School Committee chairwoman, Louise Day Hicks.[18]

Carelessly labeled a "bigot" by the media, Hicks was actually a bundle of contradictions, reflecting not only her own background but the paradoxes of modern American life. Although she came to represent the conservative values of traditional ethnic communities, her own life was hardly conventional. The only daughter of a highly successful South Boston businessman and civic leader, she married and began raising a family, then at age thirty-six entered law school and subsequently went into partnership with her younger brother. In 1961 she won a place on the School Committee on a platform pledging to "take politics out of the schools." In early 1963 she gained the committee's chair. Thus she came into the spotlight just as blacks pressed their case against *de facto* segregation. Hicks soon assumed a public position of intransigence. By rejecting black charges and demands for remedial action, she pursued a politically safe course, but the damage her stance inflicted upon the city was incalculable.

Up for reelection to the School Committee in November 1963, she topped the field, taking a record 74 percent of all votes cast, more than John Collins won in the mayor's race. Blacks organized another boycott and made use of long-ignored administrative rules to force the busing of black students to under-utilized all-white schools. In 1965, with the civil rights impulse at its peak across the nation, the Massachusetts State Education Commissioner appointed a blue-ribbon panel, which included Richard Cardinal Cushing, head of the Boston Archdiocese, to investigate the problem of school segregation in the Bay State. The group's report led to passage of the Racial Imbalance Law of 1965 which barred state aid to any school district that maintained schools with non-white student enrollments of more than 50 percent. Promising to resist this outside pressure, Hicks once more outdistanced the other candidates for the School Committee in the November 1965 election; the lone incumbent on the committee who had displayed sympathy for black causes was also the lone incumbent to lose. The *Pilot,* the newspaper of the Boston Archdiocese, characterized the voting as anti-Negro, and one nationally syndicated columnist portrayed the results as "sinister." Despite this criticism, Hicks and the School Committee continued their defiance of the Racial Imbalance Law; the state started cutting off its funds, and Hicks began preparing for the 1967 mayoralty contest.[19]

The race was wide open. Mayor Collins was not seeking a third term. With the political dividends flowing from urban renewal clearly drying up, Collins knew he faced a difficult fight. The emergence of the racial issue left Collins in even more trouble. Conservative not only fiscally, but also socially, Collins had little sympathy for the civil rights activists who were upsetting his city. Boston did escape the devastating ghetto riots that shook many big cities in the mid-1960s, but there was a weekend of looting and random violence in June 1967 after the police broke up a sit-in of black women at a municipal welfare office. Perhaps sensing that Boston was entering an era of change he could neither comprehend nor manage, Collins revealed that same month that he would step down at the end of his term.

In the charged political atmosphere ten names appeared on the preliminary ballot, but only three had a chance of making the final. One was Edward Logue, the tough urban renewal administrator, who was making his first bid for elective office. Unlike most novices, however, Logue had no recognition problem. Rather his task was "to go around and show [the voters] I don't have horns." It was a formidable assignment, but Logue was well financed by the business community which looked forward to a continuation of the Collins approach to physical and financial redevelopment.

If Logue was an outsider, then Kevin H. White was the politicians' insider. The son, grandson, and son-in-law of men long active in Boston politics, White could call upon old familial ties in making his race. He was "a man of honest Irish antecedents," despite a B.A. from Williams College and a townhouse on Beacon Hill. White had not distinguished himself during his six years as the Commonwealth's secretary of state, an elected administrative position of little consequence, but his low profile also kept him out of nasty battles and thus he had few political enemies. To most journalists White appeared incorrigibly bland ("a pleasant young man of thirty-nine who looks like the embodiment of the Boy Scout ideals") and interested in the mayoralty only as a stepping stone to the governorship, but these perceptions proved to be assets rather than handicaps in his campaign.

Clearly the person to beat was Louise Day Hicks. Fresh from her triumphs in the 1963 and 1965 School Committee races, she was the dominant figure in the city's political life. Hicks had not only staked out a popular position on the immediate school integration issue ("You know where I stand") but also made herself the spokesperson for many Bostonians who were upset over the havoc unleashed by urban renewal and the civil rights movement and who felt betrayed by their traditional institutions (e.g., the Democratic party, the Catholic Church) and alienated from academicians and the suburbs. Yet if this discontent guaranteed Hicks a runoff spot, it was far from certain that it could bring her a runoff victory.

The preliminary election boiled down to a race for second place, with Logue's can-do reputation and financing pitted against White's familiarity and promises to redress the Collins administration's neglect of ethnic neighborhoods. Both men stayed away from the racial question. Whatever chance Logue did have was lost when he bungled a legal challenge to White's nominating petitions. Logue's image as a nonpolitician was badly tarnished as White received sympathetic treatment in the press. On primary day, White easily took second and Logue finished fourth.

Hicks's triumph in the primary revealed her underlying weakness. She outpolled White by a margin of 4 to 3, but captured only 28 percent of the total vote. Since the tone of the preliminary campaign had been Hicks versus everybody else, few analysts thought that she could amass a majority of the ballots in the final with White. He was now the favorite, but the size of his victory would be closely watched as a sign of just how deep white backlash and alienation had run in Boston.[20]

Two developments dominated the weeks between the primary and runoff elections. The first was the massive support White received from the city's "Establishment." Prominent politicians from both parties endorsed his candidacy, as did the business community. Breaking its rule, dating from the 1896, of not taking a stand in elections, the *Boston Globe,* which had emerged as the city's most important media outlet, backed White. By rallying behind White in such a conspicuous fashion, the "Establishment" ran the danger of generating sympathy for Hicks as the "people's candidate" (shades of Collins in 1959), but the White campaign was sensitive to this problem and overcame it by emphasizing the theme that "You Become Important When Kevin White Is Mayor."

The second development was Hicks's blundering attempt to become something more than a one-issue candidate. By promising to increase substantially the salaries of police and firemen, without raising taxes, she displayed an abysmal lack of knowledge of city finances. When Hicks returned empty-handed from a trip to Washington, where she sought federal funds to pay for the salary hikes, her actions reinforced the widely held impression that she was not up to coping with the pressures and responsibilities of being mayor.

On election day, Kevin White defeated Louise Day Hicks 102,000 to 90,800. The turnout was the highest in the city's recent history, while the margin of victory was one of the smallest. Yet, because his triumph came at the same time that Cleveland and Gary elected the nation's first big-city black mayors, it was still taken as a sign that the nation's white backlash had passed its peak. There were other reasons for advocates of racial equality and harmony to feel good about the results. Not only did Hicks fail to run up the massive majorities in South Boston and Dorchester that observers had conceded to her, but the people of Boston also turned out the School Committee member who had been Hicks's strongest ally and elected the first black to the city council since it had gone to an at-large basis in 1951. When the chips were down, one could argue, Bostonians were not prepared to turn their back on their city's reputation for enlightened race relations.

Another interpretation of the election is possible, however. White may have won only because Hicks's salary proposal set off tax hike fears in tax-conscious Irish neighborhoods; the old issue of finances may have been decisive. Furthermore, Hicks may, ironically, have been the victim of prejudice. Surveys indicated that many of Boston's ethnic groups, including the Irish, but most particularly the Italians, were unable to accept the prospect of a woman mayor. Chairing the School Committee was one thing—education was a traditional concern for women—but being mayor was completely different. In light of these handicaps, therefore, what was most remarkable about the election was how close Hicks came to winning. She had definitely touched something in the psyche of Boston—though not as successfully as Curley had to be sure. Kevin White would have to live and govern with this fact.[21]

Dismissed by most political pundits in 1967 as cautious and shallow, White became the towering figure in Boston politics over the next sixteen years. As earlier with Curley, the politics of Boston between 1968 and 1983 essentially revolved around one man's personality; but, if Curley had been a showman, White was enigmatic. He matched Curley's record of four terms as mayor and outdid him by serving them consecutively and by building a political machine. Both had to deal with social fissures and fiscal crises, and as Curley faced legal challenges about his personal finances, so White ran into problems on the funding of his political campaigns.

Kevin White spent his first years at City Hall trying to mute racial tensions and restore the faith of ethnic neighborhoods in municipal administration. With the School Committee under fresh leadership that took less relish in confrontational tactics, the issue of integration and busing disappeared from the headlines, even though the number of racially imbalanced schools continued to increase. The new mayor rewarded the black community for its support in the 1967 election by naming blacks to posts in his administration, and he demonstrated his concern when, following the assassination of Martin Luther King, Jr., he took to the streets of Roxbury (à la New York's John Lindsay) to relieve the tension there. White understood that this might not sit well with many Bostonians, and indeed he was often referred to as "Mayor Black" by his opponents, but White was thinking of his upcoming 1970 race for governor, and he saw a strong stance on civil rights as helpful in the liberal suburbs.

As part of the delicate balancing act that characterized these early years, White sought to muster support in ethnic neighborhoods by restoring the municipal services that Collins had cut so ruthlessly. He also set up a network of Little City Halls to "bring government closer to the people." Working with neighborhood groups, the White administration opposed further highway construction in the city and resisted encroachment of the state-operated international airport into East Boston. This activism cost money, and White gambled that neighborhood residents would overlook the steep increases in the property tax rate necessary to finance it. It was a gamble he lost. The hike in taxes plus the mayor's outspoken stand on civil rights were the reasons he failed to carry Boston in his unsuccessful bid for the governorship.

Chastened by the 1970 results, White shifted gears as he prepared to run for reelection in 1971. He conspicuously toned down his rhetoric on racial issues and announced a series of budget-cutting measures similar to those Collins had imposed. The Little City Halls became *de facto* campaign offices, and White employed sophisticated campaign technology to rally his supporters. What worked most in his favor, however, was the weak caliber of White's opposition. Four candidates, including a black councilor and a Yankee councilor, ran against the mayor in the preliminary election, but White and Hicks were again the finalists. Following her defeat in 1967, Hicks had won a seat in Congress, but it was the mayoralty she wanted, and in a multicandidate field where she had always done her best, she trailed White by only 6,000 votes of the 141,000 cast. The runoff, however, proved no contest at all. While White had his organization operating at peak efficiency, Hicks had no money or organization and virtually nothing to say. On election night she stood badly beaten, 112,000 to 70,000.[22]

Two events dominated Kevin White's second term. The first was his abortive selection as George McGovern's running mate in the 1972 presidential election. Although the offer was withdrawn because of the objections of Senator Edward Kennedy, the episode generated national ambitions in White. He saw himself as one of a handful of party leaders who could hold the Democratic urban coalition together. In 1967 and again in 1971 he had won both the black and Italian vote, as well as thousands of Irish ballots. Looking ahead to 1976, he began inviting syndicated columnists and prominent politicians and academicians to Boston to discuss the country's problems and to demonstrate his mastery of the issues. These national aspirations were destroyed, however, by the inauguration of court-ordered school busing in the fall of 1974. Violence at South Boston High School, where whites tried to block the entry of blacks from Roxbury, became a staple of the network evening news, and instead of devising plans for winning the White House, Kevin White found himself trying to restore peace to Boston and salvage his political career.

White had long been aware of the dangers inherent in the school situation, but he was unwilling and unable to resolve it prior to the court action. He possessed only limited leverage over the School Committee and chose not to exercise it for fear of being blamed for the busing that was sure to be required. The mayor had tried to cast the issue in metropolitan terms, arguing that the suburbs should not be immune from the social consequences of the demographic shifts of the previous decades. When neither the state legislature nor the federal courts accepted this approach, massive intracity busing became a reality. As Boston's chief executive, White urged compliance with the court order, but he never missed an opportunity to express his dislike for the judge's ruling and sympathy for the bused children and their parents. This wishy-washy stance hardly endeared him to the fervent partisans on either side, but it allowed White to keep his disparate coalition intact and seek a third term.

Despite the intense emotions it inspired, the busing issue did not figure significantly in the 1975 mayoralty elections. Strong opponents of busing succeeded in the contests for the School Committee and council, but in the mayor's race no serious candidate with a clear anti-busing record even entered the starting gate. State Representative Raymond Flynn (South Boston), for example, who had urged that the Massachusetts compulsory education law be repealed to eliminate the legal rationale for busing, dropped plans to run when his fund-raising efforts failed. Hicks, who had made a tacit alliance with White after extremists took the anti-busing banner away from her, decided to keep the council seat she had won in 1973.

The threat to White in 1975 came from Joseph Timilty, the grandson and nephew of Boston politicians who had tied their tails to Curley's kite. Four years earlier, Timilty had run for mayor as a conservative law-and-order candidate and finished a distant third behind Hicks in the preliminary election. In the interim, however, he had undergone a political metamorphosis, championing the cause of homosexual rights and the creation of a state senate district with a black majority. He was also the sole holdout in the state senate against restoration of the death penalty. Portraying himself as the candidate of the neighborhoods, Timilty made much of the fact that his children attended public schools when the mayor's children went to private schools. Like White, he opposed "forced busing," but also like White, he went aggressively after the black vote. What Timilty offered, above all, was a fresh face. White was visibly aging, even if he was only forty-five-years old. But White could point to a record of stable tax rates and imaginative, capable administration.

White's well-oiled political machine provided him with a comfortable eleven-point lead in the preliminary contest (54 to 43 percent), but in the weeks before the final election that same political machine became an albatross around the mayor's neck. Day after day the city's newspapers, reflecting the post-Watergate mentality of the time, charged that the White campaign was underwritten by businessmen who held lucrative city contracts and by municipal employees whose salaries were directly tied to the level of their contributions to the campaign treasury. Timilty hit hard at this "climate of corruption" at City Hall, and White lashed out at the media, once his biggest supporter, for ignoring the facts of political life. The mayor nearly came unraveled as the bitter campaign drew to a close, but he hung on to gain a 81,000 to 73,700 victory.[23]

The trauma of the 1975 campaign shaped the remaining years of White's tenure in City Hall. Resigned to the fact that higher office was beyond his reach, White turned to solidifying his political power base and giving Boston a cosmopolitan image. He became obsessed with downtown revitalization as the way of establishing Boston as a "world class city," and he flaunted a lavish personal lifestyle (paid for out of public funds). When Boston celebrated its 350th anniversary in 1980, White organized a gala that invited guests from around the globe and kept neighborhood participation all but invisible.

To support this chic approach to governance, White perfected his political organization. He became a student of Richard Daley's machine. The Chicago mayor, and not John Lindsay, was now his model. If Lindsay had valued professional expertise over political savvy, White genuinely enjoyed old-fashioned arm twisting and made no apologies for heavy-handed tactics. He fired technocratic purists who were unwilling to accept the patronage deals, make the campaign contributions, and engage in door-to-door activity necessary to win elections. Politicizing the city government, White argued, made it more responsive. He even went so far as to propose that municipal elections be partisan, but the state legislature, seeing the idea as simply a power grab by the mayor, shot it down.[24]

If Kevin White was generally perceived as interested only in aggrandizing his own authority, his keen political sense also led him to abdicate responsibility. His machine allowed him to satisfy the parochial concerns of the neighborhoods, but on citywide issues City Hall grew increasingly cautious. Not only did White do little to save Boston's schools from judicial receivership, but he also stood aside as the courts took over the public housing program and the jails. The mayor saw no political gain in trying to resolve the financial and administrative ills that afflicted these arms of government. It was so much easier to let the courts devise a remedy. By the time White's third term neared its close in 1979, even the city's taxing power had come under judicial supervision.

In the election of 1979 the only real issue was Kevin White. The 1977 contests for the council and School Committee had demonstrated that, while racial tensions in the city remained high, there was no longer any political mileage in the busing question. Hicks and another incumbent, who had based his career on the city's racial divisions, lost their seats on the council, and a black candidate defeated the most vociferous opponent of busing on the School Committee.

Joe Timilty's third run for mayor generated few sparks. When he renewed his attack on White's "private political army" of municipal workers, the incumbent did not bother denying the charges and made no bones about how he thought the city should be governed. White's campaign spots usually referred to him simply as "The Mayor" and portrayed him as "The Loner in Love with His City." He held on to his personal coalition of liberals, blacks, Italians, and the elderly, added to it a sizable bloc of Irish votes, and defeated Timilty 77,000 to 65,000.[25]

Financial stringency and corruption cast long shadows over White's fourth term. The mayor had to contend with both a 1979 court decision declaring illegal the city's method of assessing commercial property (which meant the city was obliged to repay about $90 million to business taxpayers) and a 1980 statewide referendum mandating a 30 percent reduction in Boston's tax collections. Atempts to find the funds to comply with the court order started an eighteen-month battle with the council and state legislature. White had to contend with efforts to limit his power to shape the municipal budget and with the opposition of suburban representatives to new taxing authority for Boston that would hit their constituents. The mayor attempted to demonstrate the unworkability of the new voter-imposed state controls on the city's taxing capacity by concentrating the necessary personnel cuts in the police and fire departments, but when it was disclosed that White had protected the jobs of his own public relations staff and other patronage appointees, his critics claimed that this was yet another sign that the mayor was concerned more with his power than with the well-being of the city.

Growing legal problems added to White's mounting political difficulties. For years Boston had been rife with rumors about White's campaign financing. In 1981 a Republican U.S. Attorney began looking into the matter. By the middle of 1982, the press was full of stories about the extortion of contractors needing city permits, the abuse of disability pensions, the use of tax abatements to encourage political contributions, and a birthday party (canceled because of bad publicity) for Mrs. White to which city employees and people doing business with the city were expected to buy tickets. Some individuals associated with White's organization were already under indictment, others more closely tied to the mayor expected to join them, and news reports suggested that White himself faced criminal charges.

In July 1982 the *Boston Globe,* in a lengthy editorial, called upon Kevin White not to seek a fifth term the following year. Noting that it had supported White in the previous four elections, the *Globe* said that it was now "time for the mayor to leave gracefully." "The Kevin White of 1982," declared the paper, "proves Lord Acton's saying that 'Power tends to corrupt and absolute power tends to corrupt absolutely.' Of the half-dozen candidates now running, any of them would be preferable to Kevin White in 1983."

Ten months later, with his wife's abortive birthday party assuming the dimensions of a serious scandal involving allegations of laundered campaign funds, White announced he would not be a candidate for another term. Political analysts had predicted that if White ran in a crowded field he would make it into the runoff but that he would then lose the head-to-head contest. Polls showed that 44 percent of the city's electorate would not vote for him under any circumstances and 66 percent had an unfavorable opinion of the mayor. Nonetheless, his decision to withdraw came as a surprise; it was typical of White that in order to keep his intentions secret, he had taped his five-minute television announcement in New York for later broadcast in Boston. Making no mention of the corruption charges swirling around his administration, he claimed credit for the high rate of building construction in the city and said simply that the time had come "for a change" in his life.[26]

The Boston that Kevin White took over in 1968 was noticeably different from, but also remarkably similar to, the city he left in 1983. The drop in population eased somewhat in the 1960s, but picked up again in the 1970s, so that by 1980 only 570,000 people lived in the city, a loss of 230,000 residents since the war (Table A.2). As Boston's population dwindled, its composition changed dramatically. Blacks and Hispanics made up nearly a third of the total (Table A.4), and they constituted a two-third's majority in the public schools. Also on the increase was the number of young professionals making Boston their home; college graduates doubled their share of the city's population.

Economically and socially, Boston followed national trends from the 1960s to the 1980s. White had inherited a vigorous downtown redevelopment program from Collins, and construction in the central business district was booming when he departed. With a new reputation for livability and great cultural assets, Boston had become an "in-place" to work. Yet if Boston exuded prosperity, much of its population enjoyed little of it. Median income ranked near the bottom for major cities; a quarter of Boston's families fell below the poverty line. Suburban commuters held most of the well-paying jobs in town, and those professionals who did live in the city put intense pressure on an old and meager housing supply. Thousands of rental units became condominiums and ethnic neighborhoods underwent gentrification.

Kevin White largely ignored these problems, preferring the view of the new skyscrapers and relying upon his political machine to deliver votes. His city was perhaps even more sharply divided than was Curley's. As before, there was a clash of cultures: parochial versus cosmopolitan, old residents versus newcomers, rich versus poor, and, increasingly, white versus black. By withdrawing, White permitted these social and economic divisions to dominate the 1983 election.[27]

As Collins's retirement had done sixteen years earlier, White's decision not to run brought out a bevy of candidates, but three led the pack. The early front runner was radio talk-show host David Finnegan, who had family-based political connections and strong financing from building contractors. But Finnegan dissipated the advantages of name recognition and lots of advertising by remaining vague on the emerging issue of "linkage," which tied city support for downtown projects to developers' willingness to assist in the construction of low-rent housing.

Moving up were as odd a couple as Boston politics had ever seen. One was Mel King, an unsuccessful black candidate for mayor in 1975 and 1979. A former state legislator, King had carried the image of an extremist in his two prior campaigns, but in 1983 King traded his dashiki for a business suit and appealed to a "rainbow coalition" of lower-class Bostonians of all races seeking economic justice. With the city's new demographics and his more moderate stance, King rallied both blacks and liberal sympathizers, almost assuring himself a spot in the runoff. Possessing a less secure base but matching King's stress on jobs and housing was the other half of the odd couple, Councilor Ray Flynn of South Boston. Although Flynn first gained prominence in the mid-1970s for strong anti-busing and anti-abortion stands, he now emphasized economic populism. He opened his campaign at a run-down public housing project, telling the media, "You have to realize Boston is a very poor city. Kevin White has forgotten that." Flynn promised to make neighborhoods his top priority, and by campaigning in a battered 1974 station wagon, he made the contrast between himself and White a dramatic one.

In the primary King and Flynn ran a virtual dead-heat, with Finnegan finishing a close third. The results robbed the final election of any suspense—Flynn was the foregone winner. Although Flynn had come a long way from his anti-busing antics of 1974–75, King's black skin guaranteed Flynn's victory.

Flynn, the first from South Boston to win a mayor's race, defeated King by nearly 2 to 1 in a record turnout of voters. With the black vote solidly his, King needed about 40 percent of the white vote to win; he received about 20 percent. Yet, what was significant was not King's failure with whites, but his relative success. He took a larger share of the white electorate than either of the triumphant black candidates in Chicago and Philadelphia that year. With gentrification, the Boston political climate had taken a turn toward diversity and toleration, and while neither a black nor an Italian mayor was yet likely, Flynn's transformation suggested that Boston might be entering a new era of substantive, rather than symbolic, politics.[28]

When Flynn faced reelection four years later, most regarded his term as successful in terms of both politics and policy. Of Flynn's great personal success there was no question: only one serious candidate challenged Flynn in the 1987 elections, and the mayor swamped him by more than a 2 to 1 margin. The condition of Boston was not as clear-cut, but the signs were hopeful. After years of budgetary chaos under White, Flynn was able to balance the city's books because of new taxing authority from the state. With the regional economy continuing to prosper, Boston's downtown building boom went on, and Flynn began to deliver on his promise to share the benefits with the rest of the city through linkage. Boston may not have become a model of racial harmony, but racial incidents were noticeably down and Flynn fared well in polls among blacks. The mayor's ability to reshape the two-tier economy (high-paying technical and managerial jobs for a few and low-paying service jobs for the many) remained limited, but at last Boston appeared ready to discuss and act on its problems not in terms of stereotype and rhetoric, but on the basis of realism.[29]

NOTES

1. William Shannon, *The American Irish* (New York: Macmillan, 1963), pp. 182–87, 197, 207–209; Louis M. Lyons, "Boston: A Study in Inertia," in *Our Fair City*, ed. Robert S. Allen (New York: Vanguard Press), pp. 16–36; John Gunther, *Inside U.S.A.* (New York: Harper & Brothers, 1947), pp. 510–12, 518–20; Charles H. Trout, "Curley of Boston: The Search for Irish Legitimacy," in *Boston 1700–1980: The Evolution of Urban Politics,* ed. Ronald P. Formisano and Constance K. Burns (Westport, CT: Greenwood Press, 1984), pp. 165–95.

2. Constance K. Burns, "The Irony of Progressive Reform: Boston, 1898–1910," in *Boston 1700–1980,* pp. 133–64; Edward C. Banfield, *Big City Politics* (New York: Random House, 1965), pp. 39–49.

3. "The Kids of Dorchester," *Time,* December 6, 1943, p. 20; Wallace Stegner, "Who Persecutes Boston?" *Atlantic Monthly* 174 (July 1944): 45–52; Bernard De Voto, "The Easy Chair," *Harper's* 189 (August 1944): 237–240; Nat Hentoff, *Boston Boy* (New York: Alfred A. Knopf, 1986), pp. 16–21, 28–31, 65–72, 97–98; Shannon, *American Irish,* p. 230.

4. *Boston Herald,* November 7, 1945; *New York Times* [hereafter *NYT*], November 7, 1945; Jerome S. Bruner and Sheldon J. Korchin, "The Boss and the Vote: Case Study in City Politics," *Public Opinion Quarterly* 10 (1946): 1–23.

5. *Christian Science Monitor* [hereafter *CSM*], September 7, 1949; materials in Box 41.8, Henry Lee Shattuck MSS., Masschusetts Historical Society.

6. Materials in Box 41, Shattuck MSS.; William P. Marchione, Jr., "The 1949 Boston Charter Reform," *New England Quarterly* 49 (September 1976): 373–98.

7. *CSM*, November 3, 1949; John Joseph Sexton, "The Hynes Campaign: A Study in Coalition Politics" (Honors Thesis, Department of Government, Harvard College, April 1950), *passim*.

8. Edward C. Banfield and Martha Derthick, eds. *A Report on the Politics of Boston* (Cambridge: Harvard-M. I. T. Joint Center for Urban Studies, 1960), VI, 6–11, 126; Walter McQuade, "Boston: What Can a Sick City Do?" *Fortune* 69 (June 1964): 134–35; *CSM*, July 30–August 12, 1954; *NYT*, November 7, 1954.

9. McQuade, "Boston," p. 134; "Is Boston 'Beginning to Boil?' " *Fortune* 55 (June 1957): 286; Daniel S. Pool, "Politics in the New Boston: A Study of Mayoral Policy Making" (Ph.D. diss., Brandeis University, 1974), p. 66.

10. *Boston Herald*, May 6, 8, October 18, November 7, 1955.

11. Banfield and Derthick, *Report on the Politics of Boston*, II, 13–15; *CSM*, March 21, 1958, October 28, 30, 1959; *NYT*, November 1, 1959; *Boston Herald*, October 28, 1959; McQuade, "Boston," p. 136; J. Anthony Lukas, *Common Ground* (New York: Alfred A. Knopf, 1985), p. 35.

12. McQuade, "Boston," p. 134; Murray B. Levin, *The Alienated Voter: Politics in Boston* (New York: Holt, Rinehart & Winston, 1960), *passim*.

13. "Boston Bonds' Rating Slips a Notch," *Business Week*, December 19, 1959, pp. 90–94.

14. Lukas, *Common Ground*, p. 201; McQuade, "Boston," p. 134; Stephan Thernstrom, *Poverty, Planning, and Politics in the New Boston* (New York: Basic Books, 1969), p. 6; Neil R. Peirce, *The New England States* (New York: W. W. Norton, 1976), p. 108; *Boston Herald*, December 25, 1959; "What's Happening to Proper Old Boston?" *Newsweek*, April 26, 1965, pp. 77–79.

15. "What's Happening to Proper Old Boston?" p. 77; "Bold Boston Gladiator—Ed Logue," *Life*, December 24, 1965, pp. 126–34; Lukas, *Common Ground*, pp. 153–54; McQuade, "Boston," pp. 166, 169.

16. Citizens Housing and Planning Association, *Urban Renewal & Planning in Boston* (Boston: The Association, 1972), pp. 3–4; Banfield, *Big City Politics*, p. 50; *Boston Globe*, October 6, 1966.

17. Stephan Thernstrom, *The Other Bostonians: Poverty and Progress in the American Metropolis, 1880–1970* (Cambridge: Harvard University Press, 1973), pp. 179–80; Banfield and Derthick, *Report on the Politics of Boston*, I, 7–8; V, 4; VI, 47–55; Robert W. Morgan, Jr., "Over the Bridge," *Atlantic* 203 (February 1959): 73–76.

18. Thernstrom, *Poverty, Planning, and Politics*, pp. 6, 43; Peter Schrag, *Village School Downtown* (Boston: Beacon Press, 1966), *passim*; Lukas, *Common Ground*, pp. 124–28, 133.

19. Lukas, *Common Ground*, pp. 115–21, 123, 133; "Rebalancing Boston," *Newsweek*, April 26, 1965, pp. 60–61; *NYT*, November 3, 6, 1965; Peggy Lamson, "The White Northerner's Choice: Mrs. Hicks of Boston," *Atlantic* 217 (June 1966): 58.

20. "Crowded Field," *Time*, July 14, 1967, pp. 18; *NYT*, August 27, September 24, 1967; "Every Little Breeze . . . " *Newsweek*, September 18, 1967, pp. 37–39.

21. Alan Lupo, *Liberty's Chosen Home* (Boston: Little, Brown, 1977), pp. 112–13; "Narrow Margin," *Nation*, November 20, 1967, pp. 515; Jeffrey K. Hadden, Louis H. Masotti, Victor Thiessen, "The Making of the Negro Mayors 1967," *Transaction* 5 (January/February 1968): 28–29.

22. Lukas, *Common Ground*, pp. 29–35, 42–44, 132, 198–99; Arnold M. Howitt, "Electoral Constraints on Mayoral Behavior," Discussion Paper D77–4 (April 1977), Department of City and Regional Planning, Harvard University.

23. Lukas, *Common Ground*, pp. 585–89, 599–615.

24. Philip B. Heymann and Martha Wagner Weinberg, "The Paradox of Power: Mayoral Leadership on Charter Reform in Boston," in *American Politics and Public Policy,* ed. Walter Dean Burnham and Martha Wagner Weinberg (Cambridge: M.I.T. Press, 1978), pp. 280–303;

25. Howard Husock, "No More Mileage in Busing," *Nation,* December 31, 1977, pp. 710–12; Martha Wagner Weinberg, "Boston's Kevin White: A Mayor Who Survives," in *Boston 1700–1980;* pp. 215–39.

26. George V. Higgins, *Style Versus Substance: Boston, Kevin White, and the Politics of Illusion* (New York: Macmillan, 1984), pp. 189–203; *Boston Globe,* July 14, 1982; "King Kevin's Last Hurrah," *Newsweek,* June 6, 1983, p. 41.

27. Howard Husock, "Boston: The Problem That Won't Go Away," *NYT Magazine,* November 25, 1979, pp. 32–34; Edward D. McClure and Kirk Scharfenberg, "Boston for the Gentry," *Nation,* December 29, 1979, pp. 686–88; "Boston: A City of Two Tales," *Newsweek,* June 9, 1980, pp. 49–50; "A Tale of Two Cities," *Time,* August 30, 1982, p. 23.

28. "King's First Hurrah," *Newsweek,* October 24, 1983, p. 33; "Boston Wins by a Landslide," *Time,* October 24, 1983, p. 30; "Raymond Flynn's First Hurrah," *Newsweek,* November 28, 1983, p. 53.

29. *Boston Globe,* March 29, April 19, July 4, October 28, November 4, 1987; *NYT,* September 13, 1987.

IV

CHICAGO

THE COOK COUNTY DEMOCRATIC ORGANIZATION AND THE DILEMMA OF RACE, 1931–1987

Arnold R. Hirsch

Chicago's blacks have endured an ambiguous relationship with the Cook County Democratic organization and, for more than the last half century, with the party "machine" that controlled the rewards, status, and recognition that flowed through the political system. In the premigration era, blacks were not numerically very important, and, in local contests at least, they were willing to split their votes between the expected Republican beneficiaries and appealing Democrats. It was not until the twentieth century that Chicago's non-whites moved solidly into Republican ranks. Coincident with the great migration that swelled their numbers, this strong identification with the Republican party left local Democrats with a persistent electoral threat.

The architect of Chicago's modern Democratic organization, Anton Cermak, and his successor, Ed Kelly, moved to break the Republicans' grip on Chicago's black electorate during the Great Depression. Whatever their personal feelings, Cermak and Kelly included blacks within the scope of their ethnic appeals, used City Hall's considerable powers to harass and reward, and brought them into the Democratic party on a quid pro quo basis.

The cementing of the black-Democratic alliance during the New Deal, however, remained incomplete. The uncertainty governing black-white relations during Ed Kelly's tenure (1933–47), in fact, led to his dumping by the organization in December 1946 because, among other indiscretions, he went too far in appealing to the still new black Democratic vote. Local chieftains subsequently pushed the machine into a retreat on racial issues while under the distant and purely nominal leadership of Martin H. Kennelly (1947–55). In the 1950s and 1960s, Richard J. Daley forged a new accommodation, ruthlessly subordinated blacks, and raised the Democratic edifice on a barely concealed social fault line. It was a settlement that left black leadership fragmented, the masses apathetic, and black concerns unaddressed.

In transforming the Cook County Democratic organization into a vehicle for the

63

rising ethnic middle class, Daley succeeded where every other urban "boss" failed. He brought the "machine" out of the inner city, carried it to Chicago's burgeoning outskirts after World War II, and brought it stability and prosperity at a time when other urban machines found it impossible to adapt to new postwar demographic and economic realities. Confounding traditional political assumptions on the "natural" constituencies of such political organizations, Daley's machine stopped serving the poor as they became increasingly non-white. Rather than lose its bedrock of support to assimilation and new-found middle-class status, the modern Cook County Democratic organization pursued the third- and fourth-generation "ethnics" to the urban fringe, held the line on race, and defended the ethnics' interests until time, migration patterns, and the cumulative weight of its own policies brought the party down in the racial and electoral upheaval of 1983.

The signs of strain were evident even before Daley's death in 1976. But "Hizzoner's" political skill bought him time and left his neighbor and successor, the bland and considerably less adroit Michael Bilandic, to reap the whirlwind. Upset by Jane Byrne's black-supported insurgency in 1979, the machine coopted the new mayor only to suffer a crushing blow four years later. Harold Washington proved the beneficiary of a growing surge of black independence and the "reformers' " disenchantment with Byrne's political ambidexterity in his surprising 1983 *coup*.

In going after black votes, the Democrats of Ed Kelly's day were not as handicapped by history as one might suppose. In the late nineteenth and early twentieth centuries, Chicago's two Carter Harrisons—each of them five-term Democratic mayors—actively sought and won black votes. Local Democrats also found it possible before World War I to appeal to black leaders possessing their own independent political bases. Thus the Rev. Archibald Carey, a Republican and arguably the strongest black political leader on the near South Side, assisted the younger Harrison's 1911 bid for reelection as well as Edward Dunne's race for governor the following year.

The possibilities for a lasting black-Democratic rapprochement, however, were not realized immediately. The great migration brought to Chicago large numbers of southern blacks for whom the Democratic party was anathema. Moreover, rampant factionalism within black ranks shattered their nascent party organizations. Equally important, however, was the factionalism within the white Democratic community. The destruction of the Harrison wing of the party and the rise of the ethnic Irish, first under the direction of John Hopkins and Roger C. Sullivan and later under George Brennan, brought with it not continued appeals for interracial cooperation, but strident calls for white unity. From World War I to the depression, the Sullivan-Brennan Democracy openly rejected black support and brought a variety of white ethnics together in the name of racial solidarity. Particularly in the "tribal twenties," anti-black feeling provided much of the glue that held the party together.[1]

These developments coincided with changes within the Republican party and, particularly, the rise of William Hale Thompson. "Big Bill" Thompson was the primary political beneficiary of the southern blacks' trek to the Windy City. His Republican affiliation, skillful use of patronage, and ready recognition of the

"Race" earned him their overwhelming support. Black votes provided a crucial edge for Thompson, both in party primaries and in the general elections that catapulted him into City Hall in 1915, 1919, and 1927. The Thompson-black alliance, however, was hardly an unmitigated blessing for the Republican party.

The loyalty of Chicago's black voters seemed more tied to Big Bill personally than to the local Republican establishment. He could, when intraparty disputes became heated, punish his rivals within the GOP as he did in 1923 when his lieutenants delivered 60 percent of the black vote for Democratic mayoral candidate William Dever. Also, his factional opponents within the Republican party supported Progressive reforms that were strongly opposed in the black community; and their internecine battles against Big Bill could be nearly as bitter as the general elections. If fellow Republicans did not employ calliopes playing "Bye Bye Blackbird" as did the Brennan Democrats in 1927, it was a factional Republican opponent who first raised the charge that Thompson's patronage-laden City Hall was "Uncle Tom's Cabin." When combined with strains imposed from above—such as Republican President Theodore Roosevelt's autocratic handling of the Brownsville incident, the national Republican party's open courting of lily-white supporters in the South throughout the 1920s, and the Hoover administration's response to the depression— these local conditions seriously undermined the still broad, but increasingly brittle, black allegiance to the party of Lincoln.[2]

Even Thompson's generally favorable reception in and treatment of the black community had its limits. Big Bill was not quite as unreservedly pro-black as most accounts make out. In a fashion reminiscent of his later Democratic counterparts, he was a hard-nosed political operator who was willing to solicit black votes, but much less willing to share power. It was 1920 before Ed Wright earned a place of significance within the local party structure by taking over the second ward and becoming the city's first black ward committeeman. And when, after he had gained control of the neighboring third ward in 1924, Wright tried to take over the first ward two years later, Thompson broke with his former organizer. Unwilling to countenance a new rising star and potential black rival on the South Side, Thompson stripped Wright of his patronage and consigned him to political oblivion. Perhaps Wright was lucky. In the infamous "Pineapple Primary" of 1928, black attorney Octavius Grandy was gunned down by hoodlums as he ran for committeeman against Morris Eller, Thompson's city collector, in the West Side's "Bloody 20th" ward. Finally, even in matters of patronage and certainly in terms of public policy, Thompson's offerings to blacks seem meager when stacked against the massive support given him in four Republican primaries and three victorious mayoral campaigns.[3]

None of this should suggest, however, that blacks were openly dissatisfied with Thompson or leaving the Republican party on the eve of the Great Depression. With Brennan's Democrats the only alternative, there was really nowhere to go. It does indicate, however, that under the right conditions and under some new leadership, the city's Democrats could make a fair bid for black support. The economic crisis of the 1930s provided the perfect opportunity—one that was seized first by Anton Cermak, and then, even more forcefully, by Ed Kelly.

Anton Cermak was the consummate ethnic politician, and he did not exclude blacks from his constituency. In 1927, when the Brennan-led party ran a viciously racist campaign, Cermak used his perch as president of the Cook County Board of Commissioners to appoint the black publisher of the *Broad Ax* to his Civic Commission. Cermak's ultimate seizure of the party apparatus from the Brennan clique provided even greater latitude, and his first slate as party chairman in 1930 included a black along with Jews, Poles, and Italians. By the time he ran against Thompson in 1931, "what fledgling Democratic leadership" existed among blacks was, in the words of Cermak's biographer, "in his pocket—if not, indeed, his own creation." The payoff came when, in the course of his race against Big Bill, the leading black newspaper, the *Chicago Defender,* refrained from making any endorsement and gave the campaign scant coverage.[4]

During his brief tenure as mayor, Cermak used both the carrot and the stick in his continuing search for black support, although—given his nature—he wielded the club with more alacrity. Almost as soon as he entered City Hall, Cermak fired more than two-thousand temporary employees, including many blacks, and began filling South Side jails with black gamblers and policy runners. These were unquestionably acts of harassment, but not evidence of simple anti-black animus. Many of those dismissed from City Hall—particularly the black attorneys in the law department—were fired because they played crucial roles in their Republican ward organizations; and those swept up by police found the key to their release in a simple change of political affiliation. Finally, before earning lasting fame as the portly buffer separating Franklin D. Roosevelt from the assassin Guiseppe Zangara, Cermak appointed Mike Sneed of the third ward the city's first black Democratic committeeman. Finding a new generation of northern-born blacks less wary of Democratic overtures, Cermak laid the groundwork for the political revolution brought to fruition under Ed Kelly.[5]

Brought in as mayor by party chairman Pat Nash after Cermak's death in 1933, Kelly is best remembered for the corruption that marked his fourteen year administration. His biographer, Roger Biles, notes that the thievery took on "awesome proportions." The Board of Education and the public schools operated as mere appendages of the party organization by funneling contracts and jobs to the faithful and treating the task of education as incidental at best. Gambling and prostitution were notorious in Kelly's wide-open town, the police were bought and paid for, and organized crime operated with a virtual free hand. The reformers of Kelly's own age were disgusted and expected little else from a politician who avoided prosecution himself only by paying the IRS $107,000 on nearly a half million dollars of unreported income.[6]

For all his corruption, Kelly was also a master organizer and party builder who improved upon Cermak's political base, fashioned Chicago's New Deal coalition, and became a symbol of interracial amity and justice within the black community. His efforts both complemented and rivaled President Roosevelt's image on the national level. Stepping into the mainstream of twentieth-century liberal reform, Kelly obviously used his distribution of federal relief monies to further his own political interests, but blacks accepted his assistance as genuine and sincere, and the black-owned *Chicago Bee* proclaimed him a "great social force."[7] Although the certification process remained out of his hands, the mayor and his operatives did little to dissuade relief applicants from believing that political clout was a prerequisite for assistance, and they did not hesitate to wrap themselves in the New Deal's comforting mantle.

Kelly was, however, more than a mere conduit for federal resources. More than anyone else, he came closest to Big Bill Thompson in the masterful practice of symbolic racial politics. By censoring the movie *Birth of a Nation,* by declaring a Fair Employment Practices Commission Day and a Race Relations Week, and by orchestrating public ceremonies for Joe Louis and war hero Dorrie Miller, he struck responsive racial chords. Most significantly, he could speak personally before South Side audiences, reminisce about his mother, and draw "ovations" from them as he described her scrubbing floors in the large houses in Hyde Park. He conveyed the idea that he did, indeed, understand his listeners' plight.

He delivered on substantive issues as well. In 1934 Kelly ordered the Board of Education to rescind an edict segregating schools in Morgan Park and used his police to protect black students and arrest hostile white demonstrators in the ensuing furor—and he repeated this performance in the racially inspired white school boy-cotts of 1945. The mayor assumed, in short, official responsibility for maintaining social peace and, within limits, furthering racial equity—an approach institution-alized in his creation of the Chicago Commission on Human Relations (CHR) in 1943, his directed passage of a local FEPC ordinance in 1945, and the creation of a civil rights unit within the corporation counsel's office in 1946. And if there were complaints about the quality of Chicago's public schools, blacks noticed the fourteen new elementary and high schools built on the South Side during Kelly's first decade in office and the fact that the Black Belt was finally getting a disproportionately larger share of the new school seats. Finally, Kelly's appointment of blacks to the Civil Service Commission, the Board of Education, and as school principals and police and fire captains cemented his relationship to black Chicagoans.[8]

It is also crucial to note that Kelly took the first steps in the professionalization of the city's bureaucracy. One of the so-called "new breed" Irish politicians de-tected later by historian Paul Green, Kelly moved beyond the constraints of a narrowly defined ethnicity and appreciated the need for professional performance in an increasingly complex governmental administration. Indeed, even the well-known reformer Edith Abbott declared that Kelly had restrained political meddling and kept his hands off the Chicago Relief Administration (CRA). Civil service appointments filled all the vacancies in both that agency and the Cook County Bureau of Public Welfare.[9]

Kelly's desire to professionalize government and willingness to address black issues were epitomized in the operations of the Chicago Housing Authority (CHA). Not only did Kelly appoint a black professional, Robert R. Taylor, chairman of the CHA, but in pushing the construction of the Ida B. Wells Homes over white protests before World War II, the mayor provided new housing, construction jobs, and management positions for black South Siders. During the war, as Kelly's housing authority still labored under the federal "neighborhood composition rule" that prevented projects from altering the racial make-up of their neighborhoods, the

CHA actively sought integrated areas in which they could build integrated developments. While all-black projects such as Altgeld Gardens augmented the total black housing supply, the construction of mixed-residence projects such as the Robert Brooks and Frances Cabrini Homes gave evidence of the administration's willingness to accept integration. Indeed, in the postwar period the mayor and his minions even attempted to place blacks in emergency veterans' quarters in all-white areas. Kelly himself suggested that that a 10 percent quota on black occupancy in all-white communities was appropriate given the number of blacks then living in Chicago.[10]

That the CHA and its controversial executive secretary, Elizabeth Wood, were able to stake out such advanced positions was irrefutable proof of the authority's privileged status. Under Kelly, who ran both the city and the "machine" with an iron hand, the CHA led a charmed existence. The mayor protected it, kept the ward bosses off its back, and championed its proposals. City council leader John Duffy chafed under Kelly's autocratic control but acknowledged that "under Kelly, the Housing Authority submitted a proposal and that was it." Not only did the mayor offer his full support to the authority in the event their programs stirred up "racial trouble," but he ran it as a "clean" agency and refused to tap its patronage potential. Even as his administration prostituted the public school system for political advantage, Kelly kept the housing authority as his showpiece for reformers. Elizabeth Wood reveled in her independence and lorded it over the frustrated ward bosses. "They really hate us," she gloated. "They'd love to have that gravy."[11]

Kelly's vigorous brand of urban liberalism prompted two reactions of the greatest significance. The first of these was the mass movement of blacks into the Democratic party. In Chicago, at least, this electoral conversion was more the result of mayoral than presidential leadership. In 1935, in the wake of his stand in Morgan Park, Kelly polled over 80 percent of the vote in the leading black wards; and four years later he captured nearly 60 percent of the total black vote. In contrast, Franklin Roosevelt failed to win a majority of Chicago's black votes in 1936, and earned but 52 percent in 1940. Arthur Mitchell, the first black Democratic candidate for Congress in Chicago, pinpointed Kelly's appeal during his own 1934 campaign and referred to Kelly's attack on segregation in the school controversy. "The stand taken by you," he wrote Kelly

was not only manly and right, but required the highest type of courage. . . . In this matter you have made thousands of friends among the Negroes; not only for yourself but for the democratic party. Heretofore the argument has been that democrats are not sympathetic toward Negroes in matters of this kind. The work you did here stands out. There is nothing in the career of Big Bill Thompson, or any other republican, which is so heartening to Negroes.

By the late 1930s, Kelly was funneling more jobs to Oscar DePriest, the *Republican* committeeman of the third ward, than was the GOP, and Claude Barnett of the Associated Negro Press could only marvel at the strength of the local Democratic ward organizations. "County, city, sanitary district, and state patronage is democratic," Barnett wrote, and the once-proud South Side Republican organization appeared "shot."[12]

Bringing blacks into the Democratic fold, however, was not enough for Kelly— they had to be tied to *him,* not to a party label or a distant national figure. Indeed, before the end of his first full term of office the mayor was beset by serious factional reform challenges as well as the continued hostility of George Brennan's still formidable heirs. It is inconceivable that Kelly would have overlooked the potential of the growing black vote for solidifying his control of the party and turning back primary challenges. Perhaps emulating Thompson's use of the black vote in his own intraparty squabbles, Kelly's ardent New Dealism and empathy for blacks was unquestionably reinforced by a cold, pragmatic look at "the numbers" and the very real need to firm his own grip on the Democratic party machinery.

The mayor subsequently ousted the white committeeman of the second ward and replaced him with William Levi (Bill) Dawson, a renegade Republican with a strong personal organization. The move infuriated longstanding black Democrats who, after all, had joined the party when it was less than fashionable and had spent most of their careers fighting Dawson. The mayor's selection of Dawson especially infuriated rival Earl Dickerson who had been brought into the organization by Anton Cermak as an assistant attorney general and who had his own lofty ambitions. Dickerson's outspoken racial militance and his political independence, however, rendered him frighteningly unpredictable to the regulars. According to Claude Barnett of the Associated Negro Press, Kelly "want[ed] no part of Earl" and believed him to be "full of . . . crap."[13] With Kelly's patronage safely in Dawson's pocket there was little Dickerson or anyone else could do. It was a turning point for black politics in Chicago. Tenacious, skillful, and ever loyal to Kelly and the Cook County Democratic organization, Dawson eventually claimed a seat in the U.S. House of Representatives, extended his control to five wards, and became the undisputed boss of the South Side Black Belt. Kelly had certainly not planned this last development, but as long as Dawson showed no further signs of independence and continued to turn out large majorities for Kelly and the organization, the mayor allowed him to become the strongest "ethnic" politician in the city. Given the earlier Republican purge of Ed Wright, such tolerance—even with its obvious limitations—moved Kelly well beyond Big Bill Thompson as a sponsor of black political empowerment.

The second reaction to Kelly's liberalism, however, was more foreboding. An undercurrent of tension ran between white ethnics and blacks as they jockeyed for position in the city and within the Democratic party. Wartime tensions peaked in 1943 when fighting broke out near the Cabrini Homes on the North Side and whites vigorously protested CHA activity on the South Side. After the war, violence dogged every step of an enlarged black population as it searched for new housing. Between May 1944 and July 1946, forty-nine arson bombings traced but failed to maintain traditional racial borders. The attacks became so widespread that the *Defender* believed them to be part of a "systematic pattern of terrorism." By late 1946, the situation had deteriorated to the point where knowledgeable observers expected the outbreak of massive rioting.[14] With racial feelings running high in the neighborhoods, many ward bosses, already embittered by Kelly's tight discipline, needed little urging to side with their constituents.

Kelly fell victim to this irreconcilable split before the year was out. The immediate precipitant of his political demise was a racial confrontation at the Airport Homes, a temporary veterans' project that was occupied by white squatters on November 5 (election day) in the hopes of forestalling the integration of both the project and the all-white West Lawn community. Local ward politicians instigated the occupation in an attempt to use the race issue against Kelly. The mayor responded by affirming his "solid" support of the CHA's policy of nondiscrimination and ordering his police to act on the basis of that commitment. Fatefully, at the precise moment South Side ethnics were demonstrating their mortal fear of an expanding Black Belt, Kelly issued a public statement guaranteeing blacks "their right to live peaceably anywhere in Chicago."[15]

As riotous mobs surrounded the Airport project, party chairman Jake Arvey and other organization leaders polled their constituents and sealed Kelly's fate in advance of the 1947 mayoralty. Years later, when recalling the purge, Arvey spoke not of corruption, the schools, or the fevered opposition of independents and the press— all of which made Kelly's reelection problematical at best. He spoke of race and singled out Kelly's public support of open housing in the days before the party's slate-making conclave.[16] Kelly had overcome reformers and their charges of corruption before, but always with the unshakable backing of the regular Democratic organization. The desertion of his white constituency, however, precluded even an attempt at combat this time. The Democratic machine in Chicago now became a vehicle for the city's white ethnic communities. It continued to solicit black votes, but it never again pursued black interests. Kelly had defined the limits of coalition politics in Chicago and in the process had left the Cook County Democratic organization gravely weakened in the face of a postwar Republican resurgence.

Reflecting on the Kelly administration, the *Defender* speculated that the mayor's empathy for blacks was rooted in his own humble origins and mirrored the affinity of class. "He had come up from the bottom of the ladder and in the climbing he learned to understand people and it stood him in good stead," the paper declared. The editors of the *Chicago Bee* emphasized racial themes, however, and waxed even more rhapsodic. Describing an audience granted in Kelly's office, the *Bee's* editor conveyed the genuine feeling inspired by the mayor:

> As he spoke I knew that I was in a sanctuary where the equality of all men was the creed. I could scarcely listen for contemplating the man; the man who spoke out on public platform and press against lynching and mob violence; who demanded that the doors of industry open to my people; who asked the President . . . to lift my people from the yoke of rent exploitation. . . . [the man who] has given new hope to our children.

When he left office in 1947, the *Bee* concluded that Kelly could "justly be regarded as a Mayor with a heart, a sense of fairness" that was best "demonstrated in his attitude toward minorities, particularly Negroes."[17]

Kelly's hand-picked successor, Martin H. Kennelly, was, like Kelly, an Irishman born in the working-class Bridgeport community and educated in the neighborhood's DeLaSalle Institute. Beyond that, however, the two men could not have been more different. The beneficiary of postwar Republican electoral victories, the burgeoning Kelly scandals, and rebellious party operatives who felt that the mayor had gone too far in wooing blacks, Kennelly brought to City Hall a fresh face, clean image, and important connections to the business community—and he was not burdened by close ties to the regular party organization. A onetime Kelly adversary who had supported "reform" insurgencies within the party, the cool, aloof, self-made millionaire was as close as the machine could come to silk-stocking respectability. Not surprisingly, in his successful 1947 campaign Kennelly was also the beneficiary of Ed Kelly's long coattails in the black community. Though an unknown quantity on racial issues, Kennelly won black support because, as the *Defender* put it, blacks felt it important to "continue and expand the progressive and far-reaching racial policies" of Kelly. It was an act of faith that went unrewarded.[18]

Kennelly was a "white knight" in every sense. Not only did he renounce corruption, eschew narrow partisanship, and affirm his determination to rule in the public's—not the party's—interest, but he offered no resistance to the ward leaders' hostile opposition to Kelly's advanced racial positions. Fundamentally conservative, Kennelly displayed little affinity for either the social goals of the New Deal or the cause of civil rights. Willing to leave purely political matters to the regular party leadership, Kennelly, whether knowingly or not, served as a respectable "front" for a machine that had fallen into disrepute and permitted the Cook County Democratic organization to weather the postwar political crisis that threatened its hegemony. Forced to make concessions, the machine survived. "We're still in business," party chairman Arvey announced—"wholesale."[19]

Kennelly wanted nothing more than to be an efficient city manager, a nonpolitical administrator within Chicago's intensely political city government. As such, he cleaned up the schools, drove gambling out of the city or underground, and embarked upon a program of civil service reform that cost the machine thousands of patronage jobs. It was a measure of the organization's political distress that Kennelly could pursue such initiatives and still win the party's blessing for his successful 1951 reelection. It was a choice made somewhat easier by the mayor's close ties to the downtown business community, and the extraordinary corporate efforts at redevelopment that created new jobs, stimulated fresh sources of patronage, and offered opportunities in land speculation.

Kennelly's avoidance of "politics", though, crippled his administration and forced him into compromising accommodations with the ward leaders. Kennelly attacked the political cesspool at the Board of Education, for example, while keeping his hands off the machine's more vital interest in the police department. Though the department was rocked by repeated scandals, Kennelly left it untouched. He became the city's chief "booster" in public hearings on police corruption, merely appointed yet another safe "insider" to head the department when the demand for change became unavoidable, and displayed rare talent, even for a Chicagoan, in the art of looking the other way.

More important, the mayor maintained a "hands off" policy with regard to the city council. His aloofness gave machine leaders a license to seize key committee assignments and chairmanships and, especially, to control the budgetary process. It was, according to columnist Len O'Connor, a "golden era of mayoral permissiveness" in which "Big Boys" such as Tom Keane, John Duffy, and Clarence Wagner divvied up the municipal pie and graft was rampant. Indeed, Kennelly's administration was so lax that the hard men who ran the party cynically commented on the appropriateness of the mayor's tears following finance committee chairman Wagner's death in a 1953 automobile wreck. Kennelly's grief, they believed, reflected the fact that Wagner did all of his work for him.[20]

Kennelly's lack of political concern correlated well with his lack of political skill. It was not that Kennelly ignored politics as a matter of principle as his campaign rhetoric suggested, but rather that he played the game only intermittently, usually poorly, and almost exclusively in conjunction with his own electoral fortunes. Thus it was with a transparent heavy-handedness that the "reform" mayor tried to impress the new party chairman, Richard J. Daley, on the eve of the 1955 municipal elections, by pressuring the Chicago Housing Authority into appointing the chairman's cousin, John Daley, as its new counsel. Not only did Kennelly fail to make the appointment stick, but his feeble efforts to win party backing for a third term were already doomed by the new chairman's own driving ambitions.

Kennelly's attempted subversion of the CHA for political purposes also exposed a weakness on racial issues that eventually swamped his administration. The first signs of trouble came as violence erupted in changing neighborhoods. The hit-and-run attacks that bedeviled Ed Kelly had evolved into massive mob disorders in the postwar era. When confronted with this bitter white reaction to black residential expansion, the mayor refused to reaffirm his predecessor's stand against discrimination. His reaction to recurrent disorder, according to a Commission on Human Relations that openly longed for Kelly's firmer hand, consisted of little more than "appeasement and persuasion." Blaming the uprisings on subversives, Kennelly did little to end the violence or assuage black feelings.[21]

In the aftermath of one particularly serious explosion, Urban League executive Sidney Williams attacked the Kennelly administration's "ineptitude" and its "shameful failure" to protect blacks. He also called for the mayor's impeachment and organized the Committee to End Mob Violence to prod the city into greater action. Kennelly's response, it was rumored in the black community, was to use his influence in Chicago's business community to dry up white contributions to the Urban League. While it is impossible to confirm Kennelly's alleged role, the Urban League's subsequent financial distress forced it to shut down for six months and fire its entire staff, including Sidney Williams. When it opened its doors again, it had the support of the city's business leaders and, not coincidentally, a more conservative leadership.[22]

When Kennelly finally did take a stand on housing discrimination, it was to oppose an ordinance that would have banned it. Black Republican alderman Archibald Carey, Jr., introduced the measure to assure blacks that they would not be displaced by the city's slum clearance program and that they would have access to all publicly assisted housing. Kennelly maintained a silence on Carey's bill that was, according to the Chicago Council against Discrimination, "interpreted not only as opposition to the Ordinance, but also as a tacit repudiation of the platform commitments of the [Democratic] party." Loop business elites and machine politicians stood together to defeat the Carey ordinance as the former vowed to crush all threats to redevelopment and the latter feared any black initiative or expression of political power. Given such solid backing, the debate over the measure provided one of the rare occasions when the mayor stepped out of character and took the council floor to speak against pending legislation.[23]

Ultimately, however, it was not Kennelly's leadership but the lack of it that was of the greatest significance. Under his regime the ward bosses were able to reassert themselves and attack the CHA. Bereft of Kelly's protective shield, the authority renounced its original mission and became a bulwark of segregation.

The process began just weeks into Kennelly's first term when the state, at the city council's request, passed a redevelopment program that gave the council a veto over locally funded projects. The legislation threw the authority into a "new relationship" with the city and led Elizabeth Wood to anticipate "profound difficulties . . . due to the Authority's racial policy." Indeed, within months that policy led to the passage of additional state legislation that granted the city a veto over all CHA projects, even those supported by federal funds. Consequently, the precedent-setting first slate of public housing sites selected under the Housing Act of 1949 reflected the desires of a handful of council leaders who wished to contain the city's black population and halt the CHA's building program. By the fall of 1952, Elizabeth Wood acknowledged their success and characterized the CHA as a "captive Authority." Those who looked to the mayor for help discovered that he had "forsaken" their goals. Ironically, the reformers in the CHA found themselves mourning the passing of the "aggressive leadership" missing since "Mayor Kelly left office."[24]

Wood vowed to fight on but realized that she had become a controversial figure. This was because, in her view, she "made every effort to run an honest enterprise" and "tried not to discriminate." When the Trumbull Park Homes exploded in yet another racial confrontation in the summer of 1953, she found herself unable to withstand a final political assault on her independence. Demoted and rendered powerless in a reorganization inspired by one of Kennelly's "efficiency" studies, Wood attacked the hypocrisy of her superiors and their lack of resolve on racial issues. Dismissed by the authority's commissioners in 1954, Wood's removal ended the CHA's resistance to the racial demands of the city's white ward leaders.[25]

As the CHA collapsed, the mayor's disastrous relationship with Bill Dawson compounded his difficulties with the black South Side. Kennelly, who was clearly uncomfortable with blacks, never developed a political strategy to deal with them and had no basis for communicating with Dawson who was both black and a "boss." Instead, when Kennelly dealt with blacks at all, it was through more "respectable" leaders such as the *Defender*'s John Sengstacke, the housing authority's Robert Taylor, and Rev. J. H. Jackson—all individuals with strong ties to the white business community. The mayor consequently isolated himself not only from the black ward

organizations, but from the black labor movement as well—despite repeated overtures from the CIO's Willard Townsend. In his 1951 reelection bid Kennelly kept
even those blacks friendly to him at a chilly distance, organizing a committee of
black leaders only in the campaign's final weeks. Dawson could not understand
Kennelly's "disregard" for him or the mayor's willingness, in Dawson's view, to
work with "opportunists who would go either way."[26]

Kennelly's much publicized crackdown on gambling also infuriated Dawson. The
embarrassment provided by the Senate's Kefauver hearings on organized criminal
activity in late 1950 and Kennelly's 1951 reelection campaign led the mayor to
prove he was "tough on crime" by raiding South Side gambling operations that
were nominally under Dawson's protection. Even Kennelly's friendly biographer
noted that such forays simply "became a satisfactory way for creating favorable
headlines without upsetting [the larger] system of payoffs." And when Dawson
tried to curtail police pressures by offering to support Kennelly's South Side redevelopment plans, Dawson's intermediary recalled receiving nothing more than
the mayor's characteristic "blank stare" in return. The raids continued, Dawson's
opposition slowed slum clearance operations, and the mayor tightened his own
political noose.[27]

There was also more to the gambling raids than met the eye. The success of
Kennelly's raids owed a great deal to information provided by C. C. Wimbish,
Dawson's ambitious third ward committeeman. Wimbish's secret dealings with the
mayor grew out of his desire to loosen Dawson's grip on the South Side, and
Kennelly's actions projected him squarely in the middle of an internecine political
battle that directly challenged Dawson's dominance. The Cook County Democratic
organization—at Dawson's insistence—later purged Wimbish, and Kennelly succeeded only in alienating Dawson beyond redemption.[28] His powerful voice would
be the loudest among those in the party's central committee calling for Kennelly's
early retirement.

The mayor's problems in the black community, and elsewhere, surfaced during
his 1951 campaign, but they were not yet enough to deny him victory. Kennelly
lost sixteen wards in 1951, doubling the number he dropped four years before.
Significantly, not only did he lose traditionally Republican wards on the far Northwest and Southwest sides, but defections could be detected in the Black Belt and
those white wards threatened with racial transition.[29] The tally graphically revealed
the racial-political dilemma of postwar Chicago: Kennelly could not protect blacks
without alienating the still-dominant whites, nor could he ignore black concerns
without losing the support of the most rapidly growing group in the city. Eager for
a third term in 1955, Kennelly proved only that he lacked the considerable skill
necessary to handle, balance, or negate the forces at work. He never had a chance.

Going into the 1955 campaign, Kennelly suffered a number of debilitating problems. In addition to his inability to defuse the city's gnawing racial tensions which
left both blacks and whites dissatisfied, the mayor's stance on civil service and his
estrangement from organized labor made his removal from office a virtual necessity
for organization Democrats.[30] Finally, there was the consuming personal ambition
of party chairman Richard J. Daley. The result was a perfunctory four-minute

interview for the two-term incumbent mayor before the organization's slatemakers rejected him unanimously. It was a deft political beheading, executed by Daley's hand-picked committee. Stripped of the party's support, Kennelly was left virtually alone to face Daley and onetime ally Ben Adamowski in a three-cornered primary.

The white siege of South Deering's Trumbull Park Homes on the far South Side entered its second year in 1955 and provided the backdrop for the campaign. Violently protesting the presence of a handful of black families, the whites in South Deering faced a housing authority that publicly opposed discrimination but still feared disorder and the impression that its policy could be made in the streets. The CHA consequently "froze" the number of black families in the project in the futile attempt to preserve both the peace and at least a token black presence. The failure of its efforts left the CHA watching helplessly as recurrent violence lashed the community. Kennelly, doing what he did best, stood on the sidelines and ignored black protests. Believing that the "mob violence at the project was sanctioned and stimulated by the willful failure of the city administration to end it," blacks rejected Kennelly's candidacy. Indeed, not only did the *Defender* claim that Kennelly's "cowardly handling" of the Trumbull Park disorders cost him black support, but white strategists mapping Democrat-turned-Republican Robert Merriam's race in the general election also concluded that blacks deserted Kennelly because he "failed them in the Trumbull Park situation."[31]

Faced with such dim prospects in the black community, Kennelly openly courted white backlash voters. Having the sophistication to use stereotypes rather than slurs, Kennelly claimed that it was the vicelord Dawson who "pushed the controls in the 'Dump Kennelly' project." The daily press dutifully echoed the charges, claiming that "the notorious Bill Dawson" was the "chief architect" of the nefarious "plot." If Kennelly campaigned against "bossism" in general, he was counting on a white reaction to the prospect of being dominated by a black boss in particular. The *Defender* denounced Kennelly's transparent "race baiting" and attacked his strategy as "both dirty and dangerous." Even Claude A. Barnett of the Associated Negro Press, hardly a Dawson supporter, believed the campaign coverage in the white press "fanned racial hate," made the mayor's dumping a "racial issue," and merely served to rally even unsympathetic blacks to Dawson's cause.[32]

While there is no question that Dawson played an important role in the mayor's defeat, the perception that it was merely a vengeful gambling czar who was primarily responsible for an outpouring of pliable black votes merely reflects the lasting legacy of the incumbent's rhetoric and the white dailies' election coverage. The black community's dissatisfaction with Kennelly was much deeper, and its rejection of him far more profound, than such self-serving interpretations suggest.

Mobilized by the mayor's vituperative campaign and the deadly drone of disorder that echoed not only from Trumbull Park, but from Fernwood, Park Manor, and Englewood as well, black voters marched to the polls not to vote for Richard J. Daley, but to bring down Martin H. Kennelly. The distinction is important, for Daley was able to win their support with no more than the assurance that he would place the solution of Trumbull Park's troubles "at the head of his program." Indeed, it was a measure not of Daley's political skill, but of Kennelly's ineptness, that the challenger was able to pick up endorsements from both the *Defender* and the anti-black South Deering Improvement Association. With the regular organization solidly behind him, the party chairman left the mayor in an impossible situation. When it was all over, Bill Dawson's five wards turned nearly 82 percent of their votes over to Daley (58,999 to 13,437) and the rest of Daley's 100,000 vote plurality came largely from a handful of inner city, machine-controlled "river" wards.[33] With the subsequent dispatching of Democratic turncoat Merriam in the general election, Chicago had, in Richard J. Daley, its third consecutive Bridgeport-born, DeLaSalle educated, Irish mayor. His reign would be the most notable of all.

On the ropes in 1947, the machine emerged stronger than ever from eight years under the anti-organization Kennelly. It was testimony to Jake Arvey's acumen in the first instance and Richard J. Daley's considerable skills in the second. Where Ed Kelly was a party builder, Kennelly was, in a real sense, the party's savior, rescuing its precarious electoral fortunes in a time of crisis by giving the machine the veneer of respectability and the time to rebuild and recover. Daley subsequently proved to be the organization's fine tuner, striking upon a new prescription for stability and survival that functioned with unparalleled efficiency, at least in the years before 1968.

Daley took lessons from each of his predecessors. In Ed Kelly, the organization had a mayor who provided plenty of "grease" for party operatives but was dangerously out of control on racial matters; in Martin Kennelly, the organization had a mayor whose stance on labor and civil service threatened their jobs but was safe on race. In Daley, Cook County's Democrats found a leader who would be safe on both patronage and racial issues. Having survived Kelly's flirtation with civil rights and Kennelly's with respectability, the machine found a formula for success that would sustain it for another generation. It was only in the second half of Daley's twenty-one year tenure that demographic change and the tensions inherent in the machine's operations began to weaken the organization's grip on the city.

The price of survival, Daley understood, was the modernization of the Cook County Democratic organization. As saloonkeeper-alderman Mathias "Paddy" Bauler indelicately informed machine leaders in the wake of Daley's election, the boy from Bridgeport was the "dog with the big nuts" now, and the mayor moved quickly to confirm that status by refusing to surrender his position as party chairman. By controlling both the city government and the party apparatus, Daley centralized all authority in his own hands and used his unprecedented power to adapt both the machine and municipal government to mid-twentieth-century realities.

Martin Kennelly's willingness to trash the CHA for political purposes was definitive proof that the professionalization of the city's bureaucracy did not proceed in a neat or linear fashion. But Daley accelerated the professionalization of the upper levels of that bureaucracy, brought technical expertise to the increasingly complex tasks involved in running a major city, and created a layer of government beyond the reach of the traditional ward barons. In rendering the old categories of "reform" and "machine" politics meaningless, Daley pursued proposals that would have gladdened the heart of the earlier Progressives. He seized control of the budgetary process, took it out of the hands of the grasping ward and council leaders (something Kennelly never even attempted), and stripped the aldermen and committeemen of their traditional power to grant driveway permits, zoning favors, and the other necessities of political life. Daley's office even drafted an ordinance transferring the power to investigate municipal wrongdoing and crime from the council to the mayor himself. Not only had he removed from view much of the petty corruption that tarnished political life, but he had transformed his ward leaders into mere middlemen between their supplicants and the ultimate clout downtown. Even the notorious deportment of the aldermen (which included eating, sleeping, and reading racing forms on the council floor under the lax Kennelly) was dramatically upgraded. In becoming a strong executive in what was still, nominally, a "weak" mayor system, Daley accomplished what progressive reformers had only dreamed about since the turn of the century: he had centralized Chicago's political system and overwhelmed the fragmented ethnic and institutional interests that had been enshrined in the city's fifty wards.[34]

Placating the traditionally fractious feudal lords of Chicago politics was essential to Daley's exercise of such discipline. First came the jobs. Within months Daley had gutted Kennelly's civil service reforms. In a telling episode, the organization invalidated the results of a recent police exam because the questions were found in Stephen Hurley's safety deposit box after his death. Hurley had been Kennelly's incorruptible civil service commission chairman and had personally locked the exams away because he could not trust his own staff with them. In preserving the secrecy of the exams, Hurley had merely provided a pretext for claiming that their integrity had been violated. Both the exams and their results were tossed out. Eventually, labor leader and Daley confidant William Lee became director of Chicago's civil service commission, and the neighborhood cadres had no illusions as to who held the real power. If Democratic loyalists lacked the freedom they enjoyed under Kennelly, or resented the fact that Daley was even more authoritarian than Ed Kelly, they still ate well at a table set by "Hizzoner." The ample supplies of patronage "grease" also made it easier to swallow the mayor's jealously guarded monopoly of public policy.[35]

Furthermore, by adopting the pro-growth agenda of the Loop business community, Daley was able not only to satisfy established downtown interests but also to provide a steady stream of private sector opportunities for his cohorts, regular employment for politically connected unions, and an endless succession of concrete monuments to attest to the city's uninterrupted "progress." Indeed, riding the crest of a public and private construction boom that had its roots in Kennelly's administration, Daley earned a reputation as a "builder" that eclipsed those of his predecessors. Daley-era projects revitalized the commercial heart of the city, catered to powerful private interests (ranging from the *Chicago Tribune* to the University of Chicago), and serviced the machine's needs as well as the city's. If efficiency-minded, tax-conscious businessmen grumbled at Daley's emasculation of civil service, the mayor knew how to keep them happy.

Daley's handling of the Trumbull Park difficulties and the CHA gave quick evidence of his willingness to hold the line on race and appease white ethnics. Indeed, within a year of his election, the Catholic Interracial Council (CIC) found that it was "not able to get through" to Daley despite his campaign pledges, and at the end of his first term the situation remained a "running sore." The important point, though, was that the numbing violence no longer grabbed headlines. By the 1960s, a compliant housing authority slapped a low ceiling on the number of black families admitted, an obedient Commission on Human Relations lobbied against any changes that might provoke new outbursts, and what had been a celebrated cause quietly slipped from view. The actions of the CHA and the CHR were also significant because they indicated Daley's determination to enhance his political apparatus and centralize control of the city's bureaucracy. If freed from the demands of the ward leaders, those municipal operatives still reported to the man on the fifth floor of City Hall.

It was, in fact, Daley's subjugation and exploitation of the CHA that revealed most clearly the political and racial imperatives that drove his administration. Within a month of Daley's first inaugural, Elizabeth Wood's successor, General William B. Kean, agreed quietly to give each alderman the power to kill any project slated for his ward. If, somehow, a controversial site slipped through for public examination, action on the site was deferred rather than bitterly debated. All of the sites chosen for public housing during the Daley years subsequently reinforced the prevailing pattern of segregation. When the courts found the CHA guilty of discrimination in 1969, public housing construction simply ceased. Daley displayed neither the personal nor political inclination to follow in Ed Kelly's footsteps.[36]

Daley did not stop there, however. If Kean was willing to surrender on race, he was less amenable on questions of patronage. Indeed, independent alderman and Daley critic Leon Despres characterized the general's operation as one conducted "without political spoils, . . . patronage, or favoritism." Such scrupulous administration could not last. As early as 1956, the Daley-appointed commissioners on the CHA board, particularly Charles Swibel, began to harass Kean by trying to strip him of the power to hire and fire. The *Chicago Daily News* reported, even at that time, that Swibel had "his eye on the CHA chairmanship," and the cagey Swibel did not let up until he had hounded both Kean and his successor from office. By 1967, Swibel, as chairman, took control of the CHA.[37]

Swibel's rise and the decline of the CHA are a single story. Supported by close Daley associate William McFetridge of the Flat Janitors' Union, Swibel's initial appointment to the CHA board came under fire from those who felt that a slum operator was hardly an appropriate choice. The opposition withered, however, when confronted with the mayor's determined backing of Swibel's nomination. Ultimately, the critics' darkest fears became reality. By 1982, a federal study concluded that the CHA was among the "worst" managed authorities in the country due to its "high operating costs, deficits, and poor physical conditions." Under Swibel's direction the CHA had become, according to the report, an agency whose sole purpose was the "acquisition of as many Federal . . . dollars as possible for the creation of patronage jobs and financial opportunities." The authority's examiners proclaimed any attempt at reform under Swibel's direction "foolhardy," and felt his retention was "unconscionable."[38] The CHA had come a long way since the ward bosses had lifted Elizabeth Wood's scalp. A scandal-free agency that had tried to provide decent housing on an equitable basis had become a bastion of segregation and a political wasteland.

It was also instructive that Daley had precisely reversed Ed Kelly's practice of running a clean CHA while politically exploiting the schools. By Daley's era it had become clear that the CHA primarily served blacks while the schools still accommodated all of Chicago's children. It was, then, as far as Daley was concerned, easier and more expedient to make blatant political use of the former rather than the latter. Moreover, Daley's "principled" refusal to inject "politics" into Board of Education matters enabled him to distance himself from the difficult question of school desegregation.

Given the high degree of residential segregation, Chicago's "neighborhood" school system remained rigidly segregated throughout Daley's administration. In the early 1960s blacks protested the policies of the imperious school superintendant Benjamin Willis and the widespread use in crowded black areas of the temporary classrooms that became known as "Willis wagons." Daley, however, was well content with an accommodation that protected white ethnic neighborhoods and publicly—and piously—refused to "politicize" the schools. The segregation of Chicago's schools remained an open wound long after both Willis and Daley had gone.[39]

If the mayor's treatment of housing and school issues demonstrated greater concern with the health of his political organization than the welfare of the city's black residents, it was Daley's manipulation of the political system itself that revealed his determination to destroy all concentrations of power other than his own. Certainly his election in 1955 had demonstrated the dangerous potential of black political power. Indeed, Bill Dawson's pivotal role in Kennelly's defeat impressed upon Daley the need to destroy, not placate, the South Side congressman, despite the latter's pliability on racial matters. The challenge was that Daley had to trim Dawson's power while whites were rushing headlong into the suburbs and the city's black population was tripling its size.

The long term trends, however, could not overcome Daley's skill in the short run. An open housing ordinance introduced by the independent Leon Despres and later "supported" by black alderman Claude Holman provided Daley with an early opportunity. Daley, of course, had no desire for an effective open housing law, but he did want to cultivate Holman, who was using the issue to declare his independence from a disapproving Bill Dawson. Holman rallied support in the black community while Daley protected the jobs of those precinct captains willing to betray Dawson. In "freezing" patronage during this intrablack struggle, Daley took away Dawson's power to "vise" disloyal operatives and gave Holman the opportunity to build his own fourth ward organization. In return, Holman employed a variety of delaying tactics that stalled the ordinance until a watered-down version was finally passed in 1963—some seven years after Despres began working on it.

The final ordinance spoke volumes about Daley's priorities. Instead of a flat ban on discrimination, the ordinance merely regulated the city's real estate brokers and prescribed the revocation of licenses as a penalty—and that only on the recommendation of the now-domesticated CHR and after a final review by the mayor himself. Leon Despres called the ordinance a "tiny, bumbling, almost penalty-free, largely ineffectual step." But he realized that his choice was to vote for that "in-finitesimal step" or none at all.[40] In the end, Daley emerged with a loyal black lieutenant in Dawson's backyard, a law that posed no threat to the city's ethnic neighborhoods, and a symbolic gesture designed to appease civil rights advocates.

Daley continued his assault on Dawson's political control of black Chicago on the West Side. The twenty-fourth ward, Jake Arvey's old Jewish stronghold, under-went rapid racial transition after World War II due to the continued influx of southern migrants and the dislocation associated with urban renewal. In 1958 an absentee white leadership selected a Yiddish-speaking black, Ben Lewis, to fill the unexpired aldermanic term of Sidney Deutsch. Daley went even further in 1961 when he named Lewis ward committeeman in place of the now fully expired Deutsch. Tied directly to the party chairman, Lewis publicly attacked Dawson, took pride in the fact that none of his precinct captains was a "Dawson man," and earned a reputation for being "staunchly loyal" to the mayor. He worked closely with Claude Holman in the city council, and at slating time the party's central committee favored can-didates backed by the Holman-Lewis tandem over those advanced by Dawson.

The emergence of the West Side ghetto and the creation of a black political network hostile to Dawson and subservient to the party's white leadership also indicated Daley's ability to use urban renewal to political advantage. Killings in land speculation and lucrative contracts awaited the politically connected, a host of new agencies—each of them a patronage plum—came into being, and the demo-lition of slums scattered thousands of Bill Dawson's constituents. "Every time that iron ball bats down one of those slum buildings on the South Side," Ben Lewis gloated, "twenty Negro families move west." Alluding to Dawson, he added that "they don't like that on the South Side." And when Lewis was brutally gunned down just days after the 1963 primary, Daley kept a handful of potential black successors guessing, spurring each of them to turn out the vote in the mayor's own showdown with freshly-minted Republican Ben Adamowski. The black twenty-fourth ward turned out one of the city's largest pluralities for Daley in what proved to be one of his closest contests; that was "plantation politics" with a vengeance. By the mid-1960s, Dawson's empire was gone, and the congressman retained only his own seat and the patronage in his second ward home. The newer black ward leaders were Daley's own creatures, dependent upon him and forced to deal directly with him from positions of subservience and weakness. Black activists derisively dubbed those that found seats in the city council the "Silent Six," and contrasted them disparagingly to the white liberal Despres who became known as that body's "only Negro."[41]

The irony was that it was black votes that had largely catapulted Daley into city hall in 1955 and had saved him again in 1963 when the Polish Adamowski won a majority of the white vote. The volatility of Chicago's white ethnic voters, however, combined with Daley's personal predilections and the easily assumed Democratic loyalty of the black electorate to confirm the mayor's determination to maintain the racial status quo. The mayor would cater to the white ethnics streaming to the urban fringe in the effort to keep them both within the city and the Democratic party.

The result was that Daley turned the Democratic machine inside out. Initially supported by inner city machine wards, Daley's last years saw his most solid backing come from the outlying white areas on the Northwest and Southwest sides of the city. The inner city poor, whose votes had traditionally maintained machines across the country, no longer played a vital role in the Cook County Democratic organization. It was now a machine for the ethnic middle class, and the inner city poor, increasingly non-white, got little comfort from it. Black political participation subsequently dropped dramatically, and the decrease in black voting meant that not only did Daley have little to fear from black dissidents, but also that those loyal to the organization had virtually no clout within it. For Daley, it was the best of all possible worlds.[42]

The official neglect of black Chicago, however, contributed to the rise of racial tensions until the city began to snap under the strain. A fire engine, called out of its West Side station in the summer of 1965, sparked Chicago's first large riot of the civil rights era when it struck a light pole that fell and killed a young black woman. The fire department remained a white preserve under Daley's Bridgeport neighbor, fire commissioner Robert Quinn, and blacks had been protesting their exclusion when the incident triggered violence. Several days of rioting left some eighty people injured and resulted in considerable property damage. The following summer, attempts to shut off fire hydrants in the midst of a heat wave—again on the West Side—sparked another round of violence. This time there were two deaths and the National Guard had to be called out. Daley suggested that Martin Luther King, Jr.'s presence in the city might have contributed to the disorder.

King had first come to Chicago in 1965 to lend his assistance to the campaign to oust Ben Willis from the schools. When he returned in 1966 to focus his efforts on fighting housing discrimination, he moved into a West Side tenement to dramatize the conditions under which many black Chicagoans had to live. Daley deftly parried King's jabs, expressed sympathy with the black leader's goals and refused to give King the sort of confrontation that had undermined segregationist forces in the South. When King began a series of marches into the city's ethnic bungalow belt, however, Daley faced a real crisis. Violent resistance in Marquette Park, Gage Park, and Belmont-Cragin made national news, and a photograph of King being struck with a rock generated enough pressure to produce substantive negotiations. The resulting "Summit Agreement" accepted open housing in principle, but offered no effective means of implementation. King departed Chicago with nothing more than a paper declaration, leaving Daley a short-term victory. Disheartened blacks and satisfied whites subsequently played their ordained roles in Daley's fourth successful mayoral campaign in 1967—he carried all fifty wards.

In the aftermath of King's assassination in 1968, however, the West Side exploded once more, this time an eruption far more devastating than anything that had gone before. Stunned and incensed, the mayor responded with his famous order to "shoot to kill" arsonists and to shoot to "maim or cripple" looters.[43] A source of national embarrassment, the mayor's "shoot to kill" order certainly did him no damage with his bedrock ethnic constituency. Similarly, his response to the invading "Yippies" at the Democratic national convention just a few months later and his persistent refusal to compromise ethnic interests on housing or school issues further solidified his base. Whites identified with the machine's defense of their racial concerns as discouraged blacks continued to drop out.

There was a potential danger, of course, in the emphasis on racial—as opposed to party—loyalty and Daley caught a glimpse of that danger in 1972. Democratic state's attorney Edward V. Hanrahan became a symbol of racial polarization when he ran for reelection against the organization's wishes. Hanrahan's troubles stemmed from a predawn 1969 raid conducted by his officers on an apartment occupied by the radical Black Panthers. Panther leaders Fred Hampton and Mark Clark died in a hail of police bullets that later investigations found to be unjustified. Hastily dumped by the organization before the 1972 primary, Hanrahan won the Democratic nomination as white ethnic voters refused to follow the party's leadership in writing off their champion of "law and order." Black voters, enraged and mobilized by Hanrahan's candidacy, rose up to knock him down in the general election. When racial issues were so starkly drawn the machine could no longer command the loyalty of either ethnic whites or highly motivated blacks. It was the first sign of a political revolution that would be another decade in the making.[44]

Such disquieting signs were indications that the Daley organization limped into the 1970s on not one, but two, Achilles's heels. The first, clearly, was its inability to deal equitably in racial affairs. Consequently, the first halting steps toward independence by a budding handful of black leaders and a large reservoir of unregistered and apathetic black voters constituted the contradictory legacies of Daley's regime on the South and West sides. When coupled with the ongoing process of white suburbanization, it was clear that Daley's policies left the machine with a political time bomb whose faint ticking could barely be detected in the 1960s. By the 1970s, however, as the Hanrahan debacle indicated, a mobilized, organized, and highly motivated black electorate could shake the machine's very foundations.

Second, the machine's persistent corruption left it vulnerable, particularly after hostile Republicans replaced friendly Democrats in Washington D.C. A new, Republican U.S. Attorney, the politically ambitious James Thompson, did not hesitate to make his own reputation by stacking the indictments of prominent Democrats like so much cordwood—and the Cook County Democratic organization gave him a forest within which to labor. If Daley managed to survive local scandals, such as that involving the Summerdale police district "burglars in blue," he found the taint of federal wrongdoing less easily managed.

Otto Kerner, former governor and judge of the Seventh Circuit Court of Appeals, was the first to fall, convicted of tax evasion and perjury in a racetrack stock scandal. Thompson next secured indictments against Cook County Clerk Edward J. Barrett, city council finance committee chairman Tom Keane, Daley protégé Matt Danaher, Alderman Paul Wigoda, and Daley press secretary Earl Bush. Danaher's death spared him a trial, but the others were all convicted on a variety of charges including extortion, bribery, conspiracy, mail fraud, and tax evasion. Finally, in a scandal that dwarfed earlier episodes, some fifty police officers, including two district commanders, received prison sentences between 1972 and 1974 for extortion and tax evasion. Daley, in short, found himself besieged in the early 1970s by both blacks and anti-machine "good government" forces.[45]

By the mid-1970s the organization's decay paralleled Daley's own physical decline. The mayor, who suffered a stroke in 1974 just days after Tom Keane's indictment, absented himself from city hall during an extended convalescence and returned amid speculation that he might not run for an unprecedented sixth term in 1975. Daley did run, and while he remained personally untouchable, the race clearly revealed that the machine had slipped a few gears. Just four years before, Daley defeated the liberal-Democrat-turned-Republican Richard Friedman handily, winning more than 70 percent of the vote. But in 1975 he faced a primary challenge for the first time in twenty years. Independent Bill Singer took him on, as did black state senator Richard Newhouse and party renegade Ed Hanrahan. Singer won nearly 30 percent of the vote, while Newhouse took 8 percent and Hanrahan 5 percent. Daley's 463,623 votes constituted 57.8 percent of the total, his lowest marks since 1955. The lakeshore, the far North Side, and an increasing number of black wards displayed marked anti-machine tendencies. And when Daley failed to unseat Bill Dawson's rebellious successor, congressman and third ward committeeman Ralph Metcalfe, with his own black candidate the next year, it became clear that the machine had real problems. That the formerly loyal Metcalfe could survive his highly publicized break with the organization over the issue of police brutality would have been unthinkable just a few years before.[46]

Indeed, the elections in November 1976 provided Daley with a subdued last hurrah. A stunningly weak performance in important national and state contests served as the inglorious prelude to his death a month later. His last official act, fittingly, was a ribbon cutting—the opening of a new field house in Ed Vrdolyak's far South Side tenth ward. In its location, the people it served, and the alderman who claimed it as a plum, the gymnasium in which Daley sank one last basket represented everything that he was about.

There was perhaps no greater testimony to Daley's political skills than the settlement that followed his death. In hoarding and exercising his power as both mayor and party chairman, Daley created a system in which there could be no designated heir. Even before his death, there were rumblings within the ranks from such fast rising ethnic ward powers as Ed Vrdolyak and Edward Burke ("Fast" Eddie and "Slow" Eddie, respectively) who mobilized young organization loyalists disenchanted with Tom Keane's iron-fisted rule of the city council and, indirectly, with Daley's own authority. With Daley gone, the cap came off the ambitions of the most zealous ward politicians. They first made certain that no successor would inherit Daley's all-encompassing power by appointing George Dunne party chairman and Michael Bilandic of Daley's own eleventh ward as mayor. It was evident that the organization's stalwarts wanted no more of Daley's brand of authoritarianism. In rejecting the mayoral aspirations of Wilson Frost, twenty-first ward alderman and committeeman and president pro tem of the city council, the organization also showed it was not willing to surrender control to blacks, although it tried to appease both Frost and his constituents by naming him chairman of the important finance committee. The succession scramble made it obvious that one of Daley's least recognized and perhaps most notable accomplishments was his success in simply remaining on top of the grasping heap that was the Cook County Democratic organization for more than two decades. In taking public policy away from the ward politicians and strengthening the bureaucracy at the expense of the organization's political operatives, Daley kept the ward bosses at bay. Now the latter sought a return to the pre-Daley era. Still rigidly inflexible on race, the organization entered a period of contention, regression, and precipitous decline.[47]

Neither Bilandic nor the remaining political savants in the machine had the skill or ability to halt the process of political disintegration. Their unabashed conniving provoked a 1979 mayoral challenge from Jane Byrne, a high-ranking member of Daley's bureaucracy who had earlier been a mayoral confidant. Frozen out of the new inner circle after "Hizzoner's" death, Byrne campaigned against the new leadership's self-serving machinations. Doomed by their own arrogance and incompetence, the ruling clique regarded Byrne so lightly that it did not even bother to support their own "anti-machine" candidate—a black, or perhaps an "independent"—to split the organization's opposition. Their smugness proved to be a fatal mistake. The brutal winter of 1978–79, with its record breaking snow and cold, made Jane Byrne a credible mayoral challenger. As snow and ice clogged the machine's gears and brought the city to a standstill, the Bilandic administration faltered at every turn. Its callous insensitivity toward the black community became shamefully clear in the decision to maintain commuter train schedules by whisking white suburbanites non-stop into the Loop while bypassing frozen inner city residents. Riding a wave of antiadministration sentiment in the city that no longer worked, and tapping the previously unrealized potential of an enlarged and enraged black electorate, Byrne united the machine's opposition to drive Bilandic out of city hall.[48]

Once in office, however, Byrne abandoned those who had placed her there. Where she had earlier denounced the old leadership as a "cabal of evil men," she now embraced the so-called "evil caballeros" in an attempt to sustain her own administration. Playing to their ethnic constituency, she made a series of appointments and directed a ward reapportionment that assuaged their racial fears. Blacks received an occasional symbolic gesture (such as her headline-grabbing move into the Cabrini-Green housing project) but nothing more. Finally, in chasing the legend of her mentor, Byrne went after the one individual she believed endangered her plans: the late mayor's son, Richard M. Daley. In failing to defeat Daley the Younger in his race for state's attorney—and openly supporting a Republican in the process—Byrne factionalized white organization supporters and set the stage for Chicago's explosive 1983 mayoralty.

Richie Daley announced his decision to run against Byrne just a few days after the November 1982 elections. The strength of his name and that of the ward committeemen he carried with him meant that the Cook County Democratic organization faced a fratricidal bloodletting, the likes of which had not been seen in half a century. Of even greater importance, Harold Washington, a former state legislator and now a South Side congressman, tossed his hat into the mayoral ring just a few days after Daley. Washington had grown up in the organization (his father was a Democratic precinct captain who initially served Mike Sneed, Anton Cermak's first black committeeman), but he had distanced himself from it in the 1960s and survived several attempted machine purges. The chief beneficiary of a rising tide of black discontent and Democratic factionalism, Washington's campaign became a serious threat to the incumbent as blacks rallied to his cause and Daley splintered the white electorate. Just days before the election, Ed Vrdolyak tried to salvage the Byrne campaign by stating publicly that a vote for Daley was a vote for Washington. "It's a racial thing," Vrdolyak admitted. His tactics boomeranged, however, when many blacks who had supported Byrne deserted her, and late-deciding whites opted for Daley. Washington squeezed out a victory when Byrne and Daley neatly divided 63 percent of the vote.[49]

Washington's victory sent shock waves along the Cook County Democratic organization's major fault line. Immediately, the unnoticed Republican challenger, Bernard Epton, became a serious candidate as conservative ethnic whites deserted the Democratic party. Having lost control of the black vote in the primary, the machine lost the whites in the general election. The organization could no longer deliver across racial lines. The blatantly racial nature of the Epton campaign again seemed to help Washington as late-deciding white voters along the lakefront supported him and joined a wave of freshly mobilized black registrants in delivering a narrow victory. The myriad forces of political independence, suppressed and then stirred by Richard J. Daley, fed by the swelling tide of demographic change, and tapped initially by Jane Byrne in 1979, placed Harold Washington, the city's first black mayor, in city hall in 1983. For the first time in more than fifty years, the Cook County Democratic organization found itself on the outside looking in.

There were elements of tragedy and irony in all this. It was tragic that the attack on discrimination in Chicago was tied at its inception to Ed Kelly's corrupt, vulnerable administration. Unable to lead ethnic Chicago into a full and equal partnership with blacks within the Democratic party, Kelly's unsavory tenure isolated the civil rights cause from liberal, antimachine elements that should have been its natural postwar allies. And the "reform" administration of Martin Kennelly certainly did little to bring them together. That gap would not be bridged until Richard J. Daley drove blacks and antimachine forces together in united opposition. And there lay the irony: Daley, who owed so much to those who opened up the Democratic party in Chicago—to Anton Cermak's initiative, Ed Kelly's craftsmanship, and Jake Arvey's support—ended his days the political heir of George Brennan, nursing narrowly defined racial interests and antipathies. However much Daley "modernized" the organization and "professionalized" the bureaucracy, his machine survived by marching backward—not forward—from the racial positions staked out during the Depression and World War II.

In Harold Washington, however, Daley's successors more than met their match, and the famed Chicago machine's tattered remains were reduced to playing defense in their desperate efforts to stave off a final, crushing blow. They controlled twenty-nine of the city's fifty aldermen and drew on the sagacity and tenacity that had always been the organization's hallmark. Theirs would be a fight to the finish featuring a city council that could block the mayor's initiatives but not override his vetoes. Nor were organization regulars above holding the city's vital business hostage in what were, as one satirist put it, Chicago's "Council Wars"—a series of deadly political duels between Harold "Skytalker" and "Darth" Vrdolyak.

Though harassed throughout his first term, Washington succeeded in putting together a diverse, multiracial coalition that drew on a legacy of black protest that rose from the wreckage of the local civil rights movement and an antimachine reform tradition that was older than the Cook County Democratic organization itself. Exuding the street savvy and the toughness of a Cermak, a Kelly, or a Daley, Washington—as mayor—was no less a Chicagoan than a black man. By the end of his first four years, he had wrested control of the Chicago Park District, a patronage haven, from machine stalwart Edmund Kelly and thrashed the organization in the special elections called after the courts invalidated Jane Byrne's racially gerrymandered reapportionment. In a key contest that finally gave Washington control of the city council, hundreds of the machine's minions poured into a single Latino ward in the futile attempt to salvage the organization's fortunes. Safely reelected in 1987, Washington seemed poised to translate his electoral coalition into a governing one.

His sudden death less than a year after that triumphant campaign, however, breathed life back into the bedraggled opposition. More, the unstable coalition held together by the force of Washington's personality and his political skill began to unravel. The machine-oriented black politicos who found it impossible to oppose the racial hero who had downed the dragon of white dominance in Chicago had never been comfortable with the mayor's reformist tendencies; given the opportunity, they repudiated his legacy. Even as the doctors worked over the fallen Washington, the old guard worked the telephones, and—frustrated in their efforts to anoint a white pretender as acting mayor—they orchestrated the succession in concert with a handful of black colleagues who seemingly preferred business as usual. In the end, twenty-three of the council's twenty-eight whites, and six of its eighteen blacks combined to name an obviously reluctant sixth ward alderman, Eugene Sawyer, to be Chicago's second black mayor. In a performance that made Hamlet seem decisive, Sawyer allowed himself to be propped up by an organization that finally, ironically, and shamelessly donned blackface in pursuit of its self-perpetuation. The council tallied its bitterly contested vote at 4:01 A.M. as a chanting crowd of thousands besieged city hall, waved dollar bills at Sawyer, and beseeched him to cut "no deals." It was Chicago politics at its elemental best. The game goes on.

NOTES

The author wishes to acknowledge the support of the College of Urban and Public Affairs at the University of New Orleans, National Endowment for the Humanities grant no. RY–20776–84, and to thank Loyola University of Chicago for permission to draw on material previously submitted for its telecourse on Chicago history.
    1. Ira Katznelson, *Black Men, White Cities* (New York: Oxford University Press, 1973), 91–93; Charles Branham, "Black Chicago" in Melvin G. Holli and Peter d'A. Jones, eds.

The Ethnic Frontier (Grand Rapids, Mich.: William B. Eerdmans, 1977), 234–35, 257–59; Allan H. Spear, *Black Chicago: The Making of a Negro Ghetto, 1890–1920* (Chicago: University of Chicago Press, 1967), 125; Harold F. Gosnell, *Negro Politicians* (Chicago: University of Chicago Press, 1935; reprint ed., 1967) 54; St. Clair Drake and Horace R. Cayton, *Black Metropolis: A Study of Negro Life in a Northern City,* 2 vols. (New York: Harcourt Brace, 1945; reprint ed., Harper and Row, 1962), I, 347–48; William M. Tuttle, Jr., *Race Riot: Chicago in the Red Summer of 1919* (New York: Atheneum, 1970), 184–207.

2. Drake and Cayton, *Black Metropolis,* I, 346–51; Gosnell, *Negro Politicians,* 38–62 and *passim.;* Lloyd Wendt and Herman Kogan, *Big Bill of Chicago* (Indianapolis: Bobbs-Merrill, 1953); Branham, "Black Chicago," 253–54; Nancy Weiss, *Farewell to the Party of Lincoln* (Princeton, N.J.: Princeton University Press, 1984).

3. Gosnell, *Negro Politicians,* 59, 159–61, 233; Katznelson, *Black Men, White Cities,* 98–102; Spear, *Black Chicago,* 192.

4. Alex Gottfried, *Boss Cermak of Chicago* (Seattle: University of Washington Press, 1962), 93, 195, 208, 348, 400 n.90; John M. Allswang, *A House for All Peoples: Ethnic Politics in Chicago, 1890–1930* (Lexington: University Press of Kentucky, 1971), 155, 160.

5. Gosnell, *Negro Politicians,* 33, 133–35, 200–201, 232–33; Milton L. Rakove, *We Don't Want Nobody Nobody Sent: An Oral History of the Daley Years* (Bloomington: Indiana University Press, 1979), 31–32; Gottfried, *Boss Cermak,* 406 n.39; Rita Werner Gordon mistakenly claims Cermak never "sought" black votes and consequently misinterprets his actions; see Gordon, "The Change in Political Alignment of Chicago's Negroes during the New Deal," *Journal of American History* 56 (December 1969): 584–603.

6. Roger Biles, *Big City Boss in Depression and War: Mayor Edward J. Kelly of Chicago* (DeKalb: Northern Illinois University Press, 1984).

7. Ibid., 74–88; *Chicago Bee,* June 3, 1945.

8. Biles, *Big City Boss,* 89–102; *Chicago Bee,* June 24, August 26, 1945; *Chicago Defender,* February 10, 1940; Unidentified clipping, n. d., in the Christopher C. Wimbish Papers, Chicago Historical Society (CHS); author's interview with Vernon Jarrett, July 28, 1985; Mayor's Committee on Human Relations, *Report for 1945* (Chicago: City of Chicago, 1945), 15; Mayor's Committee on Race Relations, "Statement of Aims and Programs," Municipal Reference Library (MRL); Michael W. Homel, *Down from Equality: Black Chicagoans and the Public Schools, 1920–1941* (Urbana: University of Illinois Press, 1984), 43–45, 149. As was the case with Kelly's CHR, the Chicago corporation counsel's civil rights unit was apparently the first such local unit in the nation and was modeled on the civil rights section established in the Criminal Division of the Department of Justice in 1939. See the *Chicago Bee,* September 8, 1946, and the Mayor's Commission on Human Relations, *Report for 1946* (Chicago: City of Chicago, 1946), 78, 78n.

9. Paul Michael Green, "Irish Chicago: The Multi-Ethnic Road to Machine Success" in Melvin G. Holli and Peter d'A. Jones, eds., *Ethnic Chicago* (Grand Rapids, Mich.: William B. Eerdmans, 1984), 412–59; Biles, *Big City Boss,* 76.

10. *Chicago Defender,* October 26, 1940; Martin Meyerson and Edward C. Banfield, *Politics, Planning, and the Public Interest* (New York: Free Press, 1955), 122–24.

11. Biles, *Big City Boss,* 135; Meyerson and Banfield, *Politics,* 124, 128, 287.

12. Biles, *Big City Boss,* 94–95; Arthur W. Mitchell to Edward J. Kelly, October 18, 1934, Arthur W. Mitchell Papers, CHS; Associated Negro Press, press release, August 28, 1946; Claude A. Barnett to Mr. Hamilton, December 1, 1937; Barnett to Truman [K. Gibson], February 10, 1942, all in the Claude A. Barnett Papers, CHS.

13. Arthur W. Mitchell to Mr. Tittinger, January 6, 1939; James P. Durden to Mitchell, January 2, 1939, both in Mitchell Papers; Claude A. Barnett to Truman [K. Gibson], February 10, 1942, Barnett Papers; Dempsey J. Travis, *An Autobiography of Black Politics* (Chicago: Urban Research Press, Inc., 1987), 151–56; see also Charles Russell Branham, "The Transformation of Black Political Leadership in Chicago, 1864–1942" (Ph.D. diss., University of Chicago, 1981).

14. *Chicago Defender*, August 23, 1941, September 18, 1943, July 27, 1946; *New York Times*, December 11, 1946; Metropolitan Housing Council, *Biennial Report of the Metropolitan Housing Council Activities in 1943–1944* (Chicago: Metropolitan Housing Council, 1944), 6; Minutes of the Regular Meeting of the Board of Directors, April 4, May 4, 1943; Chicago Council against Racial and Religious Discrimination, "Against Discrimination" (mimeograph, August 3, 1946), all in the Metropolitan Housing and Planning Council (MHPC) Papers, University of Illinois at Chicago (UIC).

15. Mayor's Commission on Human Relations, "Memorandum on the Airport Homes" (mimeograph, n.d.), Chicago Urban League (CUL) Papers, UIC. In responding to a CHA supporter, Kelly wrote: "The criticism of people who cannot appreciate and do not adhere to decent democratic principles in government and in daily life cannot weigh very heavily against such an agency as the Chicago Housing Authority." See Edward J. Kelly to Rev. Daniel M. Cantwell, December 21, 1946, Daniel M. Cantwell Papers, CHS.

16. When asked directly by political scientist Milton Rakove, Arvey explained the dumping of Kelly from the ticket: "Kelly wanted to run. I told him that . . . if he ran, he might win but it would be by a scant margin as a result of what he had done when he took a stand on that Morgan Park open housing controversy, where he said, 'As long as I am mayor any person will be allowed to live where they want to and can afford to live.' That was laudable, but we took a poll after the 1946 election and we lost the 1946 election partly because of the resentment toward Mayor Kelly." In recalling the incident more than thrity years after it had occurred, Arvey had run a number of events together. The 1946 dispute was at the Airport Homes in West Lawn; Morgan Park perhaps stuck in Arvey's mind because of the explosive school situation there in the 1930s, and because it was the scene of racial and housing-related controversies during World War II. In any case, there is little question about the overall accuracy of his recollection, and the events he telescoped into a single incident were all real. Eugene Kennedy has also discussed Arvey's poll and the dumping of Kelly. He reported the respondents' answers in blunter terms. According to Kennedy, those refusing to back Kelly said simply: "He's too good to the niggers." See Rakove, *We Don't Want Nobody Nobody Sent*, 12; and Eugene Kennedy, *Himself! The Life and Times of Richard J. Daley* (New York: Viking Press, 1978), 80–81. See also Biles, *Big City Boss*, 146–48.

17. *Chicago Defender*, February 16, 1943; *Chicago Bee*, February 21, 1943, April 20, 1947. The *Bee* explicitly pointed to Kelly's outgoing record: "He appointed the *First* Negro member of the Board of Education; the *First* fire department captain; the *First* police captain; *First* elementary school principal; *First* civil service commissioner; *First* housing authority chairman; *First* trade school director; *First* member of the Redevelopment Authority; and *First* of the Plan Commission."

18. *Chicago Defender*, March 22, 29, 1947; *Chicago Bee*, January 5, 1947.

19. For a more detailed discussion of Kennelly's administration, see Arnold R. Hirsch, "Martin H. Kennelly: The Mugwump and the Machine" in Paul M. Green and Melvin G. Holli, eds., *The Mayors: The Chicago Political Tradition* (Carbondale: Southern Illinois University Press, 1987), 126–43.

20. Len O'Connor, *Clout: Mayor Daley and His City* (New York: Avon Books, 1975), 86; Kennedy, *Himself!*, 96.

21. Jarrett interview, July 28, 1985; Chicago Commission on Human Relations, "Memorandum on the Fernwood Park Homes" (mimeograph, n.d.), CUL Papers; "The Peoria Street Incident" (mimeograph, n.d.), MRL.

22. Sidney Williams to Homer Jack, December 1949, Archibald J. Carey, Jr., Papers, CHS; Sidney Williams to Mayor Martin H. Kennelly, November 29, 1949, Catholic Interracial Council (CIC) Papers, CHS; Arvarh E. Strickland, *History of the Chicago Urban League* (Urbana: University of Illinois Press, 1966), 172–74.

23. Chicago Council against Racial and Religious Discrimination to Martin H. Kennelly, February 24, 1949, and Archibald J. Carey to Val J. Washington, April 27, 1949, both in Carey Papers; *Chicago Defender*, March 5, 1949.

24. Elizabeth Wood to the Commissioners, July 28, 1947, Business and Professional

People in the Public Interest (BPI) Papers, CHS; Meyerson and Banfield, *Politics, passim.;* Address by Elizabeth Wood, Executive Secretary of the Chicago Housing Authority at "A Tribute to Good Government" dinner given in her honor by Chicago citizens at the Red Lacquer Room of the Palmer House on Thursday, October 9, 1952, CUL Papers; *Southeast Economist,* May 26, 1949, clipping in Cantwell Papers.

25. Address by Elizabeth Wood; Wood's firing is discussed in greater detail in Arnold R. Hirsch, *Making the Second Ghetto: Race and Housing in Chicago, 1940–1960* (New York: Cambridge University Press, 1983), 234–38.

26. Peter O'Malley, "Mayor Martin H. Kennelly of Chicago: A Political Biography" (Ph.D. diss., University of Illinois at Chicago, 1980), 147, 222–23; Willard Townsend to J. S. Knowlson, April 9, 1951; Willard Townsend to Mayor Kennelly, April 16, 1951; J. S. Knowlson to Mayor Martin H. Kennelly, June 7, 1951; [Olive M.] Diggs, Memo, March 13, 1951, all in Martin H. Kennelly Papers, Department of History, UIC.

27. O'Malley, "Mayor Martin H. Kennelly," 192; Timothy J. O'Connor to Martin H. Kennelly, January 13, 1955; Patrolman C. Ryan to Aide to the Commissioner, n.d.; Summary of Gambling Arrests Made for the Year 1951, n.d., all in Kennelly Papers; Mike Royko, *Boss: Richard J. Daley of Chicago* (New York: Signet Books, 1971), 62; author's interview with Ira J. Bach, Chicago, Illinois, July 24, 1980.

28. Jarrett interview, July 28, 1985; *Chicago Tribune,* January 13, 1952, February 6, 1955; *Chicago Sun-Times,* December 31, 1953; unidentified clipping in the Wimbish Papers.

29. O'Malley, "Mayor Martin H. Kennelly," 222; *Chicago Defender,* April 7, 1951.

30. Party leaders decided back in November 1952 that Kennelly had to go. Author's interview with Robert E. Merriam, Chicago, Illinois, September 23, 1985.

31. Report on the Community Forum's Meeting on Trumbull Park, May 23, 1954, Irene McCoy Gaines Papers, CHS; *Chicago Defender,* May 15, 1954, March 26, 1955; Elizabeth Wood to Members of the CHA Advisory Committee on Race Relations, April 27, 1954, in the BPI Papers; Duckett-Lawrence Associates et. al., "A Specialized Public Relations and Promotional Program Proposed for Robert E. Merriam, Candidate for Mayor of Chicago (Aimed at the Negro Community)," n.d., Carey Papers.

32. Kennelly campaign press release, January 30, 1955, Kennelly Papers; *Chicago Sun-Times,* January 28, 1955; *Chicago Defender,* February 5, 19, March 26, 1955; Claude A. Barnett to Frederick D. Jordan, February 21, 1955, Barnett Papers.

33. Illinois Division, American Civil Liberties Union, Executive Committee Minutes, April 7, June 16, 1955, Illinois Division-American Civil Liberties Union (ACLU) Papers, Special Collections, Regenstein Library, University of Chicago. See also *Daily Calumet,* February 21, 1955; *Chicago Defender,* February 19, 1955; O'Malley, "Mayor Martin H. Kennelly," chap. 8; O'Connor, *Clout,* 106–25.

34. Milton Rakove, "Jane Byrne and the New Chicago Politics," in Samuel K. Gove and Louis H. Masotti, eds., *After Daley: Chicago Politics in Transition* (Urbana: University of Illinois Press, 1982), 217–35; "Observations and Reflections on the Current and Future Directions of the Chicago Democratic Machine" in Melvin G. Holli and Paul M. Green, eds., *The Making of the Mayor: Chicago, 1983* (Grand Rapids, Mich.: William B. Eerdmans, 1984), 127–40; Milton L. Rakove, *Don't Make No Waves, Don't Back No Losers: An Insider's Analysis of the Daley Machine* (Bloomington: Indiana University Press, 1975); O'Connor, *Clout,* 40, 126–28.

35. O'Connor, *Clout,* 129–30; author's interview with Leon Despres, Chicago, Illinois, August 19, 1985.

36. *South Deering Bulletin,* May 5, 1955; *Daily Calumet,* February 21, 1955; Illinois Division–American Civil Liberties Union, Executive Committee Minutes, June 16, 1955; Kenneth Douty to Rev. Theodore M. Hesburgh, May 6, 1959, both in ACLU Papers; Lloyd Davis to David F. Freeman, April 9, 1956, CIC Papers; American Friends Service Committee, "Progress Report on Trumbull Park—March, 1959" (typescript, n.d.), American Friends Service Committee (AFSC) Papers, UIC; W. B. Kean, Memorandum to the Commissioners, May 23, 1955, BPI Papers; Hirsch, *Making the Second Ghetto,* 242–43, 265–66.

37. [Leon Despres], typed statement, December 28, 1956, Despres Papers; *Chicago Sun-Times,* October 31, 1956; *Chicago Daily News,* December 6, 1956, both clippings in the Despres Papers.

38. *Chicago Today,* January 17, 1970, clipping in the Despres Papers; Metropolitan Housing and Planning Council, Minutes of the Board of Governors Meeting, February 3, 1956; December 7, 1956; Minutes of the Meeting of the Executive Committee, February 20, 1956, all in MHPC Papers; Institute for Community Design Analysis, "Review and Analysis of the Chicago Housing Authority and Implementation of Recommendations: Final Report of Phase I: Recommended Changes and Resulting Savings" (March 31, 1982).

39. Mary J. Herrick, *The Chicago Schools: A Social and Political History* (Beverly Hills, Cal.: Sage Publications, 1971), 303–401; Alan B. Anderson and George W. Pickering, *Confronting the Color Line: The Broken Promise of the Civil Rights Movement in Chicago* (Athens: University of Georgia Press, 1986).

40. Author's interview with Leon Despres, Chicago, Illinois, July 25, 1984; Leon M. Despres to Philip H. Vision, October 2, 1963, Despres Papers; *Chicago Defender,* September 23, 1963, and *Chicago's American,* September 12, 1963, both clippings in the Despres Papers.

41. For black politics on the West Side, see Ernest Scribner, "Shadow of a Gunman over the 24th Ward," *Chicago Scene* (April 1963): 20–26; *Chicago Tribune,* March 1, 1963; Associated Negro Press, press release, November 7, 1962, January 30, 1963, in the Barnett Papers; *Chicago Sun-Times,* March 1, 1963, clipping in the Barnett Papers; Georgie Anne Geyer and Harry Waldo Swegle, "More and Better Black Faces, Daddy: Good-By Mister Charlie," *Chicago Scene* (September 1963): 10–16.

42. Paul Kleppner, *Chicago Divided: The Making of a Black Mayor* (DeKalb: Northern Illinois University Press, 1985), 64–90.

43. Royko, *Boss,* 146–47, 152–54, 167–70; Kleppner, *Chicago Divided,* 5; Anderson and Pickering, *Confronting the Color Line,* 208–69 and *passim.;* O'Connor, *Clout,* 201–204; Kennedy, *Himself!,* 214–22.

44. Rakove, *Don't Make No Waves,* 230; Travis, *Autobiography of Black Politics,* 407–58.

45. O'Connor, *Clout,* 4–5, 240–41, 243, 249–50, 254–55; Kleppner, *Chicago Divided,* 79.

46. Kleppner, *Chicago Divided,* 64–90, 94.

47. Ibid., 79, 91–133. See also the essays in Gove and Masotti, *After Daley.*

48. Kleppner, *Chicago Divided,* 91–133.

49. Ibid., 124–25, 134–50. See also the essays in Holli and Green, *Making of the Mayor.*

V

CINCINNATI

THE NEW URBAN POLITICS: PLANNING AND DEVELOPMENT IN CINCINNATI, 1954–1988

Zane L. Miller and Bruce Tucker

Twentieth-century American cities have served as crucibles for the practice of pluralistic social relations, and urban officials have had to incorporate changing meanings of pluralism into the design and implementation of public policy. During the thirty years before the 1950s, Cincinnati politicians and planners sought to foster the welfare of cultural groups while at the same time promoting the welfare of the city as a whole. In their efforts to do both they wrote a new city charter, created a new two-party system, and developed a metropolitan planning tradition. During the 1950s, however, politicians and planners abandoned their efforts to reconcile cultural group pluralism[1] with the welfare of the metropolis as a whole. Instead, they focused on the development of individual pluralism,[2] the idea that indivduals should seek self-fulfillment by choosing their identities and lifestyles, regardless of the group into which they might have been born. To foster the cultural autonomy of individuals, politicians and planners amended the city charter, established a *de facto* no party system, and developed a neighborhood planning tradition, all of which remain as principal characteristics of Cincinnati's politics in the 1980s.

Cincinnati entered the 1950s with a national reputation as one of the country's best governed cities. That reputation rested in large part on the pluralistic governmental and political system established in the mid-1920s during a good government revolt against the durable Cox-Hynicka Republican machine. In the late nineteenth century that organization had vested planning, policy making, administration, and personnel recruitment in a hierarchical structure dominated by the "boss" of the local GOP. The "reformers" not only captured control of city hall but also rewrote the city's charter to focus politics on the promotion of the welfare of the city as a whole as a means of fostering the coherence of the city as a pluralistic society. To accomplish this they reorganized Cincinnati's city government on horizontal pluralistic principles by setting up a city manager to coordinate the activities of the various city departments, boards and commissions, and the relationship of civic and other pressure groups with city government. In addition, the new charter established a merit system of civil service to regulate personnel matters professionally and created a nine member council to make policy, a body that chose from among its members a "weak" mayor as a presiding officer. The new charter also prescribed the election of the council through an at-large nonpartisan ballot and a system of proportional representation (PR). The elimination of ward representation through at-large elections encouraged the council to consider the welfare of the city as a whole in setting policy.[3] At the same time, the PR feature of this system, designed to secure a council seat for any organized political minority capable of garnering one-ninth plus one of the total vote, acknowledged the legitimacy of pluralism.

The new system, despite its commitment to nonpartisanship, did not eliminate two-party politics in Cincinnati. "Reform" Republicans, regular and "reform" Democrats, and independent "radicals" who created the new system promptly organized the Charter Party, which they portrayed as a pluralistic association best able to serve the welfare of the city as a whole.[4] From the mid-1920s into the mid-1950s the Charterites' opposition came from the Republican party, which also claimed to represent the best interests of the city as a whole but which tried frequently though unsuccessfully to eliminate PR on the grounds that ward representation would more accurately reflect the pluralistic nature of the city.[5]

Cincinnati also entered the 1950s with a strong metropolitan planning tradition that recognized the diversity of the region and sought to ensure its coherence through the creation by expert consultants of master plans for the welfare of the metropolis as a whole.[6] The second of these, adopted in 1948, bristled with public works proposals. The major ones called for the construction of a circumferential freeway around the metropolis and of three inter-metropolitan and commuter expressways that would converge on the riverfront. The plan scheduled the riverfront itself for clearance to make way for governmental offices, a sports stadium, a park, an historical museum, and an apartment complex and called for the separation of the entire riverfront development from downtown by a connector expressway. The plan also attacked the problem of population leakage to the suburbs by the inclusion of slum clearance and housing redevelopment projects and programs of neighborhood rehabilitation and conservation of the sort written into the federal housing acts of 1949 and 1954.

The plan of 1948 recognized that the metropolis had grown along segregated class and racial lines and proposed to perpetuate that pattern by reinforcing or creating homogeneous neighborhoods within a system of submetropolitan communities. To accomplish this, the planners proposed to merge traditional residential neighborhoods into local "communities" of 20,000 to 40,000 people and to provide each community with public schools, libraries, health clinics, recreational facilities, and a commercial and civic center. The planners also recognized that the expressway and redevelopment projects of the Master Plan would uproot thousands of families, most of them poor and black residents of the city's West End. They proposed to resolve this problem by developing more inner-city and suburban public housing projects and by assisting the private sector in constructing new single-family homes and apartments to meet the demand for additional low and moderate income accommodations. The planners intended the newly formed communities to reflect the traditional composition of the city's homogeneous neighborhoods.[7]

Between 1948 and the mid-1950s, urban redevelopment and urban renewal policy and city politics followed earlier patterns.[8] Both the Republicans and the Charterites fielded slates based on the political importance of various groups in the population. Since relatively few southern and eastern Europeans had migrated to Cincinnati at the turn of the century, each ticket usually contained German, "American," and Irish surnames (more Germans and "Americans" than Irish); Protestants, Catholics, and at least one Jew, usually of the Reform persuasion from a family of German origins; at least one black male and at least one white woman; and a representative of organized labor. This ethno-racial, religious, gender, and class balancing of party slates yielded similarly balanced city councils.

Neither these cultural factors nor policy questions, including the question of urban redevelopment and renewal, played a significant role in council campaigns, which also followed past patterns. Charterites labeled the GOP as the party of bossism and patronage politics and attacked Republicans for putting the welfare of the GOP and the election of its county, state, and national candidates above the welfare of the city. This assault suggested a Republican affinity for corruption and inefficiency in government and a cavalier approach to the important matter of civic pride and loyalty to the city as a whole. Republicans bitterly resented these insinuations and countered by describing the Charterites as self-righteous hypocrites who satisfied their lust for power by saddling the city with PR, which the GOP represented as cumbersome, confusing to voters, and un-American because of its allegedly foreign origins and because it frustrated majority rule and undermined the American two-party system.[9]

This "city as a whole" political discourse began to disintegrate in the mid-1950s as the result of two changes that helped to mold a new urban politics. First, city officials began to abandon the principles of the plan of 1948, including its focus on the welfare of the metropolis and its commitment to residential segregation and homogeneous neighborhoods. Instead they initiated a new process of planning and implementation based on the principle of community action for the welfare of neighborhoods. Second, in the mid-1950s several young Democrats undertook to reorganize the Democratic party in a process that decentralized the party apparatus and emphasized the importance of neighborhood organizations and that resulted in the emergence of the Democrats as a force to be reckoned with in Cincinnati politics. By 1960, Cincinnatians had entered a new era characterized by three-party competition for the control of city council and a drive by community councils for neighborhood autonomy in planning and implementing social, economic, and housing improvements.

The new mode of planning took neighborhoods rather than the metropolis and its subcommunities as the central elements of concern and viewed each neighborhood as endowed with a distinctive character derived from its architectural and demographic history. It also stressed the importance of treating neighborhood residents as diverse and autonomous individuals in pursuit of self-fulfillment. Principally for that reason the new mode of planning proposed community action—the participation in planning and plan implementation by all parties concerned with a particular neighborhood, especially its residents. In the view of the planners, community action provided a therapeutic device that enabled rich and poor alike to realize their aspirations for self-fulfillment and participation and thereby to secure their commitment to continued residence within the city.[10]

The reorganization of the Democratic party constituted the second step in inaugurating the new urban politics. In 1954 several young Democrats set out to revitalize the party by creating a new kind of precinct and ward organization based on the principle of decentralized and autonomous "neighborhood" organizations. The most energetic of these party organizers, John "Socko" Wiethe, oversaw the construction of a machine that covered both the "rotten boroughs" of Hamilton County, where, except for the industrial suburbs, Republicans had dominated since the 1880s, and the city's twenty-six wards. These included both the largely black wards of the second ghetto created by slum clearance and expressway construction and the old inner city wards of the first ghetto where community action in the 1950s and 1960s spawned a new generation of black political activists.

In this new mode of political organization the ward club formed the basic unit. Each club sought self-sufficiency through dues and fund-raising activities. The members of each club, not central headquarters, selected precinct leaders, who as a body formed a central committee that established party organization and elected the party leadership. This structure, which rested on a base of autonomous "neighborhood" clubs, made it difficult for one person to establish an unchallenged foothold as party "boss." It also established Democratic ward clubs as alternatives to the community councils promoted by the city government.

From this city and suburban ward club base, Wiethe emerged as chairman of the Hamilton County Democratic party. After the Republicans at last eliminated PR in 1957 he and other party leaders decided to drop out of the Charter alliance and to field a Democratic slate as a third ticket in the 1959 city elections.[11] In this effort, Wiethe tapped the energies of a group of aspiring young politicians, many of them liberals aroused in part by the prospects of a presidential bid by John F. Kennedy in 1960. In the three-way contest that ensued, the Republicans won a majority on the city council, a position they easily maintained through the 1960s as the bitterness between Democrats and Charterites engendered by their divorce prevented their reconciliation and the reestablishment of the old alliance under the Charter banner.

During their ascendancy on the city council, the Republicans worked vigorously to forestall the decline of Cincinnati as the vital core of the metropolitan area. They worried especially about economic competition from Sunbelt cities, which attracted "footloose" high technology industries and major professional sports teams and which established nationally competitive high culture facilities and tourist attractions. But the Republicans also fretted about competition from suburbs on both the Ohio and Kentucky sides of the Ohio River, especially along the expressways and near the Cincinnati international airport in Boone County, Kentucky. Suburban municipalities, such as Forest Park, Ohio, and Florence, Kentucky, attempted to attract commercial and industrial establishments and residential developments while local authorities to the northeast of Cincinnati opened their arms to auto assembly plants and to the creators of King's Island "theme" park.

To meet these Sunbelt and suburban threats, Cincinnati Republicans concentrated considerable energy on downtown revitalization. This effort gained momentum in 1964 when the City Planning Commission recommended the establishment of a Downtown Review Task Force made up of representatives of the city council, the city administration, potential developers, and downtown real estate owners. This group went over the proposed downtown plan on an item by item basis and approved a development program, thereby creating a consensus that would pave the way for the passage of the program by the council, including the first proposals for residential housing in and on the fringes of downtown. Armed with this first comprehensive neighborhood plan for downtown, council and city officials secured a bevy of new office towers, a new hotel overlooking Fountain Square and its new plaza, and a new convention center within blocks of Fountain Square. They also started an elevated pedestrian "skywalk" connecting key downtown buildings, began a new riverfront stadium with pedestrian access to downtown by way of a bridge across an expressway, and participated in a successful drive by business leaders to retain the Cincinnati Reds baseball team and to acquire a professional football franchise, the Bengals of the National Football League.

The Republicans also used historic preservation as an economic development tool by authorizing a survey of the city's historic sites and buildings and by creating an Architectural Board of Review to oversee the physical renovation of the Lytle Park area on the eastern flank of downtown as the city's first historic district. This area merited historic designation for several reasons. It occupied the former site of Ft. Washington, which for a decade in the eighteenth century served as a base of U.S. military operations against the Indians. It carried a reputation as a nineteenth-century elite residential enclave. And in the second quarter of the twentieth century it became the downtown "club district" and the site of the Taft Museum of Art, housed in a restored federal-style mansion occupied in the late nineteenth and early twentieth centuries by prominent families and civic leaders.[12]

Yet the GOP commitment to downtown did not dissipate interest in community-action neighborhood planning for the rest of the city. In 1961 the City Planning Commission, with the approval of the city council, launched a series of programs to establish community councils and to provide them technical assistance to develop and implement their own plans. These efforts began with the formation of the North Avondale Neighborhood Association (NANA) and the Clifton Town Meeting (CTM), both of which sought to preserve the distinctive historic traits of their neighborhoods and to establish themselves as two of the city's few racially integrated middle- and upper-income residential areas. They succeeded, although progress on developing plans in these and other outer neighborhoods moved slowly.

The passage by Congress of the Economic Opportunity Act of 1964 and the Model Cities legislation of 1966, moreover, gave the GOP council opportunities to endorse and expedite ambitious community action plans and programs to reha-bilitate the city's most conspicuous inner-city slums and their inhabitants. These neighborhoods consisted of the remnants of the city's first black ghetto in the West

End; the Over-the-Rhine district on the northern fringe of downtown, an area of heavy German settlement in the nineteenth century but in the 1960s occupied by poor Appalachians and blacks; and, on a hill northeast of and overlooking downtown, Mount Auburn, a nineteenth-century silk-stocking neighborhood that in the 1960s became a part of the city's second black ghetto.

The Republican majority on the council during the 1960s also presided over the violent phase of the civil rights movement.[13] This movement took shape in the 1950s with the demise of that preoccupation with intergroup relations and equity that yielded efforts between 1920 and 1950 by blacks and whites to promote intercultural understanding and tolerance. The interracial tolerance movement also sought the development of group identity, coherence, and self-sufficiency among blacks by providing them with separate but equal housing, school, and social welfare facilities and access to blue-collar jobs. In Cincinnati, as elsewhere, this form of cultural group pluralism gave way in the 1940s and 1950s to individual pluralism, a growing insistence among blacks and whites that blacks, like other autonomous individuals, should have the right to make choices about their lifestyles. This idea underlay the national drive for integration as an option for the organization of housing, schools, social welfare facilities, and labor unions and the demands that blacks should also have access to white-collar jobs as footholds on the ladder of upward social and economic mobility.

These demands manifested themselves in a variety of ways in Cincinnati during the 1950s and early 1960s, most notably in the founding of Housing Opportunities Made Equal (HOME), a nonprofit organization that worked for the elimination of racial discrimination in real estate practices and that joined other civil rights organizations to fight for the passage of local and state open housing laws. In addition, the Cincinnati chapter of the NAACP filed an unsuccessful desegregation suit against the Cincinnati School Board and joined in a successful effort by the NAACP, CORE, and the Urban League to force the management of the Coney Island amusement park to open its grounds to blacks and to persuade retail stores, especially those downtown and in the West End, to hire blacks.

While some Charterite and Democratic politicians aligned themselves with the more ardent proponents of racial integration during the late 1950s and early 1960s, the Republicans on the council took a stand for moderation and gradualism that gratified most voters. But the eruption of a four-day race riot during the summer of 1967—to which several GOP council members and judges responded with law and order rhetoric while the mayor worked feverishly to find jobs for blacks and to gain some degree of gradual integration—played a key role in altering the political balance on the council. The most intense activity in these civil disorders occurred not in the old West End ghetto, but in the second ghetto in the neighborhood of Avondale. Many analysts concluded that these uprisings stemmed from the long history of racial discrimination and segregation in Cincinnati compounded by the bitterness provoked by the uprooting of thousands of West End blacks by expressway construction and urban redevelopment and by their transplantation in the city's second ghetto. Cries of black power and community control accompanied these outbreaks, and the riots and calls for black power produced fear and resentment among whites, who responded with cries for German, Irish, and Appalachian power, and with more aggressive demands for neighborhood power, both in Cincinnati and its suburbs.[14]

One of the first victims of this ethnic rivalry and neighborhood assertiveness was the carefully wrought plan of civic leaders for the realization of an old scheme for metropolitan coherence, a form of county government designed to provide county commissioners with legislative authority (county "home rule") and a county government with a merit system of employment.[15] Many blacks in Cincinnati now asserted that county government reform might reduce their influence in Cincinnati by shifting power from the city to the county. Ironically, most white suburban township and municipal officials also thought a more effective county government would reduce their influence. Key Cincinnati Democratic officials, who counted on growing black support to capture control of the council, backed away from county reforms. The same ethnic and neighborhood rivalries stiffened voter resistance to municipal property and income tax increases and to bond levies for mass transit and other citywide improvements, especially for the benefit of Cincinnati's public schools, which had become increasingly black but which also remained under attack by civil rights advocates for allegedly maintaining a racially segregated system.

In this context some Charterites and Democrats thought that the Republican grip on the city council might be vulnerable to the charge that the city confronted a fiscal and social crisis brought on by the GOP's promotion of downtown at the expense of the neighborhoods, including inner city black ones, nearby integrated ones, and outlying white ones. Few expected, however, that the Republican majority could be ousted in three-party contests. Fewer still expected that the Charterites and Democrats could combine their forces, but that is precisely what happened in the fall of 1969.

By 1969, as Democratic party leader Sidney Weil later put it, the "go it alone" sentiment among both the Charterites and the Democrats had cooled as a result of their "getting the hell beat out of them again and again by the Republicans."[16] In addition, the presence of two black incumbents on the council, one a Charterite, the other a Democrat, suggested that a coalition of Charterites and Democrats might capitalize on black discontent, including that resulting from the GOP's law and order response to the riots, to forge a disciplined black voting bloc. Early in 1969, therefore, Charterite and Democratic leaders opened negotiations to devise a joint strategy for the fall elections. The negotiations resulted in the creation of a Democratic/Charterite coalition ticket sensitive to the concerns of residential neighborhoods. The coalition won four seats and two years later secured a majority. In the 1973 elections, the slate ran on the slogan of "44 Neighborhoods—One Great City," and won seven of nine seats. Thereafter the coalition won every council contest until 1985. Despite some Democratic victories in the suburbs, Republicans maintained their control of the county government and its three thousand employees.

Much of the strength of the coalition in city politics stemmed from the willingness of the Charter party to appeal to the new feminism. Charterites from their inception had included women civic activists in their organization and activities. Many of them espoused reform politics in the Woman's City Club, a group established in the 1910s that had concentrated until the 1950s on good city government, public school politics, the improvement of race relations, and the promotion of international peace. Leaders of this organization, like most other social reform feminists of the period, contended that in local affairs women should use their historically developed cultural capacity for nurturing to help others (usually men) devise and carry out measures promoting community and civic coherence in the pluralistic metropolis of cultural groups.

But the new feminists of the 1950s and 1960s advocated the liberation of women from the notion that women's culture imposed restraints on their roles. New feminists with civic pretensions preferred to make and carry out decisions by themselves, and many of them identified the neighborhood planning and community council movement as an ideal venue for the exercise of these ambitions. As new institutions, the community councils proved open to new civic actors, and from the inception of the community councils in the late 1950s and early 1960s women played a disproportionate leadership role in their activities. The Charterites displayed an early interest and sympathy toward the neighborhood planning movement and cultivated close relations with its leaders, including the women among them who found in the drive for neighborhood autonomy an echo of their own aspirations for personal autonomy.[17]

The coalition's attraction to the new civil rights and feminist movement gave it a decidedly "liberal" cast, and many of its candidates reflected that viewpoint, including a concern for the defense of freedom of choice and speech. This position offended Cincinnati's anti-pornography crusaders, who had staunch allies in the Republican county prosecutor's office during the 1970s and 1980s. Indeed, the leadership in that office during this period helped give Cincinnati its "squeaky clean" international reputation by suppressing the display and sale of allegedly pornographic materials, movies, videotapes, and devices, by securing a ban on the showing of the musical *Hair,* and by subjecting the activities of the Film Society at the University of Cincinnati to close scrutiny.[18] The liberal cast of the coalition also offended anti-abortion activists, who in the late 1970s organized the Cincinnati party, the candidates of which campaigned exclusively on the anti-abortion issue and sharply criticized the coalition for permitting the operation of birth control clinics that performed abortions.

Though the coalition turned back challenges from both the GOP and its other critics, internal problems made the maintenance of the coalition a difficult task for its managers. Democrats successfully insisted on naming five of the nine candidates on each council slate but never managed to elect all five, an outcome that might have ended the coalition. The coalition minimized the intramural divisiveness that always attended the selection of the mayor by agreeing that the job should be alternated annually between the Democrats and Charterites. Although the office had little power, it was and is a popular one with ambitious politicians eager for media exposure and broad name recognition.

Neither the coalition nor the Republicans, however, found a satisfactory solution to the problems of disciplining their candidates, running coherent campaigns for the ticket, and developing coherent party positions on issues before the council. Since the adoption of the nonpartisan ballot in the 1920s, council candidates had tended to compete against all other candidates, including those from their own party. But in the 1950s this tendency intensified as successful candidates developed their own campaign organizations which ran campaigns independently from the party organizations. Council members elected through their own efforts generally decided issues for themselves. If they received a very large number of votes, they pushed for the mayoralty, regardless of past procedures for handling that delicate question.

The most dramatic demonstrations of the new independence of candidates during the reign of the coalition occurred in the 1970s when two candidates who had unsuccessfully sought Democratic nominations ran as independents. In 1975 Gerald Springer, who had resigned his council seat the previous year, announced that he would run as an independent regardless of the Democratic party's wishes. During the campaign, he declared that if elected he would decide with the victorious members of the coalition, not the party leadership, whether he would caucus with the coalition.[19]

The second dramatic instance of the new independence of candidates occurred in 1979 and almost destroyed the coalition. In that year Charles Luken, a young Democrat with excellent name recognition owing to the prominence of his father, U.S. Congressman Thomas Luken, and his late uncle, council member James Luken, sought a Democratic party nomination for city council. Before the Democrats could pass on his request, Luken announced that his candidacy would proceed with or without party approval. The Charterites pushed the Democrats to repudiate Luken's bid to prevent diffusion of the Democratic vote and a Republican victory. After the decision by the Democrats not to nominate Luken, Luken announced that he would nevertheless run as an independent Democratic candidate for council, "just as Jerry Springer did in 1975 when he was elected as a Democrat without the party's endorsement."[20]

The most serious threat to the coherence of the coalition in this period, however, came in 1976 when the Charterites endorsed several Republican candidates in county races, a move that infuriated many Democrats, especially suburban ones. For their part, however, the Democrats also threatened coalition unity by reviving talk of adopting a district method of electing council members, in part to facilitate the election of black Democratic candidates. Charterites opposed district council elections because they revived fears of the logrolling they associated with the Republican regime of the early twentieth century. Some Democrats also advocated the direct election of the mayor, which Charterites opposed on the grounds that it would undermine the city manager form of government. Democratic party leaders averted a crisis by first stalling a decision on all these questions until 1977 and then by persuading the dissidents to drop the issues.

Despite its long council ascendancy the coalition made no fundamental changes in urban development policies established in the 1950s. Urban development policy had not been an issue of contention between Charterites and Republicans from the late 1920s into the 1950s, and the Charterite and Democratic minorities from 1957 to 1971 had not disagreed on the new neighborhood focus adopted in the mid-1950s. After 1971, the coalition, as worried as the Republicans before them about Cincinnati's competitive position vis-à-vis the Sunbelt and the suburbs, tried to embellish that policy with its own programs and a new slogan but did not move in a new direction. The coalition described its schemes for arresting urban decline as efforts to make Cincinnati a "livable city."[21] Part of this campaign focused on residential neighborhood preservation and development as a way of making the Queen City distinctive among major cities and a place attractive to suburbanites and newcomers. The council expanded neighborhood health and recreation facilities, supported the City Planning Commission's neighborhood planning program, and brought community council representatives into the budgeting process and onto the citizens advisory committee on Community Development Block Grant (CBGA) spending. In the early 1980s, however, a coalition city manager took the lead in creating a new Department of Neighborhood Housing and Conservation to spearhead the rehabilitation of old neighborhoods and their business districts.

But the coalition also worked vigorously to foster downtown redevelopment and rehabilitation. A coalition city manager in the mid-1970s revived the organization of big business leaders that had promoted the city's 1948 plan until that group's demise in the mid-1960s. The new association, dubbed the Cincinnati Business Committee (CBC), aimed to foster private and public sector cooperation on civic issues, especially those related to downtown and the public schools. A coalition city manager also converted the former Department of Urban Development into a Department of Economic Development, appointed a woman, Nell Surber, to head it, and made it the special trustee of the central business district. Working closely with the CBC, Surber put together local, state, and federal subsidies that underwrote the construction of two new hotels, the restoration of an elegant art deco hotel originally constructed in the 1930s, and the erection of a series of office buildings. In the early 1980s, moreover, the coalition reaffirmed its commitment to a downtown as lively by night as by day. To this end, the coalition leaders adopted a second comprehensive downtown plan which formally incorporated the central riverfront into the downtown scheme for office and retail facilities, enlarged the allotment of housing units within and on the fringe of downtown, and called for the designation of four downtown historic districts.

The coalition also took advantage of the federal Historic Preservation Act of 1966 and its later amendments providing tax credits for preservation by replacing the Architectural Board of Review with an Historic Conservation Board (HCB). It then provided the new agency with preservation ordinances regarded as models for other communities, including Milwaukee. On the recommendations of the HCB, the city council established local historic districts in residential and commercial areas, including three in the central business district and one in the nearby Mount Auburn neighborhood.

These downtown and neighborhood programs, along with efforts to encourage and regulate the development of the hillsides and the purchase and support of the transit company, proved expensive, especially as the city's population and revenue base continued to shrink. The coalition council avoided the fiscal crises that plagued New York City and Cleveland in the 1970s by passing occasional tax increases and by reducing spending on infrastructure maintenance. In addition, the city council supported the efforts of community councils to finance their own activities. The coalition also cooperated with the campaign of the University of Cincinnati to switch from municipal to state support, turned over management of the city's General Hospital to the University's medical center, and gave responsibility for the old municipal workhouse to the county government.

The juxtaposing of these cutbacks beside costly downtown improvements nettled some neighborhood leaders. Other matters worried them as well, such as a failed council attempt in the mid-1970s to spread low-income housing and its predominantly black residents more evenly across the city. These and other neighborhood concerns led to attempts to establish formal and informal citywide alliances of community councils to strengthen neighborhood lobbying efforts on citywide as well as parochial questions. Formal ones, such as the Coalition of Neighborhood Groups, did not last, but informal efforts continued. In the late 1970s school board officials recognized the critical role of concerted neighborhood lobbying when they turned to neighborhood leaders for help in securing passage of a school bond levy. Civic leaders, bureaucrats, and city council members enlisted neighborhood organizations to lead the drive for a levy to establish a separate fund to rebuild the city's infrastructure. Supporters of the Historic Conservation Board's attempt to establish a local historic district on West Fourth Street, the city's prime financial district since the early twentieth century, rallied the support of a long list of community councils with the cry that "Fourth Street is everybody's neighborhood."

This new disposition among neighborhood organizations to address citywide issues became a factor in city council elections for the first time in 1985. In that year, the Over-the-Rhine Community Council, which had been fighting the designation of that low-income area as a national and local historic district, endorsed the candidacy of a Republican who had seemed especially sympathetic to the plight of poor people regardless of their neighborhood residence. In that same campaign a coalition of neighborhoods in the populous and predominantly white and heavily Catholic western hills of the city formed a political action committee, WESTPAC. The new organization sent a questionnaire to all council candidates and endorsed those who stood with WESTPAC on both local and citywide issues, including its stand against abortion.

The election of 1985 stands out for two other reasons, the disruption of the Democratic/Charterite coalition and the surprising outcome of the contest. The falling out of the Democrats and Charterites began in 1982, when Sidney Weil, a stalwart supporter of the coalition, resigned as cochairman of the Democratic party, leaving John "Socko" Wiethe alone at the helm. The coalition remained intact through the election of 1983, a contest in which three women won seats, but in the spring of 1985 Wiethe moved to break up the coalition, an action resisted by several leading Democrats, including the incumbents, who opposed the go-it-alone policy on the grounds that it would return control of the council to the Republicans.

The three-party contest that followed yielded a new council containing no partisan majority. The new council consisted of four Republicans, two of them newcomers; four Democrats; and a single Charterite. This outcome stunned many political observers, not only because of the victories of two unexceptional Republican challengers in a Democratic city, but also because it produced an entirely male council with but one black. Blacks now comprised 33 percent of the city's population.

The selection of a mayor from this group and the reorganization of the council proved even more stunning and dramatically illustrated the irrelevance of party discipline in the new urban politics. Early in the negotiations over the mayoralty the four Democrats appeared ready to unite with the single Charterite to form a ruling majority, but the five could not agree on a choice for mayor. The deadlock finally broke when three Republicans joined with two Democrats—all five of whom had been endorsed by WESTPAC—to form a bipartisan "conservative" coalition and chose Charles Luken as mayor. In the aftermath, the leaders of both the Democratic and Republican parties claimed that they had not been parties to—indeed had not been consulted about—the deal. The remaining Democratic and Republican council members protested long and bitterly about their exclusion from important committee assignments and contended that the majority ignored past procedures for involving minority council members in the body's decision-making processes.[22]

The conservative council majority pledged that it would not raise taxes before the next election, regardless of projected reductions in municipal services and personnel. The conservative majority also sought to diminish the role of the city hall bureaucracy in policy implementation and to secure the direct election of the mayor, a proposal regarded by most observers as an effort to undermine the influence of the manager in policy making. The council majority also hired a low-profile city manager, Scott Johnson, a laconic former military officer with a degree in public administration from the University of Cincinnati and previous experience in Oklahoma City. In his new post Johnson soon came under fire for being inaccessible to the public and the network of community councils that by now numbered forty-eight.

The new majority also took "conservative" stands on so-called "family" issues. Mayor Luken, for example, refused to proclaim an official "gay rights" week, something that two previous mayors had done. Luken also wrote to the president and board of the University of Cincinnati to protest the Film Society's showing of *Hail Mary* on the grounds that the movie defamed the Virgin Mary and offended the religious sensibilities of many citizens.[23] On a five to four vote Vice-Mayor Kenneth Blackwell, the sole black on the council, pushed through a fetal disposal ordinance requiring clinics and hospitals that performed abortions to bury, cremate, or otherwise dispose of fetuses in a way approved by the health commissioner. Blackwell defended the legislation as a sanitary public health regulation, but opponents saw it as an attempt to interfere with a woman's right to have an abortion by making the procedure more expensive.[24] And the conservative majority repeatedly criticized the head of the Health Department for his management and budgetary practices. To oversee his work the conservatives appointed anti-abortionists to the board at a time when "right to life" advocates were conducting vocal demonstrations in front of birth control clinics. These demonstrations had resulted in the arrests of several demonstrators and the firebombing of two facilities. In this context, the conservative majority's "pro-family" stance led some political observers to spread the word that all five members of the new majority belonged to or had close ties to the Catholic church.

Although breaking with the past on these issues, the conservative majority did not alter the urban development policy on which the city had embarked in the mid-1950s. Like the Republican and coalition councils that preceded it, the conservative majority worried about Cincinnati's competitiveness with its suburbs and with Sunbelt and Frostbelt cities. It pursued both downtown development, including residential projects, and neighborhood housing and conservation projects proposed by the city hall bureaucracy, which remained sensitive to community council desires and committed to community action. It stood firm on the city's affirmative action policy. It continued the familiar pattern of CDBG allocations, which meant that even such notoriously unconservative agencies as HOME, which in the 1980s pursued its racial residential integration goals by filing suits against offending realtors, and the Legal Aid Society, which in the 1980s sued the Cincinnati Metropolitan Housing Authority for maintaining racially segregated projects, received support at roughly the same percentage levels as in the past. And while the conservative majority reduced the size of a proposed West Fourth Street Historic District, it did not accede to the demands of the Board of Realtors and others who regarded historic preservation as anti-growth and who wanted a moratorium on historic designations of all kinds. Nor did their "no new taxes" pledge prevent members of the conservative majority from backing a successful bond levy campaign initiated by the Cincinnati Historical Society and the Museum of Natural History to save once more historic Union Terminal railway station. Earlier developers had converted it into a shopping mall. Now it would be transformed into an up-to-date museum facility to attract tourists.

Despite the agility of the conservative majority and its adherence to traditional urban development policies, "liberal" dissatisfaction with the council leadership mounted as the election of 1987 approached. The Woman's Political Caucus vowed to elect as many women as possible to city council. Feminist and black civil rights advocates, many of them new faces who emerged from the Rev. Jesse Jackson's Rainbow Coalition presidential race of 1984, called for the reinstatement of PR, which they claimed would produce fair representation for blacks and women. Some "liberals" feared, however, that PR might yield a permanent anti-abortion majority on council because of the appeal of that issue to Catholics, evangelical Protestants, and many blacks. Disgruntled Democrats, many of them Rainbow Coalition veterans, also tried once more to oust Wiethe from the party chairmanship, and when that failed pushed him unsuccessfully to broaden membership on the Cincinnati Democratic Committee (CDC), a steering committee for city politics separate from the county organization that was established in the late 1970s.

By the summer of 1987 all three parties had put together their slates for the fall elections. The GOP nominated its incumbents plus several newcomers, including a woman, none of whom commanded broad name recognition. The Charterites endorsed their sole male incumbent and also nominated two women, including Bobbie Sterne, a fourteen-year council veteran and former mayor who had lost a reelection bid two years earlier. The Democrats had a more difficult time constructing their ticket as they struggled to reunite amid the continuing dissatisfaction with Wiethe and persisting bitterness about the defection of two Democratic council members to the conservative majority in 1985. Finally the party endorsed a slate that included a black male who ran thirteenth in 1985, three women, and all four Democratic incumbents.

The election of 1987 confirmed the persistence of political tendencies that took shape in the late-1950s. Voters ignored party lines and returned eight incumbents including four Republican, three Democrats, and one Charterite. But the ninth slot on the council went to Bobbie Sterne, who replaced incumbent James Cissell, one of the two Democratic council members of the conservative coalition. Partly as a result of her victory, negotiations for the organization of the council for the next two years yielded a variation of the theme played out two years earlier. Council members again agreed to a nonpartisan distribution of key committee chairs, and Charles Luken, who emerged as mayor, announced that he intended to maintain the conservative social and political agenda of the past two years. Neither he nor any other council member, however, could reconstruct a majority coalition, conservative or otherwise.

In 1988 the chief characteristics of the new urban politics and their influence on planning and urban development in Cincinnati since the mid-1950s stand out clearly. They consist of a de facto, no-party system and the ascendancy of independent voters, independent candidates, and independent city council members.[25] For these, the pursuit of autonomy and self-fulfillment eroded their commitment to enfeebled party organizations and of party leaders. The new urban politics also included a heightened tolerance for diversity in the form of mixed land uses and in the juxtaposition of the historic, modern, and postmodern architecture in neighborhoods and downtown; a growing legitimacy of the idea, if not the reality, of racial integration and affirmative action; and a willingness of some council members and candidates to respond, sometimes rhetorically but often with deeds, to varied and occasionally contradictory combinations of "minority" voices. The latter ranged from pro-family to pro-choice advocates and from historic conservationists to the Board of Realtors. At the same time, council members listened to the city hall bureaucracy and fostered urban development through citizens' participation in community councils.

The new urban politics also displayed a reluctance to compromise and a tendency to policy paralysis as the leaders of each neighborhood and each cause relentlessly advocated their goals. This characteristic of the new urban politics slowed the pace of urban development and with it the establishment of a distinctive "image" for the city and its downtown to foster Cincinnati's competitiveness with its own suburbs and other big cities.[26] These same characteristics of the new politics also deterred bureaucrats, council members, council candidates, and community council and civic organization leaders from reexamining postwar urban development policy. As a consequence, urban development policy per se did not become an issue, as civic actors continued to deal with familiar problems and familiar solutions.[27]

Despite the decline of the city, moreover, neither politicians, bureaucrats, community council activists, nor civic leaders called for the creation of a comprehensive economic development plan for the city as a whole. Instead, they created community action neighborhood development strategies, including one for the central business district, that included an economic component as part of the goal of making each neighborhood self-sufficient and viable. For non-downtown neighborhoods these economic plans included proposals to provide employment in the neighborhood for residents of the neighborhood and schemes to promote the development of neighborhood business districts, including sometimes projects that would attract patrons from outside the neighborhood. This community action approach cast the City Planning Department in the role of facilitator of neighborhood planning and coordinator of neighborhood plans but provided no place for a guardian of the welfare of the city as a whole. The approach also pitted each neighborhood against all the others in a contest for scarce municipal, state, and federal funds, for private and public social welfare services, and for housing and population.

While the post-1950s drive for a distinctive image and for viability has been occasionally frustrating for its proponents, it has not been fruitless. Despite its population losses, Cincinnati remains a heterogeneous and lively city. It contains middle- and upper-income residential areas, a few of which are racially integrated. Although Cincinnati's downtown area is not as lively by night as by day, it still functions as the heart of the growing metropolitan area. While rehabilitation has stalled in neighborhoods on the downtown fringe, most noticeably in Over-the-Rhine and the West End, Mount Adams continues to thrive. The riverfront has attracted restaurants and entertainment facilities, if not the housing, office, and retail outlets called for in the most recent comprehensive downtown plan. The second ghetto, moreover, did not spread into additional white neighborhoods during the late 1970s and 1980s. This stability has reduced racial tensions below their extraordinary levels of the late 1950s and 1960s. And in the mid-1980s the Department of City Planning launched an effort to develop, by means of community action, a rehabilitation and conservation program for an area the planners dubbed "Uptown," which encompassed not only the second ghetto neighborhoods of Mount Auburn, Avondale, and Corryville with their higher education and hospital complexes, but also racially integrated North Avondale and racially integrating Clifton.

In the light of this history of the new urban politics and urban development, the warnings since the mid-1950s about the imminent death of American big cities, and especially the big cities of the frostbelt, seem to have been premature. Those accounts lambasted twentieth-century urban policy makers for converting once vital and diverse big cities from their role as centers of American civilization into dumping grounds for impoverished racial minorities, the elderly, single-parent households, and the homeless, and some of them projected a future for American big city downtowns as the empty holes in the metropolitan doughnut. It is more fruitful, however, to take those warnings and projections not as descriptions of reality but as contributions to the revolt against cultural group pluralism that not only defined problems but also proposed solutions, some of which caught on and form the reality in which we yet live.

NOTES

This essay is informed in part by research and writing supported by a grant from the National Endowment for the Humanities for a project entitled "Planning and the Persisting Past: Cincinnati's Over-the-Rhine since 1940," with matching grants from the Ohio Board of Regents Urban Universities Program, the Ohio Board of Regents Linkage Grant Program, and the Murray Seasongood Foundation, Cincinnati, Ohio.

1. Advocates of cultural group pluralism contended that all "normal" individuals belong to a group (ethnic, racial, religious, class, occupational, gender) and that the identity of the group and the behavior of its members stem from its history and the influence of the social and physical environment occupied by the group. See Henry D. Shapiro, "The Place of Culture and the Problem of Identity," in Allen Batteau, ed., *Appalachia and America: Autonomy and Regional Dependence* (Lexington: University Press of Kentucky, 1983), esp. 109–128; Zane L. Miller, "Walter Prescott Webb, the Chicago School of Sociology, and Regionalism," (forthcoming).

2. The advent of individual pluralism may be seen as a revolt against the cultural group determinism of the previous era. For a sociological perspective on some of the dilemmas of individual pluralism, see Milton M. Gordon, *Assimilation in American Life: The Role of Race, Religion, and National Origins* (New York: Oxford University Press, 1984), 262–65.

3. On late nineteenth and early twentieth-century Cincinnati politics, see Zane L. Miller, *Boss Cox's Cincinnati: Urban Politics in the Progressive Era* (New York: Oxford University Press, 1968); William A. Baughin, "Murray Seasongood: Twentieth-Century Urban Reformer" (Ph.D. diss., University of Cincinnati, 1972); Andrea Tuttle Kornbluh, " 'The Bowl of Promise': Cincinnati's Social Welfare Planners, Cultural Pluralism, and the Metropolis, 1911–1952" (Ph.D. diss., University of Cincinnati, 1988); and Robert A. Burnham, "Urban Politics, Municipal Government, and Urban Development in Cincinnati, 1925–1950" (Ph.D. diss., University of Cincinnati, forthcoming).

4. Although the Charter Committee functioned as a party, by state law it could only run candidates in nonpartisan races, hence only in city council contests within Hamilton County.

5. Baughin, "Murray Seasongood," vol. II; Ralph A. Straetz, *PR Politics in Cincinnati: Thirty-Two Years of Proportional Representation* (New York: New York University Press, 1958); Wilbert J. Cameron, "Community Control of Education in Cincinnati, 1900–1921" (Ph.D. diss., University of Cincinnati, 1977); Andrea Tuttle Kornbluh, *Lighting the Way: The Woman's City Club of Cincinnati, 1915–1965* (Cincinnati: The Woman's City Club, 1986).

6. The first plan was approved in 1925. On the origins of the plan of 1948, see Robert B. Fairbanks and Zane L. Miller, "The Martial Metropolis: Housing, Planning, and Race in Cincinnati, 1940–1955," in Roger W. Lotchin, ed., *The Martial Metropolis: U.S. Cities in War and Peace* (New York: Praeger Publishers, 1984), 201–202.

7. For more detailed assessments of the plan of 1948, see Geoffrey Giglierano and Zane L. Miller, "Downtown Housing: Changing Plans and Perspectives, 1948–1980," *Cincinnati Historical Society Bulletin* 40 (1982): 167–90; and Fairbanks and Miller, "Martial Metropolis," 204–209. On the implementation of the plan, see Cincinnati Department of Urban Development, *History of Progress: Annual Report, 1965–1966* (Cincinnati: Department of

Urban Development, 1966), 6–12; and Zane L. Miller, *Suburb: Neighborhood and Community in Forest Park, Ohio, 1935–1976* (Knoxville: University of Tennessee Press, 1981), 3–45.

8. The following discussion of politics through the election of 1957 follows Straetz, *PR.*

9. In the 1957 election the GOP attacked and managed to repeal PR in a contest in which rumors circulated that the continuation of PR would eventually lead to the selection by a Charterite majority of a black as mayor, a sensitive question in a decade when the black population both increased as a result of in-migration from the South and began to move into previously white neighborhoods.

10. The new mode of planning took shape in 1954 when the Cincinnati Planning Commission and the Department of Urban Development began the long process of preparing a conservation and rehabilitation program for the neighborhoods of Corryville and Avondale. For a fuller analysis of the origins of community action in the Corryville and Avondale urban renewal plan, see Zane L. Miller and Bruce Tucker, "The Revolt against Culture and the Origins of Community Action" (forthcoming).

11. The Charter amendment repealing PR retained the nonpartisan ballot and permitted citizens to vote for up to nine candidates. The top nine vote getters comprised the city council.

12. For a general account of urban development since the mid-1950s, see Iola Hessler Silberstein, *Cincinnati Then and Now* (Cincinnati: The Voters Service Education Fund of the League of Women Voters of the Cincinnati Area, 1982), 239–303. On the Lytle Park historic district, see Jana C. Morford, "Preserving a 'Special Place': The Lytle Park Neighborhood, 1948–1976," *Queen City Heritage* 44 (1986): 3–22.

13. The most insightful analyses of the race relations and civil rights movements in Cincinnati may be found in Robert B. Fairbanks, "Better Housing Movements and the City: Definitions of and Responses to Cincinnati's Low Cost Housing Problem, 1910–1954" (Ph.D. diss., University of Cincinnati, 1981); Kornbluh, *Lighting the Way,* 71–84; Kornbluh, " 'Bowl of Promise' "; Nina Mjagkij, "Behind the Scenes: The Cincinnati Urban League, 1947–1965" (forthcoming); Robert A. Burnham, "The Mayor's Friendly Relations Committee: Race Relations as Inter-Group Relations in Cincinnati, 1943–1949" (forthcoming).

14. For an analysis of aspects of the white ethnic revival in Cincinnati, see Zane L. Miller, "Ohio's Immigrants and the Rush to an Urban Setting: Ethnicity and Community in Historical Perspective," in John Wunder, ed., *Toward an Urban Ohio,* Ohio American Revolution Bicentennial Series, V (Columbus: Ohio Historical Society, 1977), 29–34; and idem., "Cincinnati Germans and the Invention of an Ethnic Group," *Queen City Heritage* 42 (Fall 1984): 13–22. The resentment by Appalachian ethnic revivalists of black power accomplishments appeared most clearly in turf battles for control of inner-city neighborhoods, particularly Over-the-Rhine during the 1970s. See William W. Philliber and Clyde B. McCoy, eds., *The Invisible Minority: Urban Appalachians* (Lexington: University Press of Kentucky, 1981), 169–70; and Zane L. Miller, Henry D. Shapiro, and Bruce Tucker, *Planning and the Persisting Past: Cincinnati's Over-the-Rhine since 1948* (forthcoming). Appalachian advocates believed that local officials used a federal housing program to "displace" Appalachians in Over-the-Rhine and to replace them with blacks.

15. County government reformers tried once more in 1982 and failed again. For an account of these efforts, see Silberstein, *Cincinnati Then and Now,* 270–71.

16. *Cincinnati Post,* February 11, 1978, p. 1; Sidney Weil interview, March 6, 1987.

17. Kornbluh, *Lighting the Way,* 27–37; Charter Research Institute, *Community Councils of Cincinnati, 1970* (Cincinnati: Charter Research Institute, 1970); Martha S. Reynolds, "The City, Suburbs, and the Establishment of the Clifton Town Meeting, 1961–1964," *Cincinnati Historical Society Bulletin* 38 (1980): 7–32. See also Zane L. Miller, "The Role and Concept of Neighborhood in American Cities" in Robert Fisher and Peter Romanofsky, eds., *Community Organization for Urban Social Change: A Historical Perspective* (Westport, Conn.: Greenwood Press, 1981), 3–32; Patricia Mooney Melvin, *American Community Organization: A Historical Dictionary* (New York: Greenwood Press, 1986); and Robert Fisher, *Let the People Decide: Neighborhood Organizing in America* (Boston: Twayne, 1984).

18. An English publication contended in 1968 that Cincinnati, "a quiet, conservative place (*Penthouse* and *Playboy* are hidden from view at its airport's news stand) is one of America's nicest cities." *The Economist*, May 21, 1968, p. 22.

19. *Cincinnati Post*, September 2, 1975, p. 11; October 9, 1975, p. 20.

20. *Cincinnati Enquirer*, July 26, 1979, p. D1; July 31, 1979, p. A1; August 1, 1979, p. C1; *Cincinnati Post*, July 26, 1979, p. 13.

21. See Saul Pleeter, "Cincinnati: How Shall I Compare Thee . . . ?" *Urban Resources* 3 (Spring 1986): C6–C8.

22. For an example of these complaints by the minority, see *Cincinnati Enquirer*, May 3, 1987, p. B3.

23. See Robert McKay, "The Hail Mary Affair and Why the Bishop Held His Tongue," *Cincinnati Magazine* 20 (July 1987): 44–45.

24. Disposal of a fetus would cost between $154 and $2500. In July of 1987 a U.S. District Judge upheld a lower court's ban on the enforcement of the ordinance on the grounds of its vagueness and of its intent to interfere with the right to an abortion. *Cincinnati Post*, July 2, 1987, p. B3.

25. For a brief and similar analysis of the emergence of the national no-party system in presidential politics, see Richard C. Wade, "Politics in a No-Party System," *New York Times*, May 13, 1987, p. A27.

26. The notion of "image" as the creation of a "pseudo-reality" to mold the behavior of people became a problem in American civilization in the mid-1950s and early 1960s and stands as further evidence of the disdain for conformity in the era of individual pluralism. See, for example, Daniel J. Boorstin, *The Image: Or What Happened to the American Dream* (New York: Atheneum, 1962).

27. Zane L. Miller and Patricia Mooney Melvin, *The Urbanization of Modern America: A Brief History*, 2d ed. (San Diego: Harcourt Brace Jovanovich, 1987), 229–250.

VI

CLEVELAND

THE STRUGGLE FOR STABILITY

Thomas F. Campbell

In 1950 William Ganson Rose published his encyclopedic book *Cleveland: The Making of a City*. The title of his final chapter on the 1940s, "Greatness Achieved," captured the upbeat mood in Cleveland during the immediate postwar years. During World War II the city had thrived, churning out $5 billion worth of defense materiel. The Chamber of Commerce reflected the collective postwar municipal spirit when it adopted the Cleveland Electric Illuminating Company's slogan "Cleveland, the best location in the nation."

Yet lurking beneath the surface were nagging memories of the depression—collapsing banks, heartbreaking unemployment, and the spectacular fall of the Van Sweringen empire. In the words of Cleveland financier Cyrus S. Eaton, Cleveland's leadership suffered from a "depression psychosis." For decades to come, both private and public institutions displayed a fiscal conservatism that belied their optimistic pronouncements and discouraged new ventures.[1]

Cleveland's postwar political history really began in January 1945 when Mayor Frank J. Lausche became governor, and his longtime law director, Thomas L. Burke, replaced him at city hall. Tom Burke was an extremely popular and shrewd Irish-American politician in a city whose ethnic votes were primarily Democratic. Anointed by Lausche and strongly endorsed by Louis B. Seltzer, the politically powerful editor of the *Cleveland Press*, Burke served as mayor for eight years, overwhelming his Republican opponents in four elections. He left office only when Governor Lausche appointed him to fill the vacancy in the U.S. Senate created by Robert Taft's death in 1953.[2]

The years that Burke served as mayor were good years for many American cities, and Cleveland was no exception. Not only was there full employment, but during the Korean War years a severe labor shortage opened employment opportunities for blacks and whites from the southern and border states. Such prosperity might have stimulated a bold and imaginative approach to the needs of an expanding population and a deteriorating housing stock, but there was no leadership on these issues from either city hall or the business community. At a time when David

Lawrence and financier Richard Mellon created an urban renaissance in neighboring Pittsburgh, Cleveland leaders sat on their hands.

Cleveland's problems were not unknown. Mayor Burke admitted that housing, for example, was a pressing need; and utility magnate Elmer Lindseth, president of the Cleveland Electric Illuminating Company, warned his business and professional colleagues of downtown decay and neighborhood slums. Speaking in 1953, Lindseth blamed neglect and the failure to build decent rental housing, schools, and recreational facilities for the decline. He also fretted about a lack of public transit and parking facilities.[3]

In the short run, however, nothing came of these concerns. The municipal housing stock continued to deteriorate as building code violations became the norm. Both new construction and rehabilitation of old structures appeared too expensive in an era before major federal aid.

In the area of transportation planning, the Burke record was better. His administration did produce a comprehensive plan for the city that focused on highways. During the next two decades city planners engineered solutions to downtown congestion and traffic problems. To secure federal funds Burke removed the transit system from city control and created an independent transit board. In early 1952, backed by a $29 million loan from the Reconstruction Finance Corporation, the new transit system began work on a high-speed rail carrier to run from an adjacent eastern suburb through downtown Cleveland and out to the city's municipally owned airport on the far west side. When the system was completed in 1968, the city was recognized nationally for its initiative in linking the downtown area directly with its airport, but the eastern segment was built too far south of the main population centers to attract riders, and a feeder bus system did little to encourage people to ride the "Rapid" and leave their autos at home.[4]

Planning for an innerbelt freeway began in 1948, but delays surrounding the acquisition of over 1,250 parcels of land and cost disputes between the state and local government postponed construction until 1954 and completion until the mid-1960s. The new circular system successfully diverted traffic from the central business district and became a major factor in decentralizing the city's population, businesses, and industries. Over nineteen thousand residents lost their homes to the freeways. Further planning for expansion included a $35 million terminal for the municipal airport and a smaller downtown airport that planners believed would develop into a major secondary facility.[5]

With a legacy of concrete and steel in place, Burke departed Cleveland for Washington. In an ensuing election Anthony J. Celebrezze won the mayoralty. The new mayor, an Italian native, was then serving his second term as a state senator. He was a quiet, cautious lawyer who became very popular with the Cleveland voters. When he first ran in 1953 he carried the strong endorsement of Governor Lausche, Tom Burke, and Seltzer's *Cleveland Press* but not that of the Democratic party. The *Press* endorsement was particularly important because of the paper's wide circulation among "blue-collar cosmopolitans," or "cosmos" as white ethnics were then called in Cleveland. When Seltzer endorsed a candidate he threw the whole weight of the paper's news and editorial space behind his decision. The *Press* ran a banner headline proclaiming "Celebrezze is the man to get things done." Seltzer's editorial endorsement claimed Celebrezze would solve the major problem facing the city—traffic congestion caused by the failure to get the innerbelt freeway completed.[6]

Celebrezze worked effectively with the city council and its flamboyant president, Jack P. Russell, who represented the largely Hungarian sixteenth ward for almost three decades and utilized this base to become one of the most powerful politicians in the city. Russell's complete control of the council, coupled with blatant political showmanship, enraged editorial writers and good government groups, but his approach to getting elected and to controlling local government earned him an invitation as a guest lecturer at Harvard. There were few of the legislative/executive deadlocks that were to characterize succeeding administrations. Of course, no controversial issues were raised by either the mayor or the council, and blacks, who had many concerns, had no political power.[7]

Like his predecessors the new mayor tended to concentrate on bricks and mortar projects, such as the innerbelt freeway which was completed in 1965. The opening of the St. Lawrence Seaway spurred interest in making Cleveland an international seaport, and Celebrezze responded by creating the Cleveland Seaport Foundation to promote the city as a world trade center. In 1957 the city passed an $8 million bond issue to modernize the existing port facilities. Yet, despite the city's optimism and quick action, growth has been modest in recent years.[8]

Celebrezze's major impact upon Cleveland was his urban renewal program of the late 1950s and early 1960s. It initially involved three neighborhood projects on the east side of the city. Two of them were predominantly black slums located south and slightly east of the central business district (St. Vincent Center and East Woodland). The other one, called University-Euclid, lay west of University Circle, which, with its numerous cultural and educational institutions, was the cultural heart of the city. This area was largely black but not yet a slum, although the city's failure to enforce housing codes and sharp declines in municipal services soon made it one. Erieview, the fourth project, consisted of about 163 acres in the downtown business area.[9]

These urban renewal plans grew out of the enormous demographic changes that swept across midwestern metropolitan centers in the postwar period. The 1950 census recorded the city's population peak—914,808, the majority of whom were white, middle- or working-class people of European descent. There were 148,000 blacks—an increase of 75 percent since 1940. In the next decade the black population showed another increase of over 100,000, so that by 1965 there were 276,000 black citizens residing in the central city, nearly 50 percent of whom were born in the South. It is estimated that in the same postwar years approximately 80,000 white Appalachians moved into the area.[10]

The city that received this second great migration of blacks (the first was from 1916–20) had long been characterized as a "good community for blacks." The Western Reserve, of which Cleveland was the principal city, had been noted for its abolitionist record in pre–Civil War years. Until after the First World War blacks lived in many east side wards, segregated only by economics; but by the 1930s racial segregation was an established pattern. Working-class European immigrants living in ghetto neighborhoods were hostile to the influx of poor black migrants from the South.[11]

By the 1950s middle-class blacks excluded from suburbia began to move into former Jewish neighborhoods, and within a decade Glenville and Mt. Pleasant districts became largely middle-class black. These out-migrants left behind them the inner-city black ghettos where overcrowding and poverty remained. Twenty-five to 60 percent of the housing there was substandard, and one-fourth of the families had incomes below $3,000 a year. In the oldest and most dilapidated neighborhood, the West-Central area, over 60 percent of the households were below that level. Area-wide, the unemployment rate was 4.4 percent; but for black youth in the heart of the ghetto it ranged up to 27.7 percent. Among the city's six police districts, the one that contained several of the black ghettos accounted for 25 percent of all crime reported in the city. The litany of social handicaps that beset poor blacks included substandard education, illegitimate births, and juvenile delinquency.[12]

The schools, operating under a board elected at large, took great pride in the fact that they were acting in a fiscally responsible manner by not building additional schools, despite the fact that there was an increase of over 50,000 students. It was not surprising that the first significant protests of the 1960s centered on the fact that black ghetto children were forced to attend overcrowded schools in morning or afternoon shifts. Even when integration pressures mounted, officials bused black children to empty classrooms in white areas where they were kept segregated from white children and forced to use separate portable toilets. When the school board finally approved construction plans for new schools in the early 1960s, they located them in places designed to maintain segregation, thereby stimulating widespread picketing in protest. A sit-in at one of the building sites led to the accidental death by crushing of Bruce Klunder, a young white clergyman. Thereafter, a Businessmen's Interracial Committee on Community Affairs was formed in an attempt to address some of the problems facing black residents of the city; but the problems were massive, and both the city administration and the school board were insensitive, if not indifferent, to the rising tide of anguish and anger in the black community.[13]

Nowhere were conditions more desperate than in housing. Most inner-city residents lived in deteriorating rental housing in frame buildings that were built before the First World War. It was practically impossible, under the policies of the federal housing agencies and the local banks, for inner-city residents to get mortgages to buy homes or secure home improvement loans.

Hough, which was to explode in violence in the mid-1960s, was a case study in urban decay. It was a two-square-mile area between East 55th and East 105th Streets, bounded on the north and the south by Superior and Euclid Avenues, respectively. In 1910 Hough had been a fashionable upper-middle-class community of about 40,000. By 1950 it was a working- and middle-class neighborhood of over 65,000 people that included a black middle class of 3,600 and a considerable number of recently arrived white Appalachians. Dislocated by the construction of freeways and urban renewal projects and pressed by an acute housing shortage, blacks began to pour into Hough from the old Central ghetto. In the first five years of the fifties, the population of Hough soared to an estimated 82,000; and the white population, spurred by fear, racism, and the block-busting tactics of unscrupulous realty companies, fled. Not only the whites left, but also middle-class blacks.[14]

As early as 1951 the Hough Area Council had fought in vain to save its neighborhood. At the council's invitation Mayor Burke had come to hear for himself about the wide-open prostitution, the high crime rate, and the housing decay, but the shock he expressed only resulted in an empty promise of help. Hough continued its downward spiral despite several efforts by the Greater Cleveland Associated Foundation to arrest the decline. One of its funded programs, Community Action for Youth, was the result of an excellent and well developed proposal geared to involve the diverse resources of the community in solving the enormous problem of juvenile delinquency in Hough. But even this project failed to bring together the fragmented and often feuding public and private agencies whose cooperation was necessary for effective intervention in the multifaceted problems of the area.[15]

Three years later in 1966 riots broke out, and Hough went up in the flames of over 240 fires. There were four deaths, over thirty injuries, and widespread vandalism at a cost of millions of dollars. It was a week before the rioting ceased and the area returned to normal. The Hough that remained resembled heavily bombed German cities after World War II.[16]

The riots of 1966 did bring the city's political and civic leadership face-to-face with the reality of what was happening to their core city; but, while some reacted appropriately, others seemed to have learned nothing. Louis Seltzer, who headed up a special grand jury formed to investigate the riots, issued a report that noted the poor social conditions that most of the residents were forced to endure but then went on to place the blame for the riots on "outside agitators"—namely, a small group of young white communists who had opened a bookstore on the fringe of Hough. The white political structure remained similarly myopic in its approach to the city's social turmoil.[17]

Church and civic leaders were more responsive. The Businessmen's Interracial Committee for Community Affairs increased its activities by forming AIM-Jobs, a pioneering manpower-training program, in an effort to solve the chronic unemployment problems of blacks. But their analysis of the heightened racial tensions was also short-sighted. James C. Davis, a powerful establishment lawyer, charged that the racial hostility of white ethnics to blacks was responsible for blocking the city's progress. It was true that many white ethnics were hostile to the presence of blacks, both in the work place and in their neighborhoods, but, as some of their leaders pointed out, they were not responsible for the equally overt forms of discrimination that prevented minorities from getting jobs or buying homes in eastern suburbs that were dominated by the white establishment.[18]

Another cause of increased racial tensions was the worsening economic situation in the 1960s. When Celebrezze became mayor in 1953, the Korean War had just ended. The war had brought enormous economic benefits to Greater Cleveland and, as historian David Van Tassel notes, "had delayed the city's decline as an industrial and population center."[19]

By 1960 Cleveland began to suffer from a hemorrhaging of its population. At first it was only a small flow, totaling a little less than 39,000 between 1950 and 1960; but in the next two decades people flooded out of the central city to the outer rings of new suburbs. By 1980 over one-third of the largely white middle-class and blue-collar workers of native and foreign stock had fled, and with their departure went a substantial portion of the city's tax base. In the words of Harry Fagan, a former director of the city's Catholic Commission on Community Action, "the city became increasingly brown, black and broke." In the early 1950s Mayor Celebrezze and the city council, aware that the city could no longer carry the mounting welfare costs, persuaded the county commissioners to take over this responsibility, as well as that for the city hospital and the reform schools for boys and girls. Years later Celebrezze told Mayor Carl B. Stokes that in nine and one-half years he had been unable to get a tax passed. "If they want to cut back on services, go ahead and cut back," he advised Stokes.[20]

With the departure of the middle class came the decline of central city retailing and the building of suburban shopping malls that soon ringed the county. The downtown Playhouse Square area around 14th Street and Euclid Avenue suffered the loss of upscale stores, and four of its five theaters ceased operations. The two major department stores in the area also closed, and only Higbee's and the May Company, of the department stores located on Playhouse Square, survived into the 1980s. Thousands of former Clevelanders simply stopped coming downtown to shop, preferring the convenience and comfort of the enclosed malls with their free parking lots to the hazards of what they now perceived to be a crime-ridden city filled with purse snatchers, car thieves, and muggers. After 6 P.M. and on the weekend, the downtown area was practically deserted, except for black customers on Saturdays. A sign of the change was the 1964 decision of the Cleveland City Club to shift its famous free speech forum to Friday after fifty-three years of Saturday meetings because members no longer came downtown on Saturday.[21]

Not only residents were leaving the central city. New car dealers, skilled service workers, and doctors and dentists left also. On the east side, running along Euclid and Carnegie Avenues between 101st and 105th Streets, were several large office buildings where dentists, and doctors attached to nearby hospitals, had their private practice offices. These professionals now began to move out to the suburbs where their patients lived and, with their departure, thousands of square feet of office space lay empty. That section of Euclid Avenue, once a thriving shopping district, soon turned into an eyesore of boarded-up stores and cheap bars. Indeed, all of Euclid Avenue, once proudly dubbed "Millionaires Row," now was more noted for its shabby used-car lots than for the magnificent mansions of yesteryear.

During the late 1950s it was becoming evident that the city's policy of "coasting along, and . . . not doing anything very big at first, but maintaining municipal services while keeping expenses down" had been disastrous for Cleveland. Increasingly, City Hall and civic leadership rested their hope of turning the city around on the urban renewal plans put forward by the City Planning Commission under the leadership of its chairman and public housing pioneer, Ernest J. Bohn, and Planning Director James M. Lister. Yet, in reality, Lister and his staff gave little more than lip service to the neighborhood areas that were scheduled for urban renewal, for all their energy was being concentrated on the downtown project called Erieview. Composed of 163 acres, Erieview was a mixture of modest homes, hotels, apartment buildings, a few factories, some older office buildings, several fine restaurants, and lots of cheap bars.[22]

The Cleveland Development Foundation asked a leading architect, I. M Pei, to design a plan for the area. Pei told the city fathers that his approach would be "bold, aesthetic and realistic." A steady drum beat of civic boosters, from the mayor to the editor of the the the *Cleveland Press,* seized upon the plan as the one means to rejuvenate downtown and ultimately lead to other improvements across the city. A contemporary documentary film narrated by television newscaster Chet Huntley, entitled *Cleveland: A City on Schedule,* portrayed a community on the way to recovery. It showed the business and political leadership working with neighborhood people on plans to rehabilitate their homes and bulldoze those slums no longer fit for human habitation. The film ended with an artist's rendering of the finished Erieview project as Huntley predicted that by 1980 a slum-free Cleveland would be restored to its former greatness as one of America's leading cities.[23]

Despite contemporary criticism of Erieview, twenty years later City Planning Director Hunter Morrison would assert that the plan had permitted the city to put together one of the "most attractive ensembles of new buildings of any city in postwar America." Ninth Street shabbiness gave way to substantial bank and office buildings which ran from Euclid to Lakeside; and further east, Park Center, a twenty-story apartment building complete with its own enclosed shopping mall, went up along with a high rise for senior citizens. New buildings would continue to be added in the 1980s, but not all would conform to the original plan.[24]

But many people, particularly those in the neighborhoods, felt at the time that too many of the city's resources and too much administrative attention were being concentrated on this downtown project to the neglect of neighborhoods. In fact, the city planners did believe that many neighborhoods were slums that were best torn down altogether. In the University-Euclid urban renewal area the city administration adopted a deliberate policy of not enforcing housing codes and neglecting public services in order to encourage residents to leave and to drive down property costs for eventual land purchase by the city's department of urban renewal. In 1962 the U.S. Public Health Service did a study of rat and associated refuse problems in the city. In a 10 percent sample of all the city blocks, they found that 7,000 of the 25,000 premises inspected had rat infestation, and 14,000 had refuse storage deficiencies. The surveyors discovered that many residents were simply throwing garbage into their back yards. A follow-up survey in the early part of 1966 revealed that these conditions had worsened.[25]

Nevertheless, only 15 percent of the households in urban renewal areas were given relocation assistance by the city's Division of Slum Clearance. While dislocated whites were able to find housing all over the city and in the suburbs, the majority of blacks moved into adjacent areas that were already crowded. Although Cleveland had pioneered in public housing and its city council had passed an ordinance prohibiting discrimination in public housing in 1949, it never had (and still does not have) sufficient units to house all its applicants, especially those with large families. Despite the antidiscrimination law, the Cleveland Metropolitan Housing Authority continued to be blatantly discriminatory. In the 1960s, although blacks were now 47 percent of all public housing tenants, 83 percent of them were concentrated in three east side housing estates, while 99 percent of the white tenants lived in predominantly white estates across the Cuyahoga River. This pattern of segregation reflected the city as a whole. In 1965 it was estimated that 90 percent of the black community would have to be relocated in order to achieve integration in housing, and that percentage would remain the same in the 1980s.[26]

When Law Director Ralph S. Locher became mayor in 1963, following President John Kennedy's appointment of Celebrezze as Secretary of Health, Education, and Welfare, he faced an increasingly militant black population. They were angry about discrimination in jobs, segregation in schools and housing, and what blacks referred to as "negro removal." White residents on the west side were also unhappy about the damage to their neighborhoods produced by urban renewal and freeway programs. The beginning of the revolt against urban renewal and new freeways was evident in the early 1960s. A plan to demolish much of the area between West 25th and West 58th Streets was killed when the voters turned down an $8 million urban renewal bond proposal. The destruction of thousands of homes in the east side black neighborhoods and the failure to provide sufficient new homes increased tension as blacks spilled over into former white ethnic neighborhoods.[27]

The postwar period brought an end to white male domination of city council. The enlarged black population and its shift into new areas led to an increased presence on the city council. In 1945 blacks had only two representatives out of the thirty-three on the city council, and these were staunchly Republican; by 1980 blacks had increased their representation to fourteen, and there were no longer any Republicans, black or white. In 1945 there were no women on the council; by 1980 there were five, two of whom were black. In 1982 a charter amendment reduced the size of the council to twenty-one members, and the redistricting that followed resulted in a council of ten white men, one white woman, eight black men and two black women. All the blacks came from the east side wards. The white members of the council reflected the ethnic make-up of the city, with eastern and southern Europeans enjoying a large representation. There had been three Jewish members in 1945; by 1960 blacks had replaced them.[28]

Since the late 1920s the white ethnic vote has been a major factor in the political life of the city. Ethnics elected Lausche in 1941 and sustained him and his successors until the mid-1960s; but by the late 1950s their power had begun to diminish with the shift of population to the suburbs. By 1960 blacks were almost 35 percent of the city's population, making them the largest potential bloc of voters in Cleveland.[29]

Described as a "militant, principled councilman," Leo Jackson typified the changing face of black leadership. In 1957 he had won election to represent Glenville, a middle-class area which was now over 90 percent black. As urban renewal and slum clearance greatly reduced housing opportunities elsewhere in the city, Glenville began to experience the changes that had made Hough into a festering slum. Jackson, who had been active in fighting the deterioration in the Glenville

Community Council, had used city council meetings to angrily demand that the city administration tackle the rising crime rates, enforce the housing code, and provide adequate recreational facilities. But his jeremiads had been to little avail, for the police ignored Jackson's demands that black-on-black crime be halted by the arrest of black criminals, and the city did little either to enforce housing codes or to improve other city services.[30]

By the late 1950s, however, Jackson and other new black leaders were able to demonstrate the growing power of their bloc vote. In 1959 a proposal to create a metropolitan form of government was defeated. Jackson pointed out that there were no black representatives on the commission that had studied the question of metropolitan government, and the make-up of the proposed nineteen-person assembly had been weighted in favor of the suburbs. He called for its defeat because city residents, especially blacks, would lose control of their own destiny. The vote against metropolitan government was heavy in the black wards, which for the first time turned down a countywide issue. (Since that vote, no serious effort to achieve a county or metropolitan form of government has been attempted.)[31]

Blacks were increasingly angered by political racism. Their candidates for the school board always faced strong opposition in the west side wards. When the budget was cut after an operating levy failed in 1962, it was the blacks on poor relief who suffered because "to cut elsewhere would mean a loss of city jobs and bring opposition from all the councilmen. To cut the welfare budget brings only opposition from the Negro councilmen, who are not very vocal in any case."[32]

Such discrimination stimulated a rising tide of black involvement. Some took heart from the civil rights movement in the South, but most acted out of resentment at the city's failure to address the problems faced by its growing number of black citizens and their children. Despite the continual support that black voters had given to the Democratic party at local, state, and national levels, they were not sharing in the rewards. Not until 1962 were blacks appointed to cabinet positions in the city government. Although the Republican party had backed successful black candidates for both the state house and senate, the Democrats had never supported one until 1962, when Carl B. Stokes won election as a state representative.[33]

It was to be the school system that would spark Cleveland's most serious confrontation in the early 1960s. While there had long been community-wide concern about the deficiencies in the educational system, blacks had additional grievances. There were few black educators in leadership positions; teachers and students in the west side schools were nearly all white; and many black students were discouraged from taking courses that would prepare them for either skilled jobs or college. Not only were many black children attending school on a half-day basis, but the schools that were being built to relieve overcrowding were being located so as to perpetuate the existing pattern of segregation. In 1964 the racial turmoil and the racial attitude of the white-dominated school board and its president caused the resignation of the superintendent of the Cleveland public schools and the appointment of an outsider to that key position.[34]

The newcomer, Paul Briggs, had headed up the neighboring suburban Parma school system. Known for his forceful personality and strong leadership qualities, he quickly put his stamp on the school system. Briggs began by building badly needed facilities, and during his fourteen-year tenure the system added forty-three new schools. Briggs controlled the school board and was a master at getting support from the business community. He pleased the black establishment by promoting many blacks to administrative positions and by hiring minority-owned firms to design and build his new schools; but at the U.S. Civil Rights Commission hearings held in Cleveland in 1966 Briggs stated that there was nothing the school administration could do about school segregation that was the result of segregated housing patterns.[35]

In 1973 the NAACP filed a lawsuit claiming that segregation, both de facto and de jure, prevented black children from securing a quality education. Although Briggs and Arnold Pinkney, the black president of the school board, both denied that there was a deliberate policy of segregation, in 1977 Federal Judge Frank Battisti found the school system and the State Board of Education guilty of both forms of segregation and ordered remedial busing the next year.[36]

While Briggs correctly predicted that busing would cause white flight, it also caused many middle-class blacks to send their children to parochial schools or to move to the suburbs. Briggs resigned in 1978 when the voters rejected a school levy by a 2-to-1 margin. Perhaps the only bright spot in the educational system was that when busing did come, it came in a peaceful manner. Community leaders, neighborhood groups, and clergymen of all faiths were determined that no matter how they felt about busing, they did not want to see such violence as that which had occurred in Boston.[37]

During the first decade of remedial busing, the number of dropouts increased; the quality of public education declined; and chaos seemed to reign. There were frequent lengthy school strikes and constant mechanical failure of buses. Superintendents and court-appointed deputy superintendents came and went. One of the superintendents committed suicide in a school building, and another was forced to resign for incompetency. School board members were more noted for their quarrels with each other than for their concern for the quality of education. To add to the disarray one young president of the school board was ticketed for "mooning" on an interstate highway. Needless to say, the education of Cleveland's children suffered.[38]

While the mid-1960s had started out with promise for the school system, the opposite was true for the Locher administration. Ralph S. Locher, who had been born in Rumania of Swiss-Austrian parents, won easily in the special election of 1962. He was "one of the most honorable, well-meaning, personally amiable persons to hold the office of [mayor,]" but his administration was plagued by problems that neither he nor any of his appointees were able to solve. Although not himself a man of prejudice, he was unable to provide the crucial leadership so badly needed to calm the rising tide of racial friction that began with a clash between black and white youth at Sowinski Park in 1963 and ended with the Hough Riot. Mayor Locher's police chief, Richard Wagner, was convinced that black militants were training young blacks to attack policemen, and he angered blacks when he testified in favor of retaining the death penalty on the grounds that it was a necessary deterrent against black militants. Although Locher had appointed two blacks to cabinet positions and promoted others already in city jobs, he was never able to establish a good relationship with the black community.[39]

Locher inherited the failing neighborhood urban renewal programs of Celebrezze and was unsuccessful in forging new plans. When James Lister resigned as urban renewal director, the position was left vacant for months and finally filled by a man with no experience in city government or urban planning. The situation degenerated to the point that the Federal Department of Housing and Urban Renewal blocked funds until the city came up with a workable plan. Cleveland's financial position had deteriorated with the loss of more than 100,000 residents since 1950 and the removal of vast tracts of real estate from the tax rolls as a result of urban renewal and the building of tax-exempt institutions.[40]

Clearly, new monies were needed to operate the city and to improve its aging infrastructure, but Locher, faithful to the tradition of his predecessors, was opposed to raising taxes. Increasingly the business community became convinced that the Locher administration was incapable of providing the leadership needed to resolve the city's problems. Oblivious to the fact that he had alienated the majority of the black community by his support of the school building program and the arrest of the black ministers who had staged a sit-in in his office, Locher was convinced that he was doing a good job. When he was offered a federal judgeship as one way of gracefully removing himself from office, he refused, intent on vindicating himself in the election of 1965.[41]

Locher did win another term in 1965, but it could hardly be termed a great victory. His opponent was State Representative Carl B. Stokes, who was then serving his second term. He was an intelligent, attractive man who had quickly made a name for himself in the state capital by securing passage of a fair housing bill and by battling for stricter gun control. In order to avoid the Democratic primary, Stokes had run as an independent, choosing instead to face Locher and Republican Ralph Perk in the general election. The young candidate succeeded in pulling together a group of prominent black businessmen, black professionals, and white liberals who raised sufficient money to mount a major campaign. But their biggest asset was Stokes's ability on the campaign trail. West side whites were surprised to meet a well-dressed, charming, articulate black man. Early in the campaign Stokes challenged Perk's assertion that the city could meet its needs if it simply were run efficiently. Perk, who was the county auditor and a former councilman, accepted a City Club invitation to debate city finances with Stokes. Before a packed audience Stokes demonstrated a mastery of city finances and made his opponent look foolish. Although he lost the election and a subsequent recount, the narrow margin of Locher's victory and Stokes's brilliant campaigning marked him as a certain challenger in 1967.[42]

In the aftermath of the election, business leaders persuaded Locher to establish a "Little Hoover Commission" that would analyze the entire operation of the city. The resulting studies, although written in the bland language of consultants, were devastating commentaries on the administration of government in Cleveland. Locher accepted their recommendations, including one that the city seek a municipal income tax, which was subsequently approved by the voters. While Locher had tried to head off rising social tensions by appointing two blacks to his cabinet and utilizing the new tax money to expand services and facilities, these measures proved to be too little and too late.[43]

In the summer of 1966, a minor incident in Hough erupted into a major riot that shocked a complacent community and caused the business and civic leadership to look to Stokes to replace Locher and pacify the black community. The local newspapers made the Locher administration the scapegoat for all the city's problems. National newspapers portrayed Cleveland as a deeply troubled city and predicted more violence in the summer of 1967. But the ghettoes did not erupt. Blacks now had a charismatic leader and hope for the future.[44]

That year saw the end of the Lausche dynasty that had governed the city for twenty-five years. Stokes, with the financial support of the business community, the organizational skills of middle-class white liberals, and the newly aroused voting power of the black masses, overwhelmed Locher in the Democratic primary and went on to defeat the Republican candidate, Seth Taft, by a vote of 129,396 to 127,717. As the *New York Times* put it, Stokes, the great-grandson of a slave, defeated the great-grandson of a president to become the first black mayor of a major American city. Although the victory was a great personal triumph for Stokes, it had been made possible by a massive voter registration drive organized by a coalition of black and white ministers and civil rights groups. The Congress of Racial Equality received $175,000 from the Ford Foundation for the purpose of registering voters, while the Southern Christian Leadership Conference claimed to have spent $500,000 on its registration drive, a claim Stokes disputed. In any case, Stokes received more than 96 percent of the black vote and secured 19.3 percent of the white vote.[45]

The impact of his victory was immediate. The business leadership basked in the favorable publicity that the city received across the country, and the black community was in a state of exultation. But many whites were apprehensive about what they saw as a black takeover of city hall. To assuage their apprehensions, Stokes appointed an old friend and former policeman, Joseph McManamon, to the position of public safety director and another Irish-American to the key position of police chief. The stereotypical tough Irish cop, Chief Michael Blackwell had an excellent street reputation but was not the man to reform a department that the Little Hoover report of 1966 said was a shambles. The new mayor was never effectively able to control or reform the operation of the police, and after the Glenville shootout in 1968 Stokes and the department were completely alienated.[46]

But Stokes did open the doors of opportunity for black workers and middle-class professionals, both in and outside of city hall. He appointed black men and women to key administrative positions and many black professionals and businessmen were awarded city contracts. The new mayor secured the removal of Director Ernest J. Bohn of the public housing authority and replaced him with a man who was determined to end the racial discrimination that had existed for years under the old regime. Stokes utilized his political power to force banks and other companies doing business with the city to hire black employees.[47]

The mayor's most dramatic moment came in the aftermath of the assassination of Martin Luther King, Jr. While cities across the nation went up in flames, Cleveland did not. Stokes's presence in the streets of the ghetto that evening calmed an angry black community. He took advantage of the crisis to organize the "Cleveland Now" program that would subsequently raise money for housing and other social projects for the poor. Working closely with both the business leadership and the media, Stokes proposed to secure over $11 million from the business community and private individuals to leverage additional funds from government and foundations. He was to write in his autobiography that "the response was fantastic"; and, in a short time, over $5.5 million was raised. As new projects were announced, Clevelanders felt a new pride in their city. But Cleveland's feeling of euphoria vanished in the aftermath of an incident that would become known as the Glenville shootout.[48]

A grant from "Cleveland Now" funds had been given to a black nationalist named Fred Ahmed Evans who had organized a group of young blacks, ostensibly to create summer employment for ghetto youth. It was later revealed that they had used some of the money to buy weapons. On July 23, 1968, a shootout took place between the followers of Evans and members of the Cleveland Police Department who were conducting a surveillance of the group. When it ended, with the surrender of Evans, three white policemen and four black men, three of whom were allegedly involved in the gun battle, were dead; and fifteen men were wounded, including twelve policemen.[49]

Stokes later would write that "Glenville killed much of [his] public support and gave the non-supporters a chance to come out of the woodwork." He was right. The president of the city council, James V. Stanton, a tough minded Irish-American from the west side who had seized control of the council from Jack Russell in 1963, attacked the mayor, particularly over Stokes's withdrawal of white law enforcement officers and the National Guard from the Glenville area. Black policemen and prominent black citizens had patrolled the neighborhood and succeeded in ending the killing—but not the bitterness of the white police officers. That anger was evident the night of the shootout as the police radio bristled with racial epithets applied to the mayor. Stanton, who had close ties to the police department, was subsequently to turn every piece of legislation that Stokes proposed into a battle. They tangled viciously over the housing authority's plans to build more public housing on the west side, to open up the existing estates to all minorities, and to develop scattered site housing. The result was a remorseless executive/legislative deadlock.[50]

In November 1969 Stokes defeated Ralph J. Perk by 3,451 votes to win a second term which would be marked by further conflict with Stanton. The mayor pulled the eight black councilmen out of the Democratic caucus, thus releasing them from the unit rule. If Stokes vetoed a council measure, such as a zoning change designed to block public housing in a white ward, Stanton could not muster the two-thirds vote needed to override the veto. In this environment accomplishments were few, but Stokes did secure passage of an Equal Employment Opportunity Ordinance by bargaining over a zoning change for which Stanton needed the mayor's approval.[51]

The Stokes-Stanton struggle spilled over into the Democratic party in 1970 when the county organization rejected a Stokes's ally for the position of vice chairman and, instead, offered the position to a black physician who had broken with the mayor. Earlier that year Stokes had organized the primarily black Twenty-first District Caucus, named after the congressional district that his brother, Louis, had been elected to represent in the U.S. Congress. When the Democratic party met in May, the Caucus called a meeting of all elected black officials at the same time to announce their independence of the party organization. While Stokes remained mayor with patronage to hand out, the Caucus was an effective instrument of black power. But once he left the city in 1972 to become a television broadcaster in New York, it was riddled by dissension. Although the Caucus still exists, it no longer has the power it once exercised.[52]

Stokes declined to run for a third term because, he said, there was no money to do the job of rebuilding the city. He had tried to get a tax increase in 1970, but it was quickly labeled a "Stokes" tax. A young first term councilman named Dennis J. Kucinich, who had secured a popular following among ethnics by his constant attacks on the Stokes administration, played a major role in its defeat. When the accounting firm of Price Waterhouse supported Stokes's contention that the city did need additional revenues to avoid cuts in services, the council put another tax issue on the ballot. But it, too, lost.[53]

In the final analysis, Stokes's greatest accomplishment was to have given hope and jobs to black people. In 1958 a columnist writing in the English newspaper *The Observer* remarked on the death of Boston Mayor James Michael Curley that American blacks had, in cities across the land, the need for a dozen Curleys. In Cleveland, at least, Carl B. Stokes fulfilled that need.[54]

Upon Stokes's announcement of his decision to retire, Ralph Perk, who over the past few years had emerged as the champion of the white ethnics, immediately announced his candidacy. He was an easy winner over a fellow ethnic, State Representative George V. Voinovich, in the Republican primary. Arnold Pinkney, president of the school board, decided to run as an independent Democrat, thus skipping that party's primary. Stokes, while pledging his support for Pinkney, announced that in the Democratic primary he would support James M. Carney, a wealthy developer and long-time party financial backer, over both Council President Anthony Garofoli and his former police chief, Patrick L. Garity. With Stokes's assistance and a well-financed campaign, Carney secured the Democratic nomination. It was a moment of triumph for Stokes, for not only had his call to defeat Garofoli, whom he labeled a racist, been successful, but also he had eliminated several black councilmen who had opposed his scattered site program for public housing.[55]

But Stokes's primary maneuvers eventually gave Perk victory in the general election. Dennis Kucinich, who believed that a Carney victory would give the business interests complete control of the city, seized the opportunity to accuse Stokes of "willful manipulation" and announced the formation of "Democrats for Perk." Kucinich was only twenty-five years of age, but he had already mastered the art of public relations. The media, particularly television, found him good copy, for he was always ready with a brief devastating comment on the Stokes administration. Kucinich made Stokes the central focus of the Perk campaign and coined the slogan that a vote for Pinkney or Carney was a vote for Stokes. It was a racist appeal that worked. Perk got 38.8 percent of the vote to 37.7 percent for Pinkney and 28.7 percent for Carney. Twenty percent of the blacks who gave their votes to Carney did so, according to Stokes, because they were resentful of Pinkney's support of the Cleveland public schools' segregation policies.[56]

Ralph Perk became the first Republican mayor of this predominantly Democratic city in over three decades. It was a city that was bitterly divided along racial lines. The fears and anger that followed the Glenville shootout had been exacerbated by sharp conflicts between Stokes and the white city council members during his second term. The 1971 election reflected the bitterness of the times and, when it was over, whites were jubilant and many blacks were in despair. But Perk was not a racist, and there was no massive firing of the black employees hired under Stokes. In 1972 George Forbes, a shrewd and politically sophisticated black councilman, was elected president of the city council. While many Democratic council members took the position that they should do battle with the new mayor, Forbes began to work in close cooperation with the administration. Perk, in turn, helped to ease the racial tensions by lowering the tone of rhetoric and appearing at black events.[57]

Immediately upon entering office, Perk claimed that he had inherited from the Stokes administration a $27 million deficit, but the actual figure was $12.5 million. He brought in a number of belt-tightening measures, including a 10 percent pay cut, and later secured authority from the state assembly that would permit the city to issue $9.6 million in bonds to restore the pay cuts. Still, Perk was able to avoid confronting the basic fiscal problems. He sold the city-owned transit and sewer systems to newly organized regional authorities, and the city also received a massive infusion of federal revenue-sharing money in 1972. As one of the few big-city Republican mayors and a leader of ethnic Americans in a presidential election year, Perk was singled out by the Nixon administration for special attention. These monies, plus the practices of "rolling over" short-term notes and borrowing from restricted city accounts, only postponed the inevitable financial crisis.[58]

While serious students of the city's financial situation predicted that the city would be bankrupt before the end of the decade, others in the business community were content to ignore the problem. They had developed a close working relationship with both the mayor and the council president over many issues, including tax abatement, which was seen as a tool for encouraging development in the central business district.[59]

Perk's relationship with the financial establishment rankled Kucinich and soon ended their political misalliance. But Perk no longer needed the feisty young Democrat. His capture of city hall had stirred the pride of many of the sixty ethnic groups living in the Cleveland area. To please his Catholic constituents Mayor Perk banned *Playboy* from the city's airport and required the garbage collectors to distribute a pornography poll. Such antics, as well as accidental fires (in his hair at a ribbon-cutting ceremony and on an oil slick on the Cuyahoga River), sometimes made Cleveland the butt of national jokes but did not damage Perk's reputation with the voters.

Perk was easily reelected in 1973 and two years later won again, this time over Arnold Pinkney by a 10 percent margin. But time was beginning to run out for the mayor. People, industry, and businesses were leaving the city for suburbia and the Sunbelt. The population dropped from an estimated 810,857 in 1965 to 573,822 in 1980. Perk's image as the efficient administrator faded when it was discovered that $9 million of Model City money was frittered away with nothing to show for it except scandals. Neighborhood resentment at municipal neglect of services reached a symbolic peak when a group from Perk's own ward, called "Citizens to Bring Back Broadway," dumped garbage in front of the mayor's office in protest.[60]

In 1977 when Perk opened his reelection campaign by holding a $100-a-plate dinner, one of his opponents organized a ninety-nine cent kielbasa meal for representatives of neighborhood organizations. Former councilman Dennis Kucinich, now clerk of the Municipal Court, entered the race as an independent Democrat, and State Representative Edward F. Feighan carried the banner of the Democratic Party. It was the first campaign in several years built on substantive issues instead of race. Various neighborhood associations demanded in Saul Alinsky fashion that the candidates state where they stood on the issues of crime prevention, housing deterioration, dog catchers, and clogged catch basins. In addition to this nuts-and-bolts approach to municipal problems, tax abatement became a major issue, with Perk on the defensive for having granted tax abatements to two major downtown developments. Perk lost in the nonpartisan primary, and the battle became a contest between the populist Kucinich and the more moderate liberal Feighan. The latter received the blessing of the establishment as well as the support of powerful black ministers, but to the surprise and anger of many in the establishment, the *Plain Dealer* strongly endorsed its former copyboy, Kucinich. It was this endorsement and Kucinich's vigorous campaigning on a platform geared to neighborhood needs that gave him a 3,402 vote majority over his opponent (93,476 to 90,074). Most surprising was the fact that Kucinich, who had made a reputation with his attacks on the Stokes administration, received 35 percent of the votes in the black wards.[61]

The new mayor, who was of Croatian-Irish ancestry, was only thirty-one, and many of his cabinet members and staff were even younger. They were bright, aggressive, and totally inexperienced in government. Like the mayor, the cabinet members and the staff had attitudes ranging from suspicion to outright hostility toward the business community. When a number of civic leaders asked to meet with the new mayor to discuss possible areas of cooperation, Kucinich would only meet with them secretly in a hotel's private dining room, and one participant observed the mayor's police bodyguard tasting his lunch in the corridor before bringing it to him.[62]

Kucinich, who had received a Master's degree in communication, effectively used the media, and they, in turn, used him. For example, when the Growth Association (the former Chamber of Commerce) asked to see him to discuss areas of cooperation, he arranged for a breakfast meeting at his favorite eating place, Tony's

Diner, where the media had a field day covering this populist David humiliating the Goliath of the business community. But when the media began reporting on petty acts of vindictiveness perpetrated by leading members of the Kucinich administration, the honeymoon with Kucinich ended. The press revealed acts such as the midnight search of one employee's office because he was suspected of disloyalty. On another occasion Kucinich's chief adviser, Robert Weissman, who had a well-deserved reputation for his abrasive, confrontational style, unplugged a radio reporter's telephone during a press conference because he did not like his questions. And following a heated council meeting Assistant Safety Director Tonia Grdina approached George Forbes and blurted, "I hope you rot in jail." Forbes, who was under indictment at the time, did not respond but certainly was not pleased with the comment.[63]

When Kucinich appointed Richard Hongisto, a progressive sheriff from San Francisco, as police chief he was highly praised for appointing such a creative individual. The new chief quickly became popular with both the police and ordinary citizens—but not with the twenty-one-year-old Grdina. Their public disagreements and Hongisto's subsequent charge that the administration was guilty of acts of unethical conduct led Kucinich to fire his popular police chief on prime-time television.[64]

While this incident precipitated the recall movement in the spring of 1978, Kucinich's public support had been eroding for some time. The police union, which had close ties to the council, tangled with the administration over labor negotiations shortly after Kucinich became mayor. When the police subsequently were stricken with the "blue flu," Kucinich called them "crybabies." Attempts by the administration to control and manipulate neighborhood groups caused further friction. By late summer the recall movement had secured more than 60,000 signatures to place the issue of recalling the mayor on the ballot, and once again there was national and international coverage of Cleveland's "boy mayor." In an extraordinary Sunday election on August 8, 1978, the recall failed by only 236 votes out of the 120,000 votes cast.[65]

Undaunted, Kucinich claimed that he had received a fresh mandate from the people and absolutely refused to change his course of action. His repeated confrontations with the council and its president, George Forbes, resulted in an executive/legislative deadlock that alarmed the business community.

The conflict came to a head in the fall of 1978 when Cleveland went into default because the city's principal banks refused to roll over the municipal loans that had come due. At the core of the crisis was the political struggle over city ownership of the Municipal Light Plant, which Kucinich had championed even before he became mayor. The business community, as well as the Cleveland Electric Illuminating Company (CEI), saw the city's financial emergency as an opportunity to eliminate the competition provided by municipally owned power. For decades CEI had been an aggressive opponent of this legacy of the Progressive Era, but the company met its match in the young mayor who immediately ordered a "Power to the People" slogan placed in a prominent position on the Municipal Light Plant.[66]

Since the 1960s, Muny Light, as it is popularly known, had been in deep financial trouble. Its plant was outworn and the entire system suffered from rigid union work rules, frequent outages, and aggressive marketing competition from CEI. In 1965 candidate Stokes proposed its sale. None of the black wards were serviced by Muny, and the proposal pleased the business leadership; but, when Stokes became mayor two years later, he could not secure sufficient votes in the council to sell the operation. The plant's condition further deteriorated under the Perk administration, and it was increasingly dependent upon purchase of power from CEI.[67]

By 1975 Muny Light owed CEI over $16 million, and because the utility did not have the money to settle the debt, Perk and Forbes now proposed its sale. In the midst of the ensuing controversy, Kucinich organized a "Save Muny Light" committee which secured sufficient signatures to put the matter before the electorate. In the meantime, he was elected mayor and sought to take advantage of a recent Nuclear Regulatory Commission's ruling requiring that CEI "wheel" cheaper power from the Power Authority of the State of New York for use by the Municipal plant. For its part CEI, determined to collect the monies owed it, persuaded a federal court to issue liens on city property and to assess fines of $5,000 per day until the debt was paid. Blocked by the courts from issuing bonds to settle Muny's debt, which now amounted to $18 million, Kucinich began paying CEI with money from the city's operating funds.[68]

In December 1978 a federal judge ordered the city to pay the remaining $5.7 million or he would throw out a still-pending $330 million city antitrust suit that Perk had filed against CEI in 1975. Rather than face the loss of a suit he felt sure of winning, Kucinich had strained to keep up the payments; but, by this point, he had so depleted the city treasury to pay off the debt that there was no money to cover other short-term loans that were due on December 14, 1978. To head off the looming crisis, he met with the chief executive officers of the six banks that held the notes and asked them to postpone action until he could hold a special election to increase the city income tax, but M. Brock Weir of Cleveland Trust refused to accept his proposal. In a last effort to save the city from default, a few businessmen attempted to negotiate a solution, but, in the end, the entrenched hostility on both sides prevented any compromise.[69]

And so Cleveland became the first major city in America to default since the Great Depression. The refusal of the banks to roll over these notes was, in the last analysis, an exercise in political power on the part of the business establishment that had its roots in their historic hostility to public power as well as their apprehension about the policies and attitudes of the Kucinich administration. The banks had rolled over notes for preceding administrations. The difference was that those mayors had not engaged in the kind of contemptuous rhetoric that characterized the Kucinich administration. The mayor and his chief advisors also underestimated Brock Weir, who had been a paratrooper in the Normandy invasion and was not a man to be intimidated by confrontation politics.[70]

In the end Kucinich saved Muny Light, but not his mayoralty. To solve the financial crisis, the council placed two issues on a special election ballot—one to authorize the plant's sale and another to increase the city income tax by 50 percent. Kucinich organized a grass-roots campaign to prevent the sale and to pass the tax increase. Council members whose wards were not served by Muny Light campaigned for selling, as did the Citizens League and the business community, but the mayor and the business leaders worked together in an uneasy alliance to secure passage of the much needed tax increase. The voters turned down the sale of Muny Light, voting for the tax increase instead. But despite his vindication at the polls in this special issue election in the spring of 1979, Kucinich, after serving only one term, was defeated in November by Republican Lieutenant Governor George V. Voinovich.[71]

In his previous races, Kucinich had been able to count on a core vote (25–30 percent) of what might have been termed the angry urbanites (blacks and whites) resentful over their social and economic plight and distrustful of most politicians, whom they perceived as corrupt. Kucinich was an articulate spokesperson for many of those who were excluded, by class or race, from full participation in the American dream. In the election of 1977 Kucinich had won because his promise to save Muny Light and his commitment to serve the neighborhoods rather than the downtown interests attracted a broader range of voters. However, the special recall election demonstrated that he had lost a considerable number of those voters. What saved him then was the widespread attitude that the mayor deserved to be given an opportunity to serve out his full two-year term rather than be cut off after less than ten months in office. But his support was further eroded in the months following the recall effort by a heightened level of confrontational politics, further heavy-handed authoritarianism in the neighborhoods, and the financial crisis of the city. Meanwhile, as Kucinich's support fell, business and civic leaders tried to draft George Voinovich to run for mayor. Despite the fact that he was a Republican in a heavily Democratic city, Voinovich seemed an ideal candidate. Like the politically successful Frank Lausche, he was of Slovenian heritage, and, in his previous races for state representative, county auditor, and county commissioner, Voinovich had proved himself a strong candidate able to get votes across a wide spectrum of the electorate. His conservative financial views were appealing both to the business community and to many of his fellow ethnics.

Voinovich was once again to prove himself a strong campaigner. He took the Municipal Light issue away from Kucinich by opening his campaign in front of the plant to which he pledged his commitment. That question disposed of, Voinovich argued that the time had come to end confrontation politics, which was hurting a city already reeling from the loss of industrial jobs. The issue of ending confrontation was convenient for a Republican in a heavily Democratic city. Voinovich emphasized the need to forget partisan politics and work together. All his literature and placards contained the message "Together We Can Do It," in pointed contrast to Kucinich's slogan, "One Man Can Make a Difference."[72]

Kucinich campaigned in his usual manner as the champion of the "little people" and as one who had saved Muny Light and blocked the tax abatement giveaways. He pictured his opponent as the friend of "fat cat businessmen." Kucinich also produced leaflets that were frankly racist in nature. Those designed for the west side's predominantly white wards carried pictures of Pinkney and Forbes supporting Voinovich. The message presented to the heavily black wards on the east side, on the other hand, featured pictures of Forbes and former Mayor Stokes with quotations from them denouncing Voinovich as a racist. These tactics disillusioned some of Kucinich's idealistic supporters, and several members of his administration refused to distribute the literature. Roldo Bartimole, editor of the city's radical newsletter *Point of View,* commented after the election: "For one who has supported many of Kucinich's actions regarding the business community, his defeat was welcome because a win would have been a victory for racism, fear and mistreatment of people, including his own supporters."[73]

Kucinich, sure that the white ethnics were with him, concentrated on winning the black vote. In a move that surprised many, given their past relationship, Carl B. Stokes returned to the city to escort Kucinich around the black community. There was speculation that Stokes, who was leaving his New York television job, saw a chance to become the city's most influential black politician once again if he turned out a massive black vote for the mayor. Kucinich's plans for a hard-hitting attack on Voinovich in the last few weeks before the election had to be abandoned when Voinovich's young daughter was killed by a hit-and-run driver, and a tremendous wave of sympathy went out to his family.[74]

The election results showed that Kucinich's strategy in the black wards had paid off, but he had lost white voters to Voinovich. In 1977 Kucinich got 60 percent of the vote in the white wards, but in 1979 his total had dropped to 43.3 percent. In 1977 he had won 35.2 percent of the black vote, a figure that increased to 44.5 percent in 1979; but the gain was not sufficient to overcome the defection of white ethnic voters. The new mayor received 56.2 percent of the total vote of 167,000.[75]

Before Voinovich agreed to run for mayor, he had secured a commitment from the business establishment that they would join in a public/private partnership for the city's recovery. One of the key actors in shaping and implementing that partnership was the Cleveland Foundation. It funded "critical pre-audits of the city's finances, analysis of urban taxation policies, management training for city officials and a three month-long examination of all city services."[76]

After the election Voinovich organized a group of loaned executives, called the Operations Improvement Task Force, to examine the operation of major city departments. The task force came in with 650 recommendations that were calculated to save the city $37 million immediately, with the promise of an additional $57 million in savings in the years ahead. Within two years 75 percent of the recommendations had been implemented. Improvements included such measures as more efficient accounting procedures, consolidation of operations, and centralization of record keeping and purchasing.

Meanwhile, expert accountants, after spending three months auditing the city's books, reported that the total municipal debt amounted to $111 million. But, despite the clear evidence of a financial crisis and the obvious need for more money to run the city, the citizens still voted down a Voinovich proposal to increase the existing 1.5 percent income tax to 2 percent. Three months later, in February 1981, a new tax proposal was placed on the ballot and passed after Voinovich guaranteed that half of the proceeds would be reserved for badly needed capital improvements.[77]

The new mayor's cooperative style of governance produced results. One year after he was elected, the city officially ended default when the banks agreed to refinance $36.2 million in short-term debts. In July 1983 Cleveland was able to reenter the national bond market. Over a number of years, Voinovich established such good working relationships with members of the city council and its president, George Forbes, that the media would complain about the boredom of covering city hall. As the image of Cleveland began to change, the national and even the international news media ran stories with headlines such as "Troubled City Turns Itself Round" and "Cleveland Comes Back."[78]

But beneath the headlines was the grim reality that Cleveland was still hemorrhaging from population losses. The number of city residents had slipped steadily downward from its peak of 914,808 in 1950 to an estimated 535,000 in 1986 and from the continued loss of manufacturing jobs that had been the economic backbone of the Greater Cleveland community for decades. One study indicated that this area had lost 262,000 jobs between 1978 and 1982, with a good proportion of these in the central city. By 1987 the job loss had been reduced by 75,828. According to Voinovich the city had 15.4 percent of its labor force out of work in 1984—twice the national average.[79]

Cleveland was also becoming a less attractive place in which to live as both black and white middle-class residents fled. To pollsters, these departing citizens identified three factors as having influenced their decisions to move to suburbia. These were schools, safety, and services. The falling quality of education was undoubtedly the most important reason. Desegregation had weakened the traditional bonds of the neighborhood even as it failed to achieve the goal of integration. For example, in 1987 JFK High School on the east side found itself with only 81 non-blacks out of 1800 pupils. The school system that had been one of the finest in the nation in the 1940s was rapidly declining, while school superintendents and board members engaged in acrimonious public battles.[80]

For those that remained, the environment was bleak. In the 1970s residents abandoned their city housing at the rate of three units per day, and, in time, boarded-up buildings or empty lots characterized whole sections of the east side. Equally depressing was the increase in the number of people who were living below the poverty level. By 1987 the Council of Economic Opportunities reported that the number of persons living in poverty in Cuyahoga County was 65 percent greater than in 1980. The study found a sharp increase as well in the number of families headed by single women; and the unemployment rate in the city was well above the national average.[81]

All of these problems were covered by the media in print and sound and living color. The evening television news concentrated upon crime and conflict in the central city; and whenever there were fires, which was often, the television cameras were there. As one scholar observed, the media spotlighted the conflicts of the city while suburban newspapers were writing about politics by consensus. The farther suburbanites lived from the city, the more reluctant they were to venture downtown.[82]

And yet, despite this depressing picture, there were hopeful signs that the public/private partnerships were taking hold. The wasteful years of the Perk mayoralty and the destructiveness of the Kucinich era had taught the business community that they had to make a major commitment of involvement to rebuild the city. Council President George Forbes, who in the eyes of many observers had emerged as the city's most powerful politician, worked closely with Voinovich and with business leaders in formulating plans for the city's recovery.

One example of this new spirit of involvement was the decision of two major corporations with plants and headquarters located near East 40th Street and Euclid Avenue to do something about the surrounding area, which was notorious for its crime, vice, and urban blight. Two corporate leaders, Morton Mandel and Tom Roulston, organized the Mid-Town Corridor, a private economic development corporation that works closely with the city in developing the fifty-block area, which contains over 500 large and small industrial plants and businesses, strategically located near major freeways and transportation centers. Within five years rampant street prostitution was eliminated, crime rates fell by 40 percent, major street improvements were made, and a hundred new businesses located in the area.[83]

Across the mouth of the Cuyahoga River on the near west side of Cleveland, another development, which had been stalled under the Kucinich administration, blossomed. The area called the Flats, the semi-derelict industrial center of Cleveland where John D. Rockefeller had built his first oil refinery, had always had a few bars and restaurants, but by the late 1980s there were over forty on both sides of the river that were drawing hundreds of people every week. The nearby Warehouse District, which had suffered major tenant losses in the postwar years, attracted the attention of preservationists when several outstanding century-old buildings were threatened with demolition. Soon, reformers moved to save a neighborhood and transform unused warehouses into residential lofts, offices, and attractive commercial establishments. In 1988 the city, after years of failing to capitalize on the lakefront, developed an inner harbor with facilities for recreational boating and other uses.[84]

Local foundations, especially the two major ones—the Cleveland and Gund foundations—provided funds for various regenerative programs. Lexington Village, 276 new town houses for mostly middle-class residents, built in the battle-scarred and largely abandoned Hough neighborhood, was a successful project of the Cleveland Foundation, working in conjunction with the Ford Foundation, city hall, and the local councilwoman, Fannie Lewis, a former welfare mother. In nearby Glenville the construction of forty-six new homes came about because of the city's policy of giving low-interest loans and tax abatement for residences built in the city. The Cleveland Foundation, in cooperation with the Greater Cleveland Roundtable, an organization of civic leaders, gave priority to measures to improve the Cleveland public schools, including a creative scheme to award scholarship money for university education to every pupil with good grades in core academic subjects—the first such program to be implemented in the United States throughout an entire school system. In the 1987–88 academic year, this ''Scholarship in Escrow'' program raised over $13 million and credited almost $3 million to students.[85]

The universities, too, worked in partnership with the city as never before in their histories. Cleveland State University's College of Urban Affairs offered its resources to the new administration and, for a number of years, provided the city with data and programs on public finance, housing, planning, and community development until city hall reorganized and built up its own departments and staff. In addition, the college provided technical assistance to many neighborhood organizations through its Center for Neighborhood Development. Studies done by Case Western Reserve University's Center for Regional Economic Issues, which had been created by the Cleveland Foundation with the cooperation of the Federal Reserve Bank, showed that Cleveland lagged behind the rest of the country in research and development and recommended that the community assist the local universities in promoting research.[86]

By the late 1980s there were signs that Cleveland had survived the economic crisis brought about by the major decline of the metal-fabricating industries that had been the city's mainstays for over one hundred years. There had been substantial new investments in Greater Cleveland industrial plants, such as General Motors and American Steel and Wire Company. The past decade had also seen the establishment of twelve hundred new small manufacturing businesses.

According to Richard Pogue, managing partner of the city's largest law firm (and the second largest in the nation), these changes reflected

> a transformation of the underlying manufacturing base in the region. Old, obsolete facilities closed; organized labor and management learned to cooperate; and companies, especially in the automotive field, reinvested in existing facilities to make them more productive, and new companies were created in mature industries with new technology, improved labor relations and better management.

Cleveland business leaders, recognizing the city's need for a substantial manufacturing base, have resisted the siren call of an economy limited to "high tech" and services and, instead, have moved toward the development of a mixed and flexible base.[87]

Cleveland's renewed confidence in the future is apparent in its downtown building boom. The 1980s have seen an increase of over six million square feet of office space with a high percentage of occupancy. The most notable addition was the $250 million headquarters on Public Square of BP America, Inc., the wholly owned subsidiary of British Petroleum that was formerly Standard Oil.

Most important to Cleveland's recovery is a new realism about the city's problems. The civic boosterism that characterized Cleveland in the postwar period gave way to a recognition that it was not enough to call attention to the city's assets, such as its world-class art museum and symphony orchestra, its fine universities, or its public library—the second largest urban public library in the country. Business and political leaders could not neglect the neighborhoods where Clevelanders lived or the schools their children attended, nor could they sweep under the civic carpet the problems of race and poverty facing the city. As the decade came to a close there were remarkable signs of recovery. But an end to Cleveland's problems was not yet in sight.[88]

NOTES

1. Philip W. Porter, *Cleveland: Confused City on a Seesaw* (Columbus: Ohio State University Press, 1976), pp. 136–37.

2. Ibid., pp. 133–34. Lausche, in addition to being elected twice as mayor, served five terms as governor and two as U.S. senator.

3. Carol Poh Miller, "Toward the Post-Industrial City, 1930–1980," in David Van Tassel and John Grabowski, eds., *The Encyclopedia of Cleveland History* (Bloomington: Indiana University Press, 1987), xlix. Hereafter cited as *ECH*.

4. The strength of Burke's administration lay in some of the department commissioners, highly qualified and dedicated civil servants from the 1930s. The Municipal Light Plant and the Water Works were well-run operations and financial assets. The Water Works was able to supply the growing suburbs with all their water needs. (Unlike the capital city of Columbus, Cleveland did not demand annexation as the price of supplying water. So, in time, Columbus would replace Cleveland as the largest city in Ohio.) Thomas F. Campbell, "Municipal Ownership," *ECH*, pp. 701–702.

5. Porter, *Cleveland*, pp. 135–36; see also Campbell, "Municipal Ownership," pp. 700–701. Eric Johannsen, *Cleveland Architecture: 1876–1976* (Cleveland: Press of Western Reserve Historical Society, 1979), p. 216. Cleveland City Planning Commission, *Cleveland Policy Planning Report*, Vol. 1 (1975), p. 34.

6. Louis B. Seltzer, *The Years Were Good* (Cleveland: World Publishing Company, 1956), pp. 256–60; Porter, *Cleveland*, pp. 177–80, 183.

7. Martha Derthick, "Stability in City Politics: The Case of Cleveland," unpublished MS (1962?), in possession of author, pp. 8–11, 22–23; Porter, *Cleveland*, p. 248.

8. Melvin G. Holli and Peter d'A Jones, eds., *Biographical Dictionary of American Mayors, 1820–1980: Big City Mayors* (Westport, Conn.: Greenwood Press, 1981), p. 60.

9. *Hearings before the United States Commission on Civil Rights: Cleveland, Ohio, April 1–7, 1966* (Washington, D.C.: U.S. Government Printing Office, 1966), pp. 179–93. Hereafter cited as *CRH*.

10. *CRH*, pp. 645–48; Dorothy Kunkin and Michael Byrne, "Appalachians in Cleveland" (Cleveland: Institute of Urban Studies, Cleveland State University, 1972), pp. 5–6.

11. Kenneth L. Kusmer, *A Ghetto Takes Shape: Black Cleveland, 1870–1930* (Urbana: University of Illinois Press, 1976), pp. 3–35, 157–89.

12. *CRH*, pp. 645–51, 794, 837–43. See testimony of Leonard Schneiderman in *CRH*, pp. 266–68.

13. Porter, *Cleveland*, pp. 225–26; *CRH*, p. 371. See testimony of Paul Briggs, ibid., pp. 372–88; for a graphic account of the deficiencies of the Cleveland public school system in the early 1960s, see pp. 608–18.

14. Thomas F. Campbell, "History of Hough," paper delivered before Hough Area Partners in Progress, January 23, 1987, pp. 1–12. See also David A. Snow and Peter J. Leahy, "The Making of a Black Slum Ghetto: A Case Study of Neighborhood Transitions," *Journal of Applied Behavioral Science*, 16 (1980): 459–81. See also Marvin B. Sussman and R. Clyde White, *Hough, Cleveland, Ohio: A Study of Social Life and Change* (Cleveland: Press of Western Reserve University, 1959). It is interesting to compare this latter work with the Snow and Leahy study that was done three decades and one riot later.

15. Porter, *Cleveland*, pp. 226–27. Campbell, "Hough," *passim; CRH*, pp. 32–45.

16. Campbell, "Hough," passim. Porter, *Cleveland*, pp. 231–33.

17. Louis B. Seltzer, "Grand Jury Report Relating to Hough Riots, Cleveland, 1966" (Cleveland: Cuyahoga County, 1966). Louis Stokes, in a speech at the City Club on September 16, 1966, commented on the Seltzer report: "Out of the 38 riot-torn cities, only Cleveland needed the Communists to inform its Negroes that things here are bad."

18. U.S. Department of Labor, Program Report No. 7, "AIM-JOB: Cleveland's Attack on Hardcore Unemployment," 1967; James C. Davis, "Cleveland's White Problem," speech before the Cleveland Bar Association, March 1967.

19. David Van Tassel, "The Korean War," in *ECH*, pp. 599–666.

20. Earl E. Landau, "Welfare/Relief," in *ECH*, pp. 1036–1037; "The Mayoral Administration of Anthony J. Celebreeze (1953–62)," ibid., pp. 668–69; Carl B. Stokes, *Promises of Power: A Political Autobiography* (New York: Simon & Schuster, 1973), p. 251. Stokes responded, "But, Tony, the town can't survive like that." Yet Stokes, too, became weary of the day-by-day hassle of running a big city. Sidney Z. Vincent, former executive director of the Jewish Community Federation, recalls in his memoirs one incident that reflects that weariness or disillusionment. Stokes, Vincent, and Maurice Saltzman, a prominent clothing manufacturer, met to discuss problems and how the Federation could help the Stokes administration. Saltzman mentioned that he faced a difficult security situation at his factory and that if better police protection was not available he might have to move to a suburb from his central city location. Vincent wrote that he expected Stokes to say that he would look into the matter because of possible job losses. To his surprise, Carl's instant advice was to move out, expressed without regret or concern. Sidney Z. Vincent, "Personal and Professional: Memoirs of a Life in Community Service" (Cleveland: The Jewish Community Federation of Cleveland, 1982).

21. Porter, *Cleveland*, pp. 181–87. In the late 1960s these theaters were threatened with demolition, but thanks to the work of a young public school employee, Ray Shepardson, the Junior League, and the infusion of more than $6 million by the Cleveland Foundation they were saved, and three of these magnificent 1920s buildings were completely restored. They have become the home of the Great Lakes Theater Festival and the Cleveland Ballet Company—two postwar contributions to the Cleveland cultural scene. The restoration of the theaters has led to a revitalization of Playhouse Square.

22. Porter, *Cleveland*, pp. 179–80; Johannsen, *Cleveland Architecture*, p. 223.

23. Johannsen, *Cleveland Architecture*, p. 223; Chet Huntley, "Cleveland: A City on Schedule," Cleveland Development Foundation, 1962.

24. Hunter Morrison, interview with author, April 5, 1988.

25. *CRH*, pp. 137–41. Bohn and Lister were in the Robert Moses tradition of urban planners.

26. *CRH*, pp. 156–58.

27. Miller, "Toward the Post-Industrial City," li.

28. This analysis is based on an examination of the *City Record*, a weekly publication of the Cleveland City Council for the years 1945–1985.

29. "History: The Nationality Movement of Cuyahoga County" (Cleveland, unpublished MS, 1968?), *passim*.

30. Derthick, "Stability in City Politics," p. 22.

31. Ibid., pp. 22, 26–27; James A. Norton, *The Metro Experience* (Cleveland: Press of Western Reserve University, 1963), pp. 58–60.

32. Derthick, "Stability in City Politics," p. 22.

33. *CRH*, pp. 274, 278, 332–43; Porter, pp. 225–26.

34. *CRH*, pp. 371–88, 750–75. See Robert Coles's testimony on the impact of discrimination and poor social conditions on black school children, ibid., pp. 344–57. Porter, *Cleveland*, pp. 225–26. Stokes, *Promises of Power*, p. 95.

35. *CRH*, pp. 751–52. Remarks by Carl B. Stokes to author July 22, 1971.

36. *CRH*, p. 387; Stokes, *Promises of Power*, p. 247; *Reed vs. Rhodes*, 1973, *Reed vs. Rhodes*, Remedial Order, February 1978; Paul Meincke, "Desegregation in Cleveland: The School Busing Decision," seminar research paper, June 3, 1983.

37. See Meincke, for a discussion of the major impact of the bishop, James Hickey, in taking an early and repeated public stand in support of the desegregation effort. This was significant in a city that is largely Catholic. His effort was enhanced by the Greater Cleveland Interchurch Council.

38. *Plain Dealer*, August 25, 1988.

39. Porter, *Cleveland*, p. 227; Stokes, *Promises of Power*, pp. 81, 94–95.

40. Porter, *Cleveland*, p. 187; Stokes, *Promises of Power*, p. 95.

41. Porter, *Cleveland*, pp. 229–31; Stokes, *Promises of Power*, pp. 95–96.

42. Stokes, *Promises of Power*, pp. 41–73, 89–91.

43. Ibid., pp. 95–96, 157, 168–70; Porter, *Cleveland*, p. 230. There were 29 publications of the Little Hoover Commission of 1966–67. Every one was critical of the city's operation. Chapter 2 of Report No. 6 on the police department was never published in local newspapers, and Stokes claims that Police Chief Wagner persuaded the mayor and the commission not to allow its publication because it was too critical of the department's day-to-day operation. See Stokes, *Promises of Power*, pp. 168–70.

44. "Racial Powder Keg," *Wall Street Journal*, March 14, 1967; "Escape Burning," *Saturday Evening Post*, July 29, 1967.

45. *Plain Dealer*, November 8, 1967; Stokes, *Promises of Power*, pp. 96–100. The Ford grant had two other programs. These were aimed at developing training programs in community involvement for inner-city youth and adults. It appears that the only successful program was the voter registration drive.

46. Stokes, *Promises of Power*, pp. 110, 175–80; Estelle Zannes, *Checkmate in Cleveland: The Rhetoric of Confrontation during the Stokes Years* (Cleveland: Press of Case Western Reserve, 1972), pp. 115, 146–47.

47. Stokes, *Promises of Power*, pp. 123–126.

48. Ibid., pp. 128–29; Zannes, *Checkmate*, pp. 125–29.

49. Stokes, *Promises of Power*, pp. 206–24; Zannes, *Checkmate*, pp. 133–45; Louis H. Masotti and Jerome R. Corsi, *Shootout in Cleveland: Black Militants and the Police* (New York: Frederick A. Praeger, 1969), *passim*.

50. Masotti and Corsi, *Shootout in Cleveland*, pp. 146–47; Stokes, *Promises of Power*, pp. 139, 218, 223–24. For a good account of the clash between the mayor and Council President Stanton, see Chapter 9 in Stokes. It is appropriately entitled "Two Bulls," pp. 131–145. Porter, *Cleveland*, p. 248.

51. Stokes, *Promises of Power*, pp. 140–41, 240–43.

52. Ibid., pp. 241–44; Zannes, *Checkmate*, pp. 226, 239; Porter, *Cleveland*, p. 249; Todd Swanstrom, *The Crisis of Urban Growth: Cleveland, Kucinich, and the Challenge of Urban Populism* (Philadelphia: Temple University Press, 1985), pp. 105, 127.

53. Author's conversation with Stokes, April 16, 1971; Stokes, *Promises of Power*, pp. 247–52; Zannes, *Checkmate*, pp. 227–28.

54. *The Observer*, November 16, 1958. For a scholarly analysis of Stokes as a politician and mayor, see Kimball Penn, *The Disconnected* (New York: Columbia University Press, 1972), pp. 139–58. For two very negative and unfair analyses of the Stokes administration, see Porter, *Cleveland*, chapter 13, "Dreams Turned into Disaster, 1967–1971," pp. 238–54; and Zannes, *Checkmate*, pp. 114–233. For a more balanced viewpoint of Stokes's impact on Cleveland, see Michael D. Roberts, "Stokes and the Riots," *Cleveland Magazine*, July 1976.

55. Zannes, *Checkmate*, pp. 231–341; Porter, *Cleveland*, pp. 250–54; Stokes, pp. 242–44, 247.

56. Zannes, *Checkmate*, pp. 241–43; Stokes, *Promises of Power*, p. 247; Porter, *Cleveland*, p. 298.

57. Porter, *Cleveland*, pp. 297–98. Perk got 90 percent of the total vote in the white ethnic wards, while Pinkney got 90 percent in the black wards. The black vote was then between 37 and 42 percent, and, even if Pinkney got 100 percent of their vote, it was not sufficient to elect him. Perk got 88,664 to Pinkney's 74,085. For a controversial analysis of Council President George Forbes, see Edward P. Whelan, "George Forbes: An Obsession with Power," *Cleveland Magazine*, November 1986.

58. Porter, *Cleveland*, pp. 255–71, 277–78, 280–83.

59. See John Burke and Edric Weld, *Local Government Revenues and Expenditures: A Case Study of the City of Cleveland, 1961–1971* [updated to 1974] (Cleveland: Cleveland Observatory, 1974), *passim*. Professor Burke, in a City Club speech on September 27, 1974, commented, "The clock is beginning to tick away. We are going to have to repay that [borrowed] money and it will place a still greater stress on our budget." Burke was referring

to the city practice of financing its operating expenses through the sale of bonds not approved by the voters. Porter, *Cleveland,* pp. 262–63. See also Edward P. Whelan, "Mayor Ralph J. Perk and the Politics of Decay," *Cleveland Magazine,* September 1975.

60. Porter, *Cleveland,* pp. 265–69, 287, 297–99; Swanstrom, *Crisis of Urban Growth,* pp. 109–11; Eugene H. Methuen, "Cleveland Comes Back," *Reader's Digest,* March 1983.

61. See Swanstrom, *Crisis of Urban Growth,* pp. 119–35, for an excellent analysis of the political environment of the city at that time and of the political tactics employed by Kucinich. He notes correctly that seven council incumbents lost because of their support of tax abatement and for supporting the sale of Muny Light.

62. Ibid., pp. 178–80. Interview with the participant, May 4, 1988.

63. Kucinich's M. A. at Case Western Reserve University was a study of the role of some reporters in escalating the conflict between Stokes and Stanton. Swanstrom, *Crisis of Urban Growth,* pp. 215–16. This episode is a modern version of the humiliation of Holy Roman Emperor Henry IV at Canossa in 1077 by Pope Gregory VII. Brent Larkin, "Kucinich's Final Days," *Cleveland Magazine,* January 1980.

64. Swanstrom, *Crisis of Urban Growth,* pp. 214–17.

65. *Cleveland Press,* August 9, 1978. In a conversation with the author in the spring of 1982, Brock Weir said that the decision not to roll over the loans was not just financial. See John F. Lewis, "A Revision of the Default Revisionist," *Plain Dealer,* January 5, 1989, for a spirited defense of the banks and the impact the default crisis had upon Cleveland.

66. Campbell, "Municipal Ownership," pp. 701–703. See Swanstrom for a good analysis of this struggle between CEI and Muny Light Plant, *Crisis of Urban Growth,* pp. 156–74.

67. Swanstrom, *Crisis of Urban Growth,* pp. 161–63.

68. Ibid., pp. 162–67.

69. Ibid., pp. 167–71.

70. Campbell, "Municipal Ownership," pp. 702–703.

71. Swanstrom, *Crisis of Urban Growth,* pp. 171–74.

72. Interview with Will Largent, media consultant for Voinovich's 1979 campaign, November 14, 1988; Swanstrom, *Crisis of Urban Growth,* p. 220.

73. *Point of View,* November 10, 1979.

74. Swanstrom, *Crisis of Urban Growth,* pp. 219–22; Largent interview, November 14, 1988.

75. Swanstrom, *Crisis of Urban Growth,* pp. 220–24. See Larkin, "Kucinich's Final Days," for a fine analysis of the behavior of Kucinich and his chief administrators and why he lost the election. In 1981 Voinovich received 76.5 percent of the vote against state representative Patrick Sweeney, and in 1985 he defeated council member Gary Kucinich (brother of Mayor Kucinich) by getting 72 percent of the vote in the first four-year-term election.

76. Methuen, "Cleveland Comes Back." For further information on the unprecedented involvement of a community foundation in the affairs of city government, see "The Foundation and Municipal Government: Helping the City Do Its Work" (*Perspective,* Vol. IV, No. 2, Cleveland Foundation, 1984). See also their other publication, "A Trust for All Time" (1984?).

77. *New York Times,* May 10, 1980; *Christian Science Monitor,* February 29, 1980; Methuen, "Cleveland Comes Back," *passim.*

78. Swanstrom, *Crisis of Urban Growth,* pp. 247–49.

79. Leo W. Jeffres, Jean Dobos, and Jae-won Lee, "Public Perceptions of the Quality of Life," Communication Research Center, Cleveland State University, September 1988. Greater Clevelanders, when interviewed about their perceptions of the quality of life, showed increased satisfaction. For example, one poll showed that the quality-of-life rating of metropolitan Cleveland on a ten-point scale was 7.04 in 1986. Peter N. Spotts, "Troubled Cleveland Unites in Effort to Turn Itself around," *Christian Science Monitor,* February 29, 1980; Iver Peterson, "Boom and Bust Overlap in Cleveland," *New York Times,* February 5, 1982; Methuen, "Cleveland Comes Back"; Alex Brummer, "Cleveland's Kiss of Life,"

The Guardian (England), August 3, 1987; "Ten Years Later, Cleveland Is Financially Healthy," *New York Times,* December 16, 1988.

80. Jeffres et al., "Public Perceptions of the Quality of Life," *passim.* Interview with Cleveland public school teacher, Spring 1987.

81. Cleveland City Planning Commission, *Housing Abandonment in Cleveland* (October 1972); Council of Economic Opportunities, "Poverty Indicators Trend" (Cleveland: CEO Report, 1988), pp. 12–13; Swanstrom, *Crisis of Urban Growth,* pp. 248–49. See Edward W. Hill and Thomas Bier, "Economic Restructuring: Earning, Occupations, and Housing Values in Cleveland," *Economic Development Quarterly* 3 (1989), pp. 123–44, for a lower estimate of the job losses in the Greater Cleveland area.

82. Fred McGunagle, "Crime Story," *Cleveland Edition,* April 14, 1988. Even though this analysis of local television newscasts was done in February 1988, it still is reflective of local coverage over the past two decades. Swanstrom, *Crisis of Urban Growth,* pp. 215–16.

83. Interview with Margaret Murphy, executive director of the Midtown Corridor, November 17, 1988.

84. Interview with Councilwoman Helen Smith—in whose ward much of the development is taking place—December 5, 1988.

85. Cleveland Foundation Report, May 1988; The Gund Foundation Annual Report, 1988; *Plain Dealer,* January 5, 1989; *New York Times,* February 5, 1982.

86. Interview with David Garrison, director of the Urban Center of the College of Urban Affairs, November 15, 1988; *Plain Dealer,* December 22, 1987.

87. Richard W. Pogue, "Cleveland Is Scraping Off a Lot of Rust," *Plain Dealer,* September 14, 1988.

88. See also Phillip L. Clay, "Transforming Cleveland's Future: Issues and Strategies for a Heartland City," December 13, 1988, College of Urban Affairs, Cleveland State University. This monograph, by a MIT professor, has a critical but encouraging analysis of the future of Cleveland. Thomas Bier, "Housing Supply and Demand: Cleveland Metropolitan Area, 1950–2005," December 13, 1988, College of Urban Affairs, Cleveland State University, calls attention to the dimensions of changes that could occur in the Cleveland area housing market, and the author identifies policies and program options in response to those negative changes. Bier predicts that the city's population will drop to 321,000 by 2005 unless city officials act quickly to assemble large tracts of land suitable for major redevelopment.

VII

INDIANAPOLIS
SILVER BUCKLE ON THE RUST BELT

Robert G. Barrows

It is uncertain whether John Gunther's *Inside U.S.A.*, published in early 1947, ever achieved best-seller status in Indianapolis bookstores. But if residents of the Hoosier capital were not buying and reading the book that spring, they were certainly reading *about* it. In his 920 pages of text Gunther mentioned Indianapolis only briefly—but that was enough to simultaneously wound the city's pride and set off a round of introspection and self-improvement. For, while he commended the city's "several admirable book shops" and its "quite good" record in race relations, he also pronounced it "unkempt, unswept, raw"—the "dirtiest" city in the country.[1]

The response was predictable. The *Indianapolis News* decried Gunther's "invidious reference." The Jaycees invited the author to attend one of their luncheons, urging that he explain "the basis of your findings and where we differ from other cities." The *Times,* a bit less defensive, admitted that "anybody with normal vision and a modicum of candor" would agree that Indianapolis was a dirty city. But certainly not *the* dirtiest.[2] Whatever the accuracy of Gunther's observations, his public disparagement did force the city's residents to take stock. Several months later the *Star* reported on the organization of "a permanent city-wide cleanliness program." Jointly supported by several business and civic groups, the project's representatives "planned to sponsor a comprehensive program of eliminating smog, improving trash and garbage collections, and sweeping up debris on downtown streets." Though this committee was relatively short-lived, it symbolizes the many voluntary associations that have worked to improve the quality of life in the Hoosier capital since 1945. And, in this case, it inaugurated a program that ultimately was successful; in 1964 Indianapolis was designated one of the three cleanest big cities in the country.[3]

If perhaps not quite accurate in the mid-1940s, one of Gunther's adjectives—"raw"—could be fairly applied to the city during its first decades. The U.S. Congress donated four sections of land for a state capital when Indiana joined the Union in 1816 and four years later the legislature approved a wilderness site near the geographic center of the state. Surveyors platted an area one mile square in the middle of the congressional donation (the downtown is still referred to as the "Mile

137

Square'') and laid out a circle, intended for the governor's mansion, at the center of the city. Centrality in the state was the town's only natural advantage; the White River proved unsuitable for navigation, early land routes were poor, and the capital remained, through the 1830s, an "almost inaccessible village."[4]

Railroad connections secured during the 1850s, followed by the war-induced growth of the 1860s, "transformed the town irrevocably into a city." No longer a "raw" or "inaccessible" village at the close of the Civil War decade, the city's population was more than double that of its closest intrastate rival, and the state's governmental capital had become its manufacturing and commercial leader as well. During the 1890s discoveries of nearby natural gas fueled 60 percent increases in the number of city manufacturing establishments and residents. The nineties also witnessed construction of the city's most recognizable edifice: the Indiana Soldiers' and Sailors' Monument, located on the (renamed) Monument Circle in the center of the Mile Square.[5]

Two developments mitigated the exhaustion of the natural gas supply following the turn of the century: growth of the state's interurban network (of which Indianapolis was the hub), and the emergence of the automobile industry. The interurbans brought shoppers from throughout the state to the downtown business district. The automobile industry, of negligible importance in 1900, ranked second in the city twenty years later with respect to both the number of persons employed and the annual value of its product—and the fabrication of automobile parts continued as a mainstay of the city's economy until very recently.[6]

The Depression of the 1930s affected Indianapolis much as it affected other urban areas across the country. Increasingly reliant on the production and sale of consumer goods, the city's economy was sensitive to the deferral of household purchases. The interurbans were in perilous financial shape even before 1929, and one line after another shut down during the Depression decade. Starting in 1940, however, both defense dollars and defense workers began to trickle, and then pour, into the capital. As "Toolmaker to the Nation . . . Indianapolis worked hard, bought War Savings Bonds and made the best of shortages and rationing." As elsewhere in the country, the forced deferral of economic gratification during the war years, the resultant growth in personal savings and consumer demand, and the virtual cessation of public improvements would affect the city's development in the postwar years.[7]

The demographic history of the Indianapolis metropolitan area since World War II has followed the familiar national pattern of suburban growth and central city decline. Even during the war decade the suburban areas of Marion County added more residents than the city proper (see Tables 1.2 and 1.3). The 1950s and 1960s saw more of the same. The postwar explosion of pent-up housing demand, the availability of FHA and VA mortgage guarantees, the desires of baby-boom parents for detached dwellings and modern schools, and highway construction that eased commuting—all combined to push the suburbs to the county lines and beyond and to slow, and finally stop, population growth in the "old" city. During the '50s the Indianapolis city population grew by 11.5 percent, the suburban ring within the county by 78 percent. The city's growth of 49,000, however, included approximately 47,000 added by annexation; the city's *real* growth for the decade was a mere 1,600. In the 1960s the city added just 8,900 residents, a net decadal growth of only 1.8 percent.[8]

The census data for Indianapolis in Tables 1.2 and 1.3 reveal a quantum leap in the 1970 population figures—growth that reflects the implementation on January 1, 1970, of a consolidated city-county government. With the exception of a few small cities and towns excluded from the merger, the boundaries of Indianapolis and Marion County became coterminous on that date. This was the equivalent of a very large annexation, and Indianapolis soared in the national population rankings—from 26th place in 1960 to 9th place in 1970.[9]

During the 1970s the city-county experienced a net loss of population. This too is a misleading statement, however, for the decline was limited to Center Township—located, as the name suggests, in the middle of the city and county. The remainder of Marion County actually gained population, and the ring of contiguous counties gained even more. Some of the county's net loss in the 1970s was made up in the 1980s. The Center Township "core," however, continues to lose residents, exporting an estimated 3.2 percent of its population between 1980 and 1984. The suburbs, especially those in surrounding counties, continue to outpace the "old" city. As of 1986 the Census Bureau estimated the Indianapolis SMSA at 1,212,600 inhabitants, ranking it 32nd among the nation's metropolitan areas.

On the eve of World War II blacks constituted 13 percent of the city's population. During the 1940s the capital's black population grew from 51,000 to 64,000 (in part as a result of migrants from the South seeking work in war industries), and by the end of the decade the black proportion had risen to 15 percent. By 1960 the city's black population had increased to almost 100,000, or 21 percent of the capital's residents. The proportion dropped to 18 percent in 1970, but this reflected the city-county merger, not a decrease in the black population. Between 1970 and 1980 the growth of the city's black community slowed but its proportion rose to 22 percent as whites in record numbers left the city for bedroom communities in the surrounding counties. The city's white population declined in the 1970s from 608,000 to 540,000, or from 82 to 77 percent of the city's total. In 1980 the nonwhite population was 13.5 percent of the eight-county SMSA total, 22 percent of Marion County, roughly 30 percent of the area comprising the "old" city of Indianapolis, and 41 percent of Center Township. Only during the past decade or so has a sizable black migration into the northwestern quadrant of the county begun to reduce the black community's concentration in the central city.[10]

Historically, Indianapolis had a very small contingent of foreign-born residents, and little has changed in that regard in recent years. Foreign-born residents accounted for 5 percent of the city's population in 1920, 2.7 percent in 1940, and a mere 1.9 percent (13,400) in 1980. The entire eight-county SMSA recorded just under 19,000 foreign-born inhabitants in 1980, or 1.6 percent of the SMSA's population. The city does have ethnic enclaves, restaurants, groceries, and cultural organizations, and it boasts an International Center, founded in 1973, that strives to provide cross-cultural education and greater international awareness. This group sponsors an annual International Festival, a slightly incongruous event in a city of such surpassing homogeneity. This relative absence of diversity has long been a source of pride for some residents. Boosters in the early twentieth century claimed that the Hoosier capital was the "most American" city in the country. Yet, as the city recently learned, excessive homogeneity can have its drawbacks. When the United Church of Christ rejected Indianapolis as a possible headquarters site in 1986, the search committee expressed "concern for the lack of adequate racial and ethnic diversity" in the community.[11]

No event since World War II has so dramatically altered the spatial organization of Indianapolis as construction of interstate highways around and through the city. Indeed, the interstates have added a new layer of meaning to two of the city's nicknames: the "Circle City" and the "Crossroads of America." It is near the city's two circles—Monument Circle at the center and the beltway around the capital—that most development has taken place during the past fifteen years.

The Indianapolis interstates are typical of the hub-spoke-rim pattern of many urban freeway systems. The Indianapolis "rim" or beltway (I-465), a 57-mile loop, was completed in 1970 following a decade of construction. An "inner loop," finally opened in 1976, encloses the downtown on three sides and serves as a "hub" for the "spokes" of east-west I-70 and northwest-south I-65. Three other interstate "spokes"—I-69 heading northeast and I-74 to the southeast and northwest—intersect the beltway, and six U.S. highways also radiate from the city. Thus, as it was for the railroads and interurbans, Indianapolis remains a "crossroad" for a great deal of the automotive traffic traversing the Midwest. Because of its strategic location, an increasing number of warehousing companies, distribution centers, and motor and air freight firms call the city home.[12]

The I-465 beltway has become the city's Main Street, serving as a magnet for development. Motels, hotels, shopping centers, industrial parks, condos, apartment complexes, office parks—all are firmly anchored on the "outer loop." In Indianapolis, as elsewhere, interstate highways built to relieve central city congestion by diverting through traffic have helped to suburbanize the city's residents, businesses—and congestion. The city planners and consultants who studied the city's future in the late 1940s and early 1950s, and who warned against continued "decentralization" of the city's population, were already fighting a rear-guard action. The automobile and the limited access highway would quickly change the nature of the urban environment, transforming the city's focus, at least for many of its residents, from "downtown" to a peripheral, homogenized "no town."[13]

Race relations in Indianapolis since the mid-1940s have not always been harmonious, but neither have they been marked by large-scale, violent confrontation. The race-related civil strife that touched many northern cities in the 1940s, and again during the "long, hot summers" of the 1960s, never really affected the Hoosier capital.

As World War II came to a close, the Church Federation of Indianapolis organized a clinic to "analyze the problems of race relations" in the city, and to "begin effective planning of ways to meet these problems." The report of the clinic's discussions and recommendations highlights the black community's concerns in the mid-1940s and serves as something of a benchmark to measure how far the city has (and has not) come. "Housing congestion," the report noted, "is more acute among Negroes than among other minority groups because race prejudice provides an artificial check to their expansion into new areas." The group decried especially the existence of "racial restrictive covenants." The committee dealing with employment issues called for continuation of the federal Fair Employment Practices Committee and encouraged the Indianapolis school board and local utility companies "to employ Negroes and other minority groups where they do not now employ them. . . . " While "great progress [had] been made in making the various community resources, public and private, available to all citizens without regard to creed or ancestry," more could be done. Specifically, the clinic's report called for establishing "on an experimental basis" a school emphasizing intercultural education—"a foundation for consideration of long-time progress toward an undifferentiated [i.e., integrated] school system."[14]

The city's subsequent record of accomplishments in race relations and civil rights was mixed—considerable progress in some areas, relatively little in others. The Indiana legislature passed a Fair Employment Practices Act in 1945, and several cities followed suit with local ordinances. In Indianapolis, however, a proposed FEPC measure passed by the city council in 1946 was vetoed by the mayor. In 1953 the council created a Mayor's Commission on Human Relations, but failed to appropriate funds for its work. Only late in the decade did the commission get even a part-time director.[15]

Blacks' access to public accommodations was a sometime thing. In the 1940s "the general policy of all downtown restaurants was to refuse service at tables and counters" to blacks, although they might purchase food for consumption off the premises. There were occasional prosecutions for violation of the state's 1885 Civil Rights Act, but city officials were generally reluctant to press charges under this law. "By the 1950's there had been marked progress in opening theaters and restaurants in Indianapolis to all patrons without regard to race. But the situation so far as restaurants were concerned remained spotty. Negroes could by no means walk into every restaurant and be sure of being served." In hotels, too, the policies of management were Byzantine. After the early 1950s blacks visiting the city with a convention group found ready accommodations, but blacks traveling alone might find themselves barred at some hostelries. As one legislative historian has recently observed, "downtown Indianapolis did not approach full integration until the 1960s. Food and lodging equal to that which white legislators accepted as a matter of course became available to blacks only after . . . [a] public accommodations bill became law in 1961."[16]

The 1950s also saw some tentative steps in the direction of educational equality. Since the late 1920s the Indianapolis Public Schools (IPS) had been almost entirely segregated, a result of both residential patterns and official policy. When the legislature adopted a desegregation law in 1949, however, the school board abolished separate school districts for black and white children. A majority of the city's elementary schools soon had mixed enrollments (although in many of these schools the enrollment remained *predominantly* one race or the other), and by the late 1950s most of the formerly all-white high schools had undergone at least token integration. There were a few protests by white parents, some of whom headed for the suburbs, but there were no serious incidents. ''On the whole,'' wrote one observer in 1963, ''the school authorities appeared to carry out the announced purpose of the school desegregation law in good faith.''[17]

Soon, however, it had become apparent that IPS was perpetuating rather than eliminating racial segregation. In 1964, two of the city's high schools enrolled no black students; the traditionally all-black high school enrolled no whites; and teaching and administrative staffs remained largely segregated. In May, 1968, the Justice Department, acting under authority of the 1964 Civil Rights Act, filed suit against IPS in United States District Court—the first step in a complicated and protracted case that would take over twelve years to resolve. The district court's decision in 1971 found IPS guilty of *de jure* segregation, enjoined the system from further discrimination on the basis of race, and outlined several steps to implement the decision. In an effort to prevent resegregation, the court also raised the possibility of involving the outlying school corporations as part of a lasting solution. (The 1969 consolidation of city and county quite pointedly rejected a merger of IPS and the county's other school systems.) At a second trial, in 1973, the court ordered several suburban school corporations in Marion County to begin accepting black students from IPS.[18]

Appeals went on for years, but in the fall of 1981 one-way busing of IPS pupils to the suburban schools finally began. An advisory council with the acronym PRIDE (Peaceful Response to Indianapolis Desegregation Education) worked hard in the preceding months to ensure an orderly implementation of the court order. There were a few ugly incidents during the subsequent years—including the predictable cross burning—but no organized, sustained opposition. Black students have periodically complained that they are subject to more stringent disciplinary action than their white counterparts, and logistics remain a problem for inner-city students who wish to participate in extracurricular activities at their suburban schools, but, on balance, the program seems to have been a success. In fact, the parents of bused children sought and achieved the right to vote in township school elections—a rare if not unique situation.[19]

In early 1969, as the school desegregation case was just beginning and after several summers of explosive racial confrontations in northern cities, an Indianapolis radio/television station commissioned a study of the city's black community. When black residents were asked by black interviewers to name ''the three major problems of people living in Indianapolis,'' four major concerns emerged: inadequate housing; limited job opportunities and unemployment; poor schools and education; and crime, violence, and delinquency. Significantly, in light of what was happening in other cities at that time, the study reported that ''even in the presence of Negro interviewers specific concern by Negroes over segregation, discrimination, or racial tension is voiced as a major community problem by only 17 percent.''[20]

The four major concerns identified by the report in 1969 are, to varying degrees, still issues today—most notably, the lack of decent low income housing and the difficulty finding employment. Residential segregation still predominates in the Hoosier capital but has certainly become less ironclad during the past fifteen years as middle-class black families have moved out of Center Township (though seldom out of Marion County). Black unemployment, especially among young men, remains a serious concern. As the Indianapolis Urban League has noted, the city's economic growth has been of limited benefit to blacks since many of the new businesses are setting up on the fringe of the city—too far out for employment of inner-city residents reliant on public transportation. On the other hand, a recent analysis of the "economic well-being" of blacks in large SMSAs ranked the Hoosier capital eleventh out of forty-eight communities examined.[21]

Since 1943, a host of commissions, committees, associations, and consultants have visited their attentions on the Hoosier capital. The first of these was especially important, since it outlined much of the city's agenda for the next two decades. Robert H. Tyndall, who assumed office as mayor on January 1 of that year, recognized that the war-induced industrial boom could easily become a postwar bust and that the city's municipal services would require repair and expansion after years of neglect. Within months of his inauguration Tyndall appointed a 150-member committee to chart the city's postwar course.[22]

The Indianapolis Committee on Post-War Planning unveiled its initial recommendations at a gala dinner on October 20, 1944. Chairman George Kuhn, a former president of the Chamber of Commerce, began his remarks by noting that the committee had established several basic policies to guide its deliberations. First, "All its thinking, and all its plans will be geared to the goal of reversing this trend toward decentralization" of the city's population. Second, although returning servicemen might need public works jobs in the immediate postwar years, the long-range policy was to depend on the private sector for employment stability. "We don't," sniffed Kuhn, with a backward glance at the New Deal, "want a return of leaf-raking, or other non-productive projects." Finally, the committee eschewed "any recurrence of federal aid," disdaining to go "begging to Washington for any further extension of the evils of federal aid and federal domination over local units of government."[23]

Kuhn went on to detail an ambitious agenda: renovation and expansion of the sewer system; provision for broad thoroughfares into the downtown, additional off-street parking, and railroad grade separation; smoke abatement; low-income housing and slum removal via a locally financed Redevelopment Commission; and expansion of airport facilities. A year later, after subcommittees studying particular problems had completed budget estimates, the committee issued a formal report calling for expenditure of $25 million over a period of seven years. The top three priorities: sewers, redevelopment of blighted areas (soon to be known as "urban renewal"), and railroad grade separation to reduce traffic delays and congestion. Added to the previous year's wish list was a new municipal building that could replace both the City Hall and County Courthouse.[24]

Despite (or perhaps because of) the grandeur of its conception, the seven-year plan encountered difficulties. A Chamber of Commerce publication in 1947 reported few concrete accomplishments, and two years later the *Times* succinctly observed of the plan: "It failed." The proposed program was too ambitious and too expensive. But, the paper's editor noted, the plan "had the value of publicizing the city's shortcomings," and there had been *some* accomplishments. A \$2 million sewer program was underway, the Redevelopment Commission had purchased some 178 acres for slum clearance, and a new law to regulate automobile parking had just gone into effect.[25] In addition, the committee's efforts presaged the active involvement of the Chamber of Commerce in shaping the city's course, focused city attention on "decentralization" (suburbanization, "white flight"), and reinforced opposition to federal aid that remained an article of faith among the capital's leadership for two decades or more.

Having made its recommendations, the Committee on Post-War Planning died a natural death in the late 1940s. It had many successors, however, beginning with the Indianapolis Civic Pride Committee (ICPC), which emerged in response to Gunther's "dirtiest city" charge. Organized in 1948 under the auspices of a group of architects and the Chamber of Commerce, the ICPC included representatives from all the major civic organizations. Focusing on neighborhood clean-up campaigns and securing off-street parking to reduce congestion, the group "took the first steps toward changing the image of Indianapolis."[26]

The Indianapolis Civic Progress Association (ICPA) incorporated in 1955 to "enhance the attractiveness and utility of the central downtown area." The first officers were (as they continued to be) some of the leading lights of the city's business and financial community, "men pledged to make the central area of the city more virile and more vibrant and to see that it remains the business and cultural core of Indiana." Writing in 1959 one of the city's newspapers praised the ICPA for "much unseen basic planning and preparatory work." Three years later the same paper observed that many of the association's goals had been realized: old buildings razed, slums cleared, traffic flow improved, parking increased. The ICPA's tenth annual report, which summarized the highlights of the previous decade, focused on the association's work in helping to determine the routes of interstate highways through the central city, its support of a new City-County Building and a State Office Building, and planning for a civic center. Throughout the 1960s the ICPA measured "civic progress" principally in tons of brick and cubic yards of mortar, concrete, and asphalt. Indeed, its 1963 annual report called new construction "the ultimate test of our city's vitality."[27]

During the 1940s and 1950s, and even into the early 1960s, the mayor's office was not the "vital center" of Indianapolis politics that it has subsequently become. Several factors—institutional, personal, and accidental—combined to limit the influence of the city's chief executives. During these years mayors could serve only single terms. Making long-range plans, much less implementing them, was difficult when even the most competent mayor became a lame duck the day he took office. Deaths and resignations further shattered continuity: Robert Tyndall (Rep., 1943–1947) and Al Feeney (Dem., 1948–1950) both died while in office; Phil Bayt, Jr. (Dem., 1950–1951, 1956–1959) resigned twice to campaign for other positions;

and Charles Boswell (Dem., 1959–1962) left when a district postmastership became available. George Denny (Rep., 1947), Christian Emhardt (Dem., 1951), and Al Losche (Dem., 1962–1963), who served briefly to fill vacancies, had insufficient time to be more than caretakers. In addition, as a local newspaper explained in 1964, "when a new mayor is elected he finds—sometimes to his surprise—that he has no control over certain boards and commissions. Appointments are staggered, policies [already] set. . . . "[28]

There is evidence to suggest that some of these men exemplified the "Peter Principle": When they became mayor they had reached the level of their incompetence. A lengthy obituary of Feeney, for example, dwelled on his pre-mayoral days and said not a word about any accomplishments of his three years in the mayor's office. Yet if not extraordinary administrators (or even politicians), these men generally appear to have taken the job seriously and to have worked for the betterment of their community. Tyndall inaugurated planning for the postwar era. Mayor Alex Clark (Rep., 1952–1956) introduced one-way streets to improve traffic flow, began planning for a new City-County Building, and launched the annual 500 Festival (which brought attention to the city, not just the race). But Clark himself has acknowledged the limitations the city's chief executives faced for two decades after World War II, observing that his role was "more of a housekeeping job and catching up with things we hadn't been able to do."[29]

If City Hall was providing something less than vigorous leadership, who or what was filling the vacuum? The *Indianapolis Times* attempted to answer that question in 1964 with a five-part series entitled "Who Really Runs Indianapolis?"[30] The *Times* identified thirty-nine business, professional, and civic leaders—the "39 Club"—including an "inner circle" of eight men who "wield the bulk of power and influence in Indianapolis." The top eight included two industrialists, two bank presidents, two members of the Lilly pharmaceutical family, a commercial real estate developer, and the publisher of the aggressively conservative *Star* and *News*. Big business, banks, insurance, utilities, and law firms were well represented by the remaining thirty-one members of this interlocking directorate.

The *Times* was quick to point out that "there is no formal organization which calls itself or even thinks of itself as the Establishment." The 39 Club was neither "sinister" nor "all-powerful." Its members had "one cohesive interest in common—money" and "having much to conserve, most tend to be conservative." Many of the men "don't try to run anything. It just sort of happens because they control money and resources." The "tremendous influence" of Eli and J. K. Lilly, for example, "stems not so much from what they do as who they are." Of one thing the *Times* was quite certain: The members of the 39 Club "don't need public officials. More often than not, public officials need them." Through directorships of the city's banks, public utilities, real estate firms, insurance companies, and business corporations, the group exerted "direct controls over the city's economic life." "Sometimes the Republicans win," the paper noted. "Sometimes the Democrats. The Establishment wins either way."

The *Times* reported, and other sources confirm, that "the power structure's big gun" was the Indianapolis Chamber of Commerce, and the chamber's "big gun" was William Henry Book, its executive vice-president from 1934 to 1964. One knowledgeable observer of the local scene opined that "few politicians ever have had as much influence and power" and that Book "runs Indianapolis." The *Times* series, which referred to him as the chamber's "most important link with the power structure," included him in the 39 Club and reported that many observers believed he rated inclusion in the inner circle. He was also labeled "the most conservative influence in the city." During the Depression, Book had worked briefly as the state's director of unemployment relief, an experience that apparently drove him out of the Democratic party and made him a staunch opponent of "government handouts." The *Times* credited him with "selling more than with reflecting the widely held Establishment view that federal aid in such things as urban renewal weakens the moral fibre of a community." He was, by one description, "positively negative" and his motto could have been: "Do we really need that now?" An assessment reached by one student of the city's history held that "he accomplished much that was good for the city, but he also blocked hundreds of other actions that might have been."

Book helped to establish a pattern of city reliance on the Chamber of Commerce for expertise. Even after his time, city administrators often called on chamber experts for help with the budget, financing, and tax problems. Book's successor at the chamber, Carl Dortch, was said to know "more about city government than anybody in city government." One mayor is reported to have called Dortch the day before his inauguration with the invitation to "come on over tomorrow and help me out."[31]

Though certainly not viewed as epochal turning points at the time, several events in the mid-1960s marked the beginning of a watershed in the city's history: Bill Book died, Democrat John J. Barton was elected mayor, and a faction of the county Republican party took steps that eventually transformed not only the county GOP but the governmental structure of the county itself. Book's death removed an implacable foe of federal aid, and Barton, though a relatively conservative Democrat, had no qualms about seeking repatriation of Indiana's tax dollars from Washington. During the mayoral campaign in 1963 he argued that the city should seek federal monies for important projects. His administrative practice mirrored his campaign rhetoric and set an important postwar precedent. Barton and his staff revitalized the city's Housing Authority after years of desuetude, and secured assistance from HUD for many units of new public housing. The John J. Barton Apartments, the capital's first major public housing project since the New Deal, were completed just about the time the mayor was defeated for a second term.[32]

Barton's election presaged a Democratic sweep of Indiana in 1964, which in turn led to a shake-up in the Republican party. A group of young Marion County Republicans, disappointed with their party's showing, styled themselves the Republican Action Committee and sought to oust the party's leadership. Winning decisive victories for their slate of candidates at the primary of May 1966, they installed one of their own, L. Keith Bulen, as chairman of the county GOP. The next year they orchestrated the nomination of Richard G. Lugar as their mayoral candidate, and Bulen directed a well-managed campaign that led to victory over Barton by a margin of 9,000 votes.[33]

Lugar, an Indianapolis native, brought something of a "new look" to the mayor's office. He was youthful (35), bright (class valedictorian in high school and college), very well educated (a Rhodes Scholar at Oxford University), and a good extemporaneous speaker. Following a stint in the navy he returned home, entered the family businesses, and became active with local civic groups. His election to the Indianapolis school board in 1964 was the first step of a political career that led to two terms as mayor and, in 1976, to the United States Senate.

Lugar consciously brought a private enterprise approach to the administration of municipal government—especially in the areas of long-range planning and fiscal control. But following the Barton administration's precedent, Lugar and his aides also actively pursued Washington's largess. One of the few Republican chief executives of a major urban area, Lugar became known in the early 1970s as "Richard Nixon's favorite mayor." Very successful in obtaining grants from a variety of urban-oriented federal social programs (Head Start, Model Cities, Community Action Against Poverty), Lugar also made extensive use of revenue sharing funds. Brick-and-mortar projects completed or placed under construction during Lugar's tenure include Market Square Arena (home for the Indiana Pacers basketball franchise), a Convention-Exposition Center, the Indiana National Bank Tower (at 37 stories, then the tallest building in the state), and Merchants Plaza, a combination hotel-office building-bank headquarters. Beginning this serious revitalization of the downtown area was, he later said, one of the proudest achievements of his administration.[34]

Lugar and his successor, William H. Hudnut III, have been highly successful in energizing what they are wont to call a "public-private partnership" on behalf of the city. The premier mechanism used to accomplish this feat has been the Greater Indianapolis Progress Committee (abbreviated GIPC, pronounced "gypsy"). A private, not-for-profit, nonpartisan organization, funded by foundation grants and private contributions, GIPC is self-described as "an action-oriented advisory arm to the mayor's office."

Unlike the Indianapolis Civic Progress Association, which it quickly supplanted, GIPC has had from the beginning a formal, structural relationship with the city's executive branch. GIPC had its origins in the fall of 1964 when Mayor Barton appointed an advisory committee of business and civic leaders to "formulate a program of progress that makes use of the city's full potential." Frank McKinney, Sr., one of the *Times'* "inner circle" in 1964, served as the first president, and his address to the members in June, 1965, outlined many of the major projects that were to be undertaken by the city during the next two decades.[35]

Although established by Democrat Barton, GIPC grew and prospered under Republicans Lugar and Hudnut. In its early years the organization worked for development of a park and reservoir on the city's far northwest side and led the drive for the convention center. More recently, GIPC has been involved in various downtown revitalization projects. The organization's strength has been an ability to marshal the talents of private sector leaders and volunteers in support of public endeavors. A broad-based group—there are now approximately seventy-five on the mayor-appointed board of directors and over 300 members—it includes representatives of business, education, labor, government, religious bodies, social service organizations, and neighborhood groups. In spite of this diverse membership, GIPC has been subject to criticism that it is controlled by a downtown business elite unable to see beyond the Mile Square. Some also view GIPC as a sort of unelected ''shadow government''—an institution with tremendous influence over the city's agenda, but accountable to neither the electorate nor the City-County Council.[36]

John Barton, in a recent interview, called the formation of GIPC the greatest legacy of his administration. Lugar, when asked to make a similar assessment near the end of his tenure, identified a government reorganization scheme enacted by the General Assembly in 1969 as his major accomplishment. Dubbed ''Unigov'' (a contraction of ''unified government'') by local headline writers, the acronym became the popular name for an arrangement that consolidated some, but by no means all, aspects of Indianapolis and Marion County governments. Most recent observers of the Indianapolis scene have agreed with Lugar's appraisal: Unigov is the single most important political and governmental change to have been effected in the Hoosier capital since World War II.[37]

The concept of a unified city-county government did not emerge suddenly in the mid-1960s. The issue had been discussed, off and on, for over fifty years. The Committee on Post-War Planning considered the problems of government in Marion County; a ''building authority'' created in the early 1950s was charged with planning and constructing a joint city-county office building; and a Metropolitan Planning Commission, created in 1955, consolidated city and county planning and zoning functions.[38] Still, the multiplicity of governments extant by the late 1950s, with overlapping jurisdictions and duplication of functions, prompted the Indianapolis League of Women Voters to title their 1959 study of local government *Who's in Charge Here?*

Although Lugar had made no specific recommendation regarding governmental reorganization during his campaign, he soon became frustrated by the dispersion of responsibility and duplication of functions he encountered, concerns shared by the Republican presidents of the Indianapolis City Council and the Marion County Council. As government officials, party leaders, and prominent businessmen attended a series of informal policy meetings in 1968, Mayor Lugar recruited a legal team to prepare tentative drafts of the legislation required to effect government reorganization. The mayor went public with the proposed plan immediately after the general election of November 5, 1968, when he announced the creation of a Task Force on Improved Governmental Structure for Indianapolis and Marion County—a group whose primary function was to rally support for the already well-developed plan.

The Unigov bill was introduced in the 1969 General Assembly. Lugar lobbied tirelessly for the measure while other proponents successfully prevailed upon local organizations to contact legislators and express ''support for the *concept* of metropolitan government while avoiding arguments on the fine points of the bill. . . . ''[39] The measure passed by substantial majorities in both houses and went into effect on January 1, 1970. The entire public debate on the proposal had taken place remarkably rapidly, in just over four months. Among the reasons most often cited for the successful passage of the measure at this time was the fact that Republicans controlled both executive and legislative branches of government on the city, county, and state levels. This is not to suggest that the Unigov proposal encountered no Republican opposition; indeed, some of the most compelling arguments raised against the measure (at least in its initial version) originated within GOP ranks. But the final votes in the General Assembly—67 to 28 in the House, 28 to 16 in the Senate—were virtually straight party line ballots and reflected the Republicans' ability to dominate Unigov's legislative consideration.

In spite of the implications of the name, Unigov is by no means a complete consolidation of all governmental functions within Marion County. As one knowledgeable observer notes, "its actual impact is as much psychological as structural."[40] Four "excluded" cities and towns retain their own governments (although their residents pay county taxes and vote in Unigov mayoral elections and elections to the City-County Council). The Indianapolis police department and the county sheriff's department operate side-by-side, and the Indianapolis fire department coexists with semiprofessional "volunteer" departments in the townships, towns, and excluded cities. Indianapolis city schools are surrounded by the county's ten other independent school districts.

"The establishment of Unigov," note its two closest students, "was much less an act of geographic centralization than of administrative integration." The measure combined the executive offices of city and county government into six major departments and reorganized the legislative functions into a City-County Council of 29 members (25 elected from single-member districts, 4 elected at-large). The mayor appoints the six department heads; the council makes appropriations, levies taxes, passes ordinances, and confirms many mayoral appointments. Unigov thus "provides a single executive and a central policymaking council with dominant power over what had previously been many largely independent and autonomous governmental units and agencies." Perhaps more important than the (partial) integration of local governments has been the increased coherence in countywide policy formation. Indeed, some observers credit the reorganization, and especially creation of the Department of Metropolitan Development, with making possible the downtown revitalization initiatives of the late 1970s and 1980s.[41]

Unigov has not, however, received universal approbation. At the time of its passage there was some complaint that the measure had not been subjected to a popular referendum. Proponents argued, accurately, that state law did not require a referendum. This was, however, somewhat disingenuous; though not *required*, the Unigov legislation *could have* contained a provision making its operation contingent upon approval by a popular vote in the city and county. Unigov advocates obviously "wanted to avoid the difficulties, controversy, cost, and effort of a referendum campaign." They felt, in Lugar's words, that "to throw an issue which has tested the wisdom of the best constitutional lawyers in the state to persons who have not the slightest idea about what government was before or after is not wise."

And they believed, again accurately, "that they had the political muscle needed to pass the bill without a referendum provision. . . . "[42] Unigov thus became the only metropolitan consolidation in the United States during the twentieth century effected without a local referendum.

Democrats then and since have viewed the consolidation as a Republican power play ("Unigrab"). The incorporation of suburban, largely Republican voters into the city electorate, it is claimed, has ensured decades of Republican domination in the mayor's office and council. Even Lugar, who promoted Unigov as a governmental reform, admitted in the aftermath: "I know this is good for the Republicans. That is how I sold it to the legislators statewide." Republican county chairman Bulen boasted that the consolidation was his "greatest coup of all time."[43] Motivations aside, the practical political results speak for themselves: Nine of the twelve men who served as mayor between 1930 and 1968 were Democrats. Since Unigov's enactment, however, Republicans have won every mayoral contest and have generally dominated the City-County Council (where the division following the 1987 elections was 22 Republicans, 7 Democrats).

Blacks, too, have tended to view Unigov as a dilution of their political influence— if only because it turned a usually Democratic city in which blacks were developing some political leverage in the 1960s into a Republican stronghold. In 1970 blacks comprised approximately 27 percent of the "old" city's population but only about 17 percent of the entire county. Thus, in strictly numerical terms, black political weight declined when the city's boundaries expanded to the county lines. But, as a recent analysis notes, the City-County Council's single-member district system now gives blacks "a voice in suburban affairs, sometimes giving them voting leverage that can be used to bargain for support for their own programs." Whether "blacks now play significant roles in the new government," as these same analysts claim, is open to debate depending on how "significant" is defined. Blacks (and women) do currently hold high administrative positions under Unigov, however, which was seldom the case prior to consolidation. The Hudnut administration has also fought, in opposition to the Reagan Justice Department, to retain affirmative action guidelines in city hiring and promotion.[44]

While some claim that Unigov has gone too far, others argue that it has not gone far enough, that it is a mere shadow of what a thorough city-county consolidation should be. And, indeed, words such as "unified" and "consolidated" are misleading in terms of the legal realities. The expressions do, however, fairly describe the political and psychological situation: the creation of a countywide electorate, the centralization of executive and legislative authority, and the heightening of a sense of metropolitan identity and identification. As one recent study summarizes the situation: "Unigov created a structure that focused real authority in the mayor's office to provide for more efficient government. In addition, Unigov has also inspired a sense of community accomplishment that has helped to coalesce private-sector leadership."[45]

Lugar generally receives major credit for creating this new structure for city government and for strengthening public ties with the business and philanthropic communities. But it is Hudnut who gets most of the plaudits for orchestrating and overseeing the rebuilding, refurbishing, and revitalization of downtown Indianapolis during the late 1970s and 1980s. A Presbyterian minister, Hudnut became involved in politics in the early 1970s and represented the city in Congress for two years. Defeated for a second term in 1974, he jumped into the mayoral contest the following year after Lugar announced his intention to run for the Senate. Hudnut campaigned diligently and won. Reelected in 1979, 1983, and 1987, he garnered an impressive 66 percent of the vote in the last two elections. When the 1984 legislature repealed a law limiting the terms of Indianapolis mayors, pundits promptly dubbed the measure the "Hudnut Forever" bill.

Hudnut's remarkable success as the city's chief executive has not come as a result of wearing his religion on his sleeve; indeed, he has generally avoided pandering to single-issue religious extremists. Yet it is also clear that his political activity is informed by ethical and moral considerations. Although he no longer heads a church, Hudnut has written that "governmental service can be legitimately construed as a non-parish-based form of ministry." He argues that he has not left the ministry but that "it is reasonable to think of one's constituency as a large congregation which one is called to serve."[46]

Hudnut has presided over a Mile Square building spree of considerable proportions. Monument Circle, the capital's geographic and psychic center, has undergone major renovation. Union Station, architecturally significant but a crumbling eyesore by the late 1970s, has been reborn as a "festival marketplace" of shops, restaurants, and night clubs. Two downtown movie palaces, one closed and the other reduced to screening martial arts films, dodged the wrecking ball by changing into homes for a professional repertory theatre and the city's symphony orchestra. The American United Life Building, opened in 1982, is currently the state's tallest structure at 38 stories (533 feet), and a Bank One tower will soon top the skyline at 48 stories (701 feet). So many high-rise office buildings have sprouted of late, both in the central business district and along the beltway, that one journalist has proposed the construction crane for city bird.[47] An urban state park is undergoing finishing touches on the banks of White River. And the merger of two extension programs with the state's medical schools in 1969 created Indiana University-Purdue University, Indianapolis (IUPUI), now attended by some 25,000 students on a burgeoning campus adjacent to the Mile Square.

Hudnut is fond of saying that he does not want the city to become a donut—a circle with a hole in the middle—and his administration has made a conscious effort to encourage city residents to live downtown. Several new apartment and condominium complexes have recently been completed within or near the Mile Square; older apartment buildings have undergone renovation; and near-downtown neighborhoods that seemed terminally decayed fifteen years ago have become Historic Districts in the throes of gentrification. Today the city is, as cities go, clean— especially the Mile Square. A 1978 "Keep America Beautiful" award for the cleanest city with a population of over 500,000 served as a sort of community "So there!" to the ghost of John Gunther.

Lacking any geographic advantage except centrality, Indianapolis has had to seek other means to compete in the world of urban boosterism. In recent years the city has aggressively turned to sports as a path to civic visibility and economic development. Athletics in the Hoosier capital is not just fun and games these days. The city is still probably best known for its annual 500-mile automobile race, the "Greatest Spectacle in Racing." Professional sports franchises include the Indianapolis Ice (International Hockey League), Indianapolis Indians (Triple-A baseball), Indiana Pacers (basketball), and Indianapolis (neé Baltimore) Colts (football). The Colts' sudden—indeed surreptitious—move west in 1984 stunned residents of both cities and led to some nasty litigation over the team's "theft." Completion in 1983 of the 60,000 seat Hoosier Dome, an enclosed stadium located only a few blocks from the center of the city, hastened professional football's arrival. Conceived and built as an addition to the convention center, the Dome sparked hopes for an eventual pro football franchise. But there were no guarantees, or even immediate prospects, when construction began. When the risk of building a stadium for an as-yet nonexistent team paid off, it added credibility to Hudnut's description of Indianapolis as an "entrepreneurial city."

While less flashy than the NFL, amateur athletics have also contributed to the city's growing reputation as a sports mecca. The Amateur Athletic Union moved to town in the 1970s and the governing bodies of a half-dozen sports have followed. A natatorium, track and field stadium, and velodrome—all state of the art facilities—opened in the early '80s, and the city hosted the National Sports Festival in 1982 and the Pan-American Games in 1987. As Hudnut asked rhetorically in his State of the City address in the latter year: "Who would have thought 15 or 20 years ago that this city would be preparing to host the world?"[48]

Development of the sports industry has provided the capital with a welcome economic boost. As is true of other northern cities, the Indianapolis economy has been in transition during the past decade or so. From 1974 to the mid-1980s the metropolitan area lost some 24,000 manufacturing jobs, most of them in durable goods production. The nonmanufacturing sector, however, added some 111,000 jobs between 1974 and 1985—especially in service occupations and retail trade. From early 1984 to late 1985 manufacturing jobs in the metro area declined 3.3 percent while nonmanufacturing positions increased 9.5 percent. Indicative of the rather successful economic adjustment, unemployment in 1986 hovered just below 5 percent.[49]

Although this transition from manufacturing to service and high tech has been somewhat unsettling, the city as a whole has not suffered from the economic upheavals of the 1980s as much as some of its northern neighbors. This is because the city's economy was already relatively diversified compared to, say, Detroit. Durable goods manufacturing was, and is, important, but insurance, health services, pharmaceuticals, government, and education, as well as amateur and professional sports, all play significant roles in the city's economic life. The convention industry, too, is becoming increasingly important, with an economic impact on the city of $358 million in 1985.[50]

The student newspaper at Indiana University in Bloomington, 50 miles south of the capital, advised students newly arrived on campus in the early 1970s that to visit a major metropolitan area they should "go north to Indianapolis—and keep on going 'til you reach Chicago.'' The derogatory nickname "Naptown" goes back several decades; the appellation "India-no-place" is of more recent vintage. Both convey unflattering images. So it is with a mixture of gratitude and bemusement that city residents have read such descriptions of their home town in recent national publications as: "Star of the Snow Belt," "Cinderella of the Rust Belt," "Corn Belt city with Sun Belt sizzle," and "Diamond in the Rust." In the face of this external confirmation it is no wonder that the city's imagemakers have taken to using with abandon the adjective "world-class."

Such purple prose is understandable and, to some extent, justified. The city has undergone a significant transformation during the past decade or so. A downtown that used to be deserted at night is now short of parking spaces to accommodate the weekend crowds. The arts, as well as athletics, are flourishing. A 1987 survey by the National League of Cities judged Indianapolis the fifth most successful American city in terms of economic development during the preceding five years. Residents rank the city high on quality of life indices. Long a city with no image, the Hoosier capital has earned some bragging rights.[51]

Behind the hype, however, the realities of urban life remain. A local columnist, ruminating on the favorable reports of outside journalists, observes that

> virtually every big-city problem I've ever heard of exists in Indianapolis. That the problems are less pervasive and less stubborn than those in Cleveland or Chicago may owe less to the vision of our leaders than to historical accident. Indianapolis is younger, less defined ethnically, less dependent on heavy industry. Nobody planned that.[52]

The positive developments of the past decade may outweigh the negatives, but they have not eliminated them. Yes, there has been a building boom, both downtown and along the beltway—but much of what has been built is, at best, architecturally undistinguished. Yes, the city now has "world-class" athletic facilities—but no objective observer would use that adjective to describe the city's school system, newspapers, bookstores, or low-income housing. Yes, Indianapolis received national and international recognition for hosting the Pan Am Games—but the city's not-so-latent provinciality emerged when the American Legion stridently (and successfully) argued against holding the closing ceremonies on the War Memorial Plaza, one of the capital's most impressive public spaces, because foreign flags would be flown during the event. And yes, the single-minded focus of the administration and the city's movers and shakers on revitalizing the Mile Square has wrought wonders—but how much of that enormous investment of time, talent, and money has trickled down to those who neither live, work, nor play downtown?

The city's vaunted government reorganization has proved to have its drawbacks as well. The Republican domination of the City-County Council since 1970—whether viewed as a conscious goal or an incidental by-product of Unigov—has weakened the two-party system in Marion County. The Democrats' political impotence for almost two decades has, at the least, led to a reduction of thorough discussion and meaningful debate on public issues. When one party has a three or four to one plurality, year after year, the skills required to forge a bipartisan consensus can grow rusty. A more critical interpretation holds that by the mid-1980s county Republicans had fallen prey to the "arrogance of power." Evidence to support this contention was most clear in 1986 when local newspapers challenged the long-standing practice of county Republicans to conduct public business in private caucuses prior to regular council meetings. Though such activity was patently a violation of the state's Open Door law, the council's Republican majority leader refused to open the caucuses, or to stop performing official public actions in them, until mandated to do so by a court order.[53]

"Things get done smoothly and quickly around here," writes Indianapolis columnist Dan Carpenter, "because there is no dissent." That statement should be read as a bit of journalistic hyperbole. Hudnut has yet to run unopposed or to win *all* the votes. When the administration tried to pass a $46 million issue of redevelopment bonds in 1985, intended in part to finance projects for the Pan Am Games, it was defeated by a well-organized "dissent" from the usually quixotic Indianapolis Taxpayers Association. And when the City-County Council turned a bit quixotic itself and attempted to halt the sale of pornographic material in the community by declaring it a form of sex discrimination and a violation of women's rights, the courts at every level "dissented" by rejecting the plainly unconstitutional ordinance.

Still, Carpenter has a valid point. One political party dominates the council. Groups such as the Greater Indianapolis Progress Committee and the Commission for Downtown dominate the process of setting the city's agenda. And private foundations influence and ratify such decisions with the leverage of their enormous financial resources. Whereas the city's power structure has doubtless become more broad-based over the past quarter century, at the upper echelons it looks little different than that detailed by the *Times* in 1964. Some of those individuals have passed from the scene, but the institutions they represented—the major banks, Lilly—remain much the same. There are very few persons, remarks one of the city's "ten most powerful people" in a recent poll, "who have a constituency, a credibility, an influence without actually having the resources to commit." Whether called "public-private partnership," "government by consensus," "arrogance of power," or simply "money talks," the system, as Carpenter says, "seems to have worked. The real Indianapolis is a lot of what the city fathers say it is. . . . The rest of us like it here all right, but we kind of feel like spectators sometimes."[54]

NOTES

1. John Gunther, *Inside U.S.A.* (New York, 1947), pp. 387, 910.
2. *Indianapolis News,* May 21, 22, 1947; *Indianapolis Times,* May 16, 1947.
3. *Indianapolis Star,* September 11, 1947; *Indianapolis Times,* January 17, 1964.
4. Berry R. Sulgrove, *History of Indianapolis and Marion County, Indiana* (Philadelphia,

1884), pp. 97, 14; Lee Burns, *The National Road in Indiana* (Indiana Historical Society *Publications,* Vol. 7, No. 4, Indianapolis, 1919), pp. 214–22; Hugh McCulloch, *Men and Measures of Half a Century* (New York, 1888), p. 72.

5. Frederick Doyle Kershner, Jr., "A Social and Cultural History of Indianapolis, 1860–1914," Ph.D. diss., University of Wisconsin, 1950, pp. 65, 78, 122, 140; Jacob Piatt Dunn, *Greater Indianapolis* (2 vols., Chicago, 1910), I, pp. 336, 340, 441–43; Sulgrove, *History of Indianapolis,* pp. 17, 139.

6. Clifton J. Phillips, *Indiana in Transition: The Emergence of an Industrial Commonwealth, 1880–1920* (Indianapolis, 1968), pp. 194–97, 253–58; Kershner, "Social and Cultural History of Indianapolis," p. 89; U.S. Census (1920), *State Compendium: Indiana* (Washington, 1924), pp. 172–73.

7. George W. Geib, *Indianapolis: Hoosiers' Circle City* (Tulsa, Oklahoma, 1981), p. 123; Edward A. Leary, *Indianapolis: The Story of a City* (Indianapolis, 1971), p. 215.

8. Tables 1.2 and 1.3; C. James Owen and York Willbern, *Governing Metropolitan Indianapolis: The Politics of Unigov* (Berkeley, Calif., 1985), p. 17.

9. In Tables 1.2 and 1.3, the 1940, 1950, and 1960 figures for Indianapolis are for the "old," pre-consolidation city, whereas the 1970 and 1980 figures are for virtually all of Marion County. The "Metro Area" in 1940, 1950, and 1960 was Marion County, a single-county standard metropolitan statistical area (SMSA); for 1970 and 1980 it refers to an expanded, eight-county SMSA, with Marion as the central county and Indianapolis as the central city.

10. Table 1.4; Owen and Willbern, *Governing Metropolitan Indianapolis,* pp. 25–26.

11. *Indianapolis Star,* March 29, 1987, p. 17B; Table 1.4; "Foreign Stock in Indianapolis," International Report No. 2 (April, 1986), Indiana University-Purdue University, Indianapolis, Office of International Programs; U.S. Census (1980); *Indianapolis News,* September 30, 1986.

12. One writer considers the great strength of Indianapolis to be its status as a "border town" at the intersection of three distinct "nations": Dixie (the South), the Foundry (industrial Northeast), and the Breadbasket (Great Plains). Joel Garreau, *The Nine Nations of North America* (Boston, 1981), p. 71.

13. For a critical appraisal of the early effects of interstate highways on the city see Richard Hébert, *Highways to Nowhere: The Politics of City Transportation* (Indianapolis and New York, 1972), pp. 65–96. The phrase "from downtown to no town" is the subtitle of David R. Goldfield and Blaine A. Brownell, *Urban America* (Boston, 1979).

14. "Report of the Summary Committee of the Indianapolis Race Relations Clinic, June 5–6, 1945," typescript in pamphlet collection, Indiana Division, Indiana State Library, Indianapolis.

15. Emma Lou Thornbrough, *Since Emancipation: A Short History of Indiana Negroes, 1863–1963* (Indianapolis, 1963), pp. 41, 46.

16. Ibid., 90–92; Emma Lou Thornbrough, "Breaking Racial Barriers to Public Accommodations in Indiana, 1935 to 1963," *Indiana Magazine of History,* 83 (December, 1987), pp. 301–43; Justin E. Walsh, *The Centennial History of the Indiana General Assembly, 1816–1978* (Indianapolis, 1987), pp. 586–87. Jesse L. Dickinson, a black legislator from South Bend who held office throughout the 1950s, later recalled that the only place he could eat in downtown Indianapolis was at the State House snack bar. When he first came to the legislature he was forced to rent a room in a black household, which he continued to do until the downtown hotels were desegregated. Ibid.

17. Thornbrough, *Since Emancipation,* pp. 56, 61–62.

18. Unless otherwise noted, the following discussion of Indianapolis school desegregation relies upon Emma Lou Thornbrough, "The Indianapolis School Busing Case," pp. 69–92 in *We the People: Indiana and the United States Constitution* (Indianapolis: Indiana Historical Society, 1987).

19. At least some of the population growth of the surrounding counties during the 1970s

and 1980s resulted from "white flight" and the decision of white parents newly arrived in the metropolitan area to avoid even the possibility of two-way busing within Marion County.

An eight-part series assessing how school desegregation has progressed since 1981 begins in the October 25, 1987, issue of the *Indianapolis Star*.

20. "The Negro in Indianapolis," prepared for the WFBM Stations, Indianapolis, Indiana, by Frank N. Magid Associates, Cedar Rapids, Iowa, May, 1969, p. 40, transcript in Indiana Division, Indiana State Library.

21. "State of Black Indianapolis '78," *Indianapolis News*, January 21, 1978; William O'Hare, "The Best Metros for Blacks," *American Demographics*, 8 (July, 1986), pp. 27–33 ("economic well-being" is a composite index combining income, homeownership rates, and median value of homes). Several scholarly studies, based on census data, have claimed that residential segregation increased in Indianapolis between 1960 and 1970. These studies, however, apparently compared the pre-consolidation census tracts of 1960 with the post-consolidation (Unigov) census tracts of 1970. See, for example, Thomas L. Van Valey *et al.*, "Trends in Residential Segregation: 1960–1970," *American Journal of Sociology*, 82 (1977), pp. 826–44.

22. *Indianapolis Star*, July 23, 1943; "Robert H. Tyndall" (obituary), *Indianapolis News*, July 9, 1947.

23. Indianapolis Committee on Post-War Planning, *The Post-War Plan for Indianapolis* (1944), pp. 11–13. The committee's rejection of federal aid preceded by over two years a similar sentiment expressed by the Indiana General Assembly. James H. Madison, *The Indiana Way: A State History* (Indianapolis and Bloomington, 1986), pp. 313–14.

24. *The Post-War Plan for Indianapolis, passim; Indianapolis Times*, January 10, 1944; "George Kuhn" (obituary), *Indianapolis Star*, March 3, 1974; Indianapolis Committee on Post-War Planning, *Our City Improvements* (1946).

25. [Indianapolis Chamber of Commerce], *Indianapolis Looks Ahead: A Post-War Plan in Action* (1947), *passim; Indianapolis Times*, July 3, 1949.

26. *Indianapolis Times*, March 11, 1950; "Richard C. Lennox" (obituary), *Indianapolis News*, August 16, 1986.

27. *Indianapolis Star*, September 23, 1955; *Indianapolis News*, April 17, 1959, June 25, 1962; Indianapolis Civic Progress Association *Annual Report* (1965), *passim;* ibid. (1963), p. 3.

28. *Indianapolis Times*, February 18, 1964. A listing of the city's mayors through the 1960s is in Leary, *Indianapolis*, pp. 233–34.

29. *Indianapolis News*, November 13, 1950; Rick Maultra interviews with Clark, Boswell, and John Barton (Dem., 1964–1968), broadcast in October, 1987, on Channel 16, the government public access channel in Indianapolis.

30. *Indianapolis Times*, February 16–20, 1964.

31. Irving Leibowitz, *My Indiana* (Englewood Cliffs, N.J., 1964), pp. 64–65, 87; Leary, *Indianapolis*, pp. 221–22; *Indianapolis Times*, February 18, 1964; "William H. Book" (obituary), *Indianapolis Star*, April 30, 1965; *Greater Indianapolis* (June, 1965), pp. 9, 15–23.

32. William E. Anderson, "City's Growth Began with Vision of Mayors in 1950s," *Indianapolis Star*, August 2, 1987; Susan Hanafee, "Former Mayor John J. Barton Is Still Working—Quietly," ibid., June 15, 1986; Leary, *Indianapolis*, p. 228; Maultra interview with Barton (see note 29). Barton was able to run for reelection in 1967 because the Indiana General Assembly passed legislation in 1963 permitting the mayor of Indianapolis to run for a second consecutive term. *Laws of Indiana*, 1963, chapter 244.

33. Owen and Willbern, *Governing Metropolitan Indianapolis*, pp. 46–47; "Noble R. Pearcy" (obituary), *Indianapolis News*, October 1, 1987.

34. For a retrospective on the Lugar administration, see *Indianapolis Star*, November 23, 1975, *Indianapolis News*, December 16, 29, 30, 1975.

35. *Indianapolis News*, October 24, 1964, June 10, 1965.

36. *Indianapolis News*, May 7, 1975, August 9, 1979; *Indianapolis Star*, March 12, 1981; recent GIPC brochure and annual report.

37. Anderson, "City's Growth Began with Vision of Mayors in 1950s"; *Laws of Indiana*, 1969, pp. 357–448. The Unigov legislation was formally titled the Consolidated First-Class Cities and Counties Act.

38. "The Indianapolis-Marion County Approach," chapter 3 of *Experiments in Metropolitan Government*, ed. James F. Horan and G. Thomas Taylor, Jr. (New York, 1977), p. 63.

39. Richard G. Lugar, "The Need for County Leadership in County Modernization," Indiana Academy of the Social Sciences *Proceedings*, 4 (1969), p. 13; Owen and Willbern, *Governing Metropolitan Indianapolis*, pp. 90–91.

40. John W. Walls, "Indianapolis—An Analysis of Indiana's Urban Laboratory Since World War II," Indiana Academy of the Social Sciences *Proceedings*, 13 (1978), p. 26.

41. Owen and Willbern, *Governing Metropolitan Indianapolis*, pp. 107, 2; Walls, "Indianapolis—An Analysis," p. 26.

42. Owen and Willbern, *Governing Metropolitan Indianapolis*, pp. 81–82; Lugar quotation from Horan and Taylor, "The Indianapolis-Marion County Approach," p. 67.

43. Owen and Willbern, *Governing Metropolitan Indianapolis*, pp. 173, 101.

44. Ibid., pp. 180, 198.

45. Ibid., pp. 197–98.

46. William H. Hudnut III, *Minister/Mayor* (Philadelphia, 1987), p. 33.

47. Bill Pittman, "City Praised for Making It Happen," *Indianapolis News*, August 27, 1987.

48. Linda Graham Caleca, "Sports Capital Moving East," *Indianapolis Star*, July 26, 1987; "The State of the City" (editorial), *Indianapolis News*, January 17, 1987. Home-grown philanthropic assistance made possible the construction of so many new sports facilities in so short a time. The Lilly Endowment, to give the most prominent example, poured $25 million into the Hoosier Dome and donated $11 million for the natatorium.

49. *Indiana Business Review*, 61 (July, 1986), pp. 6–8, esp. Tables 1, 3; ibid., 62 (July, 1987), pp. 6–8, esp. Table 1; " 'Ghost Corridor' Tough to Bust," *Indianapolis Star*, March 31, 1987.

50. "Convention industry worth $358 million to city," *Indianapolis News*, May 14, 1986.

51. "City's Progress Ranks It Among Top Five in Nation," *Indianapolis News*, November 23, 1987; "Poll Shows High Ratings for City on Quality of Life," ibid., April 14, 1986.

52. Dan Carpenter, "Forgetting the Indy Hype for a Moment," *Indianapolis Star*, September 11, 1986.

53. *Indianapolis News*, November 20, 1986.

54. Mary Beth Moster, "Who Calls the Shots?," *Indianapolis Magazine*, 24 (January, 1987), pp. 59–75, quotation, 62; "Who's Who in City Power Structure," *Indianapolis Star*, November 28, 1976; Carpenter, "Forgetting the Indy Hype."

VIII

KANSAS CITY

A CITY IN THE MIDDLE

John Clayton Thomas

Kansas City lies near the geographic center of the United States, allowing it to readily identify with several regions. Straddling the Missouri-Kansas state line where the Missouri River bends eastward toward St. Louis, the city bridges border states to plains states, Midwest to Southwest, and Snowbelt to Sunbelt.

Kansas City may be most accurately characterized as a Snowbelt city since it lies on a latitude comparable to that of St. Louis, Cincinnati, and Washington, and averages more snowfall and lower winter temperatures than any of those three. But the city also has some of the markings of a western Sunbelt city. It developed as a western town, the starting point for both the Santa Fe and Oregon trails. It also has the frequent sunshine commonly associated with such Sunbelt cities as Dallas–Fort Worth, Tucson, and Phoenix.

This geographic perspective helps in understanding the politics and economics of the Kansas City area. Just as it combines geographic elements of both Snowbelt and Sunbelt, Kansas City also combines the different economics and politics of Snowbelt decline and Sunbelt growth.

The Kansas City area has not seen the population stagnation or decline typical for Snowbelt cities, including most of those considered in this volume. The population of the metropolitan area has grown steadily since World War II, reaching the million and a half mark in the middle 1980s. Though low by Sunbelt standards, the metro growth rate of more than ten percent per decade is well above the norm for Snowbelt cities. As in most American cities, the Kansas City area's greatest growth has come in its suburbs (see Table A.2), especially in Johnson County, Kansas, a collection of suburbs southwest of Kansas City, Missouri. The county's population grew from 62,783 in 1950 to 270,269 in 1980, and, according to recent projections, will add almost 160,000 more people by the year 2010 as the number of households doubles from its 1980 level.[1]

The central city of Kansas City, Missouri also grew through most of the postwar years, with a population decline evident only with the 1980 Census. Much of that growth was based on annexations that doubled the city's geographic area between 1940 and 1960. More annexations in the 1960s saved the city from the population decline so common in Snowbelt cities in that decade. Although the population fell within the city's 1960 boundaries between 1960 and 1970, annexations added enough people to produce a net gain.

As the central city's population grew, it became more diverse. As Table A.4 shows, the black proportion of the population of Kansas City, Missouri climbed from 12.2 percent in 1950 to 22.1 percent in 1970 and 27.4 percent in 1980. In a pattern suggestive of the Sunbelt, Hispanics have also become a significant minority, comprising 3.3 percent of the city's population in 1980.

The area economy also shows both Snowbelt and Sunbelt characteristics. Like many Snowbelt cities, Kansas City has historically depended heavily on the automobile industry, with several Ford and General Motors construction plants in the area. The decline of that industry has brought layoffs and plant closings that have hurt the local economy. In addition, the problems of American agriculture have created hardships for the large agribusiness component of the local economy, resulting in the loss of Kansas City's status as the "stocker and feeder capital of the world."[2]

Unlike many Snowbelt cities, on the other hand, Kansas City has some advantages which have sustained overall economic growth despite automobile and agribusiness problems. The area benefits, first, from a location at the nation's center that results in good access to markets, enhancing the area's attractiveness as a distribution, communication, and financial center. Adding to that advantage, Kansas City has few competitors nearby. Of the cities within a radius of 400 miles, only St. Louis has a population of more than a million people. Kansas City thus inevitably becomes an important regional center for financial, governmental, and health services.

By many measures, Kansas City also has a high quality of life. It can boast an excellent housing stock, a relatively low cost of living, many cultural amenities, and several major league professional sports franchises. One community leader has argued that the city should advertise these qualities to investors by adopting the motto, "Kansas City, the Family Capital of America."[3]

These advantages have helped to build a diversified economy. In addition to its financial, governmental, and health service components, Kansas City's economy has significant transportation, communication, and tourism sectors, as well as a substantial persisting agribusiness sector and some traditional manufacturing. The city is now the headquarters for such diverse industries as Hallmark Cards, United Telecommunications/U.S. Sprint, H & R Block, Yellow Freight, and Marion Laboratories.

One indicator of the area's economic health was the "historic $2 billion construction boom" in Kansas City, Missouri, in the early 1980s. Although based in part on "a surplus of capital looking for a place to be invested" when many other cities had been overbuilt, this investment brought a notable influx of money into the central city—to the slumping downtown as well as the desirable Southside

Country Club Plaza area—even as additional large sums went into other areas of the city.[4]

The most prominent of those other areas is Johnson County's College Boulevard office complex, the focal point of the migration of jobs and population to the west side of the state line. That area could be said by 1982 to "hold the nucleus of a new sub-city" with which the downtown would have to "play catch up."[5]

Political power in Kansas City has traditionally been very centralized. For half a century, from the 1920s into the 1970s, the central city of Kansas City, Missouri, dominated the metropolitan area, and a few leaders ran the city.

In the decades before World War II, the city was controlled by the political machine of Boss Thomas J. Pendergast, who continued Kansas City's reputation as a wide-open frontier town. Pendergast, who inherited a Northside machine when his brother Jim died in 1915, expanded its domain by providing many new social services (e.g., summer baseball leagues) to appeal to middle-class residents on the city's South Side. By the early 1930s, Pendergast controlled the city and "virtually controlled the Democratic Party in Missouri because the large block of votes he could muster at election time from Kansas City and Jackson County would make or break candidates seeking statewide offices."[6] One of the candidates sensitive to Boss Tom's wishes was a young Democratic senator, Harry S Truman.

Pendergast's power began to erode after evidence revealed that much of the machine's support in the local elections of 1934 came from "ghosts," party workers voting on behalf of names from cemetery headstones. A public outcry brought changes in state voter registration laws to make the practice more difficult. That outcry had hardly subsided when reports of financial mismanagement surfaced at city hall: "funds were being juggled so that interest payments on outstanding bonds were made while the sinking funds which were to redeem the bonds themselves were not maintained at the proper levels."[7] The final blow came from a reform-minded district attorney named Maurice Mulligan, who attacked the machine's corrupt practices through "thirty-nine cases involving 278 defendants, 259 of them convicted either by jury or by their own pleas."[8] Among those who went to jail was Tom Pendergast, convicted of tax evasion.

With the machine leadership in jail, reformers seized control of the city, winning the mayor's office and seven of the eight council seats in the municipal elections of 1940. The Citizens Association, as the reform organization was known from 1941 on, would maintain that majority for almost two decades.

A combination of factors helped the reformers hold power for so long; most notably the reform agenda was attractive to the city's voters. The first reform councils pushed for more efficient government and cut municipal spending and the city's debts, winning converts among voters and business interests still reeling from the machine's record of fiscal irresponsibility.[9] Once the city's fiscal situation was under control, the reformers found another attractive issue—the promotion of city growth. They could eventually point to a doubling of the city's geographic area between 1940 and 1960 as tangible evidence of success on that issue.

Second, the reformers built a network of neighborhood organizations to combat the machine's persisting ward organizations. These community councils, as they were known, were created by the Community Service Division of the city's Welfare Department to fight juvenile delinquency, but the reformers soon found the councils useful as an outreach arm of city hall.[10] The reformers used the councils to obtain reactions to municipal proposals, to rally voters behind bond issues, and, in general, to build support for reform government. Without the councils, the machine's ward organizations might have regained control of the city after only a few years of reform control.

Finally, the reformers were blessed with high quality leadership. That leadership came from some of its mayors—including the first reform mayor, Jack Gage—and from the city manager who held office throughout the two decades of unbroken Citizens Association control of the council. L. Perry Cookingham, named city manager by the first reform council in 1940, stayed in that job until 1959. He was probably the most powerful figure in Kansas City during those two decades, planning and administering the initial cleanup of City Hall and deciding who would go and who would stay. He then served as the principal architect of the annexations of the late 1940s and 1950s.[11]

Cookingham's power derived in part from the consensus among the city's civic leaders on where the city should be heading. With almost everyone agreed on the goals of cleaning up government and promoting growth, Cookingham knew clearly what direction to move. The structure of Kansas City's government also gave Cookingham extensive formal authority, and limited the mayor's ability to usurp that power. As is common in council-manager cities, most formal authority in Kansas City is assigned to professional administrators, led by the city manager, who are supposed to govern with "neutral competence."[12] The mayor, by contrast, makes few appointments and cannot veto city council actions. In addition, Cookingham's personality predisposed him toward strong leadership. He enjoyed negotiating agreements among various groups and wanted to lead on policy matters as well as on administrative issues.

As a consequence, although the reformers changed many things, they did not change the pattern of centralized political control of Kansas City. The power supposedly shared by the members of the Citizens Association's council majority was exerted principally by Cookingham and a few mayors.

A persisting municipal fiscal crisis brought the Cookingham era to an end in 1959. Public frustration with the city's failure to confront the crisis helped patronage-oriented Democrats, spiritual descendants of the Pendergast machine, unseat the Citizens Association majority in that year's city elections. Faced with a hostile council, Cookingham resigned.

But the end of the Cookingham era did not mean the end of reform domination. Rather than accept the loss of power, the Citizens Association regrouped behind the well-connected local lawyer Ilus W. (Ike) Davis and a new generation of business leaders, including Donald Hall of Hallmark Cards, developer Miller Nichols, William Deramus III of Kansas City Southern Industries, and bankers James Kemper and Crosby Kemper, Jr. Helped by the ineptness of a Democratic council that went through eleven city managers between 1959 and 1963, the rejuvenated Citizens Association reclaimed council control in the 1963 municipal elections, in which Ike Davis won the mayor's office.

The new reform leadership brought major physical improvements to Kansas City during Davis's 1963–71 tenure as mayor. A $150 million bond issue was passed for the development of Kansas City International Airport, which opened in 1969. Two new professional sports stadiums, the side-by-side Royals Stadium for baseball and Arrowhead Stadium for football, were built with bonds passed by Jackson County. In addition, with the aid of municipal tax abatements, Hallmark Cards built Crown Center, a large retail and office complex on the south side of the downtown.[13]

But Kansas City was changing in other ways that would soon challenge this traditional consensual, centralized reform politics. New political groups were emerging, starting a process of political fragmentation that would continue for at least a quarter century from the early 1960s to the late 1980s.

The changes began with the city's black population. Prompted by their own growing numbers and by the example of the national civil rights movement, Kansas City's blacks in 1962 formed a new political organization, "Freedom, Incorporated." Freedom quickly became a potent political force, with its election endorsements coveted by black and white candidates alike. By 1987 Freedom could "deliver more votes than any other Kansas City or Jackson County (the county containing Kansas City) political organization," including the Citizens Association.[14]

The launching of Lyndon Johnson's War on Poverty in the mid-1960s added momentum to the black push for power. With reformers having eliminated most of the local patronage—jobs and public works contracts—that had sustained insurgent political groups earlier in Kansas City's history, the poverty funding with its targeting principally to black areas served as a kind of federal "patronage" for blacks. The funds both offered an attractive target for the exercise of the new black political power and underwrote the continued growth of that power. The demise of the poverty program in the 1970s did not change matters much because federal regulations gave earlier recipients a first claim on other federal funds, such as those from the Community Development Block Grant (CDBG).

Federal programs nurtured other political groups, too. The CDBG emphasis on neighborhood development, for example, encouraged the growth of neighborhood organizations. With the CDBG program "providing a training ground for neighborhood activists," these organizations would "reach a new pinnacle of political and economic power" in Kansas City by the middle 1980s.[15] In a similar but less visible manner, a wide range of other local organizations also used federal assistance to achieve political power in the city.

The electoral structure for the city council facilitated the rise of these new groups. The twelve-member council consists of two representatives from each of six city districts, with one of the two chosen by voters from that district alone and the other by voters citywide. (The mayor is also elected citywide.) Under this system, any group with substantial numbers in a particular area of the city has a good chance to obtain council representation. Blacks, for example, won their first two council seats in 1963, only a year after the formation of Freedom, Inc.

A system that can be applauded for representing the city's new political diversity can be faulted, on the other hand, for promoting political fragmentation. Kansas City has become more difficult to govern as leaders of the several political factions often pull in different directions.

Charles (Charlie) Wheeler, Ike Davis's successor as mayor, is the most recent leader to have pulled the fragments together. Running in the aftermath of the urban riots as the candidate of minorities, neighborhoods, and Democrats, the liberal Democrat Wheeler beat a Citizens Association candidate in the 1971 election. As mayor, Wheeler encouraged the expression of the divergent views represented on the council but then was effective in finding consensus among those views.

The task of finding consensus has become more difficult since then. In the 1980s the council has grown more diverse, with the addition of several blacks, an Hispanic, and some former neighborhood activists, who have joined traditional patronage-oriented Democrats and reformers identified with the Citizens Association. Blacks elected to the council since the early 1970s have been more suspicious of efforts by white leaders to find agreement.

Wheeler's successors as mayor have been unable to overcome these centrifugal tendencies. Some local critics contend that recent mayors have simply lacked the political acumen necessary for forging agreement. Richard Berkley, mayor through the 1980s, has been described as "a nice man who often tries to do the right thing," but council members "joke about his lack of leadership . . . and do not care what he says."[16] But that explanation underestimated the importance of the limitations on mayoral powers inherent in the council-manager form of government. Unable, for example, to veto council resolutions, Kansas City's mayor has little leverage to forge a council consensus, particularly now that consensus requires agreement among several different factions.

The city manager can hardly be expected to play this role. A manager works best when charged with implementing the policies of a clear consensus. Faced with the dissensus that characterizes a factionalized council, a manager must move cautiously or risk losing the support of the majority on the council, as the recent history of city managers in Kansas City illustrates. Longtime manager Robert Kipp resigned in 1983 rather than continue to try to please the various council factions. His successor, A. J. Wilson, lasted only a year before the council became dissatisfied with his highly visible style of management. The latest manager, David Olson, has held the job since 1984 only, according to one observer, by being "extremely cautious." Olson supposedly "refrains from the decisive moves that could mark him as a more independent city manager."[17] As a consequence, the manager-dominant style of the Cookingham era has disappeared from Kansas City.

Prominent business leaders, working behind the scenes, can sometimes pull a city together when political leaders cannot, but Kansas City's business leaders usually ignore politics. According to some observers, these leaders hold to the belief in self-sufficiency—"We can go it alone"—so common in the American West. In addition, the city's business leadership is in transition from the generation of Ike Davis's era to a new generation, a transition which increases the diffusion of economic power.[18]

The political fragmentation occurring in Kansas City, Missouri parallels that of the metropolitan area as a whole. As the population outside the central city has almost tripled since 1950, Greater Kansas City has gradually divided into many jurisdictions. By one count, the area now encompasses 300 local governments, including cities, suburbs, school districts, counties, and special districts.[19]

These political subdivisions contain many different populations and interests. On the Kansas side of the state line, for example, there is the stark contrast between thriving middle to upper-class Johnson County and its languishing neighbor to the north, lower to working-class Wyandotte County, home of Kansas City, Kansas. Where Johnson County's suburbs seek to maintain quality schools and plan for growth, Wyandot County must attend more to providing social services and reviving a declining economy.

The socioeconomic contrast between city and suburbs is not as sharp on the Missouri side of the line, but differences of interest are no less pronounced. The most notable recent difference pitted the majority black Kansas City school district against many predominantly white suburban school districts in a legal battle over whether desegregation required a metropolitan solution. (The courts eventually decided against forced busing between districts, but did make suburban residents working in Kansas City subject to an earnings tax surcharge to fund school improvements.)

Differences also arise between city and county on the Missouri side, as Kansas City's political leaders often quarrel with their counterparts in Jackson County, the county which includes much of Kansas City and several of its working-class suburbs. This conflict is in part a clash of political styles: Whereas Kansas City favors reform governance for the most part, Jackson County remains a bastion of patronage politics.

A growing source of fragmentation is the state line which bisects the metropolitan area. Although Missouri retains a majority of the area's population, the greatest population growth has occurred in Johnson County, Kansas. Many forms of local cooperation now consequently require legal authorization by two distant state legislatures.

This fragmented political power has combined with the contrasts in economic health across the Kansas City area to produce broad variations in the extent to which different jurisdictions—and the same jurisdictions at different times—favor public support for economic development. At one extreme, poor economic conditions have created a consensus on the desirability of development, prompting offers of extensive incentives to developers. At the other extreme, prosperous conditions have encouraged political groups to assert different priorities, curtailing the incentives offered.

The central city of Kansas City, Missouri has seen both extremes in the recent past. A consensual pro-development perspective characterized the city's politics during hard times from the mid-1970s through the early 1980s, but a more skeptical outlook took hold when the economy improved in the mid-1980s.

The city's economy reached bottom in the late 1970s, drained by the combination of a stagnating national economy and the ongoing, long-term exodus of businesses and residents to Johnson County and elsewhere. That combination left the central city with a ''lackluster economy with persistent unemployment in major industries'' and a ''shortage of brick and mortar projects . . . , especially in the downtown area.''[20]

Persuaded by these problems, most of the city's political factions were willing to lend support to community efforts to attract new development. Black political leaders consented to loan $9 million in federal grant money, money otherwise earmarked for development of minority areas, to assist in building a luxury downtown hotel. Neighborhood leaders for their part acquiesced in the subordination of their localized CDBG projects to downtown projects.[21]

The consensus in support of economic development produced many other incentives: industrial revenue bonds, conferring federal tax breaks on developers; tax abatements, reducing the local tax burden on developers; and eminent domain privileges, permitting developers to condemn and then acquire properties at assessed market rates. (Missouri is one of two states that permit transfers of eminent domain privileges to private developers.) None of these was entirely new to the city, but the magnitude was unprecedented. One estimate puts the total public spending on special downtown projects between 1979 and early 1986 at $70 million, and that estimate does not include either tax abatements as yet unused or many other indirect supports to developers.[22]

Differences of opinion reemerged only when the city's economic outlook began to improve. Reassured by the construction boom of the early 1980s, political factions resumed the scrutiny of the inducements being offered to developers. A city-hall proposal to assist a downtown department store found black leaders conditioning their support on a minority hiring commitment by the store.[23] Proposals to fund more downtown development from CDBG funds prompted neighborhood contentions that their projects should once again take priority.[24]

The challenge to development incentives peaked in 1985–86 around a project proposed for the desirable Country Club Plaza area. The developer, R. H. Sailors & Company, initially announced a vast ''$300 million, 3 million-square-foot proposal, which called for six towers ranging in height from 11 to 52 stories,'' much higher than any other building in the area.[25] Residents, city planners, and area commercial interests all objected, forcing the company to reduce the project's scale. The city than granted zoning approval, and, following its policy on other Plaza projects, promised the company tax abatements of $40 million over 25 years and eminent domain privileges for acquiring land in the project area.

Many residents remained unhappy. Some saw the project as a threat to the beauty of the Plaza area, and others objected to giving Sailors the power of eminent domain. Perhaps the largest number—three-fourths of the city's residents, according to one poll—opposed the use of tax breaks in the prosperous Plaza area.[26] Capitalizing on these objections, a group called Citizens for Responsible Development launched a petition drive to force a voter referendum on the project.

To head off the referendum, the city council withdrew its support of the project.

Sailors officials, seeing their investment in jeopardy, then sat down with city officials and leaders of Citizens for Responsible Development and negotiated a compromise. The project size was further reduced, and the company pledged an additional $20 million in special tax payments in exchange for the tax abatements.[27] A placated council voted a new approval in early 1986.

But with the city's economy on the upswing, many residents opposed *any* municipal assistance for the project. Rejecting the agreement negotiated by their leaders, some members of Citizens for Responsible Development started a new petition drive, and succeeded in forcing an August referendum on the project.

The odds in the referendum favored the project. Its size had shrunk to 1.7 million square feet, with no building higher than 19 stories. Eminent domain was no longer an issue because Sailors had bought all of the necessary land. The tax abatements were also much reduced with Sailors committed, by the time of the referendum, to $56 million in special tax payments, leaving a net tax abatement of only $16 million. The project also won the endorsement of many organized groups, including labor unions, the Citizens Association, most neighborhood groups in the area, and the original leadership of Citizens for Responsible Development.[28]

Still, Sailors faced two-thirds voter opposition as close as a month before the vote.[29] Only a late TV blitz extolling the project's potential for jobs and development—a blitz the project's low-budget opponents could not counter—brought approval for the project by a 58 percent majority. The city's economy had not improved so much that residents would risk the loss of jobs possible if Sailors received no municipal assistance.

Traditionally, Johnson County's municipalities have also been unwilling to risk offending developers. These suburbs have competed aggressively for economic development, generating many inducements for developers. However, the inducements often take forms different from those offered by Kansas City, Missouri. Rather than providing direct financial assistance, the suburbs more often promise physical improvements on or around the land to be developed. The College Boulevard business area, for example, was developed with the help of a major governmental infrastructure investment.

That pattern changed in the mid-1980s when a booming county economy encouraged a less generous attitude toward developers. With residents understandably more skeptical of the need for development incentives, some suburbs have imposed "impact fees" on developers. These fees, which fund public improvements (e.g., streets, curbs, lights) in developing areas, represent in effect a special tax on developers.[30]

In some areas of the county, residents have even challenged the very desirability of development. Many residents of Leawood, Kansas, for example, have opposed commercial development as threatening their residential quality of life. Their opposition has slowed or blocked many projects, most of which involved no outlay of municipal funds. In other parts of the county, too, developers report "common complaints by residents . . . that developments will cause drainage, noise, and traffic problems, that property values will decline and . . . neighborhoods will suffer.'' As a consequence, developers increasingly view negotiation with residents as a routine part of project planning in the county.[31]

The Kansas City of the near future will probably look much like the Kansas City of the recent past. The pace of economic growth should continue faster than in other Snowbelt cities, but hardly as rapid as in the fastest growing Sunbelt cities. Partly as a consequence of that growth, fragmentation of power should continue to characterize the area's politics.

Several pieces of evidence points to the likelihood of continued economic growth. A national study in 1986 predicted that the rate of job growth in the Kansas City area would be ''slightly higher'' than the national rate.[32] In addition, as late as 1987, development in the central city supposedly attracted ''national investment money that could quickly fuel further growth.''[33] Kansas City has even been mentioned, in the same breath with such Sunbelt cities as Orlando, Phoenix, and San Diego as one of the likely ''boom cities'' of the near future.[34] That seems an unlikely prospect, however, given the area's continuing heavy investment in traditional Rustbelt industries.

The varying political attitudes toward development across the area are likely to affect these economic prospects only marginally. Johnson County offers so many enticements that neither impact fees nor residents' objections should slow the pace of development. The effect in the central city might be more substantial. Officials in Kansas City, Missouri can make a case for policy impact by pointing to the sequence of extensive municipal inducements immediately preceding the construction boom of the mid-1980s.

But that case is hardly persuasive. For one thing, the city's success in reviving the downtown has yet to be proved. Despite the new construction, the downtown's viability remains uncertain in the late 1980s. Second, any revival which has occurred was probably due more to national economic trends than to municipal incentives. The national economic upturn of the early 1980s undoubtedly figured in the downtown construction boom. In addition, according to some experts, the decline of the energy industry left many Sunbelt cities too ''built up,'' making Kansas City relatively more attractive as a target for construction investments.[35]

Assuming the local economy continues to grow, political power probably will remain fragmented. The fragmentation reflects a reality of multiple jurisdictions, a division between two states and ethnic and economic pluralism. Efforts to overcome those factors and pull the fragments together are unlikely to succeed if the fragmentation does not appear to prevent economic growth.

Recent events in Kansas City, Missouri support this argument. Despite widespread criticism of his inability to unite the city's political fragments, Mayor Berkley won easy reelection victories twice in the 1980s. Seeing construction booms in the downtown and the Country Club Plaza areas, voters were apparently skeptical of calls for better leadership. The mayor encouraged that outlook by taking credit for the boom in his 1985 campaign, despite the fact that civic leaders publicly discounted his role.

Voters in other parts of the metropolitan area, especially those in Johnson County, may be even less interested in repairing this political fragmentation. For political forms to change substantially in either the central city or the metropolis as a whole, the area economy would have to perform much more poorly than it has recently.

NOTES

I want to thank Robert Kipp and Richard Bernard for their detailed comments on an earlier draft of this paper. Neither, however, bears any responsibility for errors which may remain in the paper.

1. Diane Stafford, "Johnson County Expected to Lead KC Area's Growth," *Kansas City Star,* September 29, 1987.

2. This loss was noted years ago in, City of Kansas City, *A Report of the Alternative Futures Program for Greater Kansas City,* Kansas City, Missouri, 1975.

3. Tracey Leiweke, "Kansas City Should Become 'Family Capital of America,' " *Kansas City Times,* December 25, 1986.

4. For a discussion of the construction boom and its causes, see Repps Hudson, "Building Boom Goes on—But Why Here?" *Kansas City Star,* April 7, 1985.

5. Bleys Rose and Bill Turque, "Power in Kansas City," *Kansas City Magazine,* April 1982.

6. A. Theodore Brown and Lyle W. Dorsett, *K. C. A History of Kansas City, Missouri* (Boulder, Col.: Pruett Publishing Company, 1978), p. 199.

7. Ibid., p. 207.

8. Bill Gilbert, *This City, This Man: The Cookingham Era in Kansas City* (Washington, D.C.: International City Management Association, 1978), p. 12.

9. Brown and Dorsett, *K. C. A History,* p. 229.

10. Ibid, p. 231.

11. Gilbert, *This City, This Man,* pp. 125–40.

12. For an excellent analysis of this pattern, see Jeffrey Pressman, "Preconditions of Mayoral Leadership," *American Political Science Review,* 66 (June 1972), pp. 511–24.

13. Much of this detail on the Davis era comes from Brown and Dorsett, *K. C. A History,* pp. 262–65.

14. James C. Fitzpatrick, "Freedom: A Force to Reckon with," *Kansas City Times,* September 15, 1987.

15. On Kansas City, see Joe Lambe, "Neighborhoods Flex New Muscle Despite Funding Losses," *Kansas City Star,* October 3, 1984. On similar patterns in other cities, see John Clayton Thomas, *Between Citizen and City: Neighborhood Organizations and Urban Politics in Cincinnati* (Lawrence: University Press of Kansas, 1986), pp. 155–57.

16. Yael T. Aboukalkah, "The Vacuum at City Hall," *Kansas City Star,* December 13, 1987.

17. Aboukalkah.

18. Rose and Turque.

19. G. Ross Stephens, "Politics in Kansas City," pp. 216–24 in Richard J. Hardy and Richard R. Dohm, eds. *Missouri Government and Politics* (Columbia: University of Missouri Press, 1985).

20. Diane Stafford, "For City's Business Leaders, A Time for Introspection," *Kansas City Star,* December 13, 1981.

21. See: James Kuhnhenn, "Minority Groups Rip Plan for Vista," *Kansas City Times,*

May 20, 1987; and Rick Alm, "Downtown, Neighborhoods Vie for Grants," *Kansas City Star*, February 9, 1982.

22. These figures were reported by Barbara Shelly, "Proposed KC Purchase of Store Spurs Debate on Downtown Renewal," *Kansas City Star*, February 27, 1986.

23. Denise Kotula and James Kuhnhenn, "Plan for City to Buy Macy's on Main Running into Problems before Council," *Kansas City Times*, February 25, 1986.

24. Celeste Hadrick, "Allocations of Grant Fund Stir Debate," *Kansas City Star*, January 30, 1985.

25. Denise Kotula, "Plan Commission Endorses Revised Sailors Proposal," *Kansas City Times*, June 5, 1985.

26. This result came from a citywide poll, as reported by Denise Kotula, "Tax Breaks in Plaza Area under Fire," *Kansas City Times*, October 18, 1985.

27. Denise Kotula, "Sailors Finds Little Support," *Kansas City Times*, January 10, 1986.

28. These facts were summarized by Denise Kotula, "Here's What Sailors Issue Boils down to," *Kansas City Times*, August 2, 1986.

29. That finding came from a citywide poll reported by Miriam Pepper, "Sailors Project Opposed. Survey Indicates Majority Will Vote Against Project," *Kansas City Star*, July 6, 1986.

30. Lucinda Ellison, "More and More, Cities Are Asking Developers to Finance Their Growth," *Kansas City Star*, May 17, 1987.

31. Patricia Skalla, "Forging Development Compromises," *Kansas City Star*, April 10, 1987.

32. Steve Rosen, "KC Area to Add 82,000 Jobs by End of Decade, Study Says," *Kansas City Star*, June 3, 1986.

33. Joe Lambe and Chris Lester, "Development Projects in KC Area Start to Attract Outside Money," *Kansas City Star*, April 17, 1987.

34. This prediction came from the unlikely source of *The Old Farmers Almanac*. See "Getting a Head Start on Trends for 1988," *Kansas City Star*, December 4, 1987.

35. Hudson, "Building Boom Goes on."

IX

MILWAUKEE

THE DEATH AND LIFE OF
A MIDWESTERN METROPOLIS

Richard M. Bernard

The four decades that followed the Second World War mark a full generation in the life story of Milwaukee, Wisconsin, once the "German Athens" and the beer capital of America. Since 1945, the old city of ethnic neighborhoods and aging factories has given way to a modern metropolis built on the service industries.[1] Milwaukee has passed through a postwar rebirth of dreams (although conflicting ones); a boisterous youth of political change and racial conflict; and a prosperous but unsettled maturity disturbed by the infirmities of age and the challenges of suburban and Sunbelt competition. The city, which exchanged its egalitarian hopes of the late 1940s for the realities of decline in the 1970s, is now experiencing the passing of an aging leadership amid a heralded downtown renaissance. From birth to death to reincarnation, postwar Milwaukee has come full cycle.[2]

Modern Milwaukee with its new political agenda was born of an intense struggle for the mayor's office in the municipal elections of the winter and spring of 1948. Because of wartime and postwar events, the city had not had a contested mayoral race in eight years, and the eager candidates lined up fifteen deep in the February snow. Most ran on the theme of youth and change first advanced by Carl Zeidler in 1940.

In that last prewar mayoral election, Zeidler, an assistant city attorney, had swept from office the Socialist incumbent of twenty-four years, Daniel P. Hoan, winning with the respectful slogan of "Hats Off to the Past. Coats Off to the Future." Tall and blond with traditional Teutonic features, Zeidler had been a charismatic figure in the Germanic city. With a song on his lips and a warmth in his handshake, he had seemed omnipresent at fraternal, civic, and educational gatherings. Once in office, the energetic and pro-business new mayor had replaced long-time Socialist administrators with young conservatives and had begun a reexamination of the tight fiscal policies of the city government. The future had looked bright for the popular, young chief executive and his city, but that was before Pearl Harbor. As soon as possible after the Japanese bombing, Mayor Zeidler had gone into uniform. He never returned.[3]

In his stead, the low-keyed John Bohn served for six years. Seventy-five years of age when he took office in 1942, Bohn was a politician of the old school. Formerly a hotel owner, barkeeper, and real estate agent, he first won a seat on the Common Council in 1912. Elected Council President in 1940, he assumed the mayoralty two years later when his predecessor joined the war effort. The elderly Bohn accepted a caretaker role for the duration of his time in office. He was a man of few ambitions either for himself or for his aging city. Worn down by depression and war, Milwaukee and its mayor were tired out in 1948.

Surprisingly, it was the policies of the geriatric Bohn administration that set the stage for the postwar rebirth of Milwaukee politics. Primarily seeking to maintain the status quo, which in Milwaukee meant maintenance of the city's long-standing reputation for fiscal integrity, Bohn angered the area's commercial interests and inadvertently gave rise to two of the city's major postwar political issues. During the Bohn administration, the ''pay-as-you-go'' principle of financing for municipal improvements, dear to former mayor Hoan and a ''progressive bloc'' of city aldermen, caused unrest among bankers and civic leaders who feared Milwaukee would fall behind other communities in economic development. The Greater Milwaukee Committee for Community Development, which grew from a group of fifteen Rotarians in 1939 to represent the leadership of 200 of the city's largest corporations, urged public commitments in 1948 for a new civic center, library addition, baseball stadium, zoo, indoor sports arena, museum, art center, performing arts center, and an express road from the airport to downtown. Yet when new construction finally did get underway, it included the very sort of project that business leaders wanted least, public housing.

Thus, it was not surprising that the 1948 mayor campaign centered on the issues of capital spending in general and funding for public housing in particular. The leading candidate, war hero Henry Reuss, endorsed the former and, although favorable to veterans housing, remained low-keyed on the latter. Most of the other contenders followed his lead and added only a clear denunciation of public housing. Only the former mayor's brother Frank Zeidler voiced an opposing view.

The primary campaign was a bruising one. Reuss, one of a host of ex-G.I's to return from the war and run for office, headed a strong field which included the conservative leader of the Common Council, a former mayor (Hoan), and a future mayor (Henry Maier). Seemingly at the bottom of the list of hopefuls was Frank Zeidler, the political mirror image of his brother. Supported by the Municipal Enterprise Committee, a small group of old Socialists who disliked Dan Hoan's flirtation with New Deal Democrats, the 35-year-old Zeidler contrasted with his brother, both physically and philosophically. Short, dark, intellectual and blunt, Frank held political views markedly to the left of Carl's. Few took his campaign seriously.

Zeidler's victory in the primary election was a stunning tribute to the powers of name recognition and candidate placement order on the ballot. Bearer of a beloved political surname and fortunate enough to draw the top spot on the printed ballot, the former county surveyor and school board member led the field with 26 percent of the vote to runnerup Reuss' 20 percent.

In the runoff election, there were clear differences between the candidates. Zeidler favored a balanced budget at all costs as a vindication of longtime Milwaukee

Socialist policies and a recognition of the tough depression-era struggle of Mayor Hoan to bring the city out of indebtedness to its bankers. Zeidler thus argued for postponement of major city projects until there was more money in the municipal till. Reuss strongly opposed this approach, arguing that public borrowing was quite acceptable in the post-New Deal era and that borrowing for new construction was necessary to keep the beer capital in the ranks of the nation's leading cities. Down-playing public housing, Reuss looked to economic recovery as the best assistance for the poor while Zeidler endorsed government efforts at slum clearance and re-housing as humane and necessary expenditures.

Issues, however, were probably less important to the election's outcome than the inadvertent role of the city's evening newspaper in creating a backlash of sympathy for Zeidler. Strongly opposed to socialism in any form, *The Milwaukee Journal* not only editorialized against Zeidler but also went to great pains to stress his political affiliation (always identifying him as "Socialist" and Democrat Reuss as "non-partisan") and to relegate Zeidler's campaign activities to the back pages while giving Reuss free run of page one. This treatment of Zeidler evoked empathy among the losing primary candidates, who were unanimously angered by the *Journal's* coverage of their own campaigns. One by one, the endorsed Zeidler. Then on the Sunday before the election, in what seems to have been a mistake, the *Journal* ran front-page pictures of both candidates and their families. The paper's editorial page had portrayed Zeidler as a radical ogre, but its lead photograph now pictured him as the modest head of a typical American family with five charming little girls in fluffy petticoats and a well-scrubbed young son. How could such a loving family man be so awful? Two days later, the public gave the newspaper a "no confidence" vote when Zeidler won 56 percent of the ballots. He became, in all probability, Milwaukee's last Socialist mayor.[4]

Once elected, Frank Zeidler found it difficult to govern without the support of the newspapers or the conservative Democrats who controlled the Common Council. Although popular with the people, as his reelections in 1952 and 1956 demonstrated, Zeidler could neither carry other Socialists into elected office nor gain Council approval for their appointment to other positions. Nor could he push through his legislative program. In fact, given the mutual hostility of mayor and council, their collective accomplishments are remarkable.[5]

Zeidler's central concerns were the financial livelihood of the city and the comfort of its residents. More widely-read than his colleagues, Zeidler foresaw the chronic constriction of municipal funds that would result from the relocation of Milwaukee's prosperous classes to the suburbs. Better than most, he knew that these departures coupled with movement to the city of poor people, many of them nonwhite, would leave the city with ever fewer taxpayers and ever more service-users and dependent people. It was a formula for fiscal disaster. Zeidler's preferred course of action was to reverse out migration by making the city a more attractive place to live. His methods were slum clearance and redevelopment. When the mayor thought of redevelopment, he thought of new housing. Good housing, good neighborhoods, and good neighbors had long been part of the Milwaukee Socialist creed.

The council also endorsed slum clearance but for different reasons. Once demolition began, the council pushed the nonresidential construction agenda of the Greater Milwaukee Committee, thereby delaying funding for Zeidler's planned housing. Primary among these public projects were the first links in the city's interstate highway system and a public sports arena. Other projects followed: branch libraries, a public museum, and new firehouses, docking facilities, and bridges.[6]

Although he endorsed many of these projects, Zeidler maintained that he was not compromising his political principles; he was simply making adjustments based on new economic realities. He had not, after all, opposed public construction, *per se,* but rather the substantial financial obligations which usually accompanied such ventures. Postwar prosperity and the addition of thousands of new taxpayers to city revenue rolls had considerably brightened Milwaukee's financial outlook, and this fact softened the mayor's position. Thus, in 1949, the council voted to issue municipal bonds, thereby initiating a lasting capital indebtedness. Still, compared to other cities, Milwaukee's borrowing policy remained very conservative. Two decades after the Zeidler administration ended, Milwaukee still retained a coveted "AAA"-bond rating, losing it only in 1981 during a time of recession and cuts in federal urban support.

If the desire to retain middle-class taxpayers brought the mayor and council closer together on slum clearance and general public construction, the linkage of public housing to these issues only drove them back apart. In seeking better accommodations for the poor, the mayor met considerable opposition from thoughtful conservatives disturbed by the government's entry into any free enterprise industry and by the power of eminent domain through which the city could condemn and (with compensation) take over private property. Joining these ideological conservatives were shortsighted private builders, as yet unaware of the profits available to public contractors and fearful of government competition in the private housing market. Because of postwar overcrowding, these forces had let one public housing project, Hillside Terrace, slip past them, but they did not intend to allow another.

As a result of such opposition, Mayor Zeidler was able to advance only a very limited housing program. By stressing the enormous needs of returning veterans and their families, Zeidler pushed through three new projects in 1949 and 1950: Northlawn, Southlawn, and Berryland. Westlawn, a non-veterans' facility, opened in 1950. But it took another six years to gain approval for an addition to the original Hillside Terrace, and that addition proved to be the last public housing of the decade, except for some minor units for the elderly.[7]

Beyond this construction, the mayor could gain no more. In the age of McCarthyism the public was not inclined to new government experimentation. A coalition of council conservatives, private contractors, realtors, and landlords played on the fears of the citizenry and blocked further housing construction on the grounds of stopping socialism. By the mid-1950s, these early opponents gained allies among middle and working-class whites fearful that public housing projects would introduce blacks into their neighborhoods. Racism now joined with anti-communism. In the mayoral campaign of 1956, Zeidler's opponents spread a rumor that the mayor had financed the placement of billboards along southern highways promising blacks employment and equality if they would move to Milwaukee. The mayor, it was said, sought to attract these people as a means of adding voters to the Socialist rolls. The lack of truth in the rumor was irrelevant, for many saw Zeidler as a traitor to the white people of the city. His plans for expanding public housing were but the first casualties of this perception.

Rebuilding the inner city might help retain some mid-level taxpayers and entice others to return, but most new suburbanites would never voluntarily move back to Milwaukee. Rather than lose their tax dollars forever, Zeidler and the council followed the the controversial course of previous administrations and attempted to force the recalcitrants back into the city's domain. The plan was to recapture the tax dollars of urban expatriates and at the same time take in open land for future growth by the extension of municipal boundaries to surround and encompass their new residences. Carefully city officials laid plans for encouraging suburbs to consolidate with the city and for annexing unincorporated territory.

Such a course of action must have given Zeidler pause for thought: the extent to which he would succeed in reattaching middle class taxpayers to the central city would be the same extent to which he would return conservative, anti-minority voters to the city's voting rolls. The more taxpayers who returned, the greater Zeidler's own chances for defeat in coming elections. To his credit, however, the mayor never hesitated.

When Zeidler took office, Milwaukee was a city of forty-six square miles, whose population had already spilled well beyond its boundaries into other parts of Milwaukee County. During his administration, the city more than doubled its land area, growing to about ninety-six square miles by the mid-1950s. The city accomplished this with a series of annexations of unincorporated properties at its northwest and southwest corners. These annexations had the consent of the property owners and voters involved, for the areas in question were in need of city services.[8]

Most outlying residents, however, found annexation unacceptable. After all, many of them had deliberately chosen home sites outside Milwaukee's old boundaries in order to avoid the high taxes necessary to support inner-city populations. Threatened by city growth, the residents of both the incorporated suburbs and unincorporated towns moved to insulate their communities from city enticements.

As the law was written, Milwaukee could not force adjacent areas to consolidate with the city without their permission, but it could pressure its neighbors by threatening to withhold vital city services. In the mid-1950s, Milwaukee took this tact and refused a request from its incorporated neighbor to the west, the City of Wauwatosa, for supplemental water supplies. Fearing central city pressure for consolidation, the suburb appealed to a sympathetic state Public Service Commission run by Republicans from farming areas and small towns. The PSC ruled in 1958 that because of the privileged monopoly status of its utility, Milwaukee had to sell water at a fair price to any ''*municipal* water utility'' in Milwaukee County or contiguous to the city. The services weapon was useless against Wauwatosa and other municipalities. Incorporated areas were safe from consolidation.[9]

The unincorporated towns, however, came under a different ruling, a 1942 state Supreme Court edict that gave Milwaukee permission to withhold water from them. Thus, these areas remained vulnerable as long as they failed to meet the various requirements for status as cities under Wisconsin law. These provisions, most of which centered on minimum population sizes and densities, barred substantially rural towns from incorporating and gaining rights to Milwaukee's water.

Consequently in 1955, lobbyists for several towns asked the state legislature to lower the requirements for city status and thus allow quasi-rural areas near Milwaukee to incorporate and block the use of water as a weapon to force annexation. Under the leadership of the southside town of Oak Creek, the smaller areas pressed their case, winning on a 44–43 vote in the state assembly when one of Zeidler's Milwaukee opponents supported the non-urban side. The mayor then tried to play his final trump card, a promised veto from Governor Walter J. Kohler, Jr. The veto never came, and the towns won. Disarmed and surrounded by an "iron ring" of incorporated suburbs immune to consolidation pressures, Milwaukee had reached its geographic zenith. The age of growth and expansion was over, and the realities of municipal middle-age began to set in.

By the end of the 1950s, the 47-year-old Zeidler was also feeling his age and then some. Worn down by intermittent battles with the *Journal*, the city's business leaders, the Common Council, and the governments of outlying areas, Zeidler saw in 1960 the very real possibility that the issue of public housing and race might cause his defeat. His 1956 victory had been a slim one, and he faced the ever-growing wrath of white property owners frightened by the prospects of integration. Correctly identified in the public mind as friendly toward black aspirations and the resident of a neighborhood that had become predominantly nonwhite, Zeidler and his family suffered from the intensity of white frustrations. Exhausted and feeling the physical strain, he yielded to his doctor's advice and declined to run again.[10]

Zeidler's decision to step aside in 1960 opened the way for the first spirited mayoral contest in more than a decade. Again, the favored candidate was Henry Reuss, by then a congressman from Milwaukee's North and East Sides. Again, Reuss led in the primary only to lose in a runoff upset, this time to state Senator Henry W. Maier. The contest was Reuss' last chance for municipal office. Once elected, Maier remained in place for twenty-eight years, surpassing by four years Dan Hoan's previous longevity record for a Milwaukee mayor.[11]

Born Henry Walter Nelke in 1918, the future mayor took his stepfather's surname soon after high school graduation. A Navy lieutenant in World War II, Maier began his political career in college supporting 1940 Republican presidential candidate Wendel Wilkie. In the late 1940s he switched to the Wisconsin Democratic Party, which was in the throes of modernization. Traditionally the most conservative of two, three, or even four major parties in the state, the Democrats were beginning a transformation under Gaylord Nelson (later governor and senator) and Patrick Lucey (later governor) into the more liberal organization in a standard two-party system. As the Democrats moved leftward, so too did the ambitious young Maier, although he always remained a good deal to the right of Socialist Frank Zeidler.

Two years after his stillborn 1948 mayoral campaign, Maier won a seat in the state senate, and in 1953 he rose to party floor leader. Three years later, he ran unsuccessfully for the U.S. Senate against Republican incumbent Alexander Wiley. In 1960, Maier again entered the Milwaukee mayor's race, and this time he won with 58 percent of the vote. In 1968, in the wake of major racial disturbances, he reached the pinnacle of his political career, taking 86 percent of the mayoral primary vote and carrying every ward in the city. Reelected six times in all, Mayor Maier faced a serious challenge only in 1980 when former Wisconsin Secretary of Revenue Dennis Conta upset him in the primary. Maier easily won the runoff, however, with 58 percent of the vote in a high turnout election coinciding with a presidential primary.

When Maier took office in 1960, he was a "weak mayor," with only limited charter authority over appointments and budgets, but by mid-decade his power had grown to enormous proportions. It remained substantial until the waning days of his long administration.[12] The timing of his tenure brought Maier new powers that his predecessors had never held. In office during the Great Society's vast expansion of federal urban programs, Maier gained hegemony over the personnel and the budgets of scores of new federal-city cooperative programs. He placed many of these programs under the supervision of William R. Drew, his right-hand man at the Department of City Development, leaving them largely beyond the reach of other elected officials. Even the city's regular budget came under tight mayoral control with the establishment of an executive budget-review process in 1978. This coincidence of timing, together with Maier's popularity, long tenure, and like-mindedness with the council majority eventually gave him control over most city functions. The resulting powers of patronage and purse frightened away most challengers and brought many favor-seeking citizens and council members, hats in hand, to the mayor's door.[13]

Over the years, Maier and his staff refined their techniques for controlling officeholders. Like his counterpart in Chicago, Richard J. Daley, the Milwaukee mayor restricted many civil servants and commission members to temporary appointments subject to immediate termination through the use of undated letters of resignation which he required of appointees. Maier named others to charter-required fixed terms, but if they proved reliable, he then retained them in office indefinitely under the guise of awaiting appointment of successors. The continuance of those commissioners in office gave conditional status to what had been fixed-term positions. Only a newcomer in a fixed-term slot could cause trouble and even than the Maier organization was prepared. If the member of some commission strayed from the fold, that body's Maier-controlled staff, supplied by the Department of City Development, simply limited the appointee's access to information and minimized his general effectiveness until his term expired. Under these circumstances, disloyalty was no more than a short-term problem.[14]

With his lieutenants firmly in charge, Maier could have stayed above the political fray, but his combative personality rarely let him remain aloof for long. Like other astute incumbents, the Milwaukee mayor claimed credit for all good occurrences and downplayed the impact of bad news, but in Maier's case this standard practice sometimes went to the extreme. In 1982, for example, when high interest rates blocked home sales and collapsed the local real estate market, the mayor's Department of City Development made residential immobility appear as careful social planning when it proudly announced that the administration's policies had stopped the expansion of the inner-city ghetto.[15]

Sometimes it was not possible to gloss over problems. In those cases, Maier blamed failure on: (1) the suburbs or other units of local government; (2) the governor of the state (Republican or Democrat); (3) Congressman Henry Reuss, whoever was in the White House and the federal government in general; or (4) *The Milwaukee Journal* (no more Maier's friend than Zeidler's).[16] Rising city taxes, for example, became in Maier's scheme the fault of the runaway suburban middle class and the independent school board. Delays in downtown redevelopment were due to Congressman Reuss' alleged inattentiveness. Racial unrest resulted from the failure of state and federal officials to spend enough money on poverty programs and from the *Journal*'s encouragement of "outside agitators."

For Milwaukee's black community, the idea that "outside agitators" were the causes of their protests of the 1960s was laughable at best. Although clearly influenced by the national events of the Civil Rights Movement and the "urban crisis," Milwaukee blacks had plenty of reasons for protesting community conditions.

Few blacks had moved as far north as Wisconsin's southern border before World War II, although many had migrated as far as Chicago's South Side. Even in 1950 when the city had 21,772 black residents, Milwaukee ranked only twenty-third, among the nation's twenty-five largest cities, in non-white population. Ten year later there were 62,452 black Milwaukeeans, and by 1970 there were 105,088.

In the mid-1960s, Milwaukee blacks lived under the shadow of *de facto* segregation. Some 98 percent made their homes in the central city, almost all confined to an area of four square miles on the city's North Side. Housing was of poor quality, schools were segregated by neighborhood, and underemployment and crime were major problems. In a city with only 8 percent of its white population below the poverty level, one black in four was in that category.[17]

In this environment, black protest had its paradoxical origin in an attempt by Mayor Maier to head off racial trouble.[18] At Maier's urging, representatives of the city and county governments, the school board, the technical-school board and the United Fund came together in July 1963 as a Community Relations Social Development Commission to discuss the problems of the inner city. Unfortunately, an outspoken county representative chose this forum to denigrate blacks as generally detrimental to the community. His removal from the commission became the first objective of local black leaders, who suddenly discovered a following for their efforts. Their success six months later caused that support to swell.

In autumn 1963, black Milwaukeeans began efforts toward the first of what became three major civil rights objectives. Led by attorney Lloyd Barbee, blacks organized to protest the *de facto* segregation of Milwaukee schools. Soon a group called Milwaukee United School Integration Committee (MUSIC) called for blacks to boycott the schools on May 18, the tenth anniversary of the U.S. Supreme Court school desegregation ruling in *Brown v. the Topeka Board of Education.* Barbee and his group demanded an open student transfer policy, a statement from the school board opposing segregation and an end to the practice of intact busing. Under this transportation scheme children from predominately black schools were bused in groups to predominately white schools where they filled isolated classrooms. Before 1965, these bused children remained apart from those at the receiving school even during recess and lunch periods. At the end of the day the bused children rode back to their neighborhood schools, having hardly even seen white children at the receiving school.

Despite MUSIC's appeal, the board refused to denounce segregation and to end intact busing and, although it did allow open transfers, the new policy's main effect was to allow whites to opt out of schools in racial transition, thereby speeding up white flight.[19]

A year and a half later, in spring 1965, demonstrations erupted which prompted a statement from the board that integration was "administratively unfeasible." When another school boycott followed in the fall, Maier and various official and unofficial groups tried to postpone conflicts by commissioning studies of the problem and recommending changes. But neither the efforts of the protestors nor the calming words of mediators or even the condemnation of the U.S. Civil Rights Commission moved the school board to action.[20] Meanwhile, Barbee went to court.

Reviewing a case which Barbee first filed in 1965, Federal Judge John Reynolds ruled in 1976 that the Milwaukee school board was guilty of racial segregation, and he appointed a "special master" to oversee the drawing up a desegregation plan. The board appealed and won a rehearing when the appeals court required Reynolds to establish intent. After additional proceedings, Reynolds concluded in March 1978 that the city's school segregation was indeed intentional, but before he could impose a final remedy, the plaintiffs and the school board reached an out-of-court settlement. The agreement provided for partial desegregation of the schools but not to a degree which would cause white parents to withdraw their children. A decade after the original Reynolds ruling, Milwaukee public schools were 53 percent black, and they became blacker each year.[21]

The local chapter of the National Association for the Advancement of Colored People protested that this result was not sufficient. In 1983, the organization reentered the legal battle and forced an expansion of the case to include twenty-three suburban school districts. A final out-of-court settlement in 1987 brought local promises to support voluntary integration across school district lines, but it also carried an unusual commitment from the state government. The state of Wisconsin, until this suit an outsider to the controversy, agreed to encourage school desegregation by promoting residential desegregation through the provision of housing subsidies. Under the terms of the agreement, a state agency is making nearly $6 million available for mortgage and rent subsidies to families moving into areas where they will be in a racial minority. Despite the newness of the plan and a relatively low funding level that leaves its success problematic at best, the degree of Wisconsin's commitment in this area far exceeds that of all but a few of the other fifty states.[22]

In the earlier days, long before state involvement, one participant in the school segregation protests was a young Catholic priest, Father James E. Groppi, a native South Sider recently assigned to the black North Side parish of St. Boniface. Although a "white ethnic" himself, Groppi identified strongly with the people of his parish. Their cause became his cause. Groppi's arrest during the school demonstrations shocked white Milwaukeeans, but as advisor to the state and local youth chapters of the NAACP, Groppi led his "Commando" protesters in far more unsettling activities in the months ahead.

The second phase of the civil rights movement in Milwaukee began when Groppi targeted the politically potent Eagles Club for its discriminatory membership policy. The Eagles countered that theirs was a private club and that their members were free to associate with whomever they pleased. Unimpressed, the protesters demanded that, as a symbolic gesture, the area's political leaders resign their memberships.

What made their protest newsworthy was Groppi's decision to march his mostly black, teenage followers from the Eagles Club's downtown headquarters, out the city's main thoroughfare and into the white suburb of Wauwatosa to demonstrate in front of the home of a well-known Eagle, liberal Judge Robert Cannon. The sight of hundreds of young blacks in a white neighborhood drew the attention of the entire metropolis, including a violent white fringe. Police and National Guardsmen had to keep order in an atmosphere that teetered between a riot and a carnival.

Through the rest of 1966 and into 1967 the stalemate continued in a dispute that ultimately landed on the desk of Wisconsin's Attorney-General Bronson LaFollette. In the late 1970s, LaFollette threatened to nullify the Eagles' tax exempt status if they did not remove their racial ban. Soon thereafter, the Eagles granted membership to ex-prizefighter Joe Lewis of Detroit, who died in 1981 without publicly showing any awareness of the honor. Finally, in 1980, the club officially opened its doors to Milwaukee blacks and a few, mostly neighborhood politicians, did join.

As the unpleasantness at the Eagles Club went into the hands of attorneys, Groppi led Milwaukee into its third and most important civil rights controversy, open housing. As the public housing struggle of the Zeidler era demonstrated, emotions ran high on the issue of racial residence. Few blacks had ever attempted to live beyond the boundaries of the central, North Side ghetto. Almost none lived below the Menominee Valley, which bisects the city, north from south.

Although a state law from 1965 barred racial discrimination in the sale or rental of commercial properties, there was no such provision covering the single-family homes and small apartment units which comprised about two-thirds of the residences in the city. Groppi and the Commandos applied pressure for a stronger city ordinance by again marching in the streets, targeting protest at the homes and businesses of six white council members who had substantial black constituencies. But these efforts were to no avail. Beginning in 1962, Alderman Vel Phillips, the first black and the first woman to serve on the council, repeatedly introduced a mild open housing ordinance identical to state law. Each time her proposals lost. Each time hers was the lone affirmative vote.

For his part, Mayor Maier walked a tightrope of politically astute procrastination, claiming that a city ordinance passed too soon would hasten white migration to the suburbs. Maier typically pointed fingers at other units of government, calling for stronger state laws or, failing that, suburban ordinances to pave the way for city action. He promised a city ordinance once a majority of the metropolitan area's twenty-six suburban governments had acted. This careful balancing act kept Maier in favor with both whites and blacks but did little to solve the problem.

Then in the summer of 1967, a week after major rioting broke out in Detroit, Milwaukee suffered a brief explosion of racial tensions in a civil disturbance of its own.[23] It began when police broke up a scuffle outside a black night spot in the early morning hours of July 30. Their actions set off a backlash the following night when blacks went on a five-hour rampage of vandalism. In the resulting turmoil, three people died, a hundred were injured, including 47 police officers, and over 1,700 were arrested. The mayor's action in requesting 450 National Guardsmen and putting the city under curfew for ten days probably prevented further violence. Compared to the events of other cities in the hot summer of 1967, this riot was small, but it left shellshocked Milwaukeeans looking for explanations.

Some whites blamed the riot on a communist conspiracy, but there was no proof of any such radical involvement. Others blamed the media: right-wingers denouncing the media's extensive coverage of the Detroit riot and liberals blaming television for bringing home to blacks their relative lack of material goods. Reporter Frank Aukofer's story in the Sunday *Journal* the morning before the riot drew special criticism because it suggested that conditions were ripe for a Detroit-style explosion. Those who blamed Aukofer, however, assumed that the *Journal* had extensive influence among blacks, a questionable notion at best. Blacks pointed to the simplest explanation of all—the awful living conditions, discrimination, and police brutality under which they suffered. Mayor Maier and most whites, however, blamed agitators (outside or local), and especially Father Groppi, for the damage.

Acting from an ever-hardening antagonism toward the priest and his followers, Maier called together members of the black bourgeoisie to study ways to prevent riots. The document that this group produced was pure "Maierism." Observing the mayor's principle that white flight would follow, it snubbed blacks' main demand for an open housing ordinance. Instead it issued a 39-point "Marshall Plan" for the economic improvement of Black Milwaukee, in which 32 of the points called for federal or state action. In the end, the state did act, granting $4.75 million for special programs aimed primarily at inner-city schools. The federal government had already offered to include Milwaukee in the Great Society's Model Cities program, but a cautious council had refused. A rebuffed President Lyndon. Johnson now promised only a meager $50,000 rat control program which all concerned thought cynical and inadequate. To Maier, the 39-point statement voiced a solution to black problems. To Groppi, it sounded a bell for round two of the housing dispute.

A month after the riot, Groppi took to the streets again, this time choosing a far more dangerous route than the one into the suburbs.[24] His marchers now crossed the Menominee Valley's 16th Street bridge and rallied in a park in the heart of the South Side's Polish neighborhoods. Feeling defensive and threatened by Groppi's forces, South Siders were in no mood for invaders of any kind and especially not black ones.

The first night, the marchers were lucky. On August 28, they crossed the valley without incident, even at the foot of the bridge where they passed Crazy Jim's used car lot and an estimated 5,000 taunting whites. Continuing to the park and from there back across the bridge, the demonstrators heard again and again the paraphrased refrain from a traditional polka, "Eee-yi-ee-yi-eee-yi-oh, Father Groppi's got to go." They heard much worse, too. The next night the marchers were not so lucky, and their cadenced departure from the South Side disintegrated when they had to flee the violence of the counter-demonstrators in a mad chase back across the bridge. Once safe on the North Side, blacks discovered that the NAACP's Freedom House was aflame, the result of a well-placed firebomb.

Having acted decisively against black violence, Maier now equivocated as white violence mounted. The mayor issued a statement calling for white restraint but at the same time denouncing the marches as an "unworthy cause." Maier also moved to ban "demonstrations" although he allowed "peaceful assemblies" to continue in a nod to the U.S. Constitution. He left white police captains to determine which was which. It was no surprise when they identified black, but not white, gatherings as illegal "demonstrations." More protests followed.

For 200 straight nights Groppi's forces marched for open housing, and in the process they caught the attention of the national media. City officials now felt the glare of negative publicity. Finally, in December 1967, in a session charged with emotion, the council adopted Vel Phillips's open housing ordinance. Since it duplicated state law, its only effect was to put enforcement into the hands of the city's overwhelmingly white police force; yet even this mild move drew howls from opponents both inside and outside of government. After the city elections of 1968 and the assassination of Martin Luther King, Jr. in Memphis (and after twelve suburbs had passed their own housing ordinances), Maier proposed amendments which brought most of the city's housing under restrictions and added teeth to the ordinance's enforcement provisions. The new council, including seven aldermen in sensitive black districts, responded favorably.

Following the Milwaukee action, more suburbs drew up their own ordinances, and by mid-summer 1968, when the first anniversary of the city's riot passed, twenty-six communities had housing laws. In keeping with this burst of liberalism, the Milwaukee council even voted to accept Model Cities funds to rebuild black neighborhoods.

In fact, these measures had little practical effect, for Milwaukee remains one of the most segregated cities in the nation. If anything, racial attitudes may have hardened. A survey in 1980 of white Milwaukeeans found that 66 percent favored racial segregation and 78 percent believed that blacks were physically and mentally inferior to whites.[25] Still, the open housing movement had gained a symbolic victory, and for many that was enough. Racial issues faded from the attention of white Milwaukeeans, although charges of police brutality and a black-sponsored plan to create a black high school district brought revivals of protest.[26]

If Maier's handling of civil rights issues was the low point of his administration, his finest hours were certainly his successful raids on the state and federal treasuries in support of the Milwaukee city budget. Motivated by desires to meet the needs of both the city and his own power base, Maier and his aides lobbied relentlessly in Madison and Washington to increase state and federal support for municipal projects. For many years, Maier's efforts at the state level were productive, but towards the end of his time in office his productivity waned. He became increasingly critical of the state government in general and of Democratic Governor Anthony Earl in particular for being insufficiently sensitive to the mayor's views of the city's needs. Capping a long-running dispute with Earl, who had supported Maier's 1980 opponent, the mayor demonstrated both his resilient power and growing arrogance by refusing to endorse Earl for reelection in 1986. His inaction contributed significantly to Earl's defeat at the hands of a conservative rural, Republican legislator.[27]

Throughout the 1960s and 1970s, Maier's record for fund solicitation at the national level was impressive, regardless of the party in power. New to office in the heady days of LBJ's Great Society, Maier and his lieutenants quickly learned the tools of "grantsmanship," which they employed with great skill to win large categorical allotments from a generous federal establishment. President Richard Nixon, in fact, had treasury robbers such as Maier in mind when he shifted the emphasis of federal urban support away from categorical assistance and its multiple application procedures toward formula-based general revenue sharing. Maier, however, was far from discouraged. As president of the U.S. Council of Mayors, he helped lead the fight in Congress in favor of the new program, for it added a veritable wealth of discretionary funds to city budgets. In the Gerald Ford years, Maier supported Community Development Block Grants and the Comprehensive Employment Training Act because they replaced old programs carrying categorical restrictions with lump-sum grants whose disbursement was also left to city officials. Under Jimmy Carter, Maier lobbied for special aid to combat the national recession. Critics in the 1970s faulted Maier for claiming credit in Milwaukee for federal programs which were available to all cities. Yet, passage of these programs was due in no small part to the efforts of Henry Maier himself.

After the election of Ronald Reagan, Milwaukee's fortunes declined with those of most cities above the Sunbelt. In the 1980s, Maier joined with other mayors in lobbying against the president's proposed cuts in federal support for urban programs. In this struggle, Milwaukee fared no better than other Snowbelt cities whose fortunes were tied to the beleaguered social side of the national budget. Still, as a grantsman skilled at carving money from categorical programs and as a lobbyist for the fixed formula programs, Maier had brought home the bacon.[28]

One of the mayor's leaner pieces of pork was public housing, the very program that brought down Frank Zeidler. With more federal money available for such projects in the 1960s and 1970s than ever before, the problem in Milwaukee was less one of funding than of convincing the Common Council to accept Washington's largess. At first Maier moved cautiously, proposing in the 1960s projects which emphasized housing for the elderly. In the next decade, he stimulated the council's appetite with suggestions of substantial federal matching funds available on a "use them or lose them" basis.

Maier's success in this field, coming on the heels of Zeidler's failure, owed more to his public image than to any argument which he advanced. Milwaukeeans had identified Zeidler with socialism and racial integration. They never viewed Maier in the same light. Under Mayor Maier, the once-intertwined issues of public housing, government interference in private enterprise, and integration became untangled. Construction of new facilities began again. Even contractors, who now saw big profits looming in public building commitments, found merit in this form of government spending. Milwaukee soon joined the region's other big cities in developing a whole array of publicly sponsored housing initiatives, from apartment complexes to "Section 8" rent supplements. And, thanks to the dexterity with which the Maier administration manipulated federal agencies, the city did not have to spend its own money on these projects until the mid-1970s.[29]

Maier's most difficult task, however, was the economic redevelopment of this Midwestern industrial city against a backdrop of national trends favoring expansion of the suburbs and the cities of the South and West. In this effort, the Maier administration touted Milwaukee's skilled labor supply, educational facilities, and safe, family environment as counterbalances to its harsh winter climate, the high cost of its skilled labor, and the area's relatively high tax rates, mandated by the city and state's liberal approaches to social spending and by the city's growing dependent population.[30] Advancing his arguments, Maier pushed ahead with industrial solicitation aimed as much at retaining the city's current manufacturing facilities as at gaining new ones. To this end, the mayor promoted the development of a municipal land bank which bought up failing industrial properties in the Menominee River Valley and in the city's newer northwest quadrant. By purchasing the land with municipal appropriations, improving it with federal funds, and offering it to companies at below-market prices, the Maier administration hoped to reduce capital costs for industrial plants and thus retain their payrolls and tax dollars within the city's bounds.[31]

Unfortunately, relatively few companies took the bait. Most new firms, not to mention old ones planning expansion or relocation, looked well beyond Milwaukee's borders to the greener industrial parks of the suburbs and the Sunbelt. Allen-Bradley, once the city's premier manufacturer of electrical equipment, built plants in Mexico, Brazil, England, and Canada. In the 1970s, it transferred 1,200 jobs out of Milwaukee to divisions in El Paso, Texas, and Greensboro, North Carolina. About the same time, Cutler-Hammer opened a non-union plant in Florida. Allis Chalmers, the first major firm to flee to Milwaukee's suburbs, cut its West Allis employment from 20,000 in 1948 to zero in the mid-1980s and also went south.[32]

Stymied in its reindustrialization efforts, the Maier administration worked more effectively on tourism and retailing. Most successful of the former promotional activities was Mayor Maier's Summerfest entertainment program at the city's lakefront. Begun in 1968 on land cleared for urban renewal projects that never developed, Summerfest proved such a boon to both city morale and revenues that in 1978 Chicago copied the concept and hired away almost the entire Milwaukee Summerfest staff to run its program. By the late 1970s, the Milwaukee festival became so popular that the city granted use of the grounds to ethnic groups wishing to sponsor their own outdoor activites. Soon the appearance of Festa Italiana, Irishfest, Germanfest, Polishfest, and Fiesta Mexicana, among others, gave credence to a municipal slogan announcing Milwaukee as a "City of Festivals."

Also, popular was Milwaukee's summertime Circus Parade, which was something of a tradition in the 1960s and early 1970s until costs caused its discontinuance. The Common Council, over Mayor Maier's rather surprising objections, brought it back to the city in 1985. The mayor fumed about the parade's expense, but most critics hinted that Maier refused to back its return simply because he had not initiated the project.[33] Attempts to spark interest in outdoor winter festivals such as the one in St. Paul received little support from Milwaukeeans, who find little to celebrate in gray skies and slush.

If Summerfest was the city's greatest morale booster in the 1970s, the Grand Avenue Mall deserves that distinction for the 1980s, surpassing even the 1982 American League Champion Brewers baseball team for that honor. Thanks to the commitments of 46 local companies under the personal leadership of Francis Ferguson of Northwestern Mutual Life Insurance Company and the support of the Maier administration and the local newspapers, the $55 million downtown shopping mall opened its doors in 1982.[34] The mall linked together the interiors of three blocks of remodeled downtown buildings in a wonderland of upscale shops and restaurants. Catering primarily to the workday shopping needs of young business executives and secretaries, the mall showed surprising evening and weekend popularity as it pulled in metro area shoppers, especially those from the city's "unmalled" East Side. The opening of Grand Avenue also prompted new investments in office buildings, condominiums, and public facilities, including overhead walkways which brought everything within indoor walking distance of the mall, even in the fierce days of January.[35]

Encouraged by the mall's success, other developers, including the notable Houston firm of Trammell Crow, moved into the downtown area. New projects included the Milwaukee Center with its repertory theater and major hotel and office space; the Bradley Center, a $50 million facility for sports and entertainment; the 100 East office complex; and the Time Insurance building. Revitalization is well underway in the old Walker's Point and Third Ward warehouse districts near downtown, just as new construction continues on the city's western and northern fringes. Critics note the sharp decline in the revenues of both large and small retail outlets outside the mall and wonder who will occupy the new offices built in a metropolis declining in population and job opportunities. But in the late-1980s the city's redevelopment appeared more promising than it had in years.[36]

A balance sheet for the Maier administration's economic development projects, therefore, gives little credit for the city's industrial recruitment and retention efforts, but counts its promotion of Summerfest and downtown redevelopment as substantial advances. In each case, the administration made major efforts to support private entrepreneurs. The differences in outcome, therefore, may be due more to broad-range factors working against the industrial efforts of all American cities and especially those of the Northeast and Midwest.

Henry Maier had taken command as Milwaukee had entered the youthful sixties, and he had retained control long enough to see the city pass through the trials of municipal aging to an urban rebirth. By the end of his term Maier, a graying figure more like a cantankerous uncle than a kindly father, was the only municipal leader whom over half the city's population could remember. For an entire generation of Milwaukeeans, the word "mayor" was always followed by his name. The alliterative phrase "Mayor Maier" was so ingrained in local minds that the idea of another leader at City Hall seemed almost unthinkable.

Even in the 1980s, when Maier's grasp of power, and some said of reality, began to fade, his supporters far outnumbered his detractors among city voters. His constant running-battles with the Journal Company, the suburbs, the governor's office, and, near the end, the Common Council seemed to merely strengthen the loyalty of Maier's adherents.[37] His decision to retire in 1988 brought to an end years of frustration on the part of opponents and ambitious rivals.

As much excitement accompanied Maier's decision to retire in 1988 and the subsequent election of State Senator John Norquist, a 38-year old "conservative socialist," as had accompanied the last transfer of mayoral power in 1960. Whether real growth and development will follow the high anxieties of the 1980s remains a question for the new mayor and beyond him for Milwaukee's leaders of the new century.[38]

NOTES

The author wishes to thank Milwaukeeans Janet Boles, Irvin B. Charne, Norman Gill, John Gurda, David Hall, Genni McBride, Daniel McCarthy, and Frank Zeidler, and Nancy Anderson of Auburn University at Montgomery, Alabama, for their comments on this chapter.

1. Bayrd Still, *Milwaukee: The History of a City* (Madison: State Historical Society of Wisconsin, 1965) is still the best account of Milwaukee before 1948.

2. The percentage of Milwaukee's work force tied to manufacturing dropped from 36 percent in 1970 to 30 percent in 1979, but even at that rate it was the highest of any major U.S. city. "Striving to Remain a Headquarters City," *Business Week*, December 24, 1979, pp. 36–37. See also: Mary Van de Kamp Nohl, "The Turnaround Year [1985]," *Milwaukee Magazine*, December 1985, pp. 75–93 and "In Old Milwaukee: Tomorrow's Factory Today," *Time*, June 16, 1986, pp. 66–67.

3. Harold Gauer, "The Year We Beat the Mayor," *Milwaukee Magazine*, November 1983, pp. 50–57. The mayor's brother Frank Zeidler told the author that years later he learned that a German U-boat sank Carl's ship off the South African coast, November 7, 1942.

4. Hoan, who served 1916–1940, followed woodcarver Emil Seidel, who was Milwaukee's first socialist mayor, 1910–1912.

5. Generally in strong opposition to Zeidler, the *Journal* did endorse his reelection in 1956. The *Milwaukee Sentinel* joined the evening paper in bedeviling him. Zeidler's own account is the best source for material on his administration. Frank P. Zeidler Papers, Milwaukee Public Library, especially his manuscripts, "Municipal Government and Its Improvement," 3 vols., 1960, and "A Liberal in City Government," 1962.

6. Stephen F. Dragos, "Privately Funded Mechanisms for Milwaukee Redevelopment," *Urban Land* 36 (1977), pp. 15–23. At the state level, Zeidler himself became a champion of public spending for an educational television station for the Milwaukee Area Technical College. Opposition to this latter innovation came from the *Journal*, which owned a local commercial TV station, and surfaced in the Common Council, which passed a resolution to

close the school to prevent the public channel from going on the air. Despite such efforts, Channel 10 went on the air.

7. *Community Housing in Milwaukee* (Milwaukee: Department of City Development, October 1977).

8. Milwaukee peaked in population at 741,324 in 1960 about ten years after other Northeastern and Midwestern cities. Without land growth, according to an undated Department of City Development report, Milwaukee would have declined in population in 1950–60. By 1980, the city had only 636,212. In the 1970s, the entire metro area lost population and fell to below 1.4 million.

9. David D. Gladfelter, "Water for Wauwatosa," in Richard T. Frost, ed., *Casses in State and Local Government* (Englewood Cliffs, New Jersey: Prentice-Hall, 1961), pp. 280–91 and Henry J. Schmandt and William H. Standing, *The Milwaukee Metropolitan Study Commission* (Bloomington: Indiana University Press, 1965), pp. 149–167.

10. Exchanging the role of Moses for that of Jonah, Zeidler continued to speak out for government that is both honest and benevolent. For a while, he was director of the Wisconsin Department of Resource Development. In 1976, he was the Socialist Party's candidate for president. For many years he has run the Public Enterprise Committee and edited its publications which project a liberal voice, crying in the wilderness of modern urban bureaucracy.

11. Reuss went on to serve a total of 28 years in the U.S. Congress. For summaries of Maier's career see: *The Milwaukee Journal*, June 10 and 12, 1987 and *The Milwaukee Sentinel*, June 11, 1987. Bruce Murphy paints a very gloomy picture of Maier's personality in "The Unknown Mayor," *Milwaukee Magazine* (September 1987), pp. 26–32ff.

12. In Milwaukee, as compared to other cities, the political power of businessmen is relatively low. This is true for a variety of reasons, most relating historically to the city's socialist spirit of substantial government activity in matters elsewhere left to the philanthropy of private businessmen and, more recently, to the aging of chief executive officers and the takeovers of local corporations by out-of-town companies. See *The Milwaukee Journal*, May 18–22, 1980; Helen Pauly, "The Slippery Baton," *Milwaukee Magazine*, March 1985, pp. 48–56; Peter E. Marchetti, S.J., "Runaways and Takeovers: Their Effect on Milwaukee's Economy," *Urbanism Past and Present* 5, No. 2 (1980), pp. 1–11; *The Milwaukee Sentinel*, January 18–19, 1982; and, "Striving to Remain a Headquarters City," *Business Week*, December 24, 1979, pp. 36–37.

13. Henry W. Maier, *Challenge to the Cities: An Approach to a Theory of Urban Leadership* (New York: Random House, 1966) and Henry J. Schmandt, John C. Goldbach and Donald B. Vogel, *Milwaukee: A Contemporary Urban Profile* (New York: Praeger, 1971); Murphy, "Unknown Mayor."

14. William Sell, *Political and Economic Control of Social Services in Milwaukee* (Milwaukee: East Side Projects and the Board of Social Ministry of the Wisconsin-Upper Michigan Synod, LCA, 1975). For Maier's version see *Challenge*, pp. 130–151.

15. *The Milwaukee Journal*, August 22, 1982.

16. John H. Vivian, "Milwaukee's Maier and the Press," *The Masthead* 25 (Summer 1973), pp. 28–38 and "Is Milwaukee Maier's For Ever?" *The Economist*, March 29, 1980, p 68.

17. *The Milwaukee Journal*, March 18, 1981, and Harold M. Rose, "The Development of an Urban Subsystem: The Case of the Negro Ghetto," *Annals of the Association of American Geographers* 60 (March 1970), pp. 1–17 and Joseph B. Tamney, *Solidarity in a Slum* (New York: John Wiley and Sons, 1975). Even in 1980, blacks remained Milwaukee's only significant minority group. Known Hispanics by then were 26,111, only 4 percent of the population.

18. Frank Aukofer, *City with a Chance* (Milwaukee: Bruce Publishing, 1968); Peter K. Eisinger, *Patterns of Interracial Politics: Conflict and Cooperation in the City* (New York: Academic Press, 1976); and, Maier, *Challenge*, pp. 43–70.

19. Karl E. Taeuber, "Housing, Schools, and Incremental Segregative Effects," *Annals of the American Academy of Political and Social Sciences* 441 (January 1979), pp. 157–

167. Irvin B. Charne, Milwaukee School Board attorney, to R. M. Bernard, Montgomery, Alabama, November 4, 1987.

20. U.S. Commission on Civil Rights, *Racial Isolation in the Public Schools,* Vol. 1 (Washington: U.S. Government Printing Office, 1967), pp. 56–57.

21. Attorney Charne responds to the charge of partial desegregation as follows: " . . . you refer to the agreement as an attempt to substantially integrate the schools but not to a degree which would cause white parents to withdraw their children. I do not know what you believe is the basis for this statement is [sic] but I am not aware of any facts by which it can be authoritatively verified. I know that it was not a factor which was discussed in connection with the settlement negotiations. There were expressed concerns about the changing demographic patterns in the community and, therefore, a formula was developed which seemed capable of responding to these concerns." Charne to Bernard, November 4, 1987.

22. *The Milwaukee Journal,* September 18, 1987; September 4, 1977; June 1, 1978; May 4, 1979; November 6, 1987; and December 28, 1987. Bruce Murphy and John Pawasarat, "Why It Failed: School Desegregation Ten Years Later," *Milwaukee Magazine,* September 1986, pp. 34ff and Murphy, "A City Divided," *Milwaukee Magazine,* April 1986, p. 158; *New York Times,* April 21, 1987.

23. This analysis draws heavily from Aukofer. For other views, see: K. H. Flaming, *Who Riots and Why: Black Urban Perspectives in Milwaukee* (Milwaukee: Milwaukee Urban League, 1968); "Was the 1967 Rioting a Turning Point?" *The Milwaukee Journal,* July 17, 1977; and, Helen Weber, *Summer Mockery* (Milwaukee: Aestas Press, 1986).

24. "Groppi's Army," *Time,* September 15, 1967, p. 25; "Groppi's War on Milwaukee," *U.S. News and World Report,* September 25, 1967, p. 24.; and, "Priest on the March," *The Economist,* October 7, 1967, p. 48.

25. Gary Benedict, "Attitudes Toward Desegregation in Milwaukee," *Phi Delta Kappan* 61 (June 1980), p. 716; Karl E. Taeuber and Alma F. Taeuber, *Negroes in Cities: Residential Segregation and Neighborhood Change* (New York: Aldine, 1965); Annemette Sorensen, Karl E. Taeuber, and Leslie J. Hollingsworth, Jr., "Indexes of Racial Residential Segregation for 109 Cities in the United States," *Sociological Focus* 8 (April 1975), pp. 125–42; and, Sherman Park Community Association, "A Case Study of Real Estate Practices in Metropolitan Milwaukee," May 19, 1977, 27 + pp. and Metropolitan Milwaukee Fair Housing Council, "Lending Patterns in Milwaukee: A Summary Report on the Initial Findings," November 2, 1980.

26. "Accidents or Police Brutality?" *Time,* October 26, 1981, p. 70; "Milwaukee's Cops Under Fire," *Newsweek,* February 15, 1982, p. 31; and William Raspberry, "Milwaukee Ponders Black District," *Montgomery* (Ala.) *Advertiser,* November 17, 1987. Lloyd Barbee collected over a half million dollars for his work on the school desegregation case. Vel Phillips won office as Wisconsin's Secretary of State, only to face charges of incompetence and lose reelection. Father Groppi soon left the priesthood, became an Episcopalian and a bus driver, married and started a family. In 1983, on a flip of the coin after a tie vote, he became head of the county bus drivers' union. He died in 1985 of a brain tumor. Maier, who swept every ward, black and white, in the city in 1968, continued to engender black loyalty by finding places in his administration for key black leaders. Of all the major participants in the Milwaukee civil rights controversy, only the mayor continued his life relatively unaffected.

27. Overall, state funding rose from 36 percent of Milwaukee's general revenue budget in 1964–65 to 42 percent in 1974–75, then declined to 40 percent in 1984–85. U.S. Bureau of the Census, *City Government Finances in 1964–65,* Series GF-5 (Washington: U.S. Government Printing Office, 1966), Table 6, p. 60; *1974–75,* Series 75, No. 4 (1976), Table 7, p. 104; and *1984–85,* Series GF85, No. 4 (1986), Table 7, p. 100.

28. Federal support rose from 2 percent of Milwaukee's 1964–65 general revenues to 12 percent in 1974–75 and then fell to 7 percent in 1984–85. Ibid.

29. *Community Housing in Milwaukee.*

30. *The Milwaukee Sentinel,* August 18, 1982. In his "unreconstructed fondness" for

high taxes, Maier recently boasted of raising local taxes 24 times in 28 years. *The Economist*, April 9, 1988, p. 32.

31. Maier, *Challenge*, pp. 70–129 and *The Milwaukee Sentinel*, September 6–10, 1982.

32. Marchetti, "Runaways and Takeovers."

33. Charles J. Sykes, "Mayor Queeg," *Milwaukee Magazine*, February 1985, p. 126.

34. Dragos, "Privately Funded Mechanisms."

35. Helen Pauly, "Renaissance Men," *Milwaukee Magazine*, August 1985, pp. 38–46 and "The Shopping Mall Goes Urban," *Business Week*, December 13, 1982, pp. 50–52.

36. *Milwaukee, Wisconsin, Metropolitan Area . . . Today, 1987* (Washington, D.C.: The Urban Land Institute, 1987); *Report of Activities, 1980–1985* (Milwaukee: Department of City Development, September 1986); and, *Annual Reports, 1983–1986* (Milwaukee: Department of City Development, 1984–1987).

37. Charles J. Sykes: "The Losing End," *Milwaukee Magazine*, November 1982, p. 116; "The Empty Chair," *Milwaukee Magazine*, September 1984, p. 124; "Mayor Etcetera," *Milwaukee Magazine*, September 1985, p. 126, and *The New York Times*, March 29, 1988. Maier's loss of control over the council during his final term was so great that in one three-year stretch, he vetoed fifty-seven bills only to see a two-thirds majority override him thirty-three times.

38. *Economist,* op. cit.

X

NEW YORK
A TALE OF TWO CITIES

Daniel J. Walkowitz

"Everything is the biggest, the ultimate.
Nothing is higher than New York."

—Rafal Olbinski,
Polish emigré artist[1]

New York's experience has always been central to America's sense of itself; yet, the city has always been a place apart. Hollywood films such as *Miracle on 34th Street* and *Breakfast at Tiffany's* have simply confirmed the nation's view that the city is a magical place in which American dreams of opportunity, opulence, and success come true.

But New York also occupies a darker place in the American imagination. In other cinematic visions, New York loomed as a place of darkness and shadows where images of race and crime merged. Manhattan, as in Woody Allen's movie of the same name, could still be the city of aspiration, with its skyline reaching for the stars. But outside the commercial center, in the periphery and the outer boroughs, crime and danger lurked, whether it be *On the Waterfront* where the underworld contaminated sinewy longshoremen, or in an area like mid-Manhattan's Hell's Kitchen depicted in *West Side Story*, where Puerto Rican and Italian-American gangs warred. By the late 1970s, the Bronx, the borough with the largest minority percentage in its population, had come to symbolize another city, one of danger, violence, and corruption, as in *Fort Apache: The Bronx* or *The Taking of Pelham One, Two, Three*. Perhaps the best examples of the two-city vision could be seen in the immensely popular disco film, *Saturday Night Fever,* where celluloid success was idealized as possible only when one escaped the small-town confines of working-class, Italian Brooklyn for "serious" dance opportunities in cosmopolitan Manhattan.

The division of the city into ethnic, class, and racial neighborhoods was neither new to New York nor unique to it. Residential segregation existed as early as the Jacksonian era, and Charles Dickens, among others, had graphically depicted the

189

horrors of the "Five Points" slums, so reminiscent of the infamous slums of his native London. Rich and poor living next to each other remains a familiar characteristic of the American city. But the divisions within New York have taken on a new dimension in the late twentieth century, one that may prefigure and symbolize the nation's future in a world labor market. New York has become a global core city, in the words of one sociologist, one of the transformative "centers for management, control, and servicing of a world economy."[2] Like other Snowbelt cities, New York has seen its manufacturing base diminish, but as a global city, New York's experience has not simply been one of decline but of transformation, as it has experienced fundamental growth in consumer goods, finance for transnational corporations, and product diversification for corporate growth and control. The growth, however, has been uneven, and the result has been the emergence of two separate cities divided along class and racial lines.

Like other Snowbelt cities, New York has witnessed a steady decline in the number of manufacturing jobs, the traditional base of the city's "respectable" working class. In 1950, New York still accounted for approximately 7 percent of U.S. industrial employment, with over half the city's workers in blue-collar jobs ranging from apparel to printing. By 1984, the city's share of factory employment stood at under half the 1950 figure. Some jobs were only shifted to the suburbs, of course, as in the move of the New York Giants football team to the New Jersey Meadowlands, but others were lost to the region. In a move with broad symbolic meaning for a city which earlier in the century had the largest Jewish population in the world, Hebrew National Inc., announced in 1986 it was moving its rabbinically supervised kosher meat-processing operations to Indianapolis.[3]

The decline in factory jobs, however, was offset by the increase in white-collar employment, primarily in jobs for women. In 1970, approximately three hundred thousand fewer men worked in the city than had two decades earlier, but over two hundred thousand women had joined the city labor force. Many of these women found work in expanding service industries. The growth rate for producer-services industries—banking, insurance, data processing, engineering services, and the like—between 1977 and 1981 was 20.1 percent. Simultaneously, employment in the nine major service industries increased 17 percent. Historically, New York's industry has relied on cheap, seasonal labor for which the city's immigrants, women and children have been a surplus army. But transformation—growth and decline accompanied by a polarized and restructured labor force—has brought the city new challenges.[4]

Polarization has especially marked the growth in the labor market of the core city, as an army of migrants from the Caribbean basin and blacks have assumed low-paid jobs servicing the life styles of high-tech and high finance workers. As a global city, New York has become more sharply divided between an affluent, technocratic, professional white-collar group managing the financial and commercial life of an international city and an unemployed and underemployed service sector which is substantially black and Hispanic. Earlier divisions in the city were ethnic and economic; today racial and gender divisions and the growing predominance of white-collar work on the one hand and worklessness on the other hand have made

New York's labor market resemble that of a third world city. The lot of the working poor in the city has always been hard but hopeful. Today, however, a distinct labor market of underemployed persons exists who, when they work, congregate in jobs with little promise of mobility. Thus, in 1987, one of every four residents—and almost 40 percent of the city's children—lived below the federal poverty line. A study from 1984 concluded that "while New York remains a city of gold for those at the top of the economic ladder, it has become a city of despair for many elderly, for the homeless, for women and children barely subsisting on public welfare."[5]

The third world character of the polarized city extends from it workshops and board rooms to its tenements and luxury apartments. On the one hand, a real estate boom in gentrified Manhattan (and the "Manhattanizing" of adjacent areas in Jersey City, Hoboken, Long Island City, and the Park Slope and Brooklyn Heights sections of Brooklyn) accompanied the increase in professional white-collar jobs in communication, law, and finance. Blacks and to a less extent Hispanics have gained employment in government, banking, and health services. A vastly disproportionate share of racial minorities, however, who live in depressed areas like the South Bronx, East and Central Harlem, and the center of Brooklyn, face widespread unemployment and pervasive underemployment in low-paid work in maintenance and service jobs attending the offices and restaurants where the affluent professionals work and dine. As Andrew Hacker presciently wrote over a decade ago: "Whether they face up to this fact or not, New Yorkers of all ideologies have become accustomed to living off an economy built on cheap labor. . . . The wealth of New York sustains some of the best French chefs from the continent, while the maldistribution keeps families in tenements where their children risk lead poisoning."[6]

The map of inequality in New York has sharply delineated boundaries. As *Saturday Night Fever* reminded us, Manhattan is different. Although not all the rich live in Manhattan, not all of Manhattan is rich. Cheek by jowl with the corporate rich are the poor in Harlem, the aged in Washington Heights, and the dissolute in the flop houses of Times Square and the nether reaches of yet ungentrified parts of the Lower East Side. Still, the island's residents are richer, better educated, and more than twice as many are single and professional than those in any of the city's four other boroughs. Manhattanites account for almost 80 percent of the city's dividend income.[7]

Indeed, race and gender divisions of labor characterize most American cities today, but New York's ethnic and racial diversity and its large Hispanic population disproportionately concentrated in declining manufacturing sectors have provided rather archetypical social problems. New York's minority politics, for example, have also been especially complex. Mid-century balanced party slates appealed to the "three I's"—Italy, Israel, and Ireland. In the 1950 census, Italian-Americans constituted the largest bloc of New Yorkers followed by substantial Jewish and Irish groups. Blacks constituted no more than 10 percent of the population and the Hispanic percentage remained under 5 percent.

The minority population increased dramatically in the postwar era. Migrants continued to be prominent features of New York life, as the city remained a haven for the politically dispossessed from around the world. At a time when whites of foreign parentage declined from 56 percent of the total population in 1950 to 35 percent by 1980, refugees from places such as Poland and Hungary continued to arrive. Migrant Hispanics and blacks came in greater numbers. By 1950, blacks had become the third largest group in the city (25.2 percent), just behind Italians and Jews. In addition, the collapse of agriculture in Puerto Rico between 1945 and 1960 inaugurated a regular migration to the city, a flow that became a weekly stream of 1,135 by 1952. The city held its first Puerto Rican Day parade in 1959. By 1970, the shell shocked South Bronx housed nearly two out of every five of New York's 800,000 Puerto Ricans.

Other Caribbean migrants, especially West Indians, Haitians, and Cubans came in these years too, settling in New York and in nearby Paterson and Jersey City. By 1980 the Hispanic population of New York was estimated at 19.9 percent, almost 60 percent of whom were Puerto Ricans. Perhaps another 2 percent of the total population were Asians, primarily Chinese, Japanese, or Koreans. By 1970, New York had also become home to the largest Chinatown in the country. In 1950, seven of every eight New Yorkers had been of European extraction; by 1980, the ration was nearer to two in five.[8]

Poverty scarred New York's blacks and Hispanics early. Disadvantageous family lives, education, and housing limited their mobility, and discrimination blocked their opportunities. Blacks were 13 percent of the city's population in 1960 but 45 percent of those on the welfare rolls. Hispanics were 8 percent of the population and 30 percent of welfare recipients.[9] Extrapolations from fragmentary data demonstrate the necessity of work for minority mothers in particular, but perhaps nothing illustrates the problems confronting New York blacks and Hispanics more than the staggeringly high percentages of children in single-parent families, virtually all headed by mothers. While three out of every four white children lived in homes with both parents present, less than half of the Hispanic children and only two in five black kids did.[10]

Inferior minority housing, schooling, and jobs reflects the city's polarized racial experiences. Even as their numbers increased, minorities remained isolated and confined to the worst housing in the city and educated in a *de facto* segregated school system. Hispanic *machismo* also cast a long shadow over the educational experience of Hispanic girls, with its own social ramifications for the city. The percentage of New York Hispanic girls finishing high school was almost half that for their white and black counterparts, plunging to 38.3 percent![11]

The employment picture was no better. The lowest paid unskilled service jobs were always available to minorities, but even as growing numbers earned City University of New York baccalaureates, they could obtain little else. While opportunities opened for those with new communication skills, for those in the arts and for those in finance, fewer options and harsher realities confronted the majority of blacks, Hispanics, and single mothers in the city.

While the economic transformation of New York as a global city in a global economy has been scarred by polarized social experiences with racial and class divisions, certain structural conditions also shape New York's grim future and, as we shall see, shaped the political challenges of the postwar era. To begin, New York is vastly bigger than any other city. Its population of over seven million gives events in the city a practical and symbolic importance for the nation and world. As of 1986, the New York metropolitan area's almost 18 million residents continued to outrank the sprawling Los Angeles region by nearly 5 million and to double that of Chicago, the region with the third largest population.[12] A few statistics give a sense of the enormous scale on which the city functions: the city's population in 1980 was larger than that of 41 of the nation's 50 states; its annual budget of $22.7 billion (1988) is larger than that of 48 of the states; its over five thousand miles of pipes, tunnels, and water mains bring more than one trillion gallons of water into the city every day; the city has to dispose of over 20 million tons of refuse annually.[13]

New York is also the financial and communications capital of North America and, along with London and Tokyo, one of three in the world. New York City alone employed 3.6 percent of the U.S. work force in 1984—an impressive enough figure—but the city also employed fully 17.4, 22.2, and 39.1 percent of the nation's workforce in women's outerwear, advertising, and investment banking.[14] Wall Street remains the symbol of world finance; the Garment District markets American fashions (and still sews many of them, too) for 5th Avenue stores and suburban shopping malls across the country; Madison Avenue advertises these wares through New York-based radio and television networks, national news weeklies, and national newspapers such as the *Wall Street Journal* and *New York Times*. The city's 29 colleges and universities, 65 museums, 1500 galleries, and multiple theaters and dance companies make the city the nation's cultural center. When New York speaks, America listens.

Second, New York is an aged urban city dependent on ancient public works and locked into a political geography which limits its fiscal options. The city, for example, has faced enormous financial burdens to rebuild costly transportation and plumbing infrastructures first erected nearly a century ago. Unlike many Sunbelt cities, New York completed its possible geographical expansion long ago (Brooklyn was annexed last in 1898) and can not simply expand its tax base and absorb would-be competing suburbs.[15]

Rather than solving the city's problems as an annexed tax base, regional development has complicated the financial problems of the city. Suburbs have identified with the city as a metropolitan center for cultural services but have defended separateness when it came to issues such as taxes and schools. The New York Giants, for example, lured by lower New Jersey income and sales taxes and new facilities with ample parking for suburban fans, play football in the New Jersey Meadowlands. City politicians respond by offering competing tax breaks to encourage such companies to stay. Either way, city coffers suffered. As Sonny Werblin, the Jersey sports impresario and Giants owner explained, New York no longer signifies the city anyway but the greater metropolitan area in which he markets his product: "I don't believe in New York City, but in a megalopolis, stretching from Asbury Park in New Jersey to Poughkeepsie in New York and Bridgeport in Connecticut. These are the bedrooms of New York, where the tickets are billed to."[16]

The Giants illustrate in a small way the fiscal problems which have assailed postwar New York as it underwent its social and economical transformation into a global city. Some of the responsibility for New York's problems lies outside the city—in state and federal policies, in the competing regional tax bases, or in the broad structural problems endemic to older industrial cities. But what did New York politicians, moguls, and ordinary citizens do to relieve or exacerbate the situation? Where does their responsibility lie? Who held power and how did they use it? The political history of postwar New York rivals that of most nations in its complexity, dominion, intrigue, and chicanery.

As the war neared its conclusion, Mayor Fiorella LaGuardia announced in May 1945 that he would end his twelve-year reign at Gracie Mansion. After scandals beset the Jimmy Walker administration and the Tammany machine, the "little flower" had won election in 1933 by creating a Fusion party candidacy to navigate the shoals of partisan politics. New York was a staunchly Democratic city and, to win, Republican politicians such as LaGuardia had to seek an independent base, a development requiring some unusual conditions. These were not present in the late 1940s, and so more traditional political allegiances returned the Democrats to power.

The end of the war brought contradictory hopes for a new beginning and a fondness for familiar ways. William O'Dwyer's election, in November 1945 as New York City's one hundredth mayor brought both. The Irish-born O'Dwyer had won his spurs as a crusading Brooklyn D. A. who prosecuted Murder, Inc., the gangster syndicate. Ironically, his anti-corruption reputation brought him and ever corrupt Tammany Hall to power. O'Dwyer ensured his election by appealing to a new issue which would prove sacred to New York's huge renter community—rent control. Real estate interests wanted recently enacted rent control guidelines retracted. But O'Dwyer and every mayor since could count votes—three-quarters of New York residents lived in apartments—and he promised instead to extend the guidelines to protect returning servicemen.

O'Dwyer's record must be measured in the context of the particular historical moment and specific political realities in place when he assumed office. Reconversion of war industries to domestic production brought automation technologies and assembly line production which needed new facilities. But expensive land and restrictive zoning handicapped the city's chances for new facilities and made suburban tracts especially attractive. Furthermore, federal acts effectively subsidized the growth of the suburbs: the Federal-Aid Highway Act of 1944 (with the Interstate Highway Act of 1956) and the Federal Housing Act of 1949 made it cheap to move shoppers, workers, and goods to new suburban plants and provided ready mortgage money for their housing. Macy's, for example, had opened a Bronx branch even before World War II, but now it and other well-established New York consumer institutions opened branches in suburban shopping malls.[17]

In the shift of shoppers, taxpayers, and tax-producing manufacturing plants to the suburbs, New York public officials faced demands for increased services to the remaining and comparatively more needy population at the same time that the city's tax base fell. Furthermore, these services, which relied upon a decayed urban infrastructure, had to compete with those of the new suburbs and Sunbelt cities and had to do so without the expanded tax base that annexation made available in the West. New York mayors had to solve twentieth-century metropolitan urban problems with obsolete, eighteenth-century city boundaries, determined by geographic divisions rather than modern transportation networks and the long reach of regional media. Finally, a history of city-state feuds over resource allocation, not to mention inter-party sovereignty and patronage battles, limited the options of New York's mayors. State law prohibited the city from raising its own revenue without authorization from a legislature controlled by Republicans from rural and suburban areas.[18]

During most of this era, the state and federal government also took more from the city in taxes than they returned in services. In fact, federal dollars, increasingly tied to the burgeoning military-industrial complex, went disproportionately to the Sunbelt. Similarly, the interstate highway system and western irrigation projects received vast infusions of money, while mass transit and decayed urban sewer systems went begging. It was this context in which mayors such as William O'Dwyer had to work.[19]

Three particular issues during the immediate postwar years characterized the tumultuous O'Dwyer administration and foreshadowed New York's subsequent history: labor struggles, a fiscal crisis, and political corruption. The labor crisis greeted the mayor upon taking office; O'Dwyer had to mediate a tugboat strike in 1946 which had crippled the port and threatened fuel shortages. O'Dwyer's active participation in the settlement set a precedent for a new postwar mayoral role in New York labor relations.

McCarthyism during this era left another legacy for the city's labor movement. New York had always been a home for the radical part of the labor movement, and "Red" labor leaders, like Michael Quill of the TWU, deflected the vision of state legislatures away from wage demands to the "Red menace." Doing its part against the supposed communist menace, the state legislature passed the Condon-Wadlin Act in 1947, outlawing strikes by public employees.

The red scare affected city polity, too. Under the shadow of postwar McCarthyism, entrenched Tammany Hall politicians forged a new liberal alliance with a more corporatist, bureaucratic labor movement. In 1948, the Department of Welfare hired as commissioner Raymond H. Hilliard of Illinois, who was famous for prosecuting cases of fraud and saving money. In his words, Hilliard's task was to "set our house in order." Soon workers were suspended, hounded from the agency, or fired. By 1950, the Department of Welfare had withdrawn recognition of its employees' union, welcoming instead a company union which was waiting in the wings. Equally important were the shifts within the agency. Hilliard instituted efficiency drives. Measuring eligibility and counting clients became new hallmarks of welfare, a legacy which the city would pay for in mid-1960s welfare strikes and client agitation to regain benefits and reorient welfare from its obsession with eligibility back to a concern with service.[20] Thus, the city's purge of left-wing unions in welfare emasculated services at the same time as it transferred power to more conservative labor leaders who were more congenial to the Democratic machine.

The specter of McCarthyism affected more than city labor relations; it poisoned the whole public arena. Two brief examples must suffice. First, in a still largely untold story, City College and the New York City school board fired teachers accused of communist affiliations. Second, in November 1947, rather than allow the seating of another Communist Party representative (two had been seated earlier), voters approved the abolition of proportional representation on the city council. At-large candidates would now need majorities. The change gave extraordinary power to the Democrats who dominated the city, crippling both minority parties such as the Communists and hampering effective reform opposition.[21]

A second crisis which O'Dwyer confronted upon taking office was financial. He inherited a budgetary crisis, and his resolution of this crisis foreshadowed a fiscal struggle which has continued for four decades. The budget for 1945–46 of $763 million drew on revenues of only $757 million. Subway deficits increased the shortfall to $78 million, and the deficit did not include a request for higher wages from the Transport Workers' Union (TWU). This was a real crisis, and the inventive "solution" to it came from Robert Moses, a man who was reshaping the face of the city.

Though he never held elective office, Moses, a city planner with a penchant for strong-arm politics, wielded great power in the city. He created a public instrument, the Triborough Authority, which, with vast, independent funds raised through tolls, could operate in total secrecy and without accountability. This independent base gave Moses the prerogative to intimidate and cajole public officials and eventually to control virtually every public works project in the New York region from the mid-1930s through the mid-1960s. He reigned as the chair or leading committee member on nine different commissions or public works authorities. The Board of Estimate and city council, each made up of elected city officials, had to pass on any project, but as his biographer has noted, Moses "effectively dominated" both legislative bodies "through his use of the power of money"—patronage, publicity, and pork-barrel projects such as neighborhood parks. Last but not least, Moses, known both for his efficient organization and skullduggery, usually favored private developers at the expense of the working poor and minorities. All these traits and priorities became evident in his answer to the city's fiscal needs.[22]

O'Dwyer needed additional revenue, and at the same time, Moses wanted money to build a new international airport. The state had a $570 million surplus, but rather than tap into that money, Moses looked to local sources. His answer was to double the subway fare to 10 cents (the fare had not been raised in its nearly fifty years of operation) so as to permit the city's debt limit to be raised. Instead of using the money for debt service or for the overdue subway modernization and mass transit, Moses then floated bonds for roads, bridges, and airport construction with surplus revenue from the fares. Bankers, suburban commuters, and bond holders did well; transit riders and taxpayers who refunded the bondholders paid the freight.[23]

During the next twenty years, Moses's public works projects—highways, parks and housing projects—reshaped the profile of the city, intensifying the development of the two-city New York by supporting the upper classes against the poor. For example, as director of the Mayor's Committee on Slum Clearance, Moses ran the largest federal Title I housing program in the United States. By 1957, $267 million had been spent in New York City, compared to $178 million in the rest of the country. Under Title I, the city could bulldoze an individual's house in a lower-class neighborhood in order to build new housing for the community in general. Moreover, scandalous procedures sprinkled with cronyism and cost overruns enriched construction magnates while the replacement of their destroyed communities with anomic housing blocks caused the poor and minorities to pay disproportionately. Simultaneously, Moses spent over $2 billion in the building of 627 miles of roadways which could speed commuters in and around the city from the new Manhattan office buildings and back to their white suburbs. Moses built thirteen new expressways and during the postwar decade opened Idlewild International Airport (now JFK), the Verrazano Bridge connecting Brooklyn and Staten Island, and a third Lincoln tunnel tube to New Jersey. Between 1947 and 1963, builders added more than 58 million square feet of city office space in Manhattan, a total greater than that of the next 22 cities combined! Before the War, Rockefeller Center, the Chrysler Building, and Grand Central Station had marked mid-town as the center for corporate America. The glass and bronze 38-floor Seagrams building designed by Mies van der Rohe with Philip Johnson interiors and a spacious pedestrian plaza on Park Avenue, came to symbolize postwar shapes. The construction of Chase-Manhattan, Time-Life, Equitable, and the United Nations buildings began to transform midtown avenues into steel and glass caverns.[24]

While planners, politicians, and developers lauded this construction at the time as "progress," the impact was more mixed. Moses, with the approval of city legislative bodies, spent city revenues lavishly on roads, for example, but little on mass transport and education. An example from one of Moses's construction projects—the building of the Cross Bronx Expressway—suggests the uneven but devastating impact of Moses's projects. Rather than modify the planned route slightly to by-pass an ethnic, working-class residential community in the East Tremont section of the Bronx, Moses elected to tear down 159 buildings housing 1,530 families. The alternative would have moved only 6 buildings with 19 persons. Moses simply treated the 159 buildings of older, blue-collar apartments and small retail shops as a "slum." The housing was not modern, but it was roomy, solid, and affordable. As important, it was a stable community with kin networks and neighborhood services which the expressway disrupted for years and ultimately destroyed. The creation in the north Bronx of the world's largest cooperative apartment community, a 15,382-unit complex called Co-op City, further depleted the area's population. By 1970, the East Tremont community, its core gutted, had become a wasteland.

Although East Tremont had had a substantial Jewish population, Moses's Title I Slum Clearance programs disproportionately affected blacks and Puerto Ricans. In seven years, Moses forced the relocation of 170,000 people—the equivalent of a city the size of Albany. Thirty-seven percent were nonwhites (including some Hispanics), three times their percentage in the 1950 census. Moreover, public housing hardly improved the standard of living. The new high-rise housing blocks were desolate places which attracted drug dealers. The new apartments usually required higher rents, too, though Title I did nothing to find jobs for unemployed minorities.

In any case, as Robert Caro has noted, "the percentage of displaced families that had been admitted to public housing was pathetically small." Instead, minorities often found themselves shunted off into more dilapidated private rental housing, often in more segregated areas.

The social consequences of Moses's slum removal programs were disastrous for the working poor and minorities who were displaced. But not all suffered; developers captured windfall profits, especially in one famous case when no work was done. Moses's favorites gained handsomely. For example, developers offered Moses $9.58 per square foot for land for his West Side redevelopment (Lincoln Center and the Coliseum), but Moses elected to give it to one of his favored developers for $7 per square foot. In turn, he chose to purchase rather than condemn a building owned by Robert Kennedy and his sisters for $62.88 per square foot! At the same time, the Catholic Church received a tax-free, four square block parcel adjacent to Lincoln Center for its downtown Fordham campus; in exchange the Archbishop kept pressure on Washington (and President Kennedy) for federal housing funds.[25]

Other cities, we now know, accomplished much the same transformation without a czar such as Moses, but at the time the press hailed his tactics as "unique." The *Times* and others were enamored with his success—and, undoubtedly wary of his well-known political muscle and vindictiveness. Ironically, Moses's "system" may have done more to create slums than remove them:

> It is a system under which neighborhoods actually have deteriorated; it is a system under which the number of apartments, already inadequate, has been reduced for years to come. It is a system . . . beginning again the cycle of overcrowding and bad housing that creates slums.[26]

So, events in the O'Dwyer administration suggest the postwar origins of the two New York "cities." Elitist solutions to the city's fiscal plight facilitated the development of corporate services, discriminated against minority interests and consolidated Tammany's political power. O'Dwyer's precipitate resignation on August 31, 1950 resurrected yet another familiar theme in New York's history: serious urban problems did not prevent corrupt politicians from profiting. Despite O'Dwyer's prior record as a crusading D.A., he had remained remarkably chummy with gangsters. With the Senate's Kefauver Committee ready to summon him to testify, O'Dwyer, who's only proven "sin" was the shady company he kept, moved to Mexico as U.S. ambassador rather than embarrass himself or his party.[27]

The president of the city council, Vincent "Impy" Impellitteri, ascended to the mayoralty. Chosen to run with O'Dwyer largely because, as an unknown, his candidacy raised few embarrassing questions about his associations, Impellitteri now sought to establish himself in the independent LaGuardia tradition by running as a Fusion Party candidate in the special election of November 1950. He won that election, but lacking both ability and charisma, he lost in the Democratic primary in 1952 to Robert Wagner, Jr.

Wagner, son of the illustrious New York senator of the same name, had won election as Manhattan Borough president in 1949 and had become the darling of the Bronx and Manhattan Democratic machines. During his four terms (1953–1965), the politically savvy Wagner generally managed to stay on good terms with the new Tammany sachem, Carmine De Sapio, while making what have been generally regarded as unbiased political appointments of good administrators. Yet, Wagner knew his place. As capable as he might have been, outside city hall, Robert Moses presided over the physical construction of the two-city New York.

During these years, booming construction projects transformed the city. Manhattan emerged as a white collar island of steel and glass skyscrapers, while massive city-wide transportation and housing projects eviscerated some neighborhoods and promoted others. The city and the CIO had purged the militant unions during the McCarthy era, and the more conciliatory municipal and craft unions flourished in the construction boom. Indeed, Impellitteri and then Wagner ministered until 1960 with relatively few controversies, while fiscal policy remained biased towards Moses' suburban, middle-class orientation. City residents paid more and got less. Under Impellitteri, for example, subway fares went up to 15 cents, the sales tax rose from 2 to 3 percent, and the city spent only slightly more money on hospitals, schools, libraries, and the city colleges combined than on highways.

By the end of Wagner's fourth term in 1965, the conjunction between urban removal and development of a thriving commercial business center for international corporations that had laid the conditions for a divided New York could be seen in residential patterns. Three and one-half million daytime workers may have entered Manhattan's central business district (South of 59th Street) daily, but during the preceding twelve years, 800,000 white residents had fled the city for the suburbs, their numbers more than made up by additional blacks and Hispanics.[28]

By the mid-1960s the racial character of the social disjunctions in the city had become apparent. New York had traditionally been a center for radical politics, and the national civil rights movement and the anti-war protest of those years only heightened awareness of urban inequality and quickened the social response. Strong feelings generated by these movements affected New York City's mayoral election of 1965, providing the opportunity for another Republican candidate to defeat Tammany Hall.

By 1960, De Sapio had lost control of Tammany. Late to support John Kennedy in the 1960 election, De Sapio watched federal patronage slip through his hands and into the mayor's. Wagner then broke with De Sapio, running a successful anti-boss campaign in his mayoral re-election campaign (1961). Meanwhile, in Greenwich Village, liberal insurgents led by a young lawyer, Ed Koch, and others, ousted De Sapio as district leader. By the time Wagner announced he would not run for a fifth term in 1965, his appointment of independent-minded, reform Democrats put the nail in the coffin of Manhattan's Tammany machine.

The politics of race also divided the traditionally liberal Democratic constituency. During a July heatwave the preceding summer, a policeman had killed a black boy, precipitating four days of riot and fires which left a second person dead and 140 others injured. Anti-war protest and a strike by social workers that year further raised white middle-class anxieties.

In the midst of this turbulence, the Democrats nominated the conservative city comptroller, Abraham Beame, who they felt would appeal to older white ethnics. The Republicans were normally more conservative, but these were heated political times, feelings running high about the escalating U.S. role in Vietnam and the rise of Black Power militancy. This time the Republicans nominated John Vliet Lindsay, the tall, handsome WASP Congressman from the Silk Stocking District on Manhattan's Upper East Side. Lindsay, who along with Senator Javits and Governor Rockefeller represented the small, but vital liberal wing of the Republican Party, raised the hackles of a growing band on the right-wing of the Republican Party. This division did no damage to Lindsay, however, for when the conservatives left him, they split their vote between Democrat Beame and independent candidate, William F. Buckley, the renowned editor of the *National Review*. Liberals from all groups went to Lindsay.

On November 2, 1965, John Lindsay was elected the city's 103rd mayor. One week later, a power failure blacked out the city for fifteen hours. Establishing Camelot on top of a decaying urban infrastructure would be no easy task.

Lindsay led the city as if he were marching off into the sunset, a hero doing "the right thing" who could not be bothered by prosaic details of funding and politics. He took bold new initiatives on welfare and schools. He strode out into the streets of the ghetto to defuse racial violence. He promised imaginative programming and an end to political favoritism. What Lindsay promised in rhetoric, however, he lost in political savvy, often winning only the enmity of trade-union leaders, Albany legislators, Governor Rockefeller, and the city council. To many the mayor was haughty and intractable, grandstanding for a run at the presidency. Lindsay, in turn, often thought himself locked in battles with intractable opponents.

The opening day of his administration, January 1, 1966, Lindsay found himself faced with a transit strike. Refusing to negotiate while the workers struck, Lindsay chose instead to throw the long-time TWU leader, the fiery Michael Quill, in jail for twelve days. Quill made Lindsay pay for the indignation. With angry businessmen clamoring for a settlement, the union compelled the harried mayor to settle the strike by granting concessions valued at twice the union's initial request! Before the year was out, the city had also experienced a 25-day newspaper blackout, a 33-day dock strike, and a 75-day shipping delivery stoppage. To many New Yorkers and a late-night national television audience fed a steady diet of anti-New York jokes, it seemed as if the city was slowly ceasing to function. Even Mother Nature appeared to have conspired against Lindsay. The city was in the midst of a five-year drought and restaurants were only permitted to serve water on request.

Late-night humor to the contrary, the mayor was not without his successes. The years between 1965 and 1969 witnessed the biggest construction boom in the city's history. Cities across the country boiled over in riots and civil disorder, but Lindsay kept the lid on in New York. He did so with both real and symbolic actions. As noted, he walked the streets, demonstrating personal concern for the plight of the poor and the disadvantaged. More important, he initiated programs to provide services for them, services which had been withheld or cut back ever since the Hilliard era of the 1950s.

Lindsay moved to reverse years of declining services in welfare, education, and health care. Stimulated by new left college graduates who had entered social work, a welfare rights movement had spread through the city since 1964. Sensitive to the movement's demands, Lindsay appointed a new commissioner, Mitchell Ginsburg, and instructed him to reverse previous policies, insisting that all clients receive their appropriate allotment. Then, in response to claims of police brutality, the mayor inaugurated a civilian review board.

Lindsay also addressed the uneven provision of education and health care services. Beginning in the early 1950s, *de facto* discrimination had created inferior schools in black and Hispanic districts, and by 1969, the city school system had changed such that these schools were now the norm in a system where whites were in the minority. Concerned about their children's education, minority parents began to demand control over their local schools. Lindsay responded by appointing the Bundy Commission, which recommended school decentralization to give local boards community control. At the college level, the public demand was for access. Open enrollment became policy at New York's City University (CUNY), giving any high school graduate the opportunity to enter college. In regard to health care, the Municipal Hospital Corporation was established to provide medical access to all in the community.

Unfortunately, while Lindsay's programs represented a fundamental reallocation of urban resources to the needy and minorities, they were uneven successes. Local control of school boards has led to improvement only in selected districts, not generally throughout the city. The complex character of Lindsay programs can be seen in the fate of City College's (CCNY). Once the alma mater of white European ethnics, the school had had more Nobel prize winners than any other American institution of higher learning. By the mid-1980s, under open enrollment, the mission of the institution had changed from primary research to community education, in which remedial courses played a large part in the curriculum. CCNY is now a strong black institution (with a white Jewish faculty) in which blacks and Hispanics gain a foothold to mobility. Today, Caribbean blacks and Asians are the new minorities at City College.[29]

These programs cost a lot of money, stimulated serious opposition, and created political opposition to Lindsay. The neighborhood school plan, for example, resulted in a "Great School War" between the Jewish-dominated teachers' union and black communities in areas such as the Ocean Hill-Brownsville community of Brooklyn. The police were deeply offended by the Civilian Review Board, and the white middle-class in the outer boroughs complained they were "neglected." Doubled welfare rolls and costly labor contracts served others' needs; they saw only potholes and services paralyzed by striking sanitation men or teachers. Poor street cleaning after a February 1969 snowstorm embittered Queens' residents further. "Lindsay Must Go" signs sprouted around the city, as racial backlash mixed with larger social fears in a city as divided as the nation over Vietnam, inflation, and changing social roles.[30]

Neither Democrats nor Republicans wanted anything to do with the mayor. Lindsay lost the Republican primary to conservative state legislator, John Marchi, and in a five-way brawl, a little-known clubhouse politician, Mario Proccacino, won the Democratic race. Abandoned by his own party, Lindsay continued his campaign under the Liberal Party banner.

As it happened, 1969 was the year of the underdog in New York. The Mets had just completed their World Series triumph, the football Jets were on their way to winning the Super Bowl, and in a three-way mayoral race where two conservatives again cancelled each other's vote, Lindsay won reelection. Garnering 42 percent of the vote, the mayor had solved his immediate political problem, but a growing financial crisis was not so easily defeated.

As we have seen, the city's financial problems were not new; O'Dwyer had encountered them upon taking office, and subsequent mayors regularly went hat in hand to Albany and Washington to make up annual shortfalls. In 1960, the city received $150 million in federal grants, yet still had to negotiate a special infusion of funds from Governor Rockefeller to balance its budget. One-quarter of the city's income came from state and federal sources. With the election of Richard Nixon to the presidency in 1968, federal urban policy shifted dramatically toward "Middle American" projects. Money became available for increased police, the arts, and roads but not for low income housing. In New York, during 1970–75, builders started work on 34,167 housing units, but only 8,920 were for low income people. During these years, the South Bronx became a national symbol of urban blight, losing 16 percent of its housing to arson and decay, while private developers poured their money into more profitable ventures.

Federal monies dried up at the same time as more traditional revenue sources reached their practical limits. New Yorkers lamented their reputation as the most-taxed people in the nation as the city sales tax reached 7 percent and subway fares out-paced the decade's rampant inflation. More important, two severe recessions between 1969 and 1975 and massive white flight to the suburbs seriously eroded the city's tax base at the same time as minority newcomers moved into the central city. These minority newcomers not only had little taxable income, but they also needed additional services. While this residential change was in progress, large corporate taxpayers left the city. The 125 Fortune 500 corporations which made New York their home in 1970 fell to 94 by 1975. Revenue-enhancing devices such as the city-run Off-Track Betting Corporation (OTB) could not make up the difference.

Indebtedness could. The city won a measure of fiscal autonomy from the state in 1961 when the state legislature revised the city charter to give the mayor unprecedented authority to estimate (or overestimate while justifying expensive programs!) revenues and determine the level of city debt necessary to fund programs. An (1964) amendment to the City Finance Law also allowed city officials to include current expense items in their construction budget. Both provisions led to abuse, as Lindsay and his successor Abraham Beame tended to overestimate revenues. Between 1961 and 1975, city debt tripled and the cost of servicing that debt rose over 500 percent.

By 1973, Lindsay, alienated from the conservative Republican Party and sensitive to the white, middle-class backlash against his policies, changed his registration to Democrat for an aborted presidential campaign. Upon Lindsay's departure, the

Democratic comptroller, Beame, running as a man who "knows the buck!", became New York's first Jewish mayor, discounting LaGuardia, an Episcopalian who had a Jewish mother. Beame had participated in "creative financing" of the Lindsay-Beame budget for 1973–74, a budget known primarily for its gimmicks, including the transfer of a half-billion dollars of operating expenses to the capital budget which allowed a comparable overestimation of revenues for 1975.

The shortsightedness of these manipulations became clear in 1975 when New York almost went into default on its obligations. Despite their roles in creating the crisis, city officials, the municipal unions, and the poor received unfair blame from television comics, Washington politicians, and press pundits. The preconditions for the crisis lay in structural changes within the metropolitan tax base—the flight of jobs and the middle class to the suburbs—and the needs of an older decaying urban infrastructure. Mayoral financial gimmickry only exacerbated problems. A suburban-oriented federal policy under Nixon and Gerald Ford further depleted resources on which the poor depended. Finally, and ironically, those entrusted with saving the city—its bankers failed to provide proper fiscal oversight for the city's bonds. The capital expansion of the past decade had helped to ensure the city's growth as a financial and corporate center, but profit-minded bankers and state officials had encouraged the city's overindebtedness.

In 1974, Beame acknowledged the city was $430 million in the red and began policies of phased lay-offs and increased borrowing at high interest rates. "Moral obligation bonds," a device conceived by Governor Nelson Rockefeller's friend, Wall Street lawyer and Watergate-era Attorney General, John Mitchell. He permitted the city to borrow beyond its legal limit. When the state's Urban Development Corporation (UDC) collapsed in the winter of 1974–75, lawyers responsible for floating city bonds gained access to the city books. In horror at what they saw, they leaked word to the financial community. By April, Standard and Poor's suspended its A-rating for city bonds. Banks began to unload their municipal holdings, flooding the bond market. That summer the state effectively agreed to bail out the city with $2.3 billion with the condition that it be put in virtual receivership. The state-appointed Emergency Financial Control Board would handle all city finances, and the state-created Municipal Assistance Corporation (MAC), run by bankers and lawyers, would float city bonds, but only when the mayor and council agreed to impose MAC-determined fiscal prudence.

The crisis continued into the fall of 1975 as the city sought federal aid from a hostile President Ford and Congress. New York was Middle America's symbol of urban profligacy and the focus for white resentment against what was incorrectly perceived as a decade of government indulgence of minority needs. According to former Treasury Secretary William Simon, New York spent "three times more per capita" than other large American cities. Others complained about "extortionate" union contracts and indulgent welfare allowances. But when figures are adjusted for services which state and counties pay for in other cities, New York, according to economist William Tabb, compared favorably with similar older industrial cities on spending for standard functions (schools, sanitation, police, parks, etc.), wages, and welfare costs. The big cost was Medicaid (two-thirds of all city welfare costs).[31]

To the Ford White House, trade unions, welfare "malingerers," and the city itself were more obvious targets. The *Daily News* headline for October 30, "FORD TO CITY: DROP DEAD," expressed the prevailing sentiment. Only after the city and state put together an elaborate package of cut-backs and state funding did Ford propose a $2 billion loan package—with harsh repayment terms—for the city.

Before the crisis ended, 60,000 city employees went off the payroll, and social and public services suffered drastic cuts. The city had avoided default only after the teachers' union allowed its pension funds to become collateral for city loans. City banks and bond holders never lost a penny, and the banks profited more than they lost, selling bonds before the panic in 1974 and buying back into a deflated market in 1976. As one critic has reminded us, bankers were not in a conspiracy to "get" the city; they were just behaving like bankers. In the end the banks did extend maturity dates on loans and lower some interest rates.[32]

The fiscal crisis left Beame politically bankrupt. He ran for reelection in 1976, but Edward Koch, the erstwhile liberal Congressman reborn a "capital-punishment liberal," beat state senator Mario Cuomo in the Democratic primary and handily won the general election. The tone of Koch's administration was set by his variously ebullient and abrasive personality. The mayor would parade about town asking, "How am I doing?" substituting personality and bluster for social services. While blacks, Hispanics, and the artistic community grew increasingly hostile to the mayor's policies, Koch easily accommodated himself to the financial overseers at the MAC.

Indeed, Koch assumed the mantle of middle-class New York. Reversing the city trend toward increased social services in the late 1960s, Koch tried to return the city to the priorities of the 1950s. He refocused resources on building an environment accommodating to the international financiers now flocking to the city, but he did so oblivious to the peculiarities of the city's racial composition, work opportunities, labor market, and widespread poverty. In the forty years since the war the city had become an alienating and dangerous place to many old-timers. Koch's belligerence and general combativeness, however, appealed to the older Jewish, Italian, and Irish residents tired of what they felt had been coddling of criminals and the poor, a distinction too easily blurred.

The parade of the tall ships in New York harbor in celebration of the nation's bicentennial symbolized the city's return to grace. With new foreign corporations and banks settling into the city, major new hotels, such as the luxury Grand Hyatt and the super-deluxe Helmsley Palace, and a major convention center opened early in the 1980s. Real estate subsidies for converting commercial space into cooperatives and condominiums stimulated a Manhattan construction boomlet in middle-income and luxury housing. Corporations received comparable tax subsidies and zoning waivers in exchange for promises to build pedestrian plazas or renovate subway platforms. In 1986 the mammoth Javits Convention Center opened. Meanwhile the budget was balanced, even projecting a half-billion dollar surplus in 1987. New York again became a city of hope . . . for some.

But condomania was not for the army of service workers or the unemployed. To be sure, Mayor Koch, sensitive to growing crime rates, emphasized safety, but to the relative neglect of social services. True, social service continued to be a large share of a rapidly expanding budget in the late-1980s. The city spent $125 million on homeless and $200 million on homecare annually, just to give two examples. But under Koch, the Department of Welfare reduced its rolls by 5 to 10 percent, cutting off close to nine hundred thousand people in a move for "effective management." While the percentage of poor in the city continued to rise, the gulf between rich and poor also widened. The number of homeless wandering the streets of the city was greater than at any time since the depression, with estimates running over 20,000. Long lines of desperate bedraggled men waited daily in soup lines, the sleek silhouettes of the skyline at their backs. And the *Report for the Year 2000* (1987) focused on the continuing failure of city schools. These are the social conditions of the city of despair.

Recent racial incidents at Columbia University, white vigilantism against a black teenager in Howard Beach, Brooklyn, and the failure to convict William Goetz, the "subway vigilante," for shooting five black youths, symbolized the divisions between the two worlds—one a white world of affluence, the other a black and Hispanic world of poverty. (The jury did convict Goetz of carrying a firearm without a license, and his one year sentence has outraged his supporters.) Mayor Koch's combative tone and insensitivity to black problems greatly exacerbated racial tensions. But the problem in bridging these two cities lay beyond the mayor. New York City politics in the late 1980s resembled those of the Tammany Hall-Robert Moses era: Koch ruled without any effective opposition. In 1981, he won the nomination of both the Democrats and Republicans; in 1985, he won again with only token opposition. Liberalism, traditionally the backbone of reform politics in the city, languished. One of the themes of the 1980s was the evisceration of political liberalism, and New York politics reflected this: 55 percent of the city's liberals supported Koch in the 1985 election. The newspapers, especially the *Post,* but including the *Times* and the *News,* became cheering sections, lauding Koch for his "honest government." As one critic has written, "The combination of a docile press, an ineffective reform movement, and a moribund Republican Party [opposition] [has] kept the machine in power."[33]

The irony is that all the cheering seemed to drown out the sounds of jail doors closing on Koch's confidants. Koch saw his closest political allies systematically indicted or jailed for corruption, or in the tragic case of the Queens county leader, Donald Manes, commit suicide in shame. Yet, while governing amidst the highest number of high-level political indictments in recent memory, Koch retained a high level of public support.

The public response to the autocracy and corruption suggests the gap facing New Yorkers in the present. The visions of the two cities are polar: the white upper and middle classes (conservatives and often liberals) concentrated in the outer boroughs supported him, while poor blacks and Hispanics, and the intelligentsia, concentrated in Manhattan, detested him. Manhattan's liberals and a united black vote provided sufficient numbers to dethrone Mayor Koch in the 1989 Democratic primary, however. In the November election, Rudoph Guliani, the Republican candidate, who had been a crusading district attorney, narrowly failed to put together another independent fusion majority, and New York elected the liberal, soft-spoken Manhattan Borough President, David Dinkins, as the city's first black mayor. Still, at present, New York City is two cities. One a center of world finance, consumer culture, and the arts; the other, unemployed or poor and in service to the first. But, alas, the second city remains largely invisible to the first, save as an occasional nightmare of racial conflict. Bridging these two social and economic worlds is the challenge for the future.

New Yorkers of all social backgrounds share a fierce pride in their city as a tolerant, creative, international cosmopolitan center. Even the city's hectic pace and social problems must be seen in perspective. New York remains a national center of creative work in the arts. Sections of the city give wide berth to sexual, racial, and ethnic diversity. Print and television media, advertising, finance, fashion, retailing, banking, and countless other fields remain centered in New York. The city pulsates with opportunity, adventure, and power. For all the negative film images of the city, it is still "The Place Where Things Happen" when "Saturday Night Fever" subsides. This, too, is New York.

NOTES

Judith R. Walkowitz, Tom Bender, and the editor of this volume read a draft of this essay and offered helpful suggestions, for which I thank them. In particular, John Mollenkopf gave the manuscript a careful reading, graciously providing some of the more recent data and helping me refine the argument. They share credit for the essay's strengths; I alone am responsible for its deficiencies.

1. "From Poland, Emigrés Add Spirit to Arts," the *New York Times*, July 8, 1987, pp. B1, B5.

2. Los Angeles, Chicago, and San Francisco are the other U.S. core cities. Saskia Sassen-Koob, "Capital Mobility and labor Migration: Their Expression in Core Cities," in *Urbanization in the World-Economy*, Michael Timberlake, ed. (Orlando: Academic Press, 1985), pp. 231–65.

3. Andrew Hacker, *The New Yorkers: A Profile of an American Metropolis* (New York: Mason/Charter, 1975) p. 4; New York State Department of Labor, *Annual Labor, 1987*, Table 27, and *Annual labor Area Report, FY 1985*, Table 6.

4. Hacker, p. 4; and Sassen-Koob, "Capital Mobility," pp. 251, 264.

5. 1984 Report of the Community Service Society, quoted in the *New York Times*, June 11, 1987, p. B1.

6. Hacker, *The New Yorkers* pp. 2–4, 101–102.

7. Ibid., p. 42.

8. Ira Rosenwaike, *Population History of New York City* (Syracuse: Syracuse University Press, 1972), pp. 132–45; United States, Bureau of the Census, 18th Census, Census of Population: 1960, Characteristics of the Population, pt. 34, Table 21; United States, Bureau of the Census, 20th Census, Census of Population: 1980, Characteristics of the Population, pt. 34, Table 56; George J. Lankevich and Howard B. Furer, *A Brief History of New York City* (Port Washington, N.Y.: Associated Faculty Press, 1984), pp. 258–59.

9. Lankevich and Furer, *A Brief History of New York* p. 265.

10. Interestingly, Hispanics living in New Jersey replicated the family situation of whites, while black families remained uniquely troubled, with three of five children living in single-parent families. The problems of black family life extended outside the city, but New York appears to have been a special place for Hispanic mothers needing support; 20th Census, 1980, Table 117. Some scholars, like Chicago sociologist William J. Wilson (*The Truly Disadvantaged: The Inner City, the Underclass and Public Policy* [Chicago: University of Chicago Press, 1987], chs. 3–4), attribute this to unemployment, death, drugs, etc., among young black men, creating a dearth of "marriageable males."

11. Thus, the percentage of female high school graduates among whites, blacks, and Hispanics living in the New Jersey part of the SMSA ranged between 66.9 and 75 percent in 1980. It was about ten points less for New York whites and black women. Ibid.; Diane Ravitch, *The Great School Wars: New York City, 1805–1973. A History of the Public Schools as Battlefield of Social Change* (New York: Basic Books, 1974), p. 251–53; Lankevich and Furer, *A Brief History,* p. 270; and Robert Caro, *The Power Broker: Robert Moses and the Fall of New York* (New York: Knopf, 1974), pp. 969–1010.

12. 1986 U.S. Census Report in the *New York Times,* July 24, 1987, p. D19.

13. Robert C. Wood, *1400 Governments: the Political Economy of the New York Metropolitan Region* (Cambridge, Mass.: Harvard University Press, 1961), p. 14.

14. Calculated from NY State Department of Labor, *Annual Labor Area Report, New York City, Fiscal Year 1987* (December, 1987), Table 3.

15. David M. Gordon, "Capitalist Development and the History of American Cities," in *Marxism and the Metropolis,* William K. Tabb and Larry Sawers, eds. (New York: Oxford University Press, 1978), pp. 25–63.

16. *New York Times,* January 10, 1987, p. 49.

17. Edgar M. Hoover, *Anatomy of a Metropolis: The Changing Distribution of People and Jobs Within the New York Metropolitan Region* (Cambridge, Mass.: Harvard University Press, 1959), pp. 24–29, 56, 117; Caro, p. 704.

18. Wood, *1400 Governments,* pp. 70–90; and, Caro, *The Power Broker,* p. 761.

19. Kenneth T. Jackson, "The Capital of Capitalism: the New York Metropolitan Region, 1890–1940," in *Metropolis, 1890–1940,* Anthony Sutcliffe, ed. (Chicago: University of Chicago Press, 1984), pp. 346–47.

20. Daniel J. Walkowitz, "Professionalism and Class Identity: New York Social Workers Weather McCarthyism," paper delivered at the Seventh Annual North American Labor History Conference, Toronto, Canada, November 1986. On teachers, see Ellen Schrecker, *No Ivory Tower: McCarthyism and the Universities* (New York: Oxford University Press, 1986), and Marjorie Murphy, *Blackboard Unions: The AFT and the NEA, 1900–1980* (Ithaca: Cornell University Press, 1990).

21. See Martin Shefter, "Political Incorporation and the Extrusion of the Left Party: Party Politics and Social Forces in New York City," *Studies in American Political Development* 1 (1986): 50–90.

22. Wood, *1400 Governments,* pp. 162–65; and Caro, *The Power Broker,* p. 794.

23. Caro, *The Power Broker,* pp. 757–64. Governor Dewey, a Republican interested in reelection, wished to use the surplus for a tax cut.

24. Ibid., p. 850; Diana Klebanow, et al., *Urban Legacy: The Story of America's Cities* (New York: *New American Library,* 1977), pp. 352–53; Lankevich and Furer, *A Brief History,* pp. 261–64.

25. Caro, *The Power Broker,* pp. 1013–14.

26. Fred J. Cook in the *World-Telegram and Sun,* July 30, 1956, quoted in Caro, p. 1007. Caro describes the East Tremont and Title I stories in detail, pp. 851–1014 and 1151.

27. The Kefauver Report found O'Dwyer "encouraged" gangsters to operate freely in the city, but no evidence of formal malfeasance. Lankevich and Furer, *A Brief History,* pp. 256–57.

28. Hoover, *Anatomy of a Metropolis,* pp. 144–50; Hacker, *The New Yorkers,* p. 43; and Lankevich and Furer, *A Brief History,* p. 270.

29. The *Report for the Year 2000* focuses on the failure of local board control to improve the schools.

30. Charles R. Morris, *The Cost of Good Intentions: New York City and the Liberal Experiment, 1960–1975* (New York: Norton, 1980); Maurice R. Berube and Marilyn Gitell, *Confrontation at Ocean Hill-Brownsville: The New York School Strike of 1968* (New York: Praeger, 1969); Diane Ravitch, *The Great School Wars*; and Lankevich and Furer, *A Brief History*, ch. X.

31. William K. Tabb, "The New York City Fiscal Crisis," in *Marxism and the Metropolis*, Tabb and Sawyers, eds., pp. 241–66.

32. The reminder comes from William Tabb, "The New York City Fiscal Crisis," p. 254. See also Lankevich and Furer, *A Brief History*; Jack Newfield and Paul DuBrul, *The Permanent Government: Who Really Runs New York?* (New York: Pilgrim Press, 1981); and Martin Shefter, *Political Crisis/Fiscal Crisis: The Collapse and Revival of New York City* (New York: Basic Books, 1985).

33. I am particularly indebted to Newfield and DuBrul, op. cit., and Newfield's article in *The Nation*, April 4, 1987, p. 433. John Mollenkopf urged emphasis on the death of liberalism, a point made forcefully in a somewhat different context by Russell Jacoby, *The Last Intellectuals: American Culture in the Age of Academe* (New York: Basic Books, 1987).

XI

PHILADELPHIA
THE PRIVATE CITY IN THE
POST-INDUSTRIAL ERA

Carolyn Teich Adams

Writing about the American urban landscape at the turn of the century, the journalist Lincoln Steffens described Philadelphia as "corrupt and contented"[1]—a city that seemed prepared to tolerate extraordinary levels of graft and ineptitude in government, as long as it maintained its economic vigor as "the workshop of the world." When Steffens wrote in 1904, Philadelphia had already suffered fifty years of domination by a Republic machine which prospered by acting as a political buffer between the industrial capitalists whose money built the city's factories, houses, and trolley lines and the working people of all nationalities who crowded into the neighborhoods. During that era, Philadelphia had grown into an industrial giant in spite of its political machine.

In fact, in many respects, the machine's operation proved detrimental to the interests of Philadelphia commerce and industry. All of the city's major public works—including the gas works, the street railways, the water works, and the harbor—suffered at the hands of incompetent and greedy politicians who used city government to line their own pockets, leaving the city's development largely up to the private interests that operated city services through franchises. The business community's tolerance for this Republic machine extended farther into the industrial era in Philadelphia than in most American cities, and the machine retained its grip on city hall until the close of World War II. But throughout that period and even beyond, Philadelphians have generally preferred that private initiatives shape the development of the city, with only intermittent and largely ineffectual interventions by political leaders.

Sam Bass Warner was right when he characterized Philadelphia as the quintessential "private city," relying for its successes and failures upon the unplanned outcomes of the private market.[2] It was private interests, he observed, that conditioned the city's demand for workers, its capacities for dividing land, building houses, stores and factories, and its provision of public services. As well as any

American city, Philadelphia displayed the advantages of this privatism in building a thriving industrial metropolis that peaked in the 1930s. It has also demonstrated the handicaps which cities without a strong tradition of governmental activism face in the post-industrial era. As was the case during industrialization, the transition to post-industrialism has come with economic and social changes that have created not only opportunities but hardships as well. To take full advantage of the opportunities as well as to minimize the damage and dislocation that result from rapid change, the leadership of the region's government, businesses, and neighborhood and civic organizations would have had to share some goals and a general sense of the direction that development should take. This has not happened. Nor does Philadelphia's privatist tradition provide many clues as to how such a broad coalition might be built in the future.

The dimensions of the transition to post-industrialism are well-known. Like other snowbelt cities, Philadelphia has lost manufacturing jobs. Developments in the national and global economy since World War II have not favored Philadelphia's industrial base. Faced with stiffer competition than they had experienced in the 1950s, not just from Dallas and Phoenix, but from Mexico City and Taipei, Philadelphia's boosters have been handicapped by an aging plant and infrastructure and a relatively high-wage labor force. As other nations expanded industrially, the city's products have suffered in the competition for world markets. The apparel industry is a good example of one in which Philadelphia products steadily lost ground, first to the American south and then to overseas manufacturers.

The decline of manufacturing within the city was offset by strong growth in suburban industries in the 1960s, but by the 1970s even suburban plants seemed to be experiencing difficulty facing competitive pressures. During that decade, the entire metropolitan region stagnated economically, showing only 7 percent growth in total non-agricultural employment (compared with 27 percent growth in the nation as a whole). That growth took place in the service industries which have rapidly replaced manufacturing as the backbone of the regional economy. During the 1970s the proportion of the region's workforce employed in service jobs expanded from 65 to 75 percent. And while this shift from manufacturing to services was a nationwide trend, the Philadelphia region had an even larger percentage of its workers in service jobs in 1980 than did the United States.[3]

The shift to services has favored both the downtown core of the region and its suburban job nodes, while drawing economic activities away from the older commercial, industrial, and residential areas of the city. Downtown employment increased from 1960 to 1980, as legal, financial, and other business services catering to corporate offices found it advantageous to locate in the center of this large metropolitan region. Yet these same kinds of firms, which constitute the fastest growing segment of the regional economy, often find suburban office parks to be a viable alternative to center city. The suburbs' ability to compete with downtown locations is evidenced by the fact that from 1970 to 1983, the city's share of regional employment in the advanced services (e.g., computer software, finance, insurance, management consulting, etc.) dropped from about 70 to about 40 percent.[4] Over all, the balance of regional employment has shifted further in the suburban direction in this region than in most others; in comparison with 42 other leading metropolitan areas, Philadelphia has lost more jobs relative to the suburbs than the national average.[5]

These economic shifts have accompanied dramatic population shifts. After growing steadily for decades, the Philadelphia region lost over 100,000 people in the 1970s. But the population trend turned upward again in the early 1980s, so that by 1987 metro Philadelphia had regained almost 150,000 people, with almost all of the growth in the suburban counties. The city has steadily shrunk throughout the postwar period, and in more recent years the rate of decline has accelerated sharply. Whereas from 1950 to 1960 Philadelphia lost about 3 percent of its population, the losses of the 1970s amounted to over 13 percent.

The composition of the city population has changed as well. The city has become older and blacker. Persons over 65 years old composed only 8 percent of the population in 1950 but over 14 percent in 1980. During the same period, the proportion of blacks rose from 18 percent to 38 percent. Moreover, a new minority group, Hispanics, grew rapidly in the 1970s, accounting for about 4 percent of the city's total population by 1980.

While the city was losing population, the surrounding suburban counties were gaining, some quite dramatically. In 1950 Philadelphia's suburbs contained about 44 percent of the region's people. Their share rose to 64 percent by 1980. Ethnic and racial changes have affected the suburbs too, although to a much lesser extent than the city. By 1980 over one quarter of all the region's blacks, 45 percent of its Hispanics, and 61 percent of its Asians lived in the suburbs.

To the surprise of pessimists, the economic news in the mid-1980s is distinctly favorable for the region. Since 1980 the region has enjoyed a reversal of the slow growth that marked the 1970s. The shift in that decade toward a service base had positioned the region to participate in some of the fastest growing sectors of the national economy. Compared with employment growth rates of less than one percent per year in the 1970s, the region has achieved an annual growth rate of 3.5 percent in the mid-1980s. By 1985 even the city of Philadelphia was experiencing a positive growth rate of about one percent per year, as opposed to the negative changes that it suffered in the 1970s.[6] New office construction boomed in both downtown and suburban locations, and civic leaders began to evince greater optimism about the future.

The so-called "economic boom" of the 1980s, however, is not likely to resolve all the region's economic woes. For one thing, the boom is unlikely to make a serious dent in the hard core poverty that plagues many decaying neighborhoods of the inner city. Although the proportion of the city's population in poverty dipped substantially in the 1960s, that figure rose from 15 percent in 1970 to 21 percent in 1980, and it shows no sign of abating in spite of the economic upturn. One reason is the number of poor men and women who lack the education and training for jobs in the high-growth sectors. According to the census of 1980, only slightly more than half of the adults in the city (54 percent) had completed high school; the comparable figure for the region was only 67 percent.

Admittedly, the economic upturn has somewhat reduced unemployment in the region. From over 11 percent in 1980, the rate of unemployment dropped to 5.3 percent in 1986—a level so low that it led some economists to start worrying about labor shortages. Yet even those who have found jobs are not always able to rise above poverty, particularly if they have families to support. The bulk of the jobs being created in the service sector, especially entry-level jobs, pay low wages ($7,000 to $15,000) and offer no fringe benefits. Even the so-called "knowledge-based" industries like computer software, finance, and insurance, have a higher proportion of persons in low-paid jobs than did the manufacturing firms that have left the region. Thus, the growth in employment will not eliminate the need for community services and assistance for families whose incomes cannot support them.

The pattern of accelerating economic and demographic change in the region since 1950 would seem to have called for ever-more aggressive responses from the city's and region's political leadership. Ironically, however, as the challenges have mounted, the community's capacity to confront them has diminished. The high point of municipal activism since World War II came in the 1950s, a decade known to Philadelphians as "the reform era." Though short-lived, that reform impulse provided a model of public-private partnerships that subsequent generations of civic leaders have struggled unsuccessfully to duplicate. It represented a rare example of Philadelphians using the power of government to accomplish sweeping institutional and physical changes in their city.

The reforms were initiated in the late 1940s, when a group of civic and business leaders recognized the increasing economic competition facing Philadelphia and the need for an aggressive governmental response. They were emboldened by the general spirit of optimism that followed America's overseas triumph in World War II and convinced that the city could not prosper in the postwar economic climate with its obsolete downtown area, its decaying transportation and education systems, and its moldering governmental machinery. They organized to challenge the Republican machine. This coalition of lawyers, bankers, business people, and representatives of civic organizations took positions that echoed the standard reform platform of the early twentieth century. They aspired to purge municipal government of long-standing corruption, install a new professionalism in city departments, improve the efficiency of services, and minimize the influence of patronage in filling city jobs.

The reformers' opportunity came in 1948, when they managed to secure several seats on a citizens commission of the kind that Republican mayors routinely appointed to glance over the city's budget and operational needs and recommend tax increases. (Apparently, mayors thought it too risky to go to the voters for a tax increase without a commission's recommendation.) Once appointed to the study commission, the reformers insisted upon a genuine investigation of city finances. Their report, issued in early 1949, uncovered $152 million in graft payments to various city officials. Moreover, they charged that $40 million was simply missing from the city treasury, and no one could account for it. The scandal led to a series of impeachments, grand jury hearings, and state and federal investigations, and drove several city officials to suicide. The first was the head of the Amusement Tax Office, who was followed by the superintendent of the Water Department, the head of the police vice squad, and the city's chief plumbing inspector.

In the upheaval that followed these grim events, the reformers made common cause with the city's business establishment, which could no longer tolerate the machine's excesses, and with trade unionists, black leaders, and ward politicians of the regular Democratic Party, to form an electoral coalition. This unlikely alliance was animated by a common desire to unseat the Republicans.

To replace the machine's skullduggery, the city's business and civic elite proposed a revision of the city charter to create a more rational, businesslike approach to municipal government. The reformers dominated the Charter Commission which the state legislature formed in July 1949 as a result of much prodding. The resulting Home Rule Charter enhanced the power of the mayor, reorganized the city council, strengthened the civil service system, and expanded the role of the city planning commission. A few months after the new charter went into effect in 1951, the reformers succeeded in electing one of their number, Joseph Clark, as mayor and in securing fifteen seats for reform Democrats in the reorganized city council. Mayor Clark's successor was another reform Democrat, Mayor Richardson Dilworth, elected in 1955.

As in so many American cities, reform politics in Philadelphia was closely linked to an emerging planning apparatus and a program for physical renewal. One account of this period written by an insider even suggests that the reformers' interest in city planning preceded their interest in governmental reform.[7] Not long after his election, reform Mayor Clark launched a series of projects to remove outdated structures from the downtown area and to replace them with office towers, luxury housing, university buildings, and specialized shops. In effect, the reformers' plans for re-developing the city center represented their effort to transform the city's physical structure in ways that would accommodate the economic transformation already underway—the shift from manufacturing to services as the basis of the Philadelphia economy.

The city benefited from a timely convergence of political reform and the advent of the federal urban renewal program. The reformers' energetic pursuit of urban renewal gave the city a reputation as a national leader in planning and redevelopment. During the 1950s and 1960s, national meetings of architects, planners, and redevelopment officials regularly featured Philadelphia as a model for other cities to emulate. *Time, Life,* and other national magazines carried colorful accounts of Philadelphia's massive rebuilding, guided by a coalition of enlightened politicians, dedicated civic leaders, and skilled planners. Jeanne Lowe's 1967 survey of redevelopment activities in cities across the country offered this glowing assessment of Philadelphia's achievements:

> Of all the big cities, Philadelphia has come closest to a comprehensive approach to the complete challenges confronting our urban centers. . . . Perhaps more than any other big city, Philadelphia has had to rely on informed long-range plans, design excellence, aggressive action strategies for its survival.[8]

The reformers set in motion a plan for downtown renewal that guided the city's redevelopment agenda into the mid-1980s. Their vision of physical renewal, however, proved to be more powerful than their organizational base. Almost immediately after defeating the Republican machine in 1951, the triumphant Democratic coalition began to fall apart, Dilworth's victories in 1955 and 1959 notwithstanding. The coalition was, after all, an unlikely alliance tying business people, professionals, and members of the civic elite who led the reform faction, to the regular "rowhouse" Democrats who had for years tried to beat the Republican machine by emulating it. Once in office, the upper-class reformers, who were determined to stamp out patronage, came into conflict with the ward politicians, who saw patronage as the normal spoils of victory. Perhaps because they eschewed the use of patronage to maintain control of the party organization, the reformers never established a strong organization in the city's wards.

Nor did the reformers succeed in institutionalizing the strong links they had forged between city government and the business establishment. The organizational vehicle tying business activists to city hall during the reform era was the Greater Philadelphia Movement (GPM), an alliance created in 1949 to represent the views of civic-minded bankers, lawyers, and business people. As a tax-exempt organization, GPM was prohibited from direct political activity, but it made its political influence felt in all of the major undertakings of the reform movement. Many of its members, though registered as Republicans, backed the Democratic mayoral candidates Clark and Dilworth. It was the GPM that pushed for the formation of the citizens commission to redraft the city charter, and saw to it that the commission's membership included thirteen downtown businessmen and lawyers, many of them members of GPM, compared to only two elected officials.

The *Philadelphia Bulletin* admiringly labeled the GPM "the cream of civic group giants," the "powerhouse of Philadelphia's citizen elite," and "the combat and control center of the city's movers and shakers."[9] After the election of the first reform mayor in 1951, a number of GPM's members took positions in the new government, most notably as managing director and commerce director, two key cabinet appointments. One insider's history of the Philadelphia reform movement documents the constant communication and collaboration between GPM's board and Mayors Clark and Dilworth.[10]

Forged through direct personal contacts, this link between organized business and the reform politicians was, however, never institutionalized, and GPM's access to city hall virtually disappeared during the term of Mayor James H. J. Tate, an old-style patronage politician who succeeded the reformers in the early 1960s. Tate originally gained the mayoralty only because he was president of the city council when Mayor Dilworth resigned in the middle of his second term to campaign for governor. Tate was never the reformers' chosen standard bearer. After monitoring him through his own first term in office, the business community actively opposed Tate's bid for re-election in 1967. In that year most of the city's business leaders, and the GPM as an organization, supported Tate's Republican opponent.

Narrowly winning re-election, Mayor Tate broke off relations with GPM. He relied instead on alliances with the city's white ethnic groups and labor unions, particularly those of public employees. He deployed the resources made available through federal anti-poverty programs to insure that the growing sense of economic dissatisfaction within the city's black communities would not threaten his political support.

Philadelphia's Democratic coalition fragmented further when Frank Rizzo rose to power. Rizzo, whom Mayor Tate appointed as Police Commissioner, was Tate's hand-chosen successor. Rizzo's image as a tough cop cemented the loyalty of working-class and middle-class white ethnics to the Democratic Party, but it repelled blacks. During Rizzo's eight years as mayor (1971–1979), black politicians, whose loyalty had not wavered for decades, began to develop independent bases of support that allowed them to run their own campaigns for city and state offices and to take independent policy positions. The culmination of this new political independence among black voters was their united opposition to a charter referendum in 1978 that would have allowed mayors to serve more than two consecutive terms. Mayor Rizzo sought the amendment to permit him to run for an unprecedented third term. Black Philadelphians enthusiastically joined the forces opposing Rizzo and his charter change. The mayor's opponents led a massive voter registration drive in the inner city, enrolling over 62,000 new black voters, whose bloc vote against the amendment denied Rizzo a third term.

Unlike the black community, the business establishment did not at first respond negatively to Rizzo. In fact, while he was still police commissioner, the GPM had strongly supported the police department's handling of a potentially explosive "Revolutionary People's Constitutional Convention" sponsored by the Black Panthers Party at the North Philadelphia campus of Temple University. To the surprise of many Philadelphians, the three-day event concluded without violent incidents, a fact that prompted the GPM to send Commissioner Rizzo this congratulatory telegram: "Representatives of the GPM have personally observed abuse and provocation to which your men are often, on such occasions, subjected. We congratulate you and them for maintaining peace during the meetings at Temple University."[11]

But as soon as Rizzo became a candidate for mayor, his relationship with GPM began to sour. Rizzo seemed determined to assert his independence from the business establishment, refusing, for example, to respond to a questionnaire that GPM distributed to all the mayoral candidates. Rizzo publicly announced that he would not allow the city's business elite to interfere in the electoral process: "I will go directly to the people. In the end, it is the people who will accept or reject my programs."[12]

Once elected, Mayor Rizzo regained at least the lukewarm support of many Philadelphia business people because he held the line on taxes throughout his first four-year term. As soon as he was re-elected, however, his administration disclosed an \$86 million deficit that forced him to ask for a 30 percent increase in both the property tax and real estate tax. An outraged Chamber of Commerce charged the mayor with concealing the deficit in order to get re-elected, and urged him to limit the tax increases and to prune patronage employees. Mayor Rizzo responded by blaming the city's economic problems on the "ineffectuality" of unnamed business executives to promote economic development—a response that offended a large part of the business community. It is hardly surprising that the business community aided in the campaign of 1978 to defeat Rizzo's charter change. The "Charter Defense Committee" united the GPM (now called the Greater Philadelphia Partnership) with prominent black leaders. Funds supplied by the business community paid for the highly successful voter registration drives in the city's black neighborhoods and for radio advertisements opposing the charter change.

In addition to facing opposition from blacks and business people, Mayor Rizzo's city hall was the target of a neighborhood movement that gathered strength and visibility in the 1970s. Neighborhood organization was not altogether new to the city. Far from it. Philadelphia had a history of civic activism within communities. Celebrated as a "city of neighborhoods," Philadelphia had spawned hundreds of local associations that were active through the 1950s and 1960s. Yet until the 1970s, these neighborhood groups addressed themselves only to local-level issues involving housing, zoning, recreation, and schools. Rarely did they apply themselves to any wider political agenda.[13] The important departure of the 1970s was the formation of a city-wide coalition. In 1973, twelve neighborhood associations banded together to establish the Council of Neighborhood Organizations whose membership and influence soon grew. One of its major functions was to act as a watchdog over the city's budget and programs to see that neighborhood services and public works received their fair share of municipal money.

By the early 1980s, members of Philadelphia's business elite grew alarmed at the conflict and stalemate within the ruling Democratic coalition. Invigorated by their success in defeating the charter change, they launched a campaign to reassert business influence over the city's development. They acknowledged having lost the standing and the confidence that the business community had enjoyed during the reform era; their efforts had become fragmented and unfocused. A long-range planning committee of the Chamber of Commerce charged that businesses had "failed to provide the larger community with the leadership it needs" to achieve economic development.[14]

The way to re-establish corporate influence, business leaders agreed, was to reorganize as the "Greater Philadelphia First Corporation" (GPFC) and to recruit a board of directors from among the chief executive officers of the region's largest corporations. Not content simply to influence local government, the new corporation acquired its own working capital and initiated its own public projects. Each of the 27 corporations holding a seat on the board contributed a minimum of $50,000 in annual dues in order to create a pool of funds which the new group used to promote various economic development activities in the region. To direct the work of this ambitious coalition of banks, insurance companies, public utilities, and other business firms, the GPFC hired an executive director from a federal development agency, a man who had served his first political apprenticeship under reform Mayor Joseph Clark.

In forming the GPFC, members of Philadelphia's business elite openly declared that they were seeking to enhance their political and economic influence: "Of course we are interested in having a more powerful leadership position. . . . We are willing to take risks and put our reputations on the line to achieve progress and move Philadelphia ahead. This may be misunderstood as a power play for its own sake."[15]

One of their first opportunities to influence city hall came in the election of 1983, when the business community enthusiastically supported the candidacy of W. Wilson Goode, who was to become Philadelphia's first black mayor.

Here, at last, was a leader who promised to reconstruct the splintered Democratic Party. He claimed the support, not only of downtown businesses but also of neighborhood groups whose public services had improved during his term as managing director. Goode had been appointed to the position of managing director by Mayor Rizzo's successor, William Green, a Kennedy-style liberal Democrat who had become mayor in 1979 after a long congressional career. Green's Washington experience had not prepared him for the rough and tumble of big city politics. Almost as soon as he took over city hall, Mayor Green made enemies of the public employee unions by stubbornly refusing to negotiate wage increases despite marches by the police, threats of walk outs by fire fighters, and a fifty-day strike by public school teachers. He kept the feisty city council at arm's length, disdaining their brand of ward politics, and he allowed the Democrats' patronage machine to atrophy through neglect. To party regulars, Mayor Green seemed aloof—a man who avoided going into the city's neighborhoods to press the flesh. His black managing director, Wilson Goode, therefore become his emissary to the community and the city council, emerging by the end of Green's term in office as a kind of co-mayor. The white reform element saw Goode as a hard working administrator with a record for honest, efficient management of the city's operating departments, and this group joined black Democrats, lined up solidly behind this black candidate for mayor. Goode's campaign even made accommodations with the party regulars in the pro-Rizzo, working-class white wards along the river and in South Philadelphia. In return for the ward leaders' support for his candidacy, Goode offered his endorsement to some of their hand-picked candidates for lower level offices. In addition he promised patronage jobs once he was elected. Goode's coalition-building effort paid off. He took 55 percent of the vote against Republican businessman John Egan in a campaign that never took on an overtly racial tone.

Business leaders described Goode's appeal on the basis of his "apolitical and professional" approach to his previous post as managing director. They were impressed with his campaign strategy as well, particularly when, even before the election itself, Goode invited dozens of business people into a search-and-screening process to identify qualified candidates for the top city jobs. The corporate volunteers were organized into search committees which reviewed and graded thousands of resumes, guiding the mayor-elect in his choice of cabinet officers, department heads, and other key figures in his new administration. This was the most direct participation in shaping a municipal administration that the business community had exercised since the days of the reformers.

Yet a mayoralty that began with great promise was crippled almost beyond recovery in May 1985 by the city's disastrous confrontation with a small extremist commune known as "MOVE." In a largely black neighborhood of West Philadelphia that had been threatened by violence from the commune's residents, the Philadelphia police erected barricades to try to force the MOVE members to abandon their fortress-style house. The stand-off turned to tragedy when a police helicopter dropped explosives on the roof of the MOVE house, setting off a fire that killed all eleven MOVE members barricaded inside the house and subsequently destroyed two city blocks. National newscasters compared the charred wreckage to a war zone.

In addition to destroying human lives and over sixty homes, the incident also destroyed Wilson Goode's hopes of being the politician who would put the city's fractured political majority back together. No longer did Goode enjoy the unqualified support of black Democrats, some of whom saw the city's decision to drop a bomb on a residential area as a racist act. Business leaders were appalled at the lapse in managerial control that led to the incident; a blue-ribbon investigating panel accused the mayor of abandoning his command responsibilities in the emergency. Many white liberals were shocked at the use of such brutal force to quell a neighborhood disturbance. Although Wilson Goode was able to re-establish his control over municipal operations, he did not regain the personal loyalty that would have allowed him to act as a peacemaker among quarreling party factions.

Nor did Goode's re-election two years after the MOVE incident signal a healing of party factionalism. On the contrary, the contest in 1987 between Goode and Frank Rizzo (who had switched his registration to the Republican Party in late 1986 to run against Goode) produced the most racially polarized vote in Philadelphia's history. Goode won by less than 3 percent, far smaller than his margin of victory in 1983. No longer was he a coalition candidate who appealed to a wide spectrum of whites, blacks, liberals, and business leaders. He won re-election largely on the basis of his support in the black community, where his share of the vote was about 97 percent. Rizzo's candidacy had lured almost 50,000 white Democrats to re-register as Republicans and drew a vote on election day that was about 98 percent white. It remains to be seen whether the racial split in the electorate in 1987 reflects only the choice between these two particular candidates or signals a major partisan realignment.

The steady fragmentation of the Democratic Party has meant that no recent administration has been able to develop the consensus needed to pursue a coherent development strategy for the city. By and large, business leaders continue to support an emphasis on large-scale, downtown investments, including a proposed convention center and redevelopment of the city's waterfront district for tourism, offices, and high-rent housing. Such centralized investments, they reason, are sure to have spillover benefits for the rest of the city. Business groups, in short, retain their faith in the "trickle down" approach articulated in the reform plans of the 1950s.

On the other hand, members of the city council in recent years have become increasingly vocal in representing the interests of neighborhoods, even to the point of challenging the city's corporate power structure. Recent councils have exercised their authority in a number of ways that appear inimical to the interests of business. In doing so, the members of the council have reflected the suspicions and apprehensions which their constituents in the neighborhoods feel about downtown development. During the past twenty-five years neighborhood groups have mobilized time and again to protest developments which threatened their interests. Projects involving highways, high-rent housing, hospitals, universities, and office buildings have all, at one time or another, met with community opposition. As the power of district council members has increased, relative to the central leadership of the Democratic Party, it has become more common for council members, individually or in small groups, to hold up major development projects, including some endorsed by the Democratic Party leadership. Gone is the universal appeal of growth for its own sake. In the open, fragmented politics of the 1980s the question is rather: growth for whose sake?

One recent example of the Democratically controlled council's willingness to defy its own party leadership, and the business community as well, is its refusal to approve plans for a major new incinerator to burn trash and recover energy in the form of steam heat. Facing a rapidly worsening crisis in solid waste disposal, both Mayor William Green in the early 1980s and his successor, Mayor Goode, sought to persuade the council to endorse a new trash-to-steam plant at the Naval Yard in South Philadelphia. The Chamber of Commerce and other business groups, alarmed that the trash crisis had driven up the cost of doing business in the city, insisted that the trash-to-steam plant take priority on the governmental agenda.

Residents of South Philadelphia, however, vigorously opposed having the plant built in their neighborhood. Their main objection was its potential for emitting dangerous cancer-causing chemicals into the air, but they protested as well the damaging effects of traffic congestion and foul odors associated with its operation. Their district council member, allied with several at-large members of the city council, succeeded in holding up the project for over five years, despite intense lobbying by both the mayor and representatives of the business community. Finally in 1988 a stymied Mayor Goode withdrew the proposal altogether and announced that he would seek other ways to dispose of the city's trash.

The council has applied its veto power not only to projects that threatened to disrupt residential neighborhoods but also to major downtown projects, the most notable of which is a $465 million convention center. First conceived in May 1982, the project had the unqualified support of Mayor Green and the city's two most powerful business groups, the Greater Philadelphia First Corporation and the Chamber of Commerce. Despite such support for the center, the city council was not convinced it would bring anything but a massive new tax burden to their constituents in the neighborhoods. They suspected that few of its benefits would "trickle down" to the average taxpayer.

The majority of the council took the position that at the very least, the project should be structured to guarantee that a significant proportion of jobs would go to minorities, women, and city residents, and they stalled the project until builders agreed to adopt affirmative action guidelines. One influential council member warned: "I don't think the project can move forward without council support. And the position at this point is that a majority of the council favors not approving anything until they [the convention center authority] abide by affirmative action."[16] The council leadership eventually negotiated acceptable affirmative action guidelines with the convention center authority and gave its blessing to the project, but for a variety of reasons, including conflict over site acquisition and difficulties in securing state funds, the project remained stalled. By early 1988, council members worried that the six-year delay would inflate the project costs to unacceptably high levels. They established an investigating committee to review the status of the project and to recommend whether the council should withdraw its approval. Mayor Goode and business leaders accused the council of deliberately staging the hearings to galvanize the opposition to the center. That is where the matter now stands.

While delaying downtown projects, the city council has insisted that larger shares of the city's resources be invested in other parts of the city. For example, reviewing the annual capital budget that was presented to the council by Mayor Green in 1983, three of the council's most powerful black members—its president, Joseph Coleman, and his fellow members, John Street and Lucien Blackwell—joined forces to criticize the budget's downtown bias. Pointing to the heavy emphasis on central business district projects such as the proposed new convention center and waterfront development, John Street complained, "I don't call that a program that reflects any interest in the residents of the city. . . . We pay and we pay and we pay, and all we see is fancy buildings going up in the center of town."[17] The longstanding consensus on trickle-down approaches to the city's development has crumbled, but no alternative vision has majority support. The political break-throughs by new groups have not been translated into new policy directions.

The same fragmentation that frustrates business lobbyists frequently defeats the efforts of community and public interest activists as well. Neighborhood advocates, environmentalists, consumer activists, tenants rights organizations, and other similar groups find it relatively easy to gain a sympathetic hearing from one or more political leaders in the city. But what one observer has labeled the "hyper-pluralism" of urban politics makes it extremely difficult to forge effective coalitions to push for policy change. In the absence of a strong political center, "there is no mechanism to achieve or protect the goals sought by these new groups. The result is often a stalemate, which is a victory for the status quo."[18]

That same hyper-pluralism of municipal politics makes it difficult for the city to reach political accommodations with political leaders in the surrounding suburbs. Such accommodations, most observers agree, would help the region compete effectively in the national and international arenas, for in the long run, the fortunes of city and suburbs are tied together in a single economic unit. Despite its decline in recent decades, the city still defines the character of the region. The urban core performs important regional functions: it is the largest, though not the only, office center, the transportation hub, the cultural and social hub of the region, the focus of a rich array of artistic, theatrical, musical, and sports activities. Many suburban residents and investors depend on proximity to the unique assets of the central city, especially its airports, research universities, and cultural and recreational amenities. On the other hand, suburban growth provides economic opportunities to city residents because it expands the market for goods and services produced in the city. There are thus genuine interdependencies linking the separate municipalities and counties of the region.

Disparities, however, mark the region as much as interdependencies. The seven suburban counties that surround Philadelphia fall into two general categories. The high-growth counties of Bucks and Chester (in Pennsylvania) and Burlington and Gloucester (in New Jersey) have seen dramatic increases in both employment and population in the last two decades. Not surprisingly, per capita incomes in these counties (measured in constant dollars) also rose 35 to 50 percent between 1960 and 1980. In the three moderate-growth counties—Montgomery and Delaware (in Pennsylvania) and Camden (in New Jersey)—incomes were also rising during the 20-year period, though only by about 25 percent. Philadelphia, by contrast, experienced a decline of 18 percent.[19]

The combination of upward income trends in all the suburban counties with an absolute decline in the city had led by the mid-1980s to dramatic differences in the economic fortunes and the fiscal burdens of suburbs and city. According to recent estimates, Philadelphia's middle-class tax burden is about 40 percent higher than the regional average.[20] The city also places a tax burden on businesses that is far higher than in the region as a whole—45 percent higher for manufacturing, 95 percent higher for wholesale trade, and 50 to 60 percent higher for most of the services.[21]

As these discrepancies have widened, suburbanites have displayed a declining sense of loyalty to the city. More and more of them lead lives entirely outside the city's boundaries. The decreased daily interactions between Philadelphia and its surrounding counties reflect changes in commuting patterns. In 1960, 25 percent of suburban residents commuted to a job in the city. By 1980 only 18 percent of suburbanites commuted to a city job. By 1980 the census showed that there were more workers commuting between suburban counties than there were commuting from the suburbs into Philadelphia. Most, however, simply worked near their homes. In six of the seven suburban counties, most residents who had jobs worked in the same county in which they lived.

But if a smaller proportion of suburbanites are commuting inward, larger numbers of city dwellers are traveling outward. More "reverse commuters" are leaving the urban core to travel to jobs in suburban establishments. Granted, Philadelphians by the thousands have worked in manufacturing jobs in the suburbs for decades, but since 1980 large numbers have commuted long distances for low-paying, entry-level positions in shopping malls, retail stores, fast-food outlets, and corporate centers in Cherry Hill, Fort Washington, the Main Line, and the Route 202 "high-tech" corridor. The most important suburban magnets are in Montgomery County, which by 1980 had become a net importer of workers, a role previously played only by the city of Philadelphia in this region.

Although city and suburban political leaders share a common interest in promoting the economy of the region, they have been largely unsuccessful in their efforts at cooperation. No council of governments has ever been established in the region. Instead, the Delaware Valley Regional Planning Commission was created in 1965 by an interstate compact between Pennsylvania and New Jersey. It includes the seven counties of the SMSA plus one additional county in New Jersey (Mercer), and its primary functions have been clearing proposed federal projects and planning transportation for the region. Unfortunately, the representatives from the various counties and the state governments who sit on the regional commission have no authority to commit the resources of their respective units, and as a result, this body has never wielded significant power.

Public transit is the only example of a critical urban service that is operated on a regional basis. The Southeastern Pennsylvania Transportation Authority (SEPTA) controls bus, trolley, subway, and commuter rail service in the city and four suburban counties located within Pennsylvania. Organized in 1964, SEPTA is governed by an eleven member board, with two representatives from each of the five counties plus one governor's appointee. Almost since its inception SEPTA has been an arena for conflict between the city and suburbs. The central point of contention has been financing the system. Having no dedicated tax base, as many other regional transit systems around the country do, SEPTA depends entirely on annual contributions from the city, counties, and state governments. The city complains that the suburbs do not shoulder their rightful share of the cost. With about one quarter of the system's ridership, the four suburban counties furnish only about 15 percent of its local aid.

Critics argue too that suburban riders enjoy more than their share of the subsidies distributed by the authority. This happens because SEPTA is divided into a city division, which operates all the subways, trolleys, and buses in the city, and a rail division, a collection of suburban passenger trains that came under SEPTA's wing when the Penn Central and Reading Railroads went bankrupt. The SEPTA board, which oversees both divisions, allocates its revenue in such a way that suburban rail riders pay a lower proportion of the cost of running their trains than city riders pay toward the cost of their buses and subways. The authority acknowledges this apparent favoritism toward its more affluent customers, but contends that the costs are higher on the rail lines. If asked to bear this higher cost themselves, suburban riders would be likely to desert the transit system. After all, more affluent suburban commuters could simply drive to work.

To many observers, the imbalance in the treatment accorded to city and suburban divisions is an inevitable result of unequal representation on the SEPTA board. With only one quarter of the ridership, the suburbs control eight out of the eleven seats on the board. Periodically critics call on the city to pull out of the regional authority altogether and run its own buses, trolleys, and subways independently. Less extreme proposals have envisioned the expansion of SEPTA's board so that the votes would be more evenly distributed between city and suburbs. But to date there has been no reorganization, partly because the political forces within the city's majority coalition cannot agree. Neighborhood organizations, council members, and others who represent city transit riders are the most vigorous critics of SEPTA's performance. Representatives of the downtown business community, however, take the position that the heavy subsidies to the suburban railway are absolutely necessary to the survival of the core office and retail district. Without reasonably priced rail service, they argue, the central business district could not compete successfully against suburban office complexes. Without unanimity among city political forces, there is little prospect of pressuring SEPTA to change its policies.

The marked disparities between the populations and resources of the city and suburbs have made cooperation difficult on all but the least threatening activities. For example, the various governments of the region have long had agreements involving cooperation among police departments on technical and training activities, among libraries, and among water departments. But on a more controversial issue such as cooperation among the region's school systems for purposes of racial integration, there have been no significant initiatives, despite the pressure from the Pennsylvania Human Relation Commission since the early 1970s to end the pattern of segregation in the Philadelphia schools.

A difficult sticking point in any cooperative planning between Philadelphia and its suburbs is the wage tax which the city levies on suburbanites who work in the city. Throughout the postwar period the city has levied a tax on all income earned in the city, regardless of the earner's residence. Suburban politicians have always bridled at what they regarded as taxation without representation. Their constituents who commuted into Philadelphia to work have had no voice in electing the city council which set the tax rates, but they were expected to pay the tax anyway. As the suburbs grew and gained clout in the state legislature, their representatives used this forum to protest against the city's levy. In 1977 they gained a legislative cap on tax rates for non-residents working in Philadelphia. Thus, in 1983 when the city needed additional revenue, it could raise the tax rate only on its own citizens. Under the current two-tier system, city residents pay a tax of 4.96 percent on wages earned in the city, while suburbanites who hold jobs in Philadelphia pay 4.31 percent.

Not satisfied with the cap, state legislators representing the Philadelphia suburbs have continued to press for reductions in the rate levied on their constituents, and they have traded their votes on other legislation favorable to the city to gain further tax cuts. In spring 1986 several dozen state legislators from communities on the city's border tried to block a state appropriation to support the construction of Philadelphia's proposed convention center. Despite the Republican governor's contention that the project would be a boon for all of Southeastern Pennsylvania, these suburban Republicans voted against it, openly declaring that their opposition was a tactic designed to force concessions on the wage tax. While they were unable to defeat the appropriation, their success in delaying its passage added to a general climate of suspicion that marks political relations between the inner and outer rings of the region.[22]

One recent development that holds promise of breaking the city-suburban impasse on wage taxes is the Pennsylvania legislature's move in 1988 to reform the tax structure of the entire state. As part of sweeping changes in municipal taxation, the legislature proposed that wage taxes be reduced for all people who work within Philadelphia, bringing down the rate for city dwellers to 4.5 percent and the toll on suburbanites to 3.95 percent. To compensate for its revenue losses, the city government would be permitted to collect several new taxes, including a municipal sales tax and a new tax on unearned income. Subject to a voter referendum, the tax reform failed that time. Yet it represents the region's best hope of removing a longstanding obstacle to cooperation. It is no accident that the solution, if it comes in this form, will have been arrived at, not by direct bargaining between the city and suburbs but in a larger arena. When they bargain only among themselves at the regional level, political leaders seem always to be stymied by their need to protect turf.

Despite this intransigence, there are several emerging issues of major importance to the region which promise to bring city and suburban leaders together, based on hard-headed self-interest not altruism or public-spiritedness. One is the solid waste crisis that is worsening throughout the region. As the capacity of suburban landfills is rapidly exhausted, suburban counties are restricting the city's ability to dump trash within their limits in order to preserve the existing capacity for their own townships. The lack of local dump sites forces the city to haul some of its garbage as far as Maryland and Ohio. Foreseeing no easy resolution to this shortage of landfills, many of the region's communities have turned to plans for trash-to-steam incinerators such as the ill-fated one proposed for South Philadelphia. Besides taking care of their own trash problems, suburban officials expect to enrich their coffers by processing trash from outside customers. By 1987, at least sixteen such plants were under consideration within a fifty-mile radius of Philadelphia. The prospect of even half that many plants going into operation in the region has alarmed critics of the incinerator technology, who are calling for some regional agreements on when and where such plants can be built. Of the many difficulties besetting the region, this one appears the most likely to prompt concerted action.

Another looming problem that may spawn voluntary cooperation between city and suburbs is the increasing difficulty of suburban employers in hiring workers. Since the recession of 1983, the region's economic boom has added over a quarter of a million new jobs, a large number of which are retail and service jobs in suburban locations. Yet workers living in Philadelphia are unlikely to move to a suburban community in order to take such low-paying jobs. Thus, economists are predicting labor shortages in suburban counties.

True to the historical tradition of privatism, a number of Philadelphia entrepreneurs have operated outside the bounds of government to try to work out solutions to the regional labor market problem. One good example is a privately operated shuttle service created by some suburban firms to assist reverse commuters recruited from the inner city. As intriguing as these private efforts are, they will not be enough to solve the region's mismatch between job opportunities and labor pools. Like trash disposal, labor market planning is a public responsibility. Privatist formulas will not suffice to confront issues like these, which involve massive spillover effects touching all parts of the region.

The challenge to political leadership is to see beyond the sharp differences in income levels, lifestyles, and ethnic and racial composition that divide city and suburbs (and sometime divide suburb from suburb), and to recognize the opportunities for mutually beneficial cooperation. The first step toward intergovernmental cooperation must be to forge a workable political coalition inside the city, without which Philadelphia leaders have no hope of negotiating effectively with their suburban counterparts. The gradual disintegration of the ruling Democratic coalition, which started the moment the Democrats took power in 1951, has both weakened the city's role in regional affairs and hampered local government's ability to improve conditions for its own citizens. Major projects remain stalled, while basic services such as education and child welfare deteriorate.

Searching for models to guide their actions, today's political and civic leaders find few precedents for activist government in the history of this private city. The exception is the reform era of the 1950s, virtually the only time in the twentieth century when strong public officials shaped the city's future. Despite the nostalgia for that era, the formulas used by those earlier reformers cannot be easily transferred to the 1980s, a time of declining federal support and broader participation in local politics. New formulas for civic improvement must be invented—ones that tap the enormous vitality of the region's private businesses, communities, and organizations. If such new public-private partnerships are to serve the city well, they must give equal weight to public and private interests—a novel approach in a city that has traditionally elevated private welfare above the public good.

NOTES

1. Lincoln Steffens, *The Shame of the Cities* (New York: P. Smith, 1904).

2. Sam Bass Warner, *The Private City: Philadelphia in Three Periods of its Growth*, 2nd ed. (Philadelphia: University of Pennsylvania Press, 1987).

3. *Survey of Community Needs and Assets*, Community Leadership Seminars, Philadelphia, November 1985, p. 6.

4. David Elesh, William Yancey, and Janet Washbon, "The Meaning of the Industrial Transformation," Institute for Public Policy Studies Working Paper #19, Philadelphia, October 1985, p. 6.

5. Anita Summers and Thomas Luce, *Economic Development within the Philadelphia Metropolitan Area* (Philadelphia: University of Pennsylvania Press, 1987), p. 3.

6. Ibid., p. 9.

7. Kirk Petshek, *The Challenge of Urban Reform* (Philadelphia: Temple University Press, 1973), pp. 18–19.

8. Jeanne Lowe, *Cities in a Race with Time, Progress and Poverty in America's Renewing Cities* (New York: Random House, 1967), p. 313.

9. *Philadelphia Bulletin*, June 7, 1965.

10. Petshek, *The Challenge of Urban Reform*, especially ch. 2.

11. Joseph Daughen and Peter Binzen, *The Cop Who Would Be King: The Honorable Frank Rizzo* (Boston: Little, Brown and Co., 1977), p. 154.

12. Ibid., p. 166.

13. William Cutler, "The Persistent Dualism, Centralization and Decentralization in Philadelphia, 1954–1975," in William Cutler and Howard Gillette, eds., *The Divided Metropolis: Social and Spatial Dimensions of Philadelphia 1800–1975* (Westport, Conn.: Greenwood Press, 1980), p. 273.

14. Greater Philadelphia Chamber of Commerce, "Report of the Long-Range Planning Committee," 1982, p. 2.

15. Greater Philadelphia Chamber of Commerce, "Questions and Answers Regarding Long-Range Plan," March 16, 1982.

16. *Philadelphia Inquirer*, April 11, 1987.

17. *Inquirer*, April 13, 1983.

18. Barbara Ferman, *Governing the Ungovernable City: Political Skill, Leadership, and the Modern Mayor* (Philadelphia: Temple University Press, 1985), p. 211.

19. Summers and Luce, *Economic Development*, p. 22.

20. Thomas Luce and Anita Summers, *Local Fiscal Issues in the Philadelphia Metropolitan Area* (Philadelphia: University of Pennsylvania Press, 1987), p. 79.

21. Ibid., p. 86.

22. Despite strong pressure from Mayor Wilson Goode and the business community, a half dozen black Democrats representing the city of Philadelphia voted against the project, citing the failure to stipulate affirmative action quotas for the jobs and contracts to be generated by the construction.

XII

PITTSBURGH

REBUILDING A CITY:
THE PITTSBURGH MODEL

Michael P. Weber

In April 1985, Rand McNally issued the second volume of its *Places Rated Almanac*. The information it provided stunned residents of Western Pennsylvania and produced scoffers throughout the rest of the country. Pittsburgh, well known for its smoke and grime, its militant labor unions, and, more recently, for its declining industries and professional sports franchises, was named by the compilers of the *Almanac* as the most liveable city in America. Low crime rates and housing costs, and exceptionally high rankings in the arts, education, health care, and the environment enabled the former steel city to outclass cosmopolitan centers such as New York, San Francisco, and Chicago as well as the sunbelt cities of Miami, Atlanta, and Phoenix. Pittsburgh, the authors concluded "shows remarkable strength in the social indicators and is remarkably like a small town in many respects, despite its great size. Values are traditional and simple, neighborhoods tight yet friendly. . . . The result, in the 1980s, is a smoke-free city of tall office buildings set in a stunning natural setting of rugged hills and river valleys, with plenty of recreational parks and a fine waterfront. The Golden Triangle . . . is the heart of the city's business district, with scores of handsome buildings and skyscrapers."[1]

While the city's elevated ranking surprised outsiders, it was more incredible to those who know Pittsburgh well. In 1985 Pittsburgh was in a period of deindustrialization, which had seen the loss of more than 60,000 jobs in the city's basic industry—primary metals. Nearly 40,000 workers in other durable goods also lost their jobs during the same period. Unemployment hovered at nearly twice the national average. Perhaps even more disturbing was the permanency of those job losses. Pittsburgh industries, which had provided the base for the city's economy for more than a century, were closing their doors or leaving the city. Gulf Oil, swallowed up in a so-called friendly merger with Chevron Oil, transferred its operations to California. Left behind were several thousand white-collar workers, nearly five hundred scientists and staff at the firm's oil research lab, and a vacant forty-four story Gulf Building. Jones and Laughlin Steel, founded in 1861, met a similar fate at the hands of LTV and eventually shut down its Western Pennsylvania operations, putting 17,500 men and women out of work. Westinghouse Electric and Westinghouse Airbrake Companies, once the world's leading producer of electrical generators, transformers, and airbrake equipment reduced their giant East Pittsburgh works to a mere caretaking operation, idling another 15,000 workers. Other metal producing firms, such as Wheeling-Pittsburgh Steel, National Steel, and the city's industrial giant, U.S. Steel, followed the trend. Even firms which appeared immune to deindustrialization have now begun to prove vulnerable. Pittsburgh's Dravo Corporation, for example, as recently as 1979 employed 4,500 workers locally and 14,000 worldwide. The firm, with construction and engineering projects around the world, was a national leader in the production of river barges, lock and bridge building, and heavy construction. In 1980 Dravo announced that it would build a headquarters building in the Pittsburgh city center. The 54 story Dravo Building would have eventually held 5,000 company employees. Two years later, citing depressed business conditions, Dravo bowed out of the project, selling its leases to Mellon Bank. In late 1987, the company announced its third major cutback projecting a workforce of 500 in Pittsburgh and 2,750 nationally by the end of the decade. In short, the production of metals and other manufacturing goods, which employed more than 50 percent of the region's workers in 1955, now accounts for less than 20 percent of the work force. In all probability 150,000 jobs have disappeared in the past two decades.[2]

Many serious observers have criticized the Rand McNally report as sophomoric and simplistic. Nevertheless, considering the disappearance of its industrial base, a dramatic loss of tax revenues, high unemployment, failing commercial businesses, and a declining and aging population, that Pittsburgh could meet someone's test as the nation's most liveable city is a tribute to Pittsburgh's forty-year public and private partnership in urban planning and action.

Once the nation's industrial leader, the city of Pittsburgh had experienced an erratic but sustained economic decline since 1910. Growth in industrial production tapered off as the development of by-product coke ovens permitted steel firms to relocate near the source of iron ore rather than the soft coal mines. Investment capital flowed to new markets and entrepreneurial talent looked beyond the Steel City. None of the new industries which have developed in the United States since 1910 had their birth in Pittsburgh. The maturation of the Pittsburgh economy, which occurred in the second decade of the century, left the city with aging capital goods industries, highly dependent upon the condition of the national economy. This dependency heightened the vulnerability of the local population to cyclical swings. The city which experienced relatively full employment and economic growth in times of national growth—during World Wars I and II in particular—suffered more severely in periods of economic decline. After World War II national economic cycles and foreign competition further jeopardized the health of the Pittsburgh economy.[3]

The industrial decline, which weakened the city's economic structure, also left an indelible mark on the physical and social condition of the city. As many nineteenth and twentieth-century visitors testified, the indignities the physical city suffered in the name of profit illustrated the worst features of the free enterprise system. Blight and decay could be seen everywhere: in the central business district, in the neighborhoods, and in the factories themselves. A 1945 survey by the Econometric Institute of New York revealed that Pittsburgh's real property assessments had declined by $206 million during the period 1933–44. The decline cost the city nearly $6 million in tax revenues. Not a single high rise building was planned for construction during the postwar period.

In 1945 the city's central business district was in decay. Located immediately at the point where the city's three rivers join was a thirty-six acre eyesore of deteriorating buildings, warehouses, parking lots and ugly railroad trestles and tracks. The historic Blockhouse, dating from the American Revolution, stood amid warehouses and abandoned tracks. Debris including tires, automobile parts, rusting industrial artifacts, and abandoned river barges littered the potentially beautiful riverbanks. Floods covered the area nearly every spring. Further back from this warehouse district was a mixed residential, commercial, and industrial section, most of which was run down or abandoned. Blight covered the entire area. A city survey revealed that 40 percent of the structures were deteriorating and would soon be in need of major rebuilding or demolition.[4]

Pittsburgh's main business district was a mixture of venerable older buildings, such as the grand Union Trust building with its Flemish roofline, the Romanesque courthouse and jail, designed by Henry Hobbs Richardson, the more modern Gulf and Koppers skyscrapers, and a jumble of two and three story lofts and plain high rises. Excepting the historic banking district along fourth Avenue, no pattern to the placement of the buildings existed. Skyscrapers rose side by side with warehouses, commercial buildings, and service stations. Five decades of soot, smoke, and grime covered everything.

The residential neighborhoods in which most Pittsburgh families lived were no better than the business districts in which they shopped or worked. Substandard conditions and decay could be found throughout the city. An analysis of housing conducted by Philip Kline of the New York School of Social Work found fourteen neighborhoods in which one-third or more of the homes were in need of ''substantial repair or demolition.'' The worst of these, the Hill District neighborhood which ringed the central business district, was a slum. Now primarily black, this site of several generations of immigrant settlement suffered from overcrowding, inadequate sanitation, dilapidated housing structures, high incidences of disease and crime, and inadequate social services. One study concluded that ''the whole community speaks of poverty, neglect and hardship.''[5]

The decline of the economy and the decay of business and residential areas were by no means the only problems facing postwar Pittsburgh. Recurring and destructive floods, the ever present layer of smoke, health concerns, and the absence of cultural and aesthetic amenities detracted from the city's quality of life. Five major floods inundated the city between 1900 and 1945, the most serious occurring in 1936 when eleven feet of water covered the CBD. The disaster took 47 lives, injured 2,800, and left 67,500 people homeless. The U.S. Army Corps of Engineers estimated the property loss at $50 million. The frequency of minor flooding and the predictable major ones discouraged developers from investing in Pittsburgh. Solving the flood problem was perhaps the single most important step in the rebuilding of the city.[6]

Second in order of importance was smoke control. Pittsburgh's longstanding reputation as the "smokey city" was well deserved. Bituminous coal blast furnaces and open hearths, nearly 200 railroad engines which entered the city daily, and 142,000 coalburning homes produced a dense pall which constantly hung over the city. In an earlier era medical experts believed that the smoke was good for one's health; later workers and other residents accepted it as a sign of a booming economy. By 1940, however, the city's director of public health, the press, and other civic-minded groups began to call for relief. In July 1941 a city appointed smoke commission drafted a plan to force users to burn smokeless coal or use mechanical equipment to eliminate the smoke. The city council passed the ordinance one month later only to suspend its enforcement for the duration of the war. Production of the heavy metals for the war effort took precedence over clean skies.

Architect Frank Lloyd Wright was not the only observer to counsel that the wisest course of action regarding postwar Pittsburgh would be to "abandon it." Several major firms took preliminary leases on headquarters buildings in other cities and corporate heads experienced difficulty in attracting executives into the city. Even Constance Mellon, matron of the city's most prominent family, balked at returning to Pittsburgh after the war. If the city were to survive as a major metropolis immediate action was required.

While the economic, physical, and environmental problems of the city seemed insurmountable, the presence of several reform groups and a history of civic-minded voluntary associations provided some hope. Early in the century three organizations—the Civic Club of Allegheny County, the Chamber of Commerce, and the Civic Commission—sponsored city improvement projects. Smoke control, water supply, sanitation, city planning, housing, charity and tax reform all received the attention of the upper-class leaders of these groups. The Civic Commission even brought Frederick Law Olmsted to the city to produce a comprehensive plan for the redevelopment of the central business district. While nothing came of Olmsted's work, other efforts by these voluntary associations led to a number of reforms.

Civic groups continued their efforts during the interwar years but often met resistance or indifference from the governmental sector. In 1923, for example, a citizens committee developed a six-part program to improve the region's highway system, playgrounds, parks, public transit, railroads, and waterways. Only the plans for recreation and city streets were adopted by the Pittsburgh City Council. Sixteen years later the same committee, now named the Pittsburgh Regional Planning Commission (PRPC), hired Robert Moses to develop another comprehensive plan for the city. The Moses plan, although still not implemented in 1945, became the basis for the postwar redevelopment of the city.

Another civic group crucial to the postwar redevelopment of the city had its origins during the war. Started initially as a "super planning group" to coordinate postwar reconstruction of the city, the organization captured the attention and imagination of the city's foremost entrepreneur, Richard King Mellon. Mellon, who sat on the board of more than twenty Pittsburgh corporations, was recognized by all as *the* financial power of Pittsburgh. His willingness to participate in the newly formed Allegheny Conference on Community Development (ACCD) assured its viability. When he agreed to take part, all other Pittsburgh corporate heads rushed to become active members. They formed the executive committee whose members were required to attend meetings in person—substitutes were not permitted. Thus, executive-committee decisions were insured the support of corporate Pittsburgh. This important policy decision made the ACCD the preeminent private sector planning and action group in the city. By the war's end the committee had developed an outline for redevelopment of the city.[7]

The presence of several well-organized and well-financed civic associations, however, did not guarantee their success. The failure of earlier attempts at planning and urban redevelopment clearly demonstrated the need for cooperation from both the public and private sectors. A potential stumbling block was the Democratic political machine controlled by the Irish Catholic son of a blue-collar worker, David L. Lawrence. During the 1930s, Lawrence had led a Democratic takeover of almost revolutionary proportions. Since the Civil War, Democrats had won only one mayor's race and had never held a majority on the city council or the county commission. As late as 1929 Republicans held a registration edge in the city of 169,000 to 5,200.[8] But corruption within the Republican organization, the popularity of President Franklin Roosevelt, and Lawrence's own skill in building an effective Democratic organization turned the tide. In 1933 Lawrence's candidate, William McNair, became only the second Democratic mayor since the Civil War. Within the next few years, candidates backed by Lawrence won full control of the city council, county commission, state house and senate, and a governorship. Equally significant, the voter registration majority shifted substantially to the Democratic party. By the end of the Second World War, Pittsburgh became a one-party city. The inept Republican organization has never since mounted a serious challenge. In some elections the GOP has been unable to find candidates who would run against the powerful Democratic machine. In 1945, Lawrence stood virtually unopposed. Under pressure, his willingness to cooperate with the blue-blooded, all Republican, largely Protestant Allegheny Conference was in doubt.

But Lawrence gave a clear indication of his intentions when he stepped from behind the scenes to run for mayor in 1945. His seven-point platform adopted most of the ACCD redevelopment plan, and he pledged to work with that or any other group which would help in the rebuilding program. Soon after his election, Lawrence demonstrated that his statement was more than mere campaign rhetoric when he appointed key ACCD figures to prominent administrative posts. When Lawrence and Richard King Mellon agreed to cooperate, they laid the groundwork for what one group of public policy analysts called, "one of the most significant instances of public-private partnerships in the history of American cities."[9]

For twenty-five years following the election of Lawrence and the formation of the ACCD, the Pittsburgh public and private sectors worked hand in glove to create what became known as the Pittsburgh Renaissance. A formal protocol for action never existed among the groups interested in rebuilding the city. Some improvements, such as smoke and flood control were carried out primarily by the public sector. Others, such as the development of Mellon Park in the city center, came primarily from the charitable efforts of the private sector. Most, however, while largely privately financed, required the cooperation and active participation of both public and private interests.

The Lawrence administration first tackled the environmental problems which had plagued the city for nearly a century. The Democratic city and county administrations and the Republican controlled state government in Harrisburg joined forces to lobby the Truman administration to complete a series of flood control dams which Congress had authorized prior to the war. From 1947 through 1949, Lawrence made half a dozen trips to Washington to apply pressure to Congress to carry out the flood control program. The Chamber of Commerce lobbied Republican congressmen on the same issue. This joint campaign succeeded, and Congress appropriated funds during the 1948 and 1949 sessions. Work began on the projects in May 1949. Almost immediately dividends appeared. With flood control assured, the Equitable Life Assurance Society agreed to redevelop an area later known as Gateway Center. The agreement was the keystone of the entire revitalization of the city.

Achieving a flood control system was relatively simple when compared with the problems the Lawrence administration encountered in dealing with the issue of smoke. The prewar city ordinances had established a three-stage timetable for the elimination of smoke. Stages one and two targeted commercial establishments, industries, and railroads. The city encountered little difficulty in implementing most of these regulations although a reluctant Pennsylvania Railroad required the intervention of Mellon and Benjamin Fairless, President of U.S. Steel, before agreeing to convert its steam engines to diesel. Mellon and Fairless reportedly threatened to transfer all their substantial freight business to another railroad. The Pennsylvania quickly complied. A major campaign, however, was required to implement the domestic use phase. Nearly three-fourths of the city's households burned the dirty fuel, and opponents charged that the ordinance requiring smokeless fuel or conversion systems would cause a severe financial hardship on the "little Joes" of the city. Lawrence, risking political defeat in the 1949 Democratic primary, relentlessly enforced the ordinances passed by the city and county governments. Pittsburgh's newspapers also joined in the campaign by regularly running editorials and cartoons in support of smoke control legislation. Pittsburgh's sky began to clear and the city's residents at last could breathe relatively unpolluted air. By 1954 heavy smoke had declined by 98.7 percent and moderate smoke by 85.8 percent from 1946 levels.[9]

The most serious environmental issues facing the city required both public and private-sector intervention, but it was in the bricks-and-mortar rebuilding of the city that the closest cooperation occurred. In all, eight major and many minor projects were initiated during the Renaissance I period. In these the Allegheny Conference and other private sector agencies provided planning, financial projections, some funding, and occasional assistance in implementation. On the public sector side, the mayor, and the city council he dominated, provided enabling legislation when and wherever needed. The council, usually voting 9 to 0, approved every bill presented to it by the Lawrence administration during his thirteen-year tenure as mayor. In addition, an Urban Redevelopment Authority, created by Law-

TABLE 12.1
Renaissance I Urban Redevelopment Projects[a]

Project	Area (in acres)	Action Agencies	Costs (in Millions) Public Funds	Private Funds
Point Park	37	ACCD, Pa. State Govt.		
Gateway Center	23	ACCD, URA, Pgh. City Govt., City Planning, Equitable Life, PRPA	.6	118
J&L Steel Expansion	114	ACCD, URA, City Planning, J&L Steel	.11	81
Lower Hill Civic Arena	95	ACCD, URA, Pgh. Housing Authority Kaufmann family	18	90
Allegheny Ctr.	103	City Plg., ACCD, URA, Pgh. Housing Authority	24	65
East Liberty	254	City Plg., URA, ACCD Housing Authority	42	65
ALCOA/Mellon Square	.3	URA, ACCD, Mellon	.2	

[a]Robert Pease, Allegheny Conference on Community Development, Project Files. In total, Renaissance I projects affected 1018 city acres of land. The public sector provided $133 million and the private sector $500 million of the entire cost.

rence in 1946 at the suggestion of the ACCD, used its powers of eminent domain to condemn buildings, vacate streets and properties, and combine small parcels of land into larger ones suitable for major developers. Lawrence, also at the urging of the ACCD, chaired the redevelopment authority. When he named three conference members, including Mellon aide Arthur VanBuskirk, to sit on the board, he assured the continuing cooperation of the private sector. Indicative of the cooperation that was developing, the initial funding of the URA came from the sale of $150,000 in bonds to three private foundations.

The details of the major redevelopments varied (see table 12.1), but in general each followed the pattern developed in creating Gateway Center from the 23 acres of commercial slum and industrial wasteland that abutted the area which would become Point Park. Wallace Richards, Director of the Pittsburgh Regional Planning Commission suggested redevelopment to ACCD officials sometime in late 1945. Richards and VanBuskirk then approached Charles Graham, President of the West Virginia and Pittsburgh Railroad to enlist his help in a massive facelift of the area. Graham suggested that they contact Metropolitan Life Insurance, financial backer of two major housing developments in New York City. When Metropolitan proved uninterested, the pair, joined by representatives from the ACCD and the city government approached Equitable Life Insurance which eventually approved the project. The City Planning Commission certified the land as blighted and the newly created URA began condemnation proceedings to accumulate the required property. The URA also secured twenty-year leases on sixty percent of the planned floor space, an Equitable precondition to development. The Mellon interests solidified this guarantee by occupying some of the space and quietly underwriting much of the agreement. Three eleven-story cruciform buildings were completed by 1953. Another six structures and an underground parking garage were added by the end of the decade. In all the project cost $118.6 million, including only $600,000 in public funds.

In 1959, in the midst of his fourth term as mayor, Lawrence left Pittsburgh to become governor of Pennsylvania. The redevelopment program he and Mellon had spearheaded continued for another ten years, as Lawrence's handpicked successor, Joseph Barr, carried on the programs started by his mentor. In all, the first Pittsburgh Renaissance, which spanned 1945–70, produced a riverfront park of thirty-six acres at the city's point, the Gateway Center Office Complex, a center city park and office tower, an arena for sports and musical events, several major industrial expansions, a revitalized hospital complex in Oakland, and two new commercial and residential districts in the eastern and northern sections of the city. In addition, the city was now safe from floods and relatively smoke free. Several major firms had renewed their commitment to retain their national headquarters in Pittsburgh. To be sure, Renaissance I was not free from criticism. Detractors pointed to the unfinished status of the acreage surrounding the civic arena and the isolation of the black community produced by the erection of that structure. Others noted that the redevelopment had not followed a comprehensive plan but rather had occurred where developers were willing to spend money. Rebuilding was somewhat erratic, sprinkled throughout the city. In addition, neither the East Liberty nor Allegheny center commercial-residential developments have been commercial or community building successes. Both disrupted old, established neighborhoods and shopping districts. In East Liberty, the city is currently attempting to undo much of the earlier work by opening closed streets and building parking lots. Other critics charge that the Lawrence and Barr administrations failed to resolve housing problems or revive deteriorating neighborhoods. Yet, despite these problems, most objective analysts now conclude that, on the whole, Renaissance I was a remarkable achievement, accomplished with only a modest financial investment by the public sector. Redevelopment had turned the city from a rapidly deteriorating entity into one with much hope and a positive future.

Perhaps Pittsburgh was ready for a rest in 1970. Rising discontent from civil rights leaders, neighborhood groups, and special interest factions suggested that the old coalition between the Democratic machine and Republican businessmen would no longer be enough. Within the Democratic organization, contenders to fill the vacuum left by Lawrence's death in 1966 began to create division. Criticism of old-style redevelopment (bulldozing old neighborhoods and commercial districts to build new ones) began to surface both nationally and in Pittsburgh. It became difficult to find individuals or firms willing to invest in large-scale high rise office developments as the supply of office space began to outstrip the demand.

The election of the political maverick, Peter Flaherty, on a "he's nobody's boy," campaign brought about a seven-year interruption in the public-private partnership formed by Lawrence and Mellon. Although Flaherty gained his political experience within the Lawrence organization, he correctly perceived in 1969 that a break from the machine would catapult him into the mayor's office. Forging neighborhood coalitions and campaigning door to door as an independent Democrat, the attractive and affable Flaherty built an impressive personal following. His victory over the organization candidate in that year's primary was relatively close but the general election proved no contest as the Republican organization showed that it was no match for a Democrat, regardless of whether he had the endorsement of his own party. Four years later, Flaherty running on the Democratic, Republican, and Independent tickets won all three primaries. The general election in the fall was redundant.

With strong grass-roots backing, Flaherty saw no need to maintain the partnership with either corporate heads or the Democratic organization. Many business leaders, in fact, assert that the mayor went out of his way to irritate or affront the corporate community.[10] It was now clear that the old coalition could not work as long as Flaherty was at the political helm.

This lack of cooperation between the public and private sectors stemmed primarily from three sources. First, the mayor, in targeting the importance of neighborhood development at the expense of the CBD, was offering an agenda which had only limited appeal for the Allegheny Conference on Community Development. Second, the mayor and the conference became embroiled in a battle over the mode and the timing of the rapid transit system to be installed in the county. Finally, Flaherty's informal style of leadership, his unwavering emphasis on fiscal responsibility, his populist philosophy, and even his work habits contributed to the adversial relationship between corporate Pittsburgh and the administration.

The program of the new mayor promised a balanced budget, a streamlined workforce committed to a full day's work, elimination of the patronage system, no new taxes, and a reorientation of public spending toward city residents rather than corporations. Making good on his promises he reduced the city work force by more than a quarter during a seven-year period and reorganized every government bureau.[11] The streamlining began in line positions but eventually spread to directors and authority heads as well. These latter changes meant that the public and private sectors needed to develop new working relationships not only at the top—the mayor and the ACCD, for example—but at the staff level as well.

Another source of conflict revolved around the issue of the city's minorities and the neighborhoods. Racial riots and the tensions of the late 1960s made it obvious that city government could no longer ignore Pittsburgh's black community. Consistent with its business outlook, the Barr administration and the ACCD responded by sponsoring or assisting in the development of several organizations which provided help to enterprising blacks. The Negro Education Emergency Drive (NEED) provided small grants to black college students. Since 1963 this totally private organization has provided approximately $300,000 per year to needy students. Other commitments included support for the Program to Aid Citizen Enterprise (PACE), the National Alliance of Businessmen (NAB), and the Minority Entrepreneur Loan Program (MELP). Today all three provide assistance to businesses within the minority community.

When Pete Flaherty assumed office, however, he correctly asserted that such programs would not be enough to resolve the problems faced by Pittsburgh's black community. Building on activist, neighborhood-based programs started during the Barr administration, Flaherty shifted redevelopment emphasis from the CBD to the neighborhoods. His administration did complete CBD projects already underway and reluctently approved a convention center for which the federal and state governments had authorized considerable funding. Nevertheless, he gave clear indication that half of all new federal funds attracted to the city would go to the neighborhoods. Community Development Block Grant (CDBG) money spread throughout the city's neighborhoods for home improvements. Funds also built parks and recreation centers to help restore a sense of community in the city's aging ethnic and racial neighborhoods. This new policy emphasis, however, was not without problems. The practice of distributing funds throughout the city's more than fifty neighborhoods prevented the development of showplace communities. Despite efforts, housing continued to deteriorate, and two black slums desperately in need of physical rehabilitation exist in Pittsburgh today. Nevertheless, it seems clear that the neighborhood emphasis of the Flaherty administration did result in some modest improvements.

Perhaps the most significant differences among the Flaherty administration, other members of his party, and the business community revolved around two major transit projects. Flaherty's predecessor, the city council, the Democratic county commissioners, and the ACCD had all given their support to the development of an elevated, electric transit system known as skybus (similar to BART in San Francisco and the "peoplemover" at Disneyworld) to serve the region's south hills and a massive highway project in the East Street Valley to serve the north hills. Flaherty opposed both. He permanently blocked skybus and delayed the East Street Expressway for nearly a decade. The disagreements over the two issues, fought out in the courts and in the press, obscured whatever goodwill remained in the public-private partnership. While civic improvements did not totally stop during the Flaherty administration, one historian's term for this era, "the Interlude," seems overly kind.[12]

In 1976 the ambitious Flaherty left the mayor's office to become assistant attorney general in the Carter administration. Flaherty's followers, who were more committed to him than to any organization were left unprotected as new leadership stepped in. Flaherty's interim replacement, as mayor, was his political opponent from 1973, city council president Richard Caliguiri. During the next two years Caliguiri, who had pledged that he would not be a candidate for mayor, quietly built his own organization and, in 1975, announced that he had changed his mind and would run. He campaigned on the promise of another renaissance for Pittsburgh. Following a mild primary battle, Caliguiri and the Democratic regulars swept back into office. The anti-business, anti-party era had come to an end. Caliguiri intended to resurrect the spirit of cooperation which had made the city's first redevelopment a national model.

Clearly the problems Caliguiri faced were not as dramatic or even life threatening as they had been in 1945. The environment was no longer a prime issue, and while some industries were feeling the effects of foreign competition, none were threatening to leave the city. Moreover the city's aging infrastructure was still in operating condition and a large part of the city had been rebuilt.

Nevertheless, the problems the city's first mayor of Italian descent faced were formidable, and Caliguiri, while cognizant of the importance of his party ties, recognized that "politics as usual" would not bring solutions. The 1950s-style Democratic organization, based on party loyalty, political favors, and patronage could not be revived. Minority leaders, political activists, neighborhood advocates, and other groups demanded accommodation. In addition, the near unanimous city councils enjoyed by Lawrence and Barr had given way to a squabbling board, often more interested in its members' own agendas and publicity than in city redevelopment.

Moreover, even if Caliguiri could put his political house back in order, he could not turn to Pittsburgh's community for the sort of all encompassing support that his predecessors had enjoyed. There was no longer one spokesperson for the business community. The business leadership, like the city itself, was now fragmented among a number of divergent financial interests. Many were no longer certain of the role they should play. Consider, for example, the statements of four chief executive officers. "Founded here almost 100 years ago," one executive stated, "we do have a special responsibility to Pittsburgh, probably somewhat out of proportion to the number of employees as a proportion of our total employees. We have a responsibility to Pittsburgh." But, another head of an equally large corporation provided a less supportive view: "When you look at my predecessors two or three back, they would have been able to devote their time to Pittsburgh on an 80:20 ratio. Today I can afford to give Pittsburgh 20:80. Although I have an interest in Pittsburgh, I have too many things elsewhere, so that I personally can't give it that kind of attention." A third indicated that economic conditions were changing the role that corporations could play. "There's an old saying that 'survival strategies leave little room for sentiment'; and I think you could broaden that to include little room for social causes. I think, unfortunately, that many of the Pittsburgh companies really do have problems, and the more they are under the gun from other U.S. companies—and many of them foreign companies now—the less time and energy they have to devote to helping solve the problems that exist in Pittsburgh." Finally, one warned that the small number of corporations represented by the Allegheny Conference could no longer be expected to carry the full weight of a social and physical rebuilding of the city. "The biggest thing that's going to have to happen in this city is that we can't continue to ride the backs of 20 companies. We've had a slight shrinkage in the power structure. . . . We've had a growing array of demands, but we haven't altered the structure of the existing mechanisms, let alone created new ones. . . . It's going to break under its own weight."[13] In a new renaissance the public sector would probably have to play a larger role.

Like the first Pittsburgh Renaissance the second on has not developed from a comprehensive plan designed to create a model urban center. Economic conditions and demand for office space have dictated that most of the private investment funds would be allocated to the central business district. Location, building style, and type were largely left to the operations of a market driven by office occupancy rates as high as 99 percent. Nevertheless there are important differences between Pittsburgh's first and second phases of redevelopment. The fragmentation and ambivalence of the private sector, as well as changed economic and social conditions, have caused the city to play a more important role in goal setting. Four city agencies (City Planning, Housing, Economic Development, and the Urban Redevelopment Authority) became the pace setters.[14] These offices play a key role in slating areas for redevelopment, attracting funds, purchasing property, and preparing sites for development.

Mayor Caliguiri's vehicle for development was a weekly staff meeting of agency heads usually conducted by the mayor's executive secretary. This Mayor's Development Council, which includes the directors of Redevelopment, Housing, and Planning, as well as Jack Robin, chairman of the URA and program advisor to the ACCD, gave the latest city redevelopment phase the appearance of a comprehensive urban design. With the assistance of the Pittsburgh History and Landmarks Foundation, the city has studied all its existing structures to determine which ones should be restored, which could be demolished and which were in sound condition. Those areas designated for preservation, for example, included the historic districts around Market Square, on the Monongahela River bank, and the nineteenth-century financial district. The staff meeting has also developed other policies discouraging the development of single-purpose structures isolated in plazas, identifying land for public use, and setting standards for street lighting, signs, and street furniture. Renaissance II, while admittedly not facing problems so formidable as those of the Lawrence-Barr administrations, has perhaps been more successful than its predecessor. It has focused on five major elements: CBD development, transportation, neighborhoods, jobs and industry, and the creation of special multi-use zones.

The dramatic symbols of Renaissance II are the city's new high rise office complexes, but Caliguiri's programs include many more accomplishments. Central business district developments completed or nearing completion include thirteen office, restaurant, and commercial building complexes ranging in size from five to fifty-three stories, a convention center, a hotel, an open air park adjacent to the Heinz Hall opera house, a $42 million conversion of a historic theater palace into the Benedum Center for the Performing Arts, and the restoration of the eighty-year-old Pennsylvania station into inner-city luxury apartments. The total value of the new and restored structures in the CBD is approximately $2.25 billion. As in the case of Renaissance I, each project developed somewhat differently but each involved participation and encouragement from both the public and private sectors. The success of Renaissance II proved that while the makeup of the coalition was significantly different from the earlier period, common goals and interests could make the partnership workable once more. An examination of the most impressive of the Renaissance II projects (PPG Place) illustrates how the partnership works.

Early in the decade PPG Industries determined that it had outgrown its scattered offices and decided to consolidate its employees into a single office. The company considered several sites including one across the Allegheny River from the CBD and another outside the city altogether. The firm also identified a site nearly adjacent to the Renaissance I Gateway Center. PPG requested that the city use its powers of eminent domain to assemble the land then held by more than two dozen owners. Faced with an opportunity for a major redevelopment, the Caliguiri administration responded in the affirmative but added three major conditions: PPG would agree to develop an entire district of the city rather than build a single building, PPG would request no financial assistance from the city, and a joint announcement of such a comprehensive renewal had to be made to the public. The development was to include restoration of Market Square, one hundred fifty years old, and the building of an open plaza for city residents and public gatherings. PPG quickly agreed. The city through its powers and its access to PPG funds eventually relocated or bought out all commercial businesses in the redevelopment area. The New York architectural firm of Johnson and Burgee was brought in to design a signature building complex for PPG. Taking his inspiration from the firms basic product—glass— and the Gothic towers of the University of Pittsburgh, Philip Johnson created a splendid glass cathedral soaring into the Pittsburgh skyline. Five smaller cathedrals surround the building and these include a greenhouse wintergarden given over wholly to public use and displays. Workmen restored several historic buildings on the periphery, resodded Market Square Park, and repaved the roadways with brick and Belgian block.[15]

The development of PPG Place demonstrated that the city was prepared to take the leadership role in the second renaissance. The Allegheny Conference would continue to be a key player in a number of the redevelopment projects, but the city would not rely on it to initiate action. The city consulted ACCD on the PPG project, but the latter played only a limited role in its implementation. A number of other CBD and neighborhood projects followed a similar pattern.

The creation of another office-commercial complex, Oxford Place, along the city's governmental corridor, Grant Street, indicates the difficulty of keeping politics out of the business of city redevelopment. Political considerations, fortunately, have not interfered with most of Pittsburgh's redevelopment efforts, but the Oxford-Hillman controversy illustrates the importance of the public-private, apolitical partnership in Pittsburgh.

Grant Street, with its historic courthouse, traverses almost the entire city from north to south and is generally considered a key boundary for the CBD. In addition the street contains the most significant architectural structures in the city. Many consider the massive Romanesque courthouse and the adjacent jail to be Henry Hobbs Richardson's finest work. Further along the street are the City-County building with its great inner gallery and the Grant Building office tower, both designed by Henry Hornbostel. Across the street Osterling's superbly scaled and ornamented Union Trust Building (now Two Mellon Place), the elegant William Penn Hotel, and Daniel H. Burnham's Frick Building add to the architectural and historic importance of the corridor. Pittsburgh city planners identified Grant as the key street in the redevelopment process. Their plans called for the surface of the street to be redone in brick with island plantings constructed of Belgian block running the entire length. New street lighting, signage, and street furniture would enhance the historic, commercial, and legislative significance of the district. The city's largest building, USX Tower, would anchor one end, an office tower and hotel complex would join the courthouse to dominate the middle area and another major project would anchor the southern end near the Monongahela River.

The site identified for the latter project was a two-acre, open-air, ground-level parking lot, owned by Allegheny County. Although the county commissioners controlled the property, it was located in the heart of downtown Pittsburgh. Any action on it called for the collaboration of the Caliguiri administration and Democratic commissioners. Planning departments from the two agencies consulted and issued a joint request for a proposal to erect a multi-use office complex. Two developers eventually submitted full proposals. One, the Grant Land Company, was an agency created by the multi-billion dollar Hillman Corporation expressly for the purpose of developing the Grant Street project. The second was Oxford Development Corporation, a pioneer developer of shopping malls in Western Pennsylvania and throughout the nation. Both developers brought in heavy-hitting architectural firms from outside to design their projects.

Designers for Hillman offered plans and drawings for two fifty-five story office towers clad in sun-reflecting aluminum and glass. Each tower would be constructed in facing triangles so as to resemble four buildings capped with soaring, if obliquely angled, roof towers designed to capture the angles and heights of the existing city structures. The towers were in the style of I. M. Pei's Hancock buildings in Chicago and Boston. Particularly striking was the plan to mount the structures on triangular piers nine stories above the ground. At ground level the buildings were to be connected by a seven story glass and steel enclosed greenhouse-pavilion. In contrast, the Oxford Developers presented a less detailed plan for their twin towers, one of fifty-one stories, the other of forty-two. Like their competitors, the Oxford structures appeared to be several spires, minimizing their dominating effect on the street. The structures, primarily rectangles with angled corners to give an octagonal appearance, were ribboned with horizontal sections of polished aluminum and glass. Flat roofs topped off the buildings at several different levels to minimize their somewhat blunt appearance.

Architectural experts throughout the city generally praised both plans, but reached unanimous agreement that the Hillman project would be a significant piece of architecture, equal in importance to the proposed PPG complex. The Allegheny County Planning Department agreed, recommending that the commissioners select the Hillman Building over the Oxford proposal. "The building proposed by Grant Land Co. is aesthetically a different building in downtown Pittsburgh," the county planners wrote in their report to the commissioners. "The twin triangular towers would be a focal point of interest similar to the Citicorp Building in New York. . . . The Grant Land Company building is a 'hi-tech' building, sheathed in silver anodized aluminum and glass. Angles of the triangles will always be catching the sunlight. The proposed GLC building would fit in well with the image attempted to be created by the concept of Renaissance II, and would truly be a building moving the city into the 21st Century. . . . In contrast the proposed Oxford building has a number of weaknesses. While it is a curtain-wall building and a hi-tech building, its construction of bronze glass will create a rather somber building.'' The Hillman project, the planning office also pointed out, would be bigger, would generate more construction jobs, provide more permanent employment, and would start sooner and finish more quickly. It would also accommodate more parking underground while the Oxford project proposed a multi story above ground parking facility.[16]

In the end, however, company proposals weighed less than company ownership. What the report did not state, although it was widely known by political observers in Pittsburgh, was that Henry Hillman, owner of the Hillman Corporation, was the husband of Republican National Committeewoman, Elsie Hillman. For nearly a decade Mrs. Hillman had been the areas most vocal and respected Republican supporter. She had actively solicited funds and was an important contributor to both local and national Republican figures. The President of Oxford Development, on the other hand, was Edward J. Lewis, a major financial backer of former mayor Pete Flaherty and his brother, county commissioner, James Flaherty.

Several months later, ignoring the report of its own planning department, the two Democratic county commissioners announced Oxford Development Corporation as the successful bidder. Republican Commissioner Pierce voted for the Hillman project. Oxford, the majority commissioners pointed out, had submitted the initial high bid for the land, $5.5 million as compared to Hillman's $5.4 million. (Hillman eventually raised its bid to $6 million.) The county commissioners provided other justifications for their selection, but it was clear that the behind-the-scenes battle had been waged on political grounds. The Democratic majority in Pittsburgh had simply won out. While the city would still be the recipient of a major new office-commercial complex, politics, submerged during Renaissance I, had become a factor in the second redevelopment phase. Fortunately, most of the renaissance projects have not required such collaboration of the city administration and the more politically motivated county commission. In dealing with projects over which it has control, the Caliguiri administration managed to subvert political interests for the good of the project.

Developers and city administrators who travel to Pittsburgh to examine the city's continued development are impressed with its wide range and scope. Unfettered by the concerns for financial stringency, which dominated the Flaherty administration, the Caliguiri administration and its private sector partners have promoted and completed a subway and light rail transit expressway to the South Hills, a limited access busway along an abandoned Pennsylvania Railroad right-of-way to the east end, and a major crosstown expressway and limited access highway to the North Hills.

Aware of the criticism of Renaissance I, that it failed to consider the needs of the neighborhoods, the Caliguiri administration solicited the input of neighborhood groups in carrying out its community redevelopment programs. It also supported a watchdog organization, the Pittsburgh Neighborhood Alliance to provide the administration with advice and opinions. Their input has provided valuable guidance and insulated Caliguiri from charges of indifference towards the neighborhoods. Revitalization of residential areas through low interest loans, subsidized rehabilitation, and weather proofing now crisscrosses the city. Entire areas including the south and central north sides and Manchester have become redevelopment areas and have received substantial redevelopment assistance. Corrections are also underway to remedy mistakes made in the 1950s–60s in the redevelopment of East Liberty.

Of particular interest to the region has been the struggle by the public and private sectors to develop several special multi-use zones along the city's extensive waterfront. Spurred by the commercial success of the restoration of the Pittsburgh and Lake Erie Railroad terminal and warehouse on the south side of the Monongahela river (Station Square), Mayor Caliguiri, the URA, the ACCD, and others struggled to put together a financial and development package for an area known as the Strip District along the south shore of the Allegheny River and the Three River's Stadium area on the Ohio River. Both districts present large amounts of land and excellent riverfront access to would-be developers. The city is also interested in additional development of the Station Square area. A number of interesting proposals have come forth, including a science fair and amusement park around the stadium, a Baltimore waterfront type project offered by the Rouse Corporation for the Strip District, a national historic museum complex for the same area, and additional hotel and commercial development for the Station Square area. Each site would presumably offer hotels, restaurants, shopping complexes, and waterfront marinas and parks. Three major questions are retarding each of these developments. The first concerns whether the population of the Pittsburgh SMSA, and whatever tourists it might attract, can support three such developments? Should the city select one area for development or continue to support all three? A recent report suggested that the stadium area should have priority, but Mayor Caliguiri responded that he welcomed plans for all three. Second, what would be the impact of such nearby developments on the commercial, entertainment, and restaurant businesses in the CBD? Downtown Pittsburgh which boasted of an active night life as recently as 1980, has seen its evening activities fly to the suburbs, a phenomenon common to other urban areas. Would the development of another such non-CBD attraction sound the death knell of the nighttime city in Pittsburgh? Finally, and of paramount importance, who will fund these massive projects? The costs of the stadium and Strip District projects could equal that of the Gateway Center redevelopment but carry less guarantee of an attractive financial return. Several developers have studied the projects and backed away. While the city might turn to a combination of financial backers, the comprehensive nature of the projects and perhaps their attractiveness to consumers would be less certain. These projects represent major unfinished pieces of Renaissance II and the Caliguiri administration.

Perhaps the most important long range projects of Renaissance II are the attempts underway by the mayor's office, the Allegheny Conference, and others to attract new industry and employment to Western Pennsylvania. The symbolic transformation of the SMSA from a manufacturing to a service center occurred in 1980. In that year, for the first time in the region's history, the number of jobs in government, services, and finance matched the number in manufacturing. Currently the former exceed manufacturing positions by approximately 100,000. Equally important has been the redistribution of workers into different occupational levels. During the last decade (1970–1980), for example, the number of high paying and low paying jobs in the SMSA increased by about 33,000, while the number of middle-class occupations increased by only 4,000. These figures reflect the region's status as a corporate headquarters and its new emphasis on high-tech industries. They also reflect a decrease in well-paying, middle-class manufacturing jobs and the placement of displaced workers and women just entering the workforce into the low paying service categories. Minorities in the SMSA population have been hit particularly hard by this redistribution.

The necessity of attracting or creating work in the Pittsburgh SMSA is obvious and both the public and private sectors have tried hard to do just that. Penn's Southwest Organization created by the Allegheny Conference has successfully promoted the region as a suitable home for foreign firms. Fifty-five foreign companies have opened offices in Western Pennsylvania during the last decade, creating nearly 8,000 new jobs. Several of these companies, including West Germany's Bayer/ Mobay chose the area for their North American Headquarters.[17]

Recently the city and county administrations, Carnegie Mellon University, and the University of Pittsburgh, have combined efforts on a plan entitled "Strategy 21: Pittsburgh/Allegheny Economic Development Strategy to Begin the 21st Century." It provides a strategy to transform the economy of the region from a manufacturing center to one which "takes advantage of . . . trends toward advanced technology and international marketing and communications systems." Five proposed projects, estimated at a total cost of $1 billion, are to create approximately 25,000 jobs over a five year period. To initiate the project, the authors suggest the spending of some $203 million in state funds.[18] Another university-based effort, the Small Business Development Center at Duquesne University trains individuals and seeks seed funds for those wishing to start their own businesses. In addition, the state of Pennsylvania, under the direction of then Governor Richard Thornburg, created the Ben Franklin Partnership for Advanced Technology to provide start-up money to regions seeking to attract small entrepreneurial enterprises. The program provided funds to a number of educational, business, and governmental agencies for research and development in specific high-tech industries—the sort that Pittsburgh clearly sees in its future.

A final footnote to the everexpanding areas into which city and regional administrations find themselves drawn is in the roles played by the Allegheny Conference, the city administration, numerous private corporations, and a university in an attempt to keep the Pirates baseball team from leaving the city. In 1984, John Galbraith, a real estate developer from nearby Columbus, Ohio announced that, after several financially poor years, he intended to sell the Pirates. He hoped to sell to Pittsburgh interests, but if no suitable offer was forthcoming he would sell to outsiders who would likely move the team to another city. Recognizing the financial and cultural loss the city would suffer, the Caliguiri administration took an active role in putting together coalitions of local investors who would purchase the team.

After several abortive attempts to find local funding, the administration with the help of the Allegheny Conference and several key corporate chief executives developed a novel plan to "save the Pirates." A number of corporations, Carnegie Mellon University, and several individuals each pledged $2 million towards purchase of the team. In addition, the city through the Urban Redevelopment Authority, sold bonds to raise additional funds to complete the package and provide enough money to operate the team for a five-year period, after which the team would either operate at a profit or pass over to outside buyers. The team earned a small profit in 1988, a year ahead of schedule. For the present the Pirates are safe at home and their future looks secure.

The success of the redevelopment of Western Pennsylvania, coupled with a rapidly accelerating deindustrialization has created a bifurcated SMSA. Rand McNally may correctly see one Pittsburgh as comfortably affluent and oriented toward high technology, with an abundance of social and cultural amenities. Others view a city with a downwardly mobile blue-collar population, deteriorating neighborhoods, and deep pockets of poverty. Industries have closed, fallen in corporate takeovers, or moved out of the region. The area's population, too, has fallen, from a high of 2.2 million at the end of World War II to just under 2.1 million in 1987. Most of these losses have occurred in the central city which fell from its ranking as the nation's tenth largest in 1950 with 675,000 people to 41st today with just under 400,000 residents. In addition, a change in the economic base of the city has produced a major shift in its occupational distribution and created a seemingly permanent core of unemployed or underemployed workers. Old neighborhoods within the city and suburban industrial communities up and down the industrial valleys suffer from economic decay and blight. For residents of these towns the future continues to look bleak. In addition, Pittsburgh's minority population, approximately one-fourth of the inner-city total, suffers from the prejudice and economic deprivation common to blacks in most industrial cities of the Northeast. The results are familiar: high unemployment, excessive school dropout rates, a preponderance of single, young, female headed families, and socially and physically debilitating neighborhoods.

Massive economic development and the neighborhood-based rehabilitation programs sponsored by four Democratic administrations spanning forty-two years have had little impact on these hard-core pockets of poverty in Western Pennsylvania. The division created by the transitional state of the region will likely persist until the current generation of displaced blue-collar workers pass from the scene. It is a problem that will tax the ability and creativity of the current and subsequent political administrations.

Recently a potential major problem appeared when Mayor Caliguiri revealed that he was suffering from amyloidosis, a rare, incurable, and possibly fatal disease which appears to strike those of Italian descent more often than others. (Ironically, Mayor Louis Tullio of nearby Erie revealed that he too was suffering from the same disease.) Caliguiri continued to carry an impressive work load despite the installation of a pacemaker during the recent year-end holiday season. On the evening of May 5, the mayor was rushed to the hospital, the apparent victim of a heart attack. He never regained consciousness and was pronounced dead at 12:31 a.m.

Following a region-wide outpouring of sympathy, matched only by that which followed the death of David L. Lawrence, city council president Sophie Masloff was sworn in as acting mayor. Masloff at 70 years of age is the city's first female and first Jewish mayor. Like her predecessor she originally indicated that she would be content with completing Caliguiri's unexpired term and his dream of a second renaissance for Pittsburgh. After assuming office, however, she decided that she would be interested in running for a full term to begin in January 1990. Meanwhile, six other Democrats also announced that they would be candidates in the spring primary, while the virtually nonexistent Republican Party continued to play the role of a bystander. Masloff, who began the campaign as a heavy underdog, proved to be a tough street fighter. In one of the roughest Pittsburgh primaries in recent elections, she managed to hold off all contenders, although she received less than one-third of the votes cast. With no opposition in the November general election, Masloff was sworn in as the elected mayor of the city in January of 1990. Whether she will be as adept in dealing with the influential private sector groups or with the growing number of limited interest organizations as she was in sweeping aside several formidable political opponents is not yet clear. Considering the effects of the personal and policy differences of the past two mayors—Flaherty and Caliguiri—on the city's development, the fate of a number of unfinished projects and the success of attempts to attract new industries to the city lie in the answer.

NOTES

1. Richard Boyer and David Savageau, *Places Rated Almanac* (New York, 1985), p. 419.

2. Mellon Economic Report, 1981, 1984, 1986; "Pittsburgh's Old Image Goes into the Slag Pile," *U.S. News and World Report* (January 12, 1981), p. 55; *Pittsburgh Post-Gazette* (November 19, 1981, December 21, 1987); "1983–88: Six Year Development Program," Mayor's Office, City of Pittsburgh.

3. Glenn E. McLaughlin and Ralph Watkins, "The Problems of Industrial Growth in a Mature Economy," *American Economic Review,* 29 (March, 1939), p2ff.

4. Pittsburgh Housing Authority, Unpublished Report, Housing Authority Files, 1947.

5. Philip Kline, *A Social Study of Pittsburgh: Community Problems and Social Services of Allegheny County,* (New York, 1938), p. 203; Pittsburgh Housing Authority, 1947.

6. *Pittsburgh Sun-Telegraph,* April 2, 1936.

7. Shelby Stewman and Joel A. Tarr, "Four Decades of Public-Private Partnerships in Pittsburgh," Unpublished Report Prepared for the Committee for Economic Development, (Pittsburgh, July 1981); Michael P. Weber, *Don't Call Me Boss: David L. Lawrence, Pittsburgh's Renaissance Mayor* (Pittsburgh, 1988), pp203ff; "Pittsburgh's New Powers," *Fortune,* 35 (February, 1947), pp. 69ff.

8. Minute Books of the Voter Registration Commission, vol. 2, 1929.

9. Joel A. Tarr and William Lamperes, "Changing Fuel Use Behaviors and Energy Transitions: The Pittsburgh Smoke Control Movement, 1949–50," *Journal of Social History* 14 (Summer, 1981), p. 575.

10. *Don't Call Me Boss,* Interviews with corporate leaders. Located in the Archives of Industrial Society, Pittsburgh, Pa.

11. "Four Decades of Public-Private Partnerships in Pittsburgh," p. 91.

12. Ibid.

13. Roger S. Ahlbrandt Jr., Morton Coleman, "The Role of the Corporation in Com-

munity Economic Development as Viewed by 21 Corporate Executives,'' Unpublished Report, University Center for Social and Urban Research (Pittsburgh, January 5, 1987), pp. 13, 16–18.

14. The activities of the Departments of Housing and Economic Development were placed under the auspices of the Urban Redevelopment Authority in 1982.

15. For a detailed analysis of the development and Architectural evaluation of the PPG complex and other structures built during the Renaissance II period see Jonathon Barnett, ''Designing Downtown Pittsburgh,'' *Architectural Record,* (January, 1982), pp. 90ff.

16. Fred Rimington, ''Shootout over the Shape of Grant Street,'' *Pittsburgh,* (May, 1979), pp. 25 ff. See also *Pittsburgh Post-Gazette,* (November 18, 1978); ''What's Going on Downtown.'' *Pittsburgh,* (November, 1980).

17. Brian J. L. Berry, Susan Sanderson, Shelby Stewman, and Joel A. Tarr, ''The Nation's Most Liveable City: Pittsburgh's Transformation'', Gary Gappert, ed., *The Future of Winter Cities,* (Beverly Hills, 1986), pp. 190 ff.

18. Unpublished Report, ''Strategy 21: Pittsburgh/Allegheny Economic Development Strategy to Begin the 21st Century.'' (1984), pp. 2 ff.

XIII

WASHINGTON

THE BLACK MAJORITY:
RACE AND POLITICS
IN THE NATION'S CAPITAL

Steven J. Diner

It seemed an unremarkable American political ritual. On November 5, 1974, the citizens of the city went to the pools to elect their mayor and the members of their city council. Yet, in Washington, D.C., which natives refer to as "the District," it was quite extraordinary. For exactly one hundred years, federal officials had governed this city directly, denying its residents the rights taken for granted by other Americans. To reach this day, advocates of "home rule" for the city had to overcome formidable political obstacles.

Washington was almost three-quarters black, but the key congressional committee controlling its local affairs had been dominated for decades by southern segregationists determined to prevent black rule. A powerful group of local business leaders, represented by the Board of Trade, had long exercised extraordinary influence over the District's unelected government. These leaders had joined with the segregationists to maintain the *status quo* at a time when an increasingly assertive black political leadership decried poor schools, hostile police, inadequate housing and social programs, lack of community involvement in redevelopment, and a host of other big city ills. In the city, where blacks had first become a majority, it appeared that simple, representative democracy of the sort taken for granted elsewhere would bring about a major shift in political power, perhaps even a peaceful revolution in social policy.

The founders of the nation's capital expected it to become a major mercantile center, but for various reasons the city failed to develop a commercial and industrial base. Instead, by the late-nineteenth century, Washington had become a city dependent for its economic development on government employment. Its growth was most rapid in times of war or in other periods of government expansion. World War II, and the expansion of the federal government in the postwar era produced tremendous population growth. The 1940 census showed about a million people

living in the Washington metropolitan area. The area added a half-million people
to its population in the 1940s, over 600,000 in the 1950s, and just under a million
in the 1960s. By 1970, the population of the Washington metropolitan area stood
just under three million. The population growth then slowed, and by 1987, the area
total stood at 3,609,000. (See Tables 1.1–1.3.)

The overwhelming majority of this expansion, primarily a result of in-imigration,
occurred in the Maryland and Virginia suburbs. Streetcar suburbs had developed
outside the boundaries of the District in the late nineteenth century and expanded
with the growth of automobile usage in the 1920s. By 1950, the suburban population
stood at 48 percent of the metro total; by 1980 79 percent of Washington area
residents lived outside the District of Columbia. By 1950, the District had reached
its peak population of just over 800,000 people, declining by over a hundred and
fifty thousand people by 1980. In 1987 the total stood at 629,000.[1]

This familiar American pattern of population movement to the ever expanding
suburbs, driven, literally, by the growth of automobile ownership, overlapped with
another familiar American pattern, the residential segregation of black people. Racial prejudice, restrictive covenants, the social conventions of a segregated city,
the practices of mortgage lenders and government housing agencies all reinforced
a residential color line. The white population of the District increased in the 1940s
by only nine percent, in contrast to a fifty percent black increase. In the 1950s, the
white population declined 33 percent and the Black population increased by another
50 percent.[2] As early as 1957 Washington had become the first major American
city to register a black majority. By 1970, blacks made up over 70 percent of the
city's population.

The black population of the entire metropolitan area increased no faster than the
white population in these three decades, however, remaining about a quarter of the
total. The white population growth occurred in the suburbs, the black growth in
the city.

The historically confined black population of the city spread to large areas of the
District now open to it, but the surrounding suburbs remained closed. The historic
pattern of residential segregation did not change. It simply spread out over the
metropolitan area.

After the passage of federal open-housing legislation in 1968, blacks began to
move to the suburbs in substantial numbers. On the Maryland side by 1986, blacks
made up 37.3 percent of the population of Prince George's County and 8.8 percent
of affluent Montgomery County; on the Virginia side they were 9.2 percent of the
population of Arlington County and 5.9 percent of Fairfax.[3] Much of this new black
suburbanization occurred in areas that quickly became resegregated. Blacks continued to live mostly in all black residential areas.

It would be difficult to govern successfully any American city undergoing the
dramatic demographic, economic, and social changes that Washington experienced
in the postwar years. The District's peculiar governmental system made the job
nearly impossible. The federal government had ruled the city directly since 1874
through a three member Board of Commissioners, appointed by the President, which
exercised executive and quasi-legislative authority over city affairs. Two members

were civilians, who had lived in the District for at least three years. Typically they secured their appointment through political connections with the current administration or the city's influential business community. The third member was an officer of the Army Corps of Engineers. The three commissioners shared responsibility for the various city departments, but the engineer commissioner always controlled construction and physical development and therefore was the most powerful. "Don't ever let anyone tell you that city government is divided into thirds," a city official told a political scientist in the early 1960s. "It's divided into sixths—four sixths for the engineer commissioner and one-sixth for each of the others. He makes the big decisions—on urban renewal, streets, freeways, and so on. He can do anything he wants." General Alvin C. Welling, engineer commissioner from 1957 to 1960, summed up neatly how he viewed his job. "The overriding purpose of Washington," he said, "is to provide a handsome and comfortable seat for the Federal Government."[4]

Federal statutes and political realities, however, limited the power of all three commissioners. As the city grew, Congress assigned more and more responsibility for local affairs to federal agencies, so that local governmental authority became hopelessly tangled with the federal bureaucracy. A *Washington Post* writer described the situation in 1939. "The city fathers share authority with the Interior Department, the Bureau of the Budget, the army engineers, the Smithsonian Institution, the architect of the Capitol, the General Accounting Office, the Department of Justice and numerous other federal agencies." He concluded that "in many respects this community . . . is treated as just another bureau in the federal government." In the years before World War II, Congress, special consultants, and citizens groups undertook thirty different investigations of local government and proposed a dozen reorganization schemes.[5] None of them had much effect. Congress still appropriated the city's budget and legislated for the District when it could find the time.

In the postwar years, the House Committee on the District of Columbia, long chaired by Congressman John McMillan of South Carolina, became by far the most influential congressional body concerned with the District. Political scientist Martha Derthick in 1962 described the reasons for the committee's interest in local affairs:

> As Congress is pre-eminent in District government, the House District Committee is pre-eminent in Congress with respect to District affairs. It displays a deeper and more sustained interest in the District than any other Congressional committee. This interest stems from two factors: (1) The committee traditionally includes several Congressmen from neighboring districts in Maryland and Virginia whose constituents have a direct interest in District affairs; (2) it traditionally includes many Southerners who have a deep interest in the District because of the large Negro population there and the racial character of many issues in District politics. . . . The Committee is the source of more bitterness and passion than any other institution in the District.

In the 87th Congress, Derthick noted, eleven of the fifteen Democrats, including the chairman and the next four ranking members, came from southern or border states.[6]

The city's business community, represented by the Board of Trade, exercised enormous influence within this system. The board, which worked closely with the commissioners and the House District Committee, had for years been the *de facto* representative of Congress for the local population, working to keep taxes low, promote business interests, and restrict spending on social programs.

Such was the District government: unelected, limited in authority, hopelessly entwined with the federal bureaucracy, dominated by southern segregationists and conservative business leaders, its legislature an overworked congress. This government had to respond to rapid suburbanization and the emergence of a black majority in the capital, the demands of the civil rights movement, urban renewal, neighborhood change, and the host of social problems that in the 1960s was dubbed "the urban crisis."

The dramatic changes in the demography of the District occurred at the same time that civil rights advocates were waging a successful assault on legally sanctioned racial separation. Both friends and foes of civil rights recognized that the capital presented a symbolic battleground of far greater significance than its size might suggest. Because the government of the District was an agency of the federal government, the president, members of the executive branch, the Congress and the federal courts had to get involved in civil rights issues here well before they did in the southern states.

At the end of World War II racial separation seemed firmly entrenched. Schools, public playgrounds, most restaurants and hotels, theatres, and cinemas were all segregated. In 1947, the National Theatre, the target of weeks of picketing by antisegregationists, closed its doors rather than accept the demand of Actors' Equity that black patrons be admitted. Despite strong local and national protest, the city's Recreation Board refused to integrate public playgrounds. The city's public swimming pools, which in the arcane governmental system of the District were run by the U.S. Department of Interior, were technically open to both blacks and whites. When a group of black youths sought admission to the Anacostia pool in June 1949, however, the lifeguards (who were employed by the District Recreation Board) refused to admit them, and white bullies chased them away. Demonstrators for and against segregation then gathered at the pool to protest. The police dispersed them, and the pool closed for the rest of the summer.

Nonetheless, change was coming as national attention to the capital city, and the support of Presidents Truman and Eisenhower for desegregation, were having a significant impact. In 1946, a group of influential Americans (including Eleanor Roosevelt, Marshall Field, Hubert Humphrey, Walter Reuther, and Helen Hayes) formed the National Committee on Segregation in the Nation's Capital. In that same year, the U.S. secretary of labor ordered that services at the District Employment Center, a branch of the U.S. Employment Service, be integrated, and the secretary of the interior ordered the opening of a tourist camp in East Potomac Park for blacks and whites equally. Two years later, the U.S. Supreme Court declared racially restrictive covenants in the District unenforceable. And on July 26 of that year, President Truman issued a new executive order banning racial discrimination in federal government agencies.

By the early 1950s, it was widely recognized that legally sanctioned segregation in public institutions was on its way out. The real question was how quickly it would happen. In 1951, the Hecht Company opened its lunchroom to blacks, and about the same time the National Theatre, under new ownership, reopened on a desegregated basis. In 1953, in the Thompson Restaurant case, the U.S. Supreme Court upheld the validity of an 1873 District law outlawing discrimination in public accommodations. The Board of Education debated school desegregation annually, but it wasted most of its time with acrimonious debates over the transfer of underenrolled schools from the white to the colored school system. The Roman Catholic school system, on the other hand, desegregated peacefully in 1949. When in 1954, the U.S. Supreme Court outlawed school segregation, President Eisenhower asked the District Board of Education to implement the court ruling quickly, stating that Washington should be a model of desegregation for the nation.[7] Eight days later, the Board of Education voted to desegregate the schools the following fall.

The relative ease with which Washington dismantled its rigid system of apartheid belied the difficulties that lay ahead. It would not prove so easy to eliminate *de facto* segregation and discrimination or to provide adequate economic opportunities and public services to the growing low-income black population. The fate of Washington's public school system in the two decades following desegregation illustrates in microcosm the frustrating new realities.

Integrationists quickly touted the success of Washington's 1954 school desegregation. The Anti-Defamation League of B'Nai B'rith distributed a pamphlet written by a D. C. school official describing the schools' *Miracle of Social Adjustment.* The liberal press eagerly repeated the story in articles such as one in *Commentary* entitled ''Washington: Showcase of Integration.'' Southern segregationists were no less cognizant of the symbolic importance of Washington's school desegregation. Congressman James Davis of Georgia conducted infamous congressional hearings in 1956 designed to discredit Washington's desegregated schools and authored a committee report which concluded that there was ''a wide disparity in mental ability between white and Negro students,'' creating a ''most difficult teaching situation in the integrated schools'' and that ''the integrated school system of the District of Columbia is not a model to be copied by other communities.''[8]

Liberals fought back, arguing that the disparity between black and white test scores stemmed from the inadequacy of black schools under segregation, and they promised to narrow the gap in the coming years. In the meantime, however, the in-migration of blacks to the District and a high black birth rate produced dramatic increases in school enrollments and marked shifts in the socio-economic and racial mix of the D. C. schools. In 1949, total enrollment stood at 94,000 children. By 1967, it stood at 150,000 and black students accounted for all of the increase. White enrollment fell ten percent after desegregation in 1954 and by smaller percentages in each successive year, so that by 1967 whites constituted only seven percent of the total enrollment. Facilities and resources in the schools had been inadequate well before this big spurt in enrollments. Now they were hopelessly strained.[9]

Integrationists, including school superintendent Carl Hansen, had promised that black achievement would improve, and for a few years after desegregation test scores did rise modestly. Then they began to fall, and the white superintendent of schools and majority white Board of Education came under increasing attack, not only from segregationists but from militant black leaders and parents, who demanded black control of a black school system.

By the late 1960s, the school system was in crisis. School Board meetings routinely deteriorated into shouting matches, and were regularly disrupted by demonstrations, even after a popularly elected board replaced the appointed board in 1969. A string of superintendents failed to win popular support as one new educational initiative after another foundered. Standardized test scores, almost unnoticed before 1954, became the ultimate measures of school success, and they continued to fall.[10]

As visually upsetting to visitors to the nation's capital as its segregated schools was the ghetto-like environment of many of Washington's neighborhoods. Federal officials had long been anxious to eliminate the most deteriorated low-income housing, particularly the notorious alley dwellings inside central city blocks. For years, the visual cliché of the housing reform movement was a photograph of a dilapidated alley shack with the capitol dome in the background. During the New Deal, the government built some low income public housing in Washington and other cities, but interest in massive redevelopment came only after World War II. In 1945 Congress gave the city government authority to use the right of eminent domain to rebuild blighted areas.

Government officials put forth elaborate redevelopment proposals. General Ulysses S. Grant III, grandson of the former president and head of the National Capital Park and Planning Commission unveiled plans in 1947 for rebuilding the city's poorest slum area, Southwest, just west of Independence Avenue and the Mall. The commission would see, Grant announced, that "the colored population dispossessed by playgrounds, public buildings, parks, and schools" was relocated in a remote section "in the rear of Anacostia." Integrationists objected vigorously, the plan became controversial, and Congress withheld appropriations.[11]

The commission also considered urban renewal in the outlying black residential areas of Barry Farms and Marshall Heights east of the Anacostia River. Residents fearing displacement successfully appealed to Congress to scuttle urban renewal there.[12]

Turning back to Southwest, urban renewal officials developed plans for an entirely new, racially integrated middle-class community. The commission rejected as insufficiently bold an early proposal to rehabilitate a majority of the structures, moving the occupants back into their houses once work was completed. This final plan met strong opposition from black residents and white merchants in the area but got strong support from liberals who favored aggressive government action to arrest urban decay, developers, The Washington Post, the city's business establishment, and government planners. In 1954, the U.S. Supreme Court rejected a challenge to urban renewal by Southwest merchants. Liberal Justice William O. Douglas, writing for a unanimous court, stated that "it is within the power of the legislature to determine that the community should be beautiful as well as healthy, spacious as well as clean, well-balanced as well as carefully patrolled." On April 26, 1954, the first bulldozer began tearing down Southwest.[13] It had taken eight years to get to that day. It would take another five to overcome bureaucratic hurdles and complete the first building.

Southwest urban renewal accelerated the emergence of new, all-black neighborhoods in other parts of the city, although this was not the intent of many of its supporters. Low-income southwest residents moved to other parts of the city, many of them to new public housing in neighborhoods that were becoming all black, particularly east of the Anacostia River, where a good deal of land remained substantially undeveloped. In 1950, 79,000 people (82 percent of them white) lived in far southeast, the area south of Pennsylvania Avenue and east of the Anacostia River. By 1970, despite an overall decline in the city's population, this area housed 126,000 people, 85 percent of them black. In the predominantly black far northeast, north of Pennsylvania Avenue and east of the river, the population increased from 66,000 to 89,000 in these twenty years. The city placed few restrictions on growth in these areas, and schools, parks, health facilities, and other services could not keep up with the expansion of the largely low-income population. Other areas closer to downtown also experienced growth in their low-income black populations after the demolition of Southwest.

Political and bureaucratic obstacles so greatly slowed the pace of urban renewal outside of Southwest in the 1960s that a pretentiously titled urban renewal plan, *No Slums in Ten Years*, became the butt of much sarcasm. Some of these obstacles were intentionally put in place. As early as the late 1950s, local black leaders had strongly opposed Southwest-style urban renewal. In response to their criticisms and others, a liberal Congress in the 1960s mandated citizen participation in urban renewal planning. In the Shaw area, for example, an old black neighborhood just north of downtown, one political activist, Reverend Walter Fauntroy, organized ministers and local business people into the Model Inner City Community Organization (MICCO), and in 1966, he pressured urban renewal officials into designating MICCO as the authorized citizen-planning group for Shaw urban renewal.[14]

Meanwhile, private market forces were transforming many other neighborhoods adjacent to the central city into affluent, white enclaves of restored older houses, further displacing working-class and poor blacks. This process, which in the late 1970s would become known as "gentrification," had its origins in historic Georgetown, where as early as the 1920s, established residents sought to upgrade their neighborhood. Black people, who made up over forty percent of the neighborhood's population in 1930, had almost completely disappeared by 1950.

Georgetown soon became a model for the transformation of other central-city neighborhoods. Foggy Bottom, the area just east of Georgetown and adjacent to George Washington University, a working class neighborhood from the earliest days of the city, was by 1950 predominantly black. In the following two decades it changed completely, not so much because of the restoration of private homes as the construction of private offices, luxury apartments, the John F. Kennedy Center for the Performing Arts, and the expansion of the university campus.[15] Dupont Circle and Adams-Morgan in northwest, and Capitol Hill in southeast soon followed suit.[16] By the early 1970's, these areas formed an affluent, predominantly white residential ring three quarters of the way around the commercial and governmental center of the city, even as the overall white population of the District declined. By the middle 1970s, many blacks pointed to this white influx as evidence of a plan to turn Washington back into a majority-white city.

Rising black expectations in a black majority city, fears of racial displacement, severe social and economic ills, an unelected and unresponsive government, and the growing success of the national civil rights movement—these elements produced a volatile mix in the nation's capital just as Washington became a mecca for aspiring young black leaders. The nation's capital had a black majority and venerable black institutions such as Howard University. Small wonder that it attracted from elsewhere a new generation of local civil rights leaders, who would first transform the black organizational and political life of the city itself.

In the 1950s, the NAACP and the Urban League dominated black institutional activities. The Urban League worked closely with local business leaders in programs to improve the economic status of black people.

From 1956 on, Sterling Tucker led the league, and he became a leading spokesman for black Washington. Like so many of the new black leaders, Tucker was not a native Washingtonian. Born and raised in Akron, Ohio, he worked for the Akron and Canton Urban League chapters, leaving Ohio in 1956 to head the League's Washington office. Under his leadership, the Washington Urban League greatly expanded its budget and programs for the poor. White businessmen and government officials regularly turned to Tucker for the views of the black community. In a 1961 interview, Tucker summed up his organization's approach. "I don't regard the League as conservative at all," he said. "We beat people on the head, but with facts, public opinions, and programs."

The Washington chapter of the NAACP undertook more militant political action. Rev. E. Franklin Jackson, another migrant and pastor of one of the largest black churches in the District, headed this group in the 1960s. A native Floridian, Jackson held a pulpit in Buffalo before coming to Washington. He became NAACP president in 1958, and in that year led a one-day boycott of downtown stores which had refused to hire blacks. He also led a campaign against police brutality in the black community. "We're the sledge hammer for the Urban League," he said in 1961. "They do the statistics; we apply the pressure."[17]

These and other black leaders of the 1950s and early 1960s worked closely with a new generation of liberal, white political leaders. In the late 1950s, a bi-racial insurgent group under the leadership of Joseph Rauh took over control of the D. C. Democratic Party. The son of immigrant Jews, Rauh grew up in Cincinatti and came to Washington during the New Deal to clerk for Supreme Court Justice Felix Frankfurter. In the postwar period, he became one of the nation's most prominent liberal lawyers and political activists. Polly Shackelton, a Boston native, worked closely with Rauh in the D. C. Democratic Party. When, in 1956, the District began electing representatives to the national party committees, Shackelton won the post of national committeewoman, winning reelection throughout the 1960s.[18]

Within a few years, still newer leaders and tactics eclipsed the militance of Jackson's NAACP and the biracial leadership of the D. C. Democratic Party. Walter

Fauntroy, one of the few native Washingtonians to assume leadership in these years, was born and raised in the Shaw neighborhood. A graduate of Yale Divinity School, Fauntroy returned to the old neighborhood in 1959 as pastor of his boyhood church, and he immediately plunged into civil rights work. In 1961 he became the head of the Washington chapter of Martin Luther King's Southern Christian Leadership Conference (SCLC). He joined in sit-ins and picketed stores to force the integration of public accommodations and to increase the number of blacks hired by downtown merchants. He oversaw local arrangements for the 1963 March on Washington, and sought to prevent Southwest-style displacement of blacks from Shaw. In 1960, Fauntroy first used the phrase that would become a rallying cry for blacks nationally. "Urban renewal," Fauntroy said, "means Negro removal."[19]

Like Martin Luther King, Fauntroy was more unsettling to the white establishment than were the leaders of the Urban League and the NAACP, but less so than a still newer group of secular militants. Two very different individuals of the latter type gained attention in the 1960s and early 1970s—Julius Hobson and Marion Barry.

Hobson came to Washington from Birmingham, Alabama to major in economics at Howard University. "I studied the economics of the working man," he later recalled, and he became a socialist. In the 1950s, Hobson followed the established avenues of civic involvement. He served as a PTA president, a member of the executive committee of the NAACP, and vice president of the Federation of Civic Associations. Convinced that the established organizations were too tame—he later referred to the Federation of Civic Associations as "a pasteurized, frightened black group of people who worry about street lights, garbage cans, and good manners"— Hobson in 1960 became head of the Washington chapter of the Congress of Racial Equality, a militant civil rights group. In the next four years, he led a campaign to force downtown merchants to hire black sales clerks, running eighty-five picket lines and gaining the employment of over 5,000 people. "When we started out a Negro clerk downtown was as rare as a white crow. When we finished you could knock on any door and find them."

Hobson became the master of the big bluff. In 1961, he threatened to clog Maryland Route 40 with demonstrators unless the restaurants there desegregated. "I set up a bank of telephones which were not connected to anything, . . . and I had girls very carefully sitting by those phones and keeping their hands on them so no reporter could pick them up and see that they were dead," he confessed years later. In the mid-1960s, he agitated for a rat control program in poor black neighborhoods by catching rats in Shaw and placing them on top of station wagons, threatening at a rally to release hundreds of them in Georgetown. "Actually, what we were doing was drowning the hell out of those rats after dark," he admitted later, but the city immediately began a rat extermination program.

In the mid-1960s, Hobson turned his attention to the D. C. public schools. In 1963, he sued Superintendent Carl Hansen, claiming that the predominantly white schools west of Rock Creek Park had smaller classes, better teachers, and more resources than the schools attended by poor black children. He also objected to the "tracking system" in which children were grouped on the basis of ability, claiming that it consigned the poor black children placed disproportionately in the lowest tracks to "the economic and social junk heap." The established civil rights groups, including the NAACP and the Urban League, would not join Hobson's suit. In 1967, Judge J. Skelly Wright struck down the tracking system, and ordered the busing of children from overcrowded black schools to schools west of the park. The Board of Education refused to appeal the decree, and Hansen resigned. Hobson later returned to court in the early 1970s and won a new decree mandating equal spending per pupil.[20]

Marion Barry came to Washington in 1965 to head the Washington office of the Student Nonviolent Coordinating Committee (SNCC). Born in a small town in Mississippi, Barry spent most of his childhood in Memphis, where he had completed college before undertaking graduate work in chemistry at Fisk.

A relative latecomer to the pool of local civil rights activists, Barry joined the movement with a splash. Six months after his arrival, he organized a successful boycott of D. C. Transit buses to protest a fare increase. He harshly criticized police brutality against blacks and was arrested several times. In 1967, Barry went on trial for destruction of public property. The government claimed that he kicked a police wagon during an altercation with authorities. The jury acquitted him.

Despite his militant image, reinforced by the dashiki that became his signature, Barry quickly turned from protest to direct work with ghetto residents. In 1967, he helped to organize Pride, Inc., which used a large federal grant to help poor young black men find jobs.[21]

By 1968, Washington's black community had become highly politicized. A diverse group of leaders, with different styles and tactics, shared the same goals—making black people equal participants in Washington life. This would happen, they believed, if only the residents of the District could gain the same political rights as other Americans. Therefore, the local struggle for civil rights and black power became intertwined in the 1960s with the movement for voting rights and home rule.

By 1960, a well organized coalition supported the movement for an elected local government (home rule) and for elected District representation in the federal government. The coalition included civil rights and black groups, a majority of the neighborhood associations, the League of Women Voters, organized labor, Americans for Democratic Action, many religious groups, and the District Democratic Party. The District Republican Party favored representation, but took an ambivalent position on home rule. The Board of Trade favored representation but vigorously opposed home rule, and the House District Committee, dominated by segregationists, opposed both. Six times between 1948 and 1966, the Senate passed home rule bills, but each time the bill died in the House.

The first breakthrough came in 1960, when Congress approved a constitutional amendment giving the District three electoral votes for president. With broad bipartisan support, the necessary thirty-eight states ratified the twenty-third amendment in nine months. The only opposition came in the south, where segregationists opposed it because it would grant voting rights to blacks.[22]

The election of President John F. Kennedy heartened home rule supporters because Kennedy had long sympathized with their cause. But the House District

Committee, under the chairmanship of John McMillan, steadfastly refused to report out a home rule bill. When Lyndon B. Johnson defeated Barry Goldwater in the 1964 landslide, carrying a liberal Democratic majority with him in both houses of Congress, home rule supporters believed that their time had come.

Johnson urged Congress to approve home rule legislation, and once again the Senate passed a home rule bill. Chairman McMillan refused to schedule hearings, but home rule supporters secured enough congressional signatures on a discharge petition to move the legislation to the floor of the House. At this point, McMillan, at the urging of the Board of Trade, reported to the floor a bill to provide for the local election of a commission to draft a home rule charter, which would then require approval of Congress. This bill passed the House, which then refused to go to conference with the Senate. Once again, home rule legislation died.[23]

During the 1965 congressional consideration of home rule, the Board of Trade sent a letter of opposition to newspapers around the nation. "The fact is," the board wrote, "that a great many Washingtonians—including the overwhelming majority of local, civic, professional, and business leaders—are opposed to pending home rule legislation." A group of prominent local civil rights leaders, after meeting with representatives of the board, issued a statement accusing the board of waging "a stepped-up campaign" to defeat home rule because it did not want to relinquish its "inordinate power" over "the affairs of the city."

At this point, Marion Barry organized a "Free D.C. Movement" to boycott local businessmen who opposed home rule. Barry explained the tactic:

> We want to free D.C. from our enemies, the people who make it impossible for us to do anything about lousy schools, brutal cops, slumlords, welfare investigators who go on midnight raids, employers who discriminate in hiring and a host of other ills that run rampant through our city. Southern white segregationists have gotten together with the moneylord merchants of this city to oppose our right to vote. We can't hurt McMillan . . . but we can hurt the moneylord merchants. . . .

The movement asked businessmen to sign a petition in favor of home rule, display a "Free D.C." emblem in their store windows, and contribute money to the group, and it picketed stores whose owners refused. The tactic drew considerable criticism, even from some home-rule supporters who called it blackmail, but a number of local businessmen did publicly disavow the Board of Trade position.[24]

With home-rule legislation dead for the moment, President Johnson submitted to Congress a reorganization plan for the District government which replaced the Board of Commissioners with a single commissioner (popularly known as the mayor) and a nine-member city council. Even though these new officials would still be accountable to Congress and the president, Johnson wanted to create a structure that more closely approximated an elected city government. The change went through despite opposition from McMillan and the Board of Trade. Johnson then appointed a black man, Walter Washington, as mayor-commissioner, and a majority black city council that included Sterling Tucker and Walter Fauntroy, as well as white supporters of civil rights like Polly Shackleton.[25]

In Walter Washington, Johnson picked a trained public administrator to head the new District government. Born in Georgia but reared in Jamestown, New York Washington had come to the capital to study at Howard University and had married into a prominent local black family. After graduate study, he went to work for the Alley Dwelling Authority, moved up in the city's housing bureaucracy, and in 1961 became director of the National Capital Housing Authority. This was the highest administrative position then held by a black person in the District government. In 1966, Washington left the city to become head of the public housing agency in New York. Lyndon Johnson gave Washington only one directive before taking office: "act like you were elected."[26]

Walter Washington had his work cut out for him. By 1968 the city had become racially polarized, and tensions between the black community and the police were mounting. The danger of a riot was apparent to all. Washington began working around the clock to reduce tensions, using his extensive networks in both the black and white communities. By temperament and background, he was uniquely suited to mediate between militant blacks and frightened whites. He immediately promoted black officers within the police force and aggressively sought black recruits.

On March 31, Martin Luther King spoke in Washington. "I don't like to predict violence, but if nothing is done between now and June to raise ghetto hopes," he said, "I feel this summer will not only be as bad but worse than last year." Four days later he died, and the violence so many feared began.

Within hours of the grim announcement on April 4, 1968, of his assassination in Memphis, mobs of black people had begun smashing windows, looting stores, and setting fires in ghetto areas of the central city. The eruption of this violence "ten blocks from the White House" on that terrible night and in the days that followed should hardly have been surprising. From 1964 on, when black residents of Harlem rioted after the shooting of a black man by New York police, such disturbances became common in cities with significant black populations—Los Angeles' Watts neighborhood in 1965, Detroit, Newark, and New Haven in 1967, to name only a few. Washington itself had already experienced several racial disturbances in which large-scale violence was narrowly averted, as in the early hours of August 1, 1967, when youths threw bottles and stones at police officers and fire fighters and smashed windows in the ghetto area between 7th and 14th Streets, Northwest.

It is difficult two decades after to understand why the riot occurred. Probably about 20,000 people participated. Most of those arrested were young men, and a majority of them had jobs. Some even worked for the federal or District governments. Few of the unemployed and the very poorest people were among the large number arrested. Most rioters were also long-time residents or natives of Washington.

Why did they riot? The *Washington Post* interviewed a number of rioters afterwards and received different explanations. A seventeen-year-old girl said, "It had nothing to do with Dr. King's murder. The manager [of the store she looted] was nasty and mean." A nineteen-year-old girl said, "I knew I could get away with it and . . . everybody was doing it." A seventeen-year-old boy said, "I did it because everybody else did it. . . . The people on H Street were out there to get what they could.'' A high school senior stated: ''All those windows were broken and all those stores were open, so why not take what you could get?'' A Howard University student was ''not sorry about anything. . . . All the white stores in town could burn down. . . . I felt like striking back.'' Another Howard student reported that ''I was able to make quite a bit of money out of it.''[27]

Certainly the riots cannot be attributed simply to despair. The conditions under which poor and working-class blacks lived were improving modestly, and there was more cause for hope than there had been ten or twenty years earlier. The rioters did not have any immediate political objectives, and black leaders did not incite the rioters. Indeed black leaders sought to calm tensions once the news of King's assassination spread. Nonetheless, black protest over the previous decade had politicized the city's black population. Blacks had been made more conscious of their deprivation; they had been politicized. When the opportunity presented itself, they felt justified in taking what was there.

The riot greatly escalated the city's racial tensions. The police cordoned off the riot area to keep the destruction from spreading but refrained from using direct force against the rioters themselves. Many of the whites who owned businesses in the area later complained bitterly that the police had failed to protect their property. Blacks were also bitter. While city officials struggled to provide immediate relief for residents of the area and to develop a plan for reconstruction of the riot corridors—a decade later a journalist would describe the rebuilding plan as ''hurry up and wait''—militant black leaders insisted that blacks must own the businesses in their rebuilt neighborhoods. ''White people should be allowed to come back only if the majority of ownership is in the hands of blacks,'' said Marion Barry. ''That is, they could come back and give their experience and expertise—and then they should leave.''

By the fall of 1968, Washington was a city coming apart at the seams but, in that same year, Congress moved to restore social and political stability. It passed legislation providing for an elected Board of Education. Home-rule advocates hailed this as a move toward self government. McMillan supported it to stave off pressure for greater reform.

The city held its first local elections in almost a century in fall 1968, and selected an eleven-member board, most of whose members were black. The best known winner was Julius Hobson. Three years later, Marion Barry headed a school board slate that deposed that initial board in a move that soon gave Barry the board's presidency.[28]

President Richard M. Nixon announced his support for home rule shortly after his election, and he reappointed Walter Washington, Sterling Tucker, and a black majority to the city council. In 1969, Congress provided for the election of a nonvoting delegate to the House of Representatives from the District, and in the 1970 elections, Walter Fauntroy defeated Julius Hobson and several other candidates for the post. The appointed city government, the elected Board of Education, and the position of delegate became fast-track, training grounds transforming black activists into public office holders.[29]

The 1972 congressional elections once again raised hopes that home rule might finally come. In a turn-of-events that belied Barry's earlier statement that blacks could not "hurt McMillan," the veteran congressman lost the Democratic primary in his district because recently enfranchised blacks voted him out. Walter Fauntroy and other black leaders had gone to McMillan's district to campaign for his opponent. In 1973, a black congressman, Charles Diggs of Michigan, became the chair of the House District Committee and Congress passed a new District charter which granted partial home rule through an elected mayor and city council.

The District still had no voting representation in Congress, and the home rule charter left significant control over local affairs in the hands of Congress.[30] Under the home rule charter, Congress could veto any act of the city council, and the budget of the city government had to be explicitly approved as part of the federal budget process. The President of the United States appointed the judges of the local courts, and the U.S. Attorney for the District of Columbia, another presidential appointee, served also as the city prosecutor.

In electing their first local government in a hundred years, Washington voters chose a familiar cast. Walter Washington, having served as appointed mayor for seven years, won election to the post in his own right. Sterling Tucker won the chairmanship of the city council. Marion Barry, Julius Hobson (elected from a party advocating statehood for the District), Douglas Moore of the Black United Front, Polly Shackleton, and activists such as David Clarke, Willie Hardy, and John Wilson won seats on the council. Walter Fauntroy continued as delegate to Congress.

If activists dominated the new Washington government, they were nonetheless quite experienced activists. The previous seven years had provided a transition to home rule in which a new leadership group had gained political and administrative experience. Mayor Washington had already served as the city's chief executive. Several members of the council, including Tucker, Shackelton, and Reverend Jerry Moore, had served on the appointed council, as had Delegate Fauntroy. Several other council members had experience on the elected Board of Education, including Hobson and Board President Marion Barry.

City politics quickly took on a liberal-activist flavor. The city charter provided for the election of Advisory Neighborhood Commissions (ANC's) to give neighborhoods more say in city affairs. In some neighborhoods, residents demonstrated a new assertiveness on such issues as zoning and development. The council passed a variety of new laws, tightening rent controls and housing code enforcement, requiring that a substantial percentage of city contracts be awarded to minority firms and that firms awarded urban renewal contracts have minority partners, ensuring gay rights, mandating that city employees live in the city, and prohibiting the use of public funds for travel to states that had not ratified the Equal Rights Amendment. Senior positions in the District government now went mostly to blacks.

The dire predictions of the Board of Trade and other home rule opponents proved unfounded. Mayor Washington, his successor Mayor Marion Barry, and the members of the council all showed keen sensitivity to the concerns of the city's business community, recognizing that the city needed a vigorous business sector to maintain its tax and employment base. They also recognized that the business community could be a major source of campaign contributions. Thus, the city government worked hard for the construction of a convention center, despite considerable citizen opposition, and pushed forward with an extensive downtown urban renewal program. The council, over the objections of organized labor, decreased benefits under the city's workers compensation law to bring them into line with neighboring states (a longstanding concern of the business community). Until stopped by a public referendum, the council also tried to loosen rent controls. A *Washington Post* business reporter, interviewing the city's business leaders on the tenth anniversary of home rule, found that "there appears to be a consensus in the business community that home rule has improved relations between the local government and business." He also found, "general agreement in the private sector that the D.C. government is more responsive to business than it was ten, or even five years ago."[31]

When home rule began in 1975, the business community trusted Walter Washington and Sterling Tucker but still feared radicals like Marion Barry. Four years later, Barry challenged both Washington and Tucker in a three-way primary race for the Democratic Party nomination for mayor and narrowly defeated his rivals. Although most business leaders had backed Tucker, the Barry administration gained substantial credibility in their eyes by its handling of a financial crisis shortly after taking office. During the many years of federal rule of the District, deficits from revenue shortfalls had been carried over from one year to the next. Upon taking office in 1979, Barry discovered an accumulated deficit of $284 million, which increased a year later by $105 million. Taking tough steps to control spending and reduce the number of city employees, Barry brought the deficit under control and began to retire the accumulated debt.[32]

If the predictions of nay sayers were wrong about the effects of black home rule on business, they proved equally amiss in their warnings of white flight. The relative proportion of blacks and whites in the city remained fairly stable under home rule. Both Mayor Washington and Mayor Barry appointed whites to key positions and exerted considerable effort to win white political support and unify the city. As a result, Washington politics, although profoundly shaped by racial consciousness, has not polarized along racial lines. A majority black electorate has elected several whites to city-wide office, including council Chairman David Clark, a longtime civil rights activist and graduate of Howard University. Clark won most of the black endorsements in his race in 1982 for chairman against two black candidates.

There were, of course, significant differences in black and white voting patterns, and racial consciousness remained high in the city. Marion Barry received heavy support from white areas in his first race for mayor. However, amidst corruption scandals and allegations that the mayor uses drugs, he has failed since to carry the white vote. Black voters still supported him overwhelmingly; but by early 1989, Barry's erratic behavior and a new set of allegations that he had consorted with a drug dealer were threatening significant defections of black political and business leaders from the mayor's camp.

Racial voting is also apparent on referendums. In 1987, a ballot initiative requiring return deposits on beverage containers illustrated once again the power of racial appeal in local politics. The beverage industry defeated the initiative in this overwhelmingly liberal city by convincing black voters that the initiative was sponsored by whites and would raise beverage costs for poor blacks who had more serious problems to worry about than litter control.

More fundamentally, many blacks still fear that they will be displaced from the city and that black political control will prove shortlived. Race remains a critical factor in Washington politics, but racial differences do not divide the city politically. Race relations are much better than they were before the advent of home rule.

With the establishment of an elected government in 1973, the people of Washington gained a measure of political power, but District residents still enjoyed considerable less self government than other Americans. The fight was not finished. In the aftermath of the civil rights struggle that had brought suffrage to the District in the years after 1960, the city's traditional home rule leadership won what appeared to be another major victory in 1978. In that year, Congress approved a resolution for a constitutional amendment granting the District two senators, voting representation in the House, and the right to ratify constitutional amendments.

Even as the District sought ratification of this amendment in the state legislatures, another approach to self-government—statehood—began to win support within the city. Julius Hobson had organized the Statehood Party in 1970 and won a council seat as the party's candidate in 1974. He and his supporters argued that it would at once give District residents rights equal to those enjoyed by other Americans by providing congressional representation and by giving the District the same authority over its local affairs as that enjoyed by the other states.

In 1980, the Statehood Party used a new initiative procedure to place the issue on the D.C. ballot, and the voters approved the election of a constitutional convention to write a statehood constitution. The convention, dominated by grassroots activists, pushed aside established political leaders and wrote a controversial document opposed even by some statehood supporters. The voters narrowly approved the constitution in 1982 after several key political officials promised to amend it (it did better among blacks than among whites), and the mayor submitted to Congress a petition for admission of the state of "New Columbia" to the union. It has gone no farther.[33]

The extraordinary progress of the statehood movement within the District shows the extent to which local citizens now demanded full political rights. By the late 1970s, however, the national consensus in favor of civil rights, which had fueled the District's drive for suffrage, had given way to a new conservatism that viewed government, and particularly the federal government, with suspicion. As a result, sympathy for greater District self-government began to wane. Conservatives argued that District representation in Congress would result in increased federal spending because District senators would have an unusual economic stake in a large federal government. Furthermore, with the Senate closely divided between Democrats and Republicans after 1980, Republicans and conservative Democrats showed no eagerness for two new senators who would almost certainly be black, liberal Democrats, and champions of urban causes.[34] And in 1988, Congress showed its restiveness with the liberal city government by attaching amendments to the District appropriations act which overturned a law prohibiting discrimination against homosexuals, barred the use of local tax revenues to fund abortions for poor women, and required the city to repeal a law mandating that all city employees live in the District.

By the late 1980s, a new Washington had emerged. Its black political leaders had overcome a legacy of severe racial tension and black exclusion and had established an environment in which business could prosper and in which upper-middle class professionals could enjoy the capital's extraordinarily rich cultural and social life. Racial tensions remained just below the surface, however, and some wondered out loud whether home rule had really made any difference to the daily lives of the city's large poor and working-class population. The city still enjoyed only partial self-government. Although no one ruled out the possibility that racial tensions might again be politicized, Washington in the late 1980s displayed a degree of racial accommodation and political maturity unthinkable two decades earlier.

NOTES

Some might question why an essay on Washington D.C. would be included in a volume on "Snowbelt cities." Washington is the most southerly city discussed in this volume, and its metropolitan area, like those in the Sunbelt, has grown very rapidly since the start of World War II because of the proliferation of government and private sector employment dependent upon government. It has an information based, post-industrial economy. Yet the central city of Washington has more in common with the older industrial cities of the northeast and midwest than it has with the newer sunbelt cities. Like the older northern cities, it is physically compact with an aging physical infrastructure. Like its northern neighbors, it could not annex suburban territory and faced quite early the problems of white flight and the deterioration of the central city tax base; black political insurgency followed quickly. Its efforts to address the problems of crime and police-community relations, public housing and urban renewal, welfare, and employment resemble those of northern cities, as does its liberal politics.

1. Eunice S. Greer, *People and Government: Changing Needs in the District of Columbia, 1950–1970* (Washington Center for Metropolitan Studies, 1973), pp. 9–11; *Population Trends, District of Columbia, 1940–1960* (Washington Biostatistics Division, D.C. Department of Public Health, 1961), pp. 1–5; *The People of the District of Columbia* (Washington D.C. Office of Planning and Management, 1971), pp. 1–9; Robert A. Harper and Frank O. Ahnert, *Introduction to Metropolitan Washington* (Washington: Association of American Geographers, 1968), pp. 15–21. Janice Hamiltion Outtz, *Data Book for Washington Area, 1982* (Washington: Greater Washington Research Center, 1982, pp. 3–27; Greater Washington Research Center, *Market Trends*, Vol. 3, No. 9 (1987).

2. Outtz, *Data Book, 1982*, pp. 50–52.

3. Ibid., pp. 58–63.

4. Martha Derthick, *City Politics in Washington, D.C.* (Harvard/MIT Joint Center for Urban Studies and Washington Center for Metropolitan Studies, 1962), pp. 48–53.

5. Steven J. Diner, *Democracy, Federalism and the Governance of the Nation's Capital, 1790–1974* (Washington: Center for Applied Research and Urban Policy, University of the District of Columbia, 1987), pp. 37–41; Constance M. Green, *Washington: Capital City,*

1879–1950 (Princeton, N.J.: Princeton University Press, 1963), pp. 431, 440; Merlo J. Pusey, *The District Crisis* (Washington Post, 1937), pp. 3–4.

6. Derthick, *City Politics in Washington*, pp. 48, 53.

7. Constance M. Green, *The Secret City: A History of Race Relations in the Nation's Capital* (Princeton, N.J.: Princeton University Press, 1967), pp. 274–308.

8. Steven J. Diner, *Crisis of Confidence: The Reputation of Washington's Public Schools in the Twentieth Century*, (Washington: D.C. History and Public Policy Project, University of the District of Columbia, 1982), pp. 25–30; Carl F. Hanson, *Miracle of Social Adjustment* (New York: Anti-Defamation League of B'nai Birth, 1957); Erwin Knell, "Washington: Showcase of Integration," *Commentary* 27 (March 1959), pp. 194–202; U.S. House Committee on the District of Columbia, *Investigation of Public School Conditions* (Washington: Government Printing Office, 1957), pp. 44–46.

9. Steven J. Diner, *The Governance of Education in the District of Columbia: An Historical Analysis of Current Issues* (Washington: D.C. History and Public Policy Project, University of the District of Columbia, 1982), pp. 35–36; Martha S. Swaim, "Desegregation in the District of Columbia Public Schools" (M.A. Thesis, Howard University, 1971).

10. Diner, *Crisis of Confidence*, pp. 30–40.

11. Howard Gillette, Jr., "A National Workshop for Urban Policy: The Metropolitanization of Washington, 1946–1968," *The Public Histroian*, 7 (Winter, 1985), pp. 7–27; Frederick Gutheim, *Worthy of the Nation: A History of Planning for the National Capital*, (Washington: Smithsonian Institution Press, 1977), pp. 313–17; Green, *Secret City*, pp. 279–280; William Barnes, "A National Controversy in Miniature: The District of Columbia Struggle Over Public Housing and Redevelopment, 1943–46," *Prologue* 9 (Summer 1977), pp. 91–104.

12. Jerome S. Paige and Margaret M. Reuss, "Safe, Decent and Affordable: Citizen Struggle to Improve Housing in the District of Columbia, 1980–1982," in *Housing Washington's People: Public Policy in Retrospect*, ed. by Steven J. Diner and Helen Young (Washington: D. C. History and Public Policy Project, University of the District of Columbia, 1983), pp. 85–89.

13. Jeanne R. Lowe, *Cities in a Race with Time: Progress and Poverty in America's Cities* (New York: Random House, 1967), pp. 164–231; Eugene L. Meyer, "Urban Renewal and Housing: Rhetoric and Reality," in *The Federal Social Dollar in its Own Back Yard*, ed. by Sar Levitan (Washington, D.C.: Bureau of National Affairs, 1973), pp. 238–41; Gutheim, *Worthy of the Nation*, pp. 317–23.

14. Paige and Reuss, "Safe, Decent and Affordable," pp. 93–99; James W. Rouse and Nathaniel Keith, *No Slums in Ten Years* (Washington, 1955).

15. Eileen Zeitz, *Private Urban Renewal: A Different Residential Trend* (Lexington, Mass: Lexington Books, 1979); Suzanne B. Sherwood, *Foggy Bottom, 1800–1975* (Washington: George Washington University, 1978), pp. 26–37.

16. Jeffrey R. Henig, *Gentrefication in Adams Morgan: Political and Commercial Consequences of Neighborhood Change* (Washington: George Washington University, 1982). Paul Herron, *The Story of Capital Hill* (Coward-McCann, 1963), pp. 183–202.

17. Derthick, *City Politics in Washington*, pp. 95–98.

18. "Mr. Rauh is Joe Liberal," *Washington Post*, January 16, 1971; "The Long Drive to Self-Determination" [interview with Polly Shackleton], *Washington Times*, January 28, 1985; *Current Biography, 1979* (New York: The H. W. Wilson Company, 1979), pp. 124–27.

19. Paige and Reuss, op. cit.

20. Susan Jacoby, "Julius Hobson: The Man Behind the Month," *Washingtonian* 4 (April, 1969), pp. 37–39, 59–60; Charles N. Conconi, "Goodby, Mr. Hobson: The Last Interview," *Washingtonian* 12 (May 1977), pp. 136–41; Oral History Interview with Julius Hobson, July 3, 1967, Civil Rights Documentation Project, Mooreland-Spingarn Research Center, Howard University; "Top Achievement: Change in Hiring Practices" [Interview of Julius Hobson], *Washington Post*, July 4, 1972.

21. David Blum, "Barry, Barry, Not Contrary," *The New Republic* (November 1978), pp. 10–14; "Barry's Rise Unbroken String of Victories," *Washington Star-News,* December 5, 1974; "Marion Barry, Activist," *Washington Post,* December 10, 1978.

22. Anthony J. Thompson, "The Story of the Twenty Third Amendment," unpublished paper [1965], copy in Washingtonian Division, Martin Luther King, Jr. Public Library; *Washington Star,* March 21, 1961.

23. U.S. House of Representatives, *Home Rule for the District of Columbia: Communication from the President of the United States.* House Document No. 254 (Government Printing Office, August 8, 1965); Mike McManns, "Bill Press: The Quiet Power Man of the Board of Trade," *Washingtonian* 5 (November 1969), p. 47; James Irwin Moore, "The 1967 Reorganization of the District of Columbia Government," (Research Paper, Department of Political Science, University of Oklahoma), pp. 31–33, copy in Washingtonian Division, Martin Luther King, Jr. Public Library.

24. Steven J. Diner, *The Center of a Metropolis: Washington Since 1954* (Washington: Associates for Renewal in Education, 1980), pp. 42–54.

25. Moore, "1967 Reorganization of D.C. Government," p. 9.

26. Ibid, p. 136; U.S. House Committee on Government Operations, *Reorganization Plan No. 3 of 1967: Hearing, June 13–22, 1967* (Washington: Government Printing Office, 1967), p. 194; U.S. House Committee on Government Operations, *Reorganization Plan No. 3 of 1967: Committee Report* (Washington: Government Printing Office, 1967); U.S. House Committee on the District of Columbia, *D.C. Reorganization Proposals: Hearings, July 31, 1967* (Washington: Government Printing Office, 1967), p. 220; Steven J. Diner and Helen Young, eds., *Managing the Nation's Capital* (Washington: Center for Applied Research and Urban Policy, University of the District of Columbia, 1986).

27. Ben W. Gilbert, *Ten Blocks From the White House: Anatomy of the Washington Riots of 1968* (New York: Praeger, 1969), pp. 10–12.

28. Diner, *Democracy, Federalism and Governance of the District.* pp. 55–56.

29. Ibid, pp. 57–59.

30. Ibid, pp. 59–61; Jason I. Newman and Jacques B. DuPuy, "Bringing Democracy to the Nation's Last Colony: The District of Columbia Self-Government Act," *The American University Law Review,* 24 (Spring 1975), pp. 537–47; U.S. House Committee on the District of Columbia, *District of Columbia Self-Government and Governmental Reorganization Act: Report* (Washington: Government Printing Office, 1973).

31. "Business, Government Ties Strong Under Home Rule," *The Washington Post,* December 31, 1984.

32. Diner and Young, ed., *Managing the Nation's Capital,* pp. 18–19.

33. Phillip Schragg, "By the People: The Political Dynamics of a Constitutional Convention," *Georgetown Law Journal* 72 (February 1984), pp. 819–1108.

34. Diner, *Democracy, Federalism and the Governance of the District,* pp. 65–66.

APPENDIX TABLES

TABLE A.1

**Populations of Consolidated
Metropolitan Statistical Areas in the Northeast and Midwest, 1970–80,
with Black and Hispanic Percentages for 1980**

| | Total Population | | | 1980 | |
CMSA*	1970	1980	1987	% Black	% Hispanic
New York	18,192,819	17,539,344	18,053,800	16.1	11.7
Chicago	7,612,314	7,937,326	8,146,900	19.6	8.0
Philadelphia	5,749,093	5,680,768	5,890,600	18.2	2.6
Detroit	4,788,369	4,752,820	4,629,400	19.4	1.6
Boston	3,939,029	3,971,736	4,092,900	4.4	2.3
Cleveland	2,999,811	2,834,062	2,766,900	15.0	1.5
St. Louis	2,429,376	2,376,998	2,458,100**	17.2	0.9
Pittsburgh	2,556,029	2,423,311	2,296,400	7.5	0.5
Cincinnati	1,613,414	1,660,278	1,714,600	11.2	0.6
Milwaukee	1,574,722	1,570,275	1,562,100	10.5	2.6
Kansas City	1,373,146	1,433,458	1,546,400**	12.6	2.3

*The 1980 Consolidated Metropolitan Statistical Areas (CMSAs) are: New York-Northern New Jersey-Long Island, NY-NJ-CT: Chicago-Lake County, IL-IN-WI; Philadelphia-Wilmington-Trenton, PA-NJ-DE-MD; Detroit-Ann Arbor, MI; Boston-Lawrence-Salem, MA-NH; Cleveland-Akron-Lorain, OH; St. Louis-East St. Louis-Alton, MO-IL; Pittsburgh-Beaver Valley, PA; Cincinnati-Hamilton, OH-KY-IN; Milwaukee-Racine, WI; and Kansas City, MO-Kansas City, KS.

**After 1980, the U.S. Census Bureau downgraded the St. Louis and Kansas City CMSAs to MSAs.

Sources: U.S. Department of Commerce News (CB 88–157), September 30, 1988; U.S. Department of Commerce, Census of Population: 1980, *Supplementary Report: Metropolitan Statistical Areas (as defined by the Office of Budget and Management in 1983)*, PC 80-S1-18 (Washington: U.S. Government Printing Office, December 1984), Table 3 and, U.S. Bureau of the Census, *Census of Housing: 1970*: Vol. I, *Housing Characteristics for the States, Cities and Counties*, Parts 10, 15, 16, 22–25, 27, 34, 37, 40, and 51 (Washington: U.S. Government Printing Office, 1972), Tables 1, 5.

TABLE A.2.
Populations of Major Metropolitan Areas
in the Northeast and Midwest, 1940–1986

Metro Area*	1940	1950	1960	1970	1980	1986
New York						
Metro Area	8,706,917	9,555,943	10,694,633	11,571,899	8,274,961	8,473,400
New York	7,454,995	7,891,957	7,781,984	7,894,862	7,071,639	7,262,700
Outer Area	1,251,922	1,663,986	2,912,649	3,677,037	1,203,322	1,210,700
Chicago						
Metro Area	4,569,643	5,117,868	6,220,913	6,978,947	6,060,387	6,188,000
Chicago	3,396,803	3,620,962	3,550,404	3,366,957	3,005,072	3,009,530
Outer Area	1,172,835	1,556,906	2,670,509	3,611,990	3,055,315	3,178,470
Philadelphia						
Metro Area	3,199,637	3,671,048	4,342,897	4,817,914	4,716,818	4,825,700
Philadelphia	1,931,334	2,071,605	2,002,512	1,948,609	1,688,210	1,642,900
Outer Area	1,268,303	1,599,443	2,340,385	2,869,305	3,028,608	3,182,800
Detroit						
Metro Area	2,377,329	3,016,197	3,762,360	4,199,931	4,488,072	4,334,700
Detroit	1,623,452	1,849,568	1,670,144	1,511,482	1,203,339	1,086,220
Outer Area	753,877	1,166,629	2,092,216	2,688,449	3,284,733	3,248,480
Boston						
Metro Area	2,209,608	2,410,572	2,589,301	2,753,700	2,805,911	2,824,200
Boston	700,816	801,444	697,197	641,071	562,994	573,600
Outer Area	1,438,792	1,609,128	1,892,104	2,112,639	2,242,917	2,250,600
Washington						
Metro Area	967,985	1,464,089	2,001,897	2,861,123	3,250,822	3,563,000
Washington	663,091	802,178	763,956	756,510	638,333	626,000
Outer Area	304,894	661,911	1,237,941	2,104,613	2,431,804	2,937,000
Cleveland						
Metro Area	1,267,270	1,465,511	1,796,595	2,064,194	1,898,825	1,850,200
Cleveland	878,336	914,808	876,050	750,903	573,822	535,830
Outer Area	388,934	550,703	920,545	1,313,291	1,325,003	1,314,370
St. Louis						
Metro Area**	1,464,111	1,719,288	2,060,103	2,363,017	2,376,998	2,438,000
St. Louis	816,048	856,796	750,026	622,236	453,085	426,300
Outer Area	648,063	862,492	1,310,077	1,740,781	1,923,913	2,011,700
Pittsburgh						
Metro Area	2,082,556	2,213,236	2,405,435	2,401,245	2,218,870	2,122,900
Pittsburgh	671,659	676,806	604,332	520,117	423,938	387,490
Outer Area	1,410,897	1,536,430	1,801,103	1,881,128	1,794,932	1,735,410

TABLE A.2. (*Continued*)

Metro Area*	1940	1950	1960	1970	1980	1986
Mpls.-St. Paul						
Metro Area	967,367	1,151,053	1,482,030	1,813,645	2,137,133	2,295,200
Mpls.	492,370	521,718	482,872	434,400	370,951	356,480
St. Paul	287,736	311,349	313,411	309,980	270,230	263,680
Outer Area	187,261	317,986	685,747	1,069,267	1,495,952	1,675,040
Baltimore						
Metro Area	1,139,529	1,405,399	1,727,023	2,070,670	2,199,531	2,280,000
Baltimore	859,100	949,708	939,024	905,759	786,775	752,800
Outer Area	280,429	455,691	787,999	1,164,911	1,412,756	1,527,200
Cincinnati						
Metro Area	787,044	904,402	1,071,624	1,138,851	1,401,491	1,418,600
Cincinnati	455,610	503,998	502,550	452,524	385,457	369,750
Outer Area	331,434	400,404	569,074	686,330	1,016,034	1,048,850
Milwaukee						
Metro Area	829,629	956,948	1,194,290	1,403,688	1,390,143	1,379,700
Milwaukee	587,472	637,392	741,324	717,099	636,212	605,090
Outer Area	242,157	319,556	452,966	686,589	753,931	774,610
Kansas City						
Metro Area**	686,643	814,357	1,039,493	1,253,916	1,433,458	1,517,800
KC, Mo.	399,178	456,622	475,539	507,087	448,159	441,170
Outer Area	287,465	357,735	563,954	746,829	985,299	1,076,630
Columbus						
Metro Area	388,712	503,410	682,962	916,228	1,243,883	1,299,400
Columbus	306,087	375,901	471,316	539,677	564,871	566,030
Outer Area	82,625	127,509	211,646	376,551	679,012	733,370
Indianapolis						
Metro Area	460,926	551,777	697,567	1,109,882	1,166,575	1,212,600
Indpls.	386,972	427,173	476,258	744,624	700,807	719,820
Outer Area	73,954	124,604	221,309	365,258	465,768	492,780

*The 1940–60 data use 1960 boundaries. The 1970, 1980 and 1986 data use boundaries from their respective years. These changes can artificially affect the data as in the case of New York, 1970–80.

**For the 1980 Census, the U.S. Census Bureau labelled the St. Louis and Kansas City areas as CMSAs. Thereafter, they reverted to MSA status.

Sources: Table 1.1; *U.S. Department of Commerce News* (CB 87-165), October 16, 1987; and, U.S. Bureau of the Census, *U.S. Census of Population, 1960,* Vol. 1, *Characteristics of the Population,* Part I, U.S. Summary (Washington: U.S. Government Printing Office, 1964), Table 33.

TABLE A.3.
Growth Rates of Major Metropolitan Areas
in the Northeast and Midwest, 1940–1986

Metro Area*	1940–1950	1950–1960	1960–1970	1970–1980	1980–1986
New York					
Metro Area	9.8	11.9	8.2	−28.5	2.4
New York	5.9	−1.4	1.5	−10.4	2.7
Outer Area	32.9	75.0	26.2	−67.3	0.6
Chicago					
Metro Area	20.1	13.3	12.2	−13.2	2.1
Chicago	6.6	−1.9	−5.2	−10.7	0.1
Outer Area	32.7	71.5	35.3	−15.4	4.0
Philadelphia					
Metro Area	14.7	18.3	10.9	−2.1	2.3
Philadelphia	7.3	−3.3	−2.7	−13.4	−2.7
Outer Area	26.1	46.3	22.6	5.6	5.1
Detroit					
Metro Area	26.9	24.7	11.6	6.9	−3.4
Detroit	13.9	−9.7	−9.5	−20.4	−9.7
Outer Area	54.8	79.3	28.5	22.2	−1.1
Boston					
Metro Area	9.1	7.4	6.3	1.9	0.7
Boston	4.0	−13.0	−8.1	−12.2	1.9
Outer Area	11.8	17.6	11.7	6.2	0.3
Washington					
Metro Area	51.3	36.7	42.9	13.6	9.6
Washington	21.0	−4.8	−1.0	−15.6	−1.9
Outer Area	117.1	87.0	70.0	15.5	20.8
Cleveland					
Metro Area	15.6	22.6	14.9	−8.0	−2.6
Cleveland	4.2	−4.2	−14.3	−23.6	−6.6
Outer Area	41.6	67.2	42.7	0.9	−0.8
St. Louis					
Metro Area	17.4	19.8	14.7	−2.0	2.6
St. Louis	5.0	−12.5	−17.0	−17.2	−5.9
Outer Area	33.8	51.9	32.9	10.8	4.6
Pittsburgh					
Metro Area	6.3	8.7	−0.2	−7.6	−4.3
Pittsburgh	0.8	−10.7	−13.9	−18.5	−8.6
Outer Area	8.9	17.2	4.4	−4.6	−3.3

Metro Area*	1940–1950	1950–1960	1960–1970	1970 1980	1980–1986
Mpls.-St. Paul					
Metro Area	19.0	28.8	22.4	17.8	7.4
Minneapolis	6.0	−7.4	−10.0	−14.6	−3.9
St. Paul	8.2	0.7	−1.1	−12.8	−2.4
Outer Area	69.8	115.7	55.9	39.9	12.0
Baltimore					
Metro Area	23.3	22.9	19.9	6.2	3.7
Baltimore	10.5	−1.1	3.5	−13.1	−4.3
Outer Area	62.5	72.9	47.8	21.3	8.1
Cincinnati					
Metro Area	14.9	18.5	6.3	23.1	1.2
Cincinnati	10.6	−0.3	−10.0	−14.8	−4.1
Outer Area	20.8	42.1	20.6	48.0	3.2
Milwaukee					
Metro Area	15.3	24.8	17.5	−0.1	−1.2
Milwaukee	8.5	16.3	−3.3	−11.3	−4.9
Outer Area	32.0	41.7	51.6	9.8	2.7
Kansas City					
Metro Area	18.6	27.6	20.6	14.3	5.9
KC, Missouri	14.4	4.1	6.6	−11.6	−1.6
Outer Area	24.4	57.6	32.4	31.9	9.3
Columbus					
Metro Area	29.5	35.7	34.2	35.8	4.5
Columbus	22.8	25.4	14.5	4.7	0.2
Outer Area	54.3	66.0	77.9	80.3	8.0
Indianapolis					
Metro Area	19.7	26.4	59.1	5.1	3.9
Indianapolis	10.4	11.5	56.3	−5.9	2.7
Outer Area	68.5	77.6	65.0	27.5	5.8

Sources: Tables 1.2 and 1.3.

TABLE A.4.
Black Percentages of the Populations of Major Metropolitan Areas
in the Northeast and Midwest 1940–1980, with Hispanic Percentages for 1980

Metro Area	1940	1950	% Black 1960	1970	1980	% Hispanic* 1980
New York						
Metro Area	5.9	8.6	11.5	16.3	23.1	17.7
New York	6.1	9.5	14.0	21.1	25.2	19.9
Outer Area	4.5	4.4	4.8	5.9	10.2	4.9
Chicago						
Metro Area	6.6	10.3	14.3	17.6	22.3	8.6
Chicago	8.2	13.6	22.9	32.7	39.8	14.0
Outer Area	2.1	2.8	2.9	3.6	5.2	3.2
Philadelphia						
Metro Area	10.5	13.1	15.5	17.5	18.8	2.5
Philadelphia	13.0	18.2	26.4	33.6	37.8	3.8
Outer Area	6.6	6.5	6.1	6.6	8.1	1.7
Detroit						
Metro Area	7.2	11.9	14.9	18.0	19.9	1.6
Detroit	9.2	16.2	28.9	43.7	63.1	2.4
Outer Area	2.9	4.9	3.7	3.4	4.1	1.4
Boston						
Metro Area	1.6	2.2	3.0	4.6	5.8	2.4
Boston	3.1	5.0	9.1	16.3	22.4	6.4
Outer Area	0.8	0.7	0.8	1.1	1.7	1.4
Washington						
Metro Area	23.7	23.1	24.3	24.6	26.8	2.9
Washington	18.2	35.0	53.9	71.1	70.3	2.8
Outer Area	13.8	8.6	6.1	7.9	17.3	3.2
Cleveland						
Metro Area	6.9	10.4	14.3	16.1	18.2	1.4
Cleveland	9.6	16.2	28.6	38.3	43.8	3.1
Outer Area	0.8	0.8	0.7	3.4	7.1	0.6
St. Louis						
Metro Area	10.4	12.6	14.3	16.0	17.2	0.9
St. Louis	13.3	17.9	28.6	40.9	45.6	1.2
Outer Area	6.6	7.2	6.1	7.2	5.9	0.6
Pittsburgh						
Metro Area	5.4	6.2	6.7	7.1	7.7	0.5
Pittsburgh	9.3	12.2	16.7	20.2	24.0	0.8
Outer Area	3.6	3.5	3.4	3.5	3.8	0.5

Metro Area	1940	1950	% Black 1960	1970	1980	% Hispanic* 1980
Mpls.-St. Paul						
Metro Area	0.9	1.1	1.4	1.8	2.3	1.0
Minneapolis				4.4	7.7	1.3
	1.1	1.5	2.5			
St. Paul				1.0	4.9	2.9
Outer Area	0.1	0.1	0.1	0.2	0.6	0.7
Baltimore						
Metro Area	17.5	19.3	21.9	23.7	25.5	1.0
Baltimore	19.3	23.7	34.7	46.4	54.8	1.0
Outer Area	11.8	10.1	6.7	6.0	9.2	1.0
Cincinnati						
Metro Area	8.7	10.5	12.0	13.4	12.4	0.6
Cincinnati	12.2	15.5	21.6	27.6	33.8	0.8
Outer Area	4.0	4.2	3.4	4.0	4.3	0.5
Milwaukee						
Metro Area	1.1	2.3	5.3	7.6	10.8	2.5
Milwaukee	1.5	3.4	8.4	14.7	23.1	4.1
Outer Area	0.2	0.2	0.2	0.2	0.5	1.1
Kansas City						
Metro Area	9.8	10.7	11.2	12.1	12.6	2.3
KC, Mo.	10.4	12.2	17.5	22.1	27.4	3.3
Outer Area	9.0	8.9	5.9	5.2	5.8	1.9
Columbus						
Metro Area	10.0	10.3	11.7	11.6	11.0	0.7
Columbus	11.7	12.4	16.4	26.5	22.1	0.8
Outer Area	3.8	3.9	1.5	1.8	1.8	0.5
Indianapolis						
Metro Area	11.3	11.8	14.3	12.4	13.5	0.8
Indianapolis	13.2	15.0	20.6	18.0	21.8	0.9
Outer Area	1.1	0.9	0.8	0.8	1.1	0.6

*Hispanic data for 1980 are for people with Spanish origins (self-defined). U.S. Census figures undercount all minorities, especially Hispanics.

Sources: Tables 1.1 and 1.2; U.S. Department of Commerce, *1980 Census of Population, Supplementary Report: Metropolitan Statistical Areas as defined by the Office of Management and Budget in 1983)*, PC 80-51-18 (Washington: U.S. Government Printing Office, December 1984), Tables 1–3; and, U.S. Bureau of the Census, *U.S. Census of Population: 1960, Selected Area Reports, Standard Metropolitan Statistical Areas, Final Report PC (3)-1D* (Washington: U.S. Government Printing Office, 1963) Table 1.

CONTRIBUTORS

Carolyn Teich Adams is Professor and Chair of Geography and Urban Studies at Temple University and coauthor of *Comparative Public Policy: The Politics of Social Choice in Europe and America*, 3rd ed. (1990).

Joseph L. Arnold is Professor of History at the University of Maryland–Baltimore County and author of *The New Deal in the Suburbs: A History of the Greenbelt Town Program, 1935–1954* (1971).

Robert G. Barrows, an editor at the Indiana Historical Bureau during the preparation of his essay for this volume, is now Assistant Professor of History at Indiana University-Purdue University, Indianapolis. He is the author of "Beyond the Tenement: Patterns of American Urban Housing, 1870–1930," *Journal of Urban History*, 9 (August 1983), pp. 395–420.

Richard M. Bernard is Professor of American History and Dean of the Faculty at Bethany College (West Virginia). He is coeditor of *Sunbelt Cities: Politics and Growth since World War II* (1983).

Thomas F. Campbell is Professor of History at Cleveland State University and coeditor of *The Birth of Modern Cleveland, 1865–1930* (1988).

Steven J. Diner is Professor of History at George Mason University and author of *Housing Washington's People: Public Policy in Retrospect* (1983).

Mark I. Gelfand is Associate Professor of History at Boston College and author of *A Nation of Cities: The Federal Government and Urban America, 1933–1965* (1975).

Arnold R. Hirsch is Professor of History and Urban Studies at the University of New Orleans and author of *Making the Second Ghetto: Race and Housing in Chicago, 1940–1960* (1983).

Zane L. Miller is Professor of History and Co-Director of the Center for Neighborhood and Community Studies at the University of Cincinnati and author of *Suburb: Neighborhood and Community in Forest Park, Ohio, 1935–1976* (1981).

John Clayton Thomas is Professor of Public Administration and Director of the L. P. Cookingham Institute of Public Affairs at the University of Missouri–Kansas City. He is author of *Between Citizen and City: Neighborhood Organizations and Urban Politics in Cincinnati* (1986).

Bruce Tucker is Associate Professor of History at the University of Windsor (Canada) and Visiting Research Associate in the Center for Neighborhood and Community Studies at the University of Cincinnati. He is author of "The Reinvention of New

England, 1601–1770,'' *The New England Quarterly* 59 (September 1986), 315–340.

Daniel J. Walkowitz is Professor of History and Director of Metropolitan Studies at New York University and author of *Worker City, Company Town: Iron and Cotton-Worker Protest in Troy and Cohoes, New York, 1855–84* (1978).

Michael P. Weber is Vice President for Academic Affairs at Duquesne University and author of *Don't Call Me Boss: David L. Lawrence, Pittsburgh's Renaissance Mayor* (1988).

	DATE DUE		